Business
Plans
Handbook

Business Plans Handbook

A COMPILATION OF ACTUAL BUSINESS PLANS DEVELOPED BY BUSINESSES THROUGHOUT NORTH AMERICA

VOLUME

14

**Lynn M. Pearce,
Project Editor**

GALE
CENGAGE Learning

Detroit • New York • San Francisco • New Haven, Conn • Waterville, Maine • London

Business Plans Handbook, Volume 14

Project Editor: Lynn M. Pearce

Product Manager: Jenai Mynatt

Product Design: Jennifer Wahi

Composition and Electronic Prepress: Evi Seoud

Manufacturing: Rita Wimberley

For product information and technology assistance, contact us at
Gale Customer Support, 1-800-877-4253.
For permission to use material from this text or product,
submit all requests online at **www.cengage.com/permissions.**
Further permissions questions can be emailed to
permissionrequest@cengage.com

Gale
27500 Drake Rd.
Farmington Hills, MI, 48331-3535

ISBN-13: 978-07876-9503-3
1084-4473

Printed in the United States of America
1 2 3 4 5 6 7 12 11 10 09 08

Contents

Highlights

Business Plans Handbook, Volume 14 (BPH-14) is a collection of actual business plans compiled by entrepreneurs seeking funding for small businesses throughout North America. For those looking for examples of how to approach, structure, and compose their own business plans, *BPH-14* presents 20 sample plans, including plans for the following businesses:

- Academic Testing Improvement Service
- Art Gallery
- Cafe and Gas Station
- Courier Service
- Ethanol Fuel Production
- Fantasy Book & Memorabilia Store
- Food and Beverage Vending Company
- Greenhouse and Flower Shop
- Home Furnishing Manufacturer
- Interior Renovation Company
- Organic Grower and Supplier
- Pet Sitting Service
- Residential and Commercial Painting Service
- Shoe Store
- Smoothie and Juice Shop
- Tattoo & Body Piercing
- Used Clothing, Furniture, and Antique Store
- Water Purification System Distributor
- Website Designer
- Wooden Furniture Manufacturer and Supplier

FEATURES AND BENEFITS

BPH-14 offers many features not provided by other business planning references including:

- Twenty business plans, each of which represent an owner's successful attempt at clarifying (for themselves and others) the reasons that the business should exist or expand and why a lender should fund the enterprise.
- Two fictional plans that are used by business counselors at a prominent small business development organization as examples for their clients. (You will find these in the Business Plan Template Appendix.)

- A directory section that includes: listings for venture capital and finance companies, which specialize in funding start-up and second-stage small business ventures, and a comprehensive listing of Service Corps of Retired Executives (SCORE) offices. In addition, the Appendix also contains updated listings of all Small Business Development Centers (SBDCs); associations of interest to entrepreneurs; Small Business Administration (SBA) Regional Offices; and consultants specializing in small business planning and advice. It is strongly advised that you consult supporting organizations while planning your business, as they can provide a wealth of useful information.

- A Small Business Term Glossary to help you decipher the sometimes confusing terminology used by lenders and others in the financial and small business communities.

- A cumulative index, outlining each plan profiled in the complete *Business Plans Handbook* series.

- A Business Plan Template which serves as a model to help you construct your own business plan. This generic outline lists all the essential elements of a complete business plan and their components, including the Summary, Business History and Industry Outlook, Market Examination, Competition, Marketing, Administration and Management, Financial Information, and other key sections. Use this guide as a starting point for compiling your plan.

- Extensive financial documentation required to solicit funding from small business lenders. You will find examples of: Cash Flows, Balance Sheets, Income Projections, and other financial information included with the textual portions of the plan.

Introduction

Perhaps the most important aspect of business planning is simply doing it. More and more business owners are beginning to compile business plans even if they don't need a bank loan. Others discover the value of planning when they must provide a business plan for the bank. The sheer act of putting thoughts on paper seems to clarify priorities and provide focus. Sometimes business owners completely change strategies when compiling their plan, deciding on a different product mix or advertising scheme after finding that their assumptions were incorrect. This kind of healthy thinking and re-thinking via business planning is becoming the norm. The editors of *Business Plans Handbook, Volume 14 (BPH-14)* sincerely hope that this latest addition to the series is a helpful tool in the successful completion of your business plan, no matter what the reason for creating it.

This fourteenth volume, like each volume in the series, offers genuine business plans used by real people. *BPH-14* provides 20 business plans used by actual entrepreneurs to gain funding support for their new businesses. The business and personal names and addresses and general locations have been changed to protect the privacy of the plan authors.

NEW BUSINESS OPPORTUNITIES

As in other volumes in the series, *BPH-14* finds entrepreneurs engaged in a wide variety of creative endeavors. Examples include a proposal for a pet sitting service, a tattoo and bodypiercing shop, and a vending machine operation. In addition, several other plans are provided, including a residential and commercial painting serivce, a greenhouse and flower shop, and an art gallery.

Comprehensive financial documentation has become increasingly important as today's entrepreneurs compete for the finite resources of business lenders. Our plans illustrate the financial data generally required of loan applicants, including Income Statements, Financial Projections, Cash Flows, and Balance Sheets.

ENHANCED APPENDIXES

In an effort to provide the most relevant and valuable information for our readers, we have updated the coverage of small business resources. For instance, you will find: a directory section, which includes listings of all of the Service Corps of Retired Executives (SCORE) offices; an informative glossary, which includes small business terms; and a cumulative index, outlining each plan profiled in the complete Business Plans Handbook series. In addition we have updated the list of Small Business Development Centers (SBDCs); Small Business Administration Regional Offices; venture capital and finance companies, which specialize in funding start-up and second-stage small business enterprises; associations of interest to entrepreneurs; and consultants, specializing in small business advice and planning. For your reference, we have also reprinted the business plan template, which provides a comprehensive overview of the essential components of a business plan and two fictional plans used by small business counselors.

SERIES INFORMATION

If you already have the first thirteen volumes of *BPH*, with this fourteenth volume, you will now have a collection of over 300 real business plans (not including the one updated plan in the second volume, whose original appeared in the first, or the two fictional plans in the Business Plan Template Appendix section of the second, third, fourth, fifth, sixth, and seventh volumes); contact information for hundreds of organizations and agencies offering business expertise; a helpful business plan template; a foreword providing advice and instruction to entrepreneurs on how to begin their research; more than 1,500 citations to valuable small business development material; and a comprehensive glossary of terms to help the business planner navigate the sometimes confusing language of entrepreneurship.

ACKNOWLEDGEMENTS

The Editors wish to sincerely thank the contributors to BPH-14, including:

- Juan C. Falquez
- Sutton Lasater
- Scott MacArthur
- Tracy Reynolds
- Mary Green
- Andrea Hibbeler
- Bryan King
- Arilova Randrianasolo
- Adam Theurer
- Alex Wander
- John Benoist
- Gustavo Ramis
- Christopher Lee Aubuchon
- Ryan Franklin
- Justin Gimotea
- Elliot Smith
- Gerald Rekve, Corporate Management Consultants

The editors would also like to express their gratitude to Jerome Katz and his colleagues Trey Goede, Tim Hayden, Paul Scheiter, Dr. Jintong Tang, and Vincent Volpe of the Cook School of Business at Saint Louis University. They have been instrumental in finding and securing high–quality, successful business plans for inclusion in this publication.

COMMENTS WELCOME

Your comments on *Business Plans Handbook* are appreciated. Please direct all correspondence, suggestions for future volumes of *BPH*, and other recommendations to the following:

Managing Editor, Business Product
Business Plans Handbook
The Gale Group
27500 Drake Rd.
Farmington Hills, MI 48331-3535
Phone: (248)699-4253
Fax: (248)699-8052
Toll-Free: 800-347-GALE
E-mail: BusinessProducts@gale.com

Academic Testing Improvement Service

Academic Assistance

20 Elmstead Ln.
Madison, Wisconsin 53705

Juan C. Falquez, Sutton Lasater, Scott MacArthur, and Tracy Reynolds

Academic Assistance is a LLC created with the intention of helping students throughout school. Our mission is to foster the improvement of students' performance during test taking by means of tools that would help them perform more efficiently and effectively.

EXECUTIVE SUMMARY

Business Overview

Academic Assistance is a LLC created with the intention of helping students throughout school. Our mission is to foster the improvement of students' performance during test taking by means of tools that would help them perform more efficiently and effectively. We decided to form a LLC to get all the benefits of forming a corporation and avoid drawbacks such as double taxation and excessive paperwork.

Our reason for existence is the constant need for students' academic improvement. Nowadays, advertisers would have you believe that through study techniques and/or nutritional supplements, students are able to study for a test within a night, take it in matter of minutes and still get an A or B grade. Unfortunately, the reality for many students is different. While many students can finish their test in an average of twenty minutes, others are not able to finish it within the time given. Some students would study really hard for days and still would not get a good grade. We felt that students within this segment were under-represented and not given the attention that they deserve. We feel that with the use of the *Precise Pencil*, their needs will be more fully met and we would be solving a test time problem.

PRODUCTS & SERVICES

Precise Pencil

The *Precise Pencil* is the first product of our company. It intends to replace the No. 2 pencil, normally used on tests that require the use of a Scantron sheet. Eventually, we hope that the *Precise Pencil* will become the standard utensil for test taking. The *Precise Pencil* is very user friendly. When the student is ready to fill in the blank circles, all he/she needs to do is to place the pencil right on the circle he/she wishes to fill in and then push down. The mechanism inside the pencil will make the graphite lead twist down, applying enough pressure to leave a solid mark, simulating the action of a stamper.

The concept of the *Precise Pencil* is one that is a little difficult to create because it is the first one of its kind. In order to perfect and utilize the *Precise Pencil* to the fullest, the prototype works along the same concepts as the mechanical pencil. The *Precise Pencil* takes the traditional mechanical pencil model, and alters it so that instead of the user clicking on the top part of the base unit, there is another tubular base that fits within the original base, which makes it possible for the user to push down to activate the movement of the pencil lead out of the base. Additionally, one of the primary modifications made to the prototype is the twisting action as the pencil lead descends from the base unit, which accounts for the way the mark on the Scantron sheet is made. In order to make this possible, the *Precise Pencil* has a spring loaded twisting action that occurs when the inner base is pressed inward. One of the other key differences in this product is the 3 mm lead required to operate the device. This is the size needed to fill in the entire Scantron bubble. A common question that comes to the floor is if it will be possible to replace the lead within the *Precise Pencil*. At Academic Assistance, we have figured out a way around that. Each time the pencil deploys lead, the track holding the lead returns to approximately half of the original length of deployment. This will cause the lead to continue to move closer and closer to the bottom of the base, until the time is needed for a replacement of the lead.

After running several test–trials, we realized that the majority of students focus most of their time in the actual test and leave little time to fill in the blanks of the Scantron sheet. We also found that on average, a student takes between four to seven minutes to fill in the circles of a Scantron sheet of a fifty question test. Time is an important element during test taking and we hope that the *Precise Pencil* helps reduce this time down to one to two minutes.

In order to manufacture this product, any pencil manufacturer that makes mechanical pencils would suffice because of the similarities in the design. Some of the companies that have facilities already set up that could handle a product like this are: Kingways Stationary Company Ltd (China, Taiwan), Guangdong Genvana Stationary Company Ltd (China), Shenzhen Acme Pen Co Ltd (China), Blue Bond Technology Industry Co Ltd (Taiwan). Because there are more parts involved in the creation of the *Precise Pencil*, Academic Assistance has to charge a mildly higher price based on complexity of the prototype design.

This product is very revolutionary because it is the first one of its kind to do something this user–friendly. The *Precise Pencil* is so easy to use that all a user has to do is place the base over the desired Scantron bubble and push down to fill in the necessary bubble. The *Precise Pencil* is a practical and time saving solution to long Scantron tests, which could greatly benefit anyone.

MARKET ANALYSIS

The pencil industry is comprised of numerous producers which include, but are not limited to: Paper Mate, BIC, Faber–Castell, Musgrave Pencil Company, General Pencil Company, Dixon Ticonderoga Pencil Company, Liberty Pencil Company Limited, and the American Pencil Company. Although all of these companies and more manufacture pencils as well as other writing utensils, there is not a single business in the industry that creates a *Precise Pencil* or similar product, which is a void in the market that we hope to fill.

Currently, the pencil industry is growing every year. Although more and more people are using word processors instead of using a wooden pencil (which dates back to over 400 years ago), the industry is still experiencing growth. The industry has about a $220 million dollar market, and some companies have been increasing production, some by up to 12 percent from 2006 to 2007. In 2007, it is estimated that over 15 billion pencils were sold worldwide. Some financial numbers in the industry are as follows:

- Industry Average Annual Sales: $6,263,945

- Cost of Sales: $3,679,442

- Gross Profit: $2,584,503

Clearly, the pencil industry is one that can offer high profits and large growth. At Academic Assistance, we feel that entrance into this large market, especially with our new product, will not be associated with high risk or threat of failure.

Customers

The market for our product is mainly focused on students at institutions that use Scantron exam sheets. We could market our product to students as well as schools, which may opt to buy our product to offer to their students for no cost. This would be especially beneficial to schools in low–income areas where students don't have the disposable income to buy our product. Across the United States, there are 56,888,700 million students in 128,300 public, private, and chartered primary and secondary schools. About $489 billion will be spent per year related to their education. As far as post–secondary schools, there are eighteen million two and four year college students in private and public institutions and full-time and part-time programs. There are 4,314 post secondary schools which includes private, public, two year schools and four year schools. The market for our product is clearly very large and, if properly marketed and manufactured, our product has the potential to help any of the aforementioned students with test taking.

Academic Assistance has the option of marketing the *Precise Pencil* to schools or to the students themselves. Marketing to schools may provide our business with more sales since schools may like to provide this product to all of their students, as to give all of them a better test–taking advantage. Marketing to students, however, may provide our company with the option to create a "hot trend" in the school supply market. When back–to–school shopping, many students race to get the hot new products, and we believe that our product had the potential to become one of the latest back–to–school trends.

Another potential market that Academic Assistance may have for the *Precise Pencil* is to sell to office supply stores. Some office supply stores that we may focus on selling our product to include, but are not limited to: Office Max (900 stores), Staples (2,000 stores), Office Depot (1,600 stores), Target (1,500 stores), and Wal–Mart (6,900 stores). The benefit of marketing our product to office supply stores is that Academic Assistance would not need to focus on direct sales to the consumer, but rather sell in bulk quantities.

At Academic Assistance, we have also been researching selling our product to Scantron, who would then be able to sell our product with their Scantron sheets. Approximately 80 percent of schools across the country at all levels use Scantron sheets, which is about 59,910,960 students. If Academic Assistance can effectively market to these students and can earn sales from even one half of one percent of them, there is the potential to sell 299,544 *Precise Pencils*. By selling our pencils to Scantron, they can use the market ties that they have already established and sell our product to supplement theirs.

Strengths and Weaknesses

A thorough analysis of the strengths, weaknesses, opportunities, and threats of our product can be seen below. This analysis demonstrates areas that are positive to our company as well as possible limitations or areas in which to improve.

Strengths

- No product like this on the market

- Potentially raises students' grades by giving them more time to focus on the test itself

- Students are becoming more competitive with academics and want to have the best scores possible

Weaknesses

- Possible lack of need for product since it hasn't yet been developed

- Unsure about darkness of the lead mark left on Scantron sheet

- The No. 2 pencil has been around for over 400 years and has survived the introductions of ball point pens and computers

- Poor economy encourages people to be thrifty rather than frivolous (*Precise Pencil* may be considered a frivolous item)

BUSINESS STRATEGY

In order to determine what we needed to do next in terms of our future action plan we turned to Stanley Rooke. Stanley Rooke is the Associate Director and head of Intellectual Property at Suburban University. We went to him to discuss how to keep our idea safe from being copied, what procedures we would need to go through, and any other information that he could give to us.

After meeting with Stanley Rooke, our next step is to apply for a utility patent (1.16A1). A utility patent protects any new invention or functional improvements on existing inventions. This can be to a product, machine, a process, or even composition of matter. The basic filing fee for a utility patent is $150.00. The process to be granted a utility patent takes anywhere from six months to one year. Once we are granted a utility patent it is good for twenty years.

Once we have filed for our utility patent, our next step will be to create non–disclosure agreements. These are extremely important to create because they ensure that, while our patent is being processed, nobody that works on this project can steal our idea. We will draft a document that anyone that has any interaction with this project will have to sign. These could be our engineers that we have physically creating the product, attorneys that are helping us with legal issues, or counterparts. We will make sure not to discuss this project and/or idea with anyone that has not signed or that refuses to sign our non–disclosure agreement.

In congruence with the non–disclosure agreement, we will be contracting a mechanical engineer. Once again, before the engineer begins working on this project and before we discuss it with him/her we will have them sign a non–disclosure agreement. We are contracting a mechanical engineer so that they will be able to design and build our initial prototype. We will then be able to take this prototype with us to explain how our product works, to help gain more funding, and for our sales pitches. Once we have a prototype it will be much more feasible for us to be able to gain investor interest and expand our product. This way we will allow people to see and use the prototype so that they are able to gain a better understanding of how it works.

Once we have our prototype, we will apply for a design patent (1.16B1). A design patent protects the ornamental design, configuration, improved decorative appearance, or shape of an invention. A design patent also grants the exclusive right to manufacture or sell your design. The basic filing fee for a design patent is $210.00. The process to be granted a design patent takes anywhere from six months to one year. Once we are granted a design patent it is good for fourteen years.

Once we have filed for all of our patents and we have our initial prototype completed, it will be time to conduct some market research. We want to conduct market research in order to gauge the response to our new pencil. We want to be able to make sure that consumers like it, that universities find it to be a beneficial tool, and that people would actually use it. In order to conduct this market research we are going to conduct focus groups. These focus groups will consist of eight to ten people. We will give them a questionnaire to answer on a Scantron sheet and also provide them with our new pencil. Once they are finished using it we will be able to talk to them and see what they thought of it. Throughout the time they take the test we will also be observing to make sure that the pencil is working properly and that nobody is having problems with it. We will also conduct surveys and hand out prototypes in classrooms since our main target market is to universities and students.

FINANCIAL ANALYSIS

In order to fund our costly endeavor we have come up with various outlets. We plan to apply for United States' grants that are geared towards education advancement. We feel that our product can enhance the achievement of students across the nation with their education and, because of this, we feel that we would be the perfect candidates to receive a grant that is geared towards educational advancement.

We also plan on getting in contact with the Educational Testing Service. The Educational Testing Service is the organization that proctors tests such as the SAT, GRE, and TOEFL. We hope to present our prototype to them to be able to form some type of a partnership. Many of the tests that this organization proctors are administered on Scantron sheets, which are what our new pencil is compatible with. We hope that the Educational Testing Service will be interested in a partnership in order to make their testing methods easier for those taking the test.

Lastly, we would like to talk with university investors. With the help of the Educational Testing Service, high schools and universities will gain interest and invest in the product of their respective schools. All schools are interested in ways to advance their level of education and we feel that this would be an appropriate use of their funds. One set of university investors that we especially would like to get in contact with are the Investors of Suburban University (ISU). Seeing that we are all students at this university, we feel that we would have a good chance of gaining funds from them for a product that was not only developed by their own students but that will benefit their students for years to come.

CONCLUSION

In conclusion, once we have the funding that we need to cover the start up costs for the *Precise Pencil*, we will find a low–cost manufacturer to mass produce the prototype. Then we will find a distributor to distribute to the office supply store chains, such as Office Depot and Office Max. We also plan to market the *Precise Pencil* to universities in order to further the advancement of educational tools. We will market to Scantron as well, in hopes to create a bundle package. Anyone that would purchase the Scantron sheets and machines from the company would then be able to get the *Precise Pencil* as well.

Art Gallery

COOKE GALLERY

4312 Main St.
Seattle, WA 98103

Gerald Rekve

Cooke Gallery will strive to sell superior quality, traditional artworks to tourists and local clients, while providing educational information, value, and excellent customer service as a profit- and growth-oriented business.

EXECUTIVE SUMMARY

Company History

Cooke Gallery was established in April 2007 with the goal of providing a place to sell local art from the rich tradition of the area. The owner, Mr. Harthow, is retiring and selling the gallery to long–time associate and friend Ms. Cooke. During the last few years, the gallery operation was focused more on limited edition art, and the sales numbers showed weakness. Ms. Cooke believes that a new approach with fresh, original art supplied by local artists will garner new interest from art lovers in the city and catapult sales into a new growth phase.

Cooke Gallery is a limited liability company operating in a beautiful 1,700 square foot traditional art gallery within the high tourism area of central Seattle; this area attracts thousands of tourists each day. Mr. Harthow, current owner of Cooke Gallery, wishes to sell the gallery to Dorthea Cooke who has been the gallery's manager for the past seven years.

Cooke Gallery has been operating since 2000 in the same central Seattle location, within a storefront facility. The interior has been renovated to suitably display high-quality local art works including gold and silver jewelry, carvings, prints, clothing, paintings, glass sculpture, and other art works. All merchandise has a standardized retail mark–up of 100 percent. The business has realized annual sales increases of approximately 19 percent since inception and anticipates similar sales increases to continue.

A new lease is being negotiated as part of the sale. The monthly rent will remain the same at $700.00, and fair market triple net taking effect after the three years of operation. The new lease will also include a five–year renewable term provided by the building landlord.

Cooke Gallery currently employs one full–time employee, five part–time employees, and two seasonal employees. Ms. Cooke and her daughter will maintain their employment; however Dorthea will also try to employ and train as many people as she deems necessary and who are currently in the local art market.

CUSTOMERS

Cooke Gallery provides high-quality local art works at fair prices and is committed to providing high levels of customer service. This has resulted in a strong and loyal client base that includes repeat customers and has endeared them with the thousands of tourists who frequent central Seattle. Finally, Cooke Gallery is the only local art gallery owned in central Seattle with no direct competition in the region. The Cooke Gallery facility is in a location with many other businesses that suit the art gallery and will draw like clients to the store.

The primary client base for Cooke Gallery is made up of 80 percent tourists. According to *Seattle Tourism Journal*, tourists are primarily from within a 700 mile radius. Business in the area is continually growing at a rate of 11 percent per annum and this number is expected to increase as a result of even more attractions that have recently been added to the area or are in the planning stages. This is due in large part to the recently completed new highway bypass and the growing tourism economy within Seattle.

According to *Washington Statistics*, in 2005, the tourism sector contributed $2.4 billion dollars (constant 2000 dollars) to the Seattle economy, a 3.2 percent increase from 1997. This was the strongest growth seen in the tourism industry since 1991. In addition, wholesale and retail trade realized a 3.1 percent growth in their contribution to tourism GDP, which has been positive for the past nine years.

The secondary client base for the gallery, or the remaining 20 percent, is local residents and repeat clientele. *Washington Statistics* reports that the population equals 190,010 with an average income of $56,070.00.

FINANCIAL ANALYSIS

Start–up Expenses

Item	Cost
Purchase	$100,000
Total required	$100,000
Less owners equity	$ 25,000
Bank loan	$ 75,000
Total required	**$100,000**

The purpose of the bank loan is detailed in the table below.

Purchase	$100,000.00
Total required	$ 25,000.00
Less owners equity	$ 25,000.00
Total conventional financing required	**$ 75,000.00**

Sales

The expected sales from the first three years of operations are shown below. These figures are based upon historical revenues for 2004–2006, with anticipated increases of 3 percent to 5 percent per annum.

Year 1	Year 2	Year 3
$250,000	$266,000	$280,000

Monthly Start-Up Expenses

Rent	$ 800
Advertising	$ 2,000
Inventory	$20,000
Accounting	$ 500
Legal	$ 1,000
Utilities	$ 500
Store renovations	$10,000
Signage	$ 2,000
Office supplies	$ 400
Office equipment	$ 1,200
Payroll	$ 4,500
Production materials	$ 1,000
Auto	$ 500
Travel and entertainment	$ 2,000
Website development	$ 2,000
Software	$ 1,500
Retail supplies	$ 500
Postage and mailing	$ 1,000
Paint and other supplies	$ 500
Total	**$51,900**

The gallery will be structured as a corporation, with Dorthea Cooke having 100 percent ownership.

PRODUCTS

Cooke Gallery sells a diverse range of high–quality local art works to tourists, local clients and collectors at fair mark–up prices. The gallery's largest pieces include oil paintings, large candles, masks, paintings and sculptures. The majority of the gallery space is devoted to smaller, more affordable pieces such as finely drawn watercolors, acrylics, and limited edition prints; the consistently high quality of these items ensures that tourists are encouraged to purchase anywhere from $10 to $5,000 items, without sacrificing either end of the potential market and its respective client groupings.

All products sold at Cooke Gallery are made on the West Coast, with 95 percent of the inventory coming from local artists and companies. The highest selling products are hand–carved silver jewelry (rings, bracelets, earrings, and pendants), prints for both watercolor and oil paintings, clothing, and gift items such as frames, vases, and framed art cards. Overall sales are broken down into the following nine categories, in order of revenue generated:

1. Miscellaneous small items

2. Jewelry

3. Clothing

4. Artwork

5. Carvings

6. Cards

7. Masks

8. Books

9. Music

Cooke Gallery also sells commissioned special order pieces for customers, local and abroad, and provides national and international shipping services to anywhere in the world. Following the gallery's dedication to customer service policy, custom orders are commissioned with the client's interests incorporated into the piece.

MISSION

To sell superior quality, traditional artworks to tourists and local clients, while providing educational information, value, and excellent customer service as a profit– and growth–oriented business.

MARKET ANALYSIS

The West Coast's artwork is a strong cultural component for Seattle's local art and has been developed for sale over many years. Within the last thirty years there has been a growing awareness and appreciation of people's art and history. The market in North America for traditional art, specifically Seattle local art, is growing steadily and has a long, proud, complex history. While traditions remain strong, innovations flourish among contemporary artists.

Currently, international recognition of, and appreciation for, the West Coast's cultural riches is at the forefront of the market's growth, with many opportunities for export within the well–established markets of Canada, Asia, Europe, South America and the Middle East. Cooke Gallery has planned for this growing market and has established a website, which will continue to be refined to develop this opportunity further.

Success Factors

Cooke Gallery has a strong and proven history of success, based upon strong management and customer service. The company has a unique market position with various competitors in the region, but it is the only traditionally-owned gallery in Seattle and is thriving in a growing tourism industry. The purchase of this business is based on the new owner's excellent understanding of how the business operates and desire to further develop of the business' cultural component.

Within the industry, retail galleries fall into the category of wholesale and retail trade; this sector realized a 3.3 percent growth in their contribution to tourism GDP in 2006 and has been positive for the past nine years. This is consistent with the strong tourism statistics, which according to *Washington Statistics* increased 3 percent from 2004 to 2005. This was the strongest growth seen in the tourism industry since 1995. Overall, Cooke Gallery has a proven formula for success that will continue to flourish and thrive under the new ownership of Ms. Dorthea Cooke and her continued management.

Competition

There are many indirect competitors in Seattle; however, traditionally-owned galleries in central Seattle are non–existent—thus the gallery has no direct competition.

MANAGEMENT SUMMARY

Ms. Cooke will continue as Gallery Manager. Ms. Cooke possesses seven years experience as Gallery Manager and is responsible for all aspects of operations including all inventory controls, purchasing, payroll, management of staff, sales training, and cultural education and training. Ms. Cooke possesses excellent interpersonal and organizational skills and is committed the highest quality customer service. Ms. Cooke is also dedicated to training the staff and educating her customers on the cultural aspects of each piece sold, and it is this level of customer service that is the basis of the business's success. Her management expertise will continue to provide the company a strong basis of operations while strengthening the cultural component of operations.

The company has a strong and dedicated staff of seven part–time and casual sales associates—each has worked with the gallery for several years. The staff has established a strong working relationship with the new owner and will continue working at the gallery in the same capacity.

The management and staff of the Cooke Gallery are committed to providing excellent customer service, based upon caring and respectful relationships. The current staff has been with Cooke Gallery for many years and is developing their knowledge and skills regularly. The staff's enjoyment for their work is passed on to the customers who come into the store. There is always a positive atmosphere in the gallery with the very friendly and helpful staff. As well as discussing the artwork and the native culture, they willingly help tourists find their way around and give travel advice.

OPERATIONS

The Cooke Gallery operates seven days a week from 9AM–5 PM. As a retail operation, there is a wide range of daily activities that include selling, buying, custom orders, inventory controls, marketing, customer relations and merchandising.

The manager of the gallery is responsible for all aspects of operations including customer relations, meeting with artists daily, buying artwork, inventory control, ordering special customer requests, and researching cultural information for staff and customers on different subjects. In addition, Ms. Cooke manages all financial transactions of day–to–day sales and accounts payable. Ms. Cooke will be responsible for the management of promotions, sales, cultural education, and marketing.

The staff is responsible primarily for customer service, conveying inventory needs, trends and requests. Strict adherence to ensuring a high level of customer service and dynamic inventory ensures that customers are well taken care of, receive fair value and return regularly. The golden rule is that visitors are given the best customer service and respect within Cooke Gallery, making it a fun place where customers can feel comfortable browsing while they gain background and knowledge about the artwork and culture of Seattle.

MARKETING & SALES

Cooke Gallery's overall market is based upon two primary client groups of tourists and local clients. Tourists to the region represent the first market, and the second is local clients from the central Seattle area.

Tourists want to take something home with them that represents the West Coast. Native art and its content have become the symbol of the West Coast. People connect with the different representation from their own experiences. Within this market *Washington Statistics* reported in 2006 that tourism is a strong and growing industry in Seattle. This is due in large part to the recently completed upgrades to the highway and the growing tourism economy within Washington. Further, the tourism sector GDP increased 3 percent from 2004. This was the strongest growth seen in the tourism industry since 1999. In addition, wholesale and retail trade realized a 3 percent growth in their contribution to tourism GDP, which has been positive for the past nine years.

Advertising

Cooke Gallery has adopted an aggressive marketing campaign that includes high quality business cards, brochures, regular mail outs of newsletters, periodical advertising, a comprehensive website, and charitable events. These marketing tools have been adopted over the last decade and have proven successful for the gallery. Ms. Cooke will continue to evolve her marketing strategy based on customer feedback and the success of existing tools.

We will also focus our advertising dollars in the areas of tourism publications where the gallery will get the maximum exposure to the desired clients. For example, we will focus on bus and taxi advertising where the Cooke Gallery name will be in front of the driving traffic while they are in the city either as tourists or as business travellers.

Target Sales

All products are marked up 100 percent; layaway and custom order terms include a 50 percent deposit with the balance due upon delivery of the product. We will also investigate art placement as a way to drive higher revenue. This is where we rent the art to be placed in either business and/or city locations like hospitals, government buildings, and the like. This is not included in this plan but we will add this service once we get all the details on the business model.

Target sales are tracked monthly and are compared weekly and monthly against actual. Cooke Gallery anticipates sales increases of 10 percent for 2007–2008, with 5 percent per annum increases per month thereafter.

CONCLUSION

Business Feasibility

A detailed explanation of our strengths, weaknesses, opportunities, and threats is noted below. We feel our strengths and opportunities greatly outweigh our weaknesses and threats, leaving our business poised for success.

Strengths:	• Our art will be of the higher scale, catering to clients who like art that is traditional. This market is strong and does not suffer the ups and downs of niche art.
	• Our art is organized and placed in visually appealing ways throughout the store
	• We have an excellent proven history and sales
	• We have a strong client base
	• We offer medium to high pricing
	• We have no direct competition
	• We boast an excellent central location
	• We have educated and loyal staff
Weaknesses:	• Slow seasons. Management knows this and plans accordingly
Opportunities:	• Enhance cultural training and activities
	• Enhance international sales through website marketing
	• Develop catalogue for international and corporate sales
Threats:	• Downturns in tourism economy

Growth Strategy

Cooke Gallery has a long history as a successful art gallery and, with our tourism client base, we are assured of long-term success in the business. With the demographic boom in this area carrying on for the past 10 years, we are certain that this going to be a solid place for our business to be. In addition, the company operates with competition in the area that has no direct product similarities and has a high volume of vehicle traffic and two tourism seasons.

Future plans for Cooke Gallery include some major renovations to the facade and store displays. In addition, the company will continue to develop its advertising through magazines, newspapers, and the internet.

Cafe and Gas Station
TROON CAFE AND GAS STATION

56 Lakeview Circle
Indian River, Michigan 49749

Gerald Rekve

The Troon Cafe and Gas Station will be a full–service and self–serve facility that will sell gasoline, boat fuel, motor oils, lubricants, and confectionery and will house a 45 person cafe. The cafe will be based on a 1950s diner to appeal to the aging baby boomers. The use of colors, seating, and counter will mimic the traditional 1950s diner.

EXECUTIVE SUMMARY

Business Overview

The Troon Cafe and Gas Station will be a full–service and self–serve facility that will sell gasoline, boat fuel, motor oils, lubricants, and confectionery and will house a 45 person cafe. The cafe will be based on a 1950s diner to appeal to the aging baby boomers. The use of colors, seating, and counter will mimic the traditional 1950s diner.

The business owner of The Troon Cafe and Gas Station is Wanda Fretter. The city council has approved the planning phase of the Cafe and Gas Station. The approval is conditional based on obtaining above–ground gas tanks that are in compliance with the Fire Services Act and securing the necessary financing. Thomasson Oil, based in Mackinac City, will supply both oil and gas to the facility. We will also sell a full range of cigarettes and pipe tobacco. The menu items will be all fast–food type, therefore allowing for quick turnover of the customers in our 45 seat cafe.

OPERATIONS

The gas station will be an incorporated business owned and managed by Wanda Fretter. The gas station is located on the main route going through Indian River, Michigan and the hours of operation are 5:00AM to 1:00AM, seven days per week. The proposed site measures 250 feet by 210 feet, and offers easy access from the local highway. There will be 6 self–serve pumps, 6 full–service pumps, a convenience store that measures 200 square feet, and public washroom facilities. The cafe will be 680 square feet.

The funding will be used for various purposes as outlined below:

- Site preparation: $150,000

- Equipment (purchase and installation): $200,000

- Fuel: $30,000

- Build convenience store: $150,000

- Inventory: $13,000

- Insurance: $1,000

The business will begin when all of the start–up capital is in place. An environmental assessment will be completed by the local government office responsible for gas station businesses.

Once all the business processes are started, we will begin site excavation to install the gas tanks and lines. Then once this is done, the building for the cafe and gas station will be constructed. We will use the most current technologies to build the location's structures.

Management Summary

Wanda Fretter will be the manager of the business and will work full–time at Troon Cafe and Gas Station. Mrs. Fretter has extensive experience in the business, having worked as a manager for Perky's Restaurant Chain for four years and as a manager with Tricky Speedy Stores for six years. Wanda's management experience will be a valuable asset to the business.

The business will hire the following:

- 12 part–time employees, each with 4 to 35 hours per week

- 7 full–time employees, each with 37.5 hours per week

- 3 full–time cooks, each with 40 hours per week

Eventually, a bookkeeper will also be hired for the business. The position will be filled in 2010, pending completion and approval of the environmental assessment and secured financing. The position will be part–time, consisting of 4–8 hours per week.

PRODUCTS & SERVICES

The Troon Cafe and Gas Station will be a full–service and self–serve facility; the initial focus will be fuel sales, including regular, premium, and diesel fuel.

The station will also sell motor oils and accessories, such as coolants and lubricants. According to the Petroleum Communication Foundation, the profits realized on fuel sales are marginal and with such small markups, the main way to stay in business is to sell huge volumes. (An average urban station sells from three to six million gallons of gasoline per year or 400–800 gallons an hour.) Despite huge volumes, margins are so thin that virtually all filling stations depend on non–fuel products, such as snack foods, to increase revenues and margins. For this reason, the secondary product line will include convenience items such as magazines, tobacco, maps, ice, soft drinks, and candy.

The fuels will be contained in above ground tanks. Underground fuel storage tanks usually fail from rust perforation due to several effects of water inside the tank. External rust, unless very heavy, isn't highly correlated with internal rust. Leaks can occur due to tank damage or at piping connections and a new tank involves significant expense.

Automobile Fuel

According to the American Petroleum Products Institute (APPI), automobile fuel consumption is constant. With the minimal profit margin on automobile fuels, the business will also target recreational boaters and fishers by selling boat fuel. Another focus of the business will be convenience store sales and cafe sales.

Boat/marine fuel

Sport fishing and recreational boat use in Michigan is a multi–million dollar industry. Boating attracts tens of thousands of visitors every year. Recreational fishing and related activities are not only of economic importance, it is part of the city of Indian River's history. With the wide variety of fish and fishing environments and facilities available, it is no question that Northern Michigan's reputation as an fisher's paradise is unchallenged.

Water Sports Participation in 2006

Percent of population participating at least once in 2006

Water sports participation (15 and up)

Water sports	Men	Women
Swimming	46%	41%
Fishing (others)	28%	23%
Canoeing	16%	10%
Fishing (fly)	5%	2%
Water skiing	16%	13%
Sailing	22%	18%
Scuba diving	24%	15%
Board sailing	26%	24%

Other Services

The gas station/convenience store combination will offer confectionery, hot and cold beverages, news-papers and magazines, and prepared food items in addition to industry staples like gas and other car accessories.

MARKET ANALYSIS

The Troon Cafe and Gas Station will be the only gas station in the area that is easily visible and accessible from the local highway. The Troon Cafe and Gas Station will target several different types of customers. The travel and tourist market will be one target market. The town of Indian River doubles in size in the summer months, and the traffic through the town is substantial. The visibility and location of the station will ensure a constant flow of traffic through the station.

The additional two target markets are local citizens and the residents of the area surrounding Indian River; through these two markets we anticipate a constant stream of business for gas and food purchases.

The business will be a success for the following reasons:

- Lack of comparable competition

- Nice new store and cafe built with traditional decor

- Convenient store sales

- Visible, easily accessible location

- Cafe that looks like it was built in the 1950s, yet is new construction

COSTS

Below is a detailed explanation of the different costs associated with starting this business.

Financial information

Item	Cost
Environmental assessment, prepare site	$ 150,000
Install equipment (pumps etc.)	$ 200,000
Convenience store construction	$ 150,000
Inventory for convenience store	$ 13,000
Business insurance, permits, licenses	$ 1,000
Purchase fuel	$ 30,000
Total required	**$ 544,000**

History of the Industry

Crude oil is the raw material from which gasoline is distilled. Crude oil makes up more than 99 percent of the volume of most gasoline and it contributes a significant portion of the final price. Crude oil prices behave much as any other commodity with wide price swings in times of shortage or oversupply. The crude oil price cycle may extend over several years.

Refining costs are the component of price added by the refining company to cover its costs and profit margin. Refiner margins average 10 to 15 percent of the total pump price. This money pays for refinery capital costs, refinery fuel, wages and salaries, profits and corporate taxes.

Retail costs are the price that is retained by the retailer. The majority of motorists see little or no difference between brands of gasoline. If competing gasoline stations are about equal in service, convenience and cleanliness, many motorists will switch stations for two–tenths of a cent per gallon. This means competition is based almost exclusively on price and the best way to attract customer is to sell for less. As a result, gasoline retailers must keep their markup razor–thin. Markups, which are less than 10 percent, cover: land, salaries, buildings, fuel delivery, site maintenance, profit (about one cent per gallon). With such small markups, the main way to stay in business is to sell huge volumes, and the primary way to increase volumes is to reduce retail margins.

Competition

There are almost 55,500 retail gas outlets in the United States. Retail gas through these outlets accounts for 37 percent of overall petroleum demand in the country. In Michigan there are 769 gas outlets, and in the Indian River area there are 5 gas stations.

As with much of the retail sector, the retail gas industry has undergone some major changes over the past 20 years.

Some factors that affect gas stations are:

*   Increased/longer operating hours
*   Strategic location adjacent to supermarkets/malls
*   Increased numbers of gas stations in urban centers
*   Shifts in customer demand for more products and services (ATMs, etc.)

Independent and corporate gas stations have met with these demands and the result is increased competition. The competition is most intense in cities and larger towns. An independent company like The Troon Cafe and Gas Station can still be profitable in a smaller, rural and less competitive setting.

Although competition has increased over the past few years, fuel sales continue to increase annually. The most intense competition is in larger urban centers (large supermarkets with gas bars take the lead).

This leaves opportunity for independents in smaller rural settings. To be successful, location on a main highway with significant through traffic is a key factor. Easy access, convenient and plentiful parking, and high visibility are also very important.

There are many things that must be done to assure that the business can be successful and efficient, as noted below:

- Convenience store equipment turned on as necessary
- Count float, open daily records, check tallies recorded from previous evening
- Initialize and turn on pumps
- Do an inspection of pumps, site and equipment
- Order fuel; inventory control done automatically by fuel company
- Store inventory control; order as necessary
- Dip measurement to check fuel level at night
- Measurement checked to daily usage (as per cash machine); balance as necessary

Supplies

Below is a list of proposed suppliers, the products they offer, and the terms.

Supplier	Products	Terms
Western Transportation System	Fuel, petroleum, boat fuel, diesel	Net 15
Pepsi Canada	Soft drinks	Net 15
Canadian Confectionery	Chocolate bars, candies	Net 15
Coca Cola	Soft drinks, bottled water	Net 30
Fresh Meats Inc.	All kitchen rest foods	Net 15
Confectionary Inc.	All confectionary Items	Net 15
BONZOS	Chips and other snacks	
Bats Inc	Chips, snack foods, chip dips	Net 30
Fresh Sandwich's Inc.	Made daily sandwiches	Net 0—paid on delivery
Auto Trader	Car magazines	Net 0—paid on delivery

Customers

The Troon Cafe and Gas Station is located in the heart of the major tourism destination—Indian River is a popular summer–time vacation destination. The area's population itself almost doubles in size during the summer, turning this small city into something more like a large city.

Location

The location allows for maximum visibility and easy access. Motorists will see the station from the highway in time to access the station safely. It will have excellent forecourt lighting for nighttime customers and will be built on flat land that will facilitate access. There will be ample room to enter and exit the station without difficult or abrupt turns. Prominent signage on the site will list the services offered and their prices. Strategically placed road signage will direct highway traffic to the gas station.

MARKETING & SALES

Advertising

To attract business, we will employ the following methods:

- Business cards
- Flyers

- Internet website
- Weekly contest—"Free Gas Draw"
- Yellow pages
- Radio advertising
- Signage on local highway and surrounding areas

For the first six months of business, the customers will be polled as to how they found the business and the most inefficient advertising and marketing techniques will be eliminated.

Pricing Strategy and Target Sales

The Troon Cafe and Gas Station will make every effort to be competitive in its pricing. External factors such as the price of international crude oil affect gas prices and are beyond control of our business, but we will maintain a fixed profit margin. Higher transport costs will be reflected in our prices; therefore, our pricing will be somewhat higher than most urban centers. This will not affect sales due to the limited competition and the strong customer base from local residents.

The industry standard for markups, less than 10 percent, will be followed. This standard 10 percent covers land, salaries, buildings, fuel delivery, site maintenance, and profit. With this in mind, the convenience store will offer promotions to local residents to increase sales volumes. These promotions will include contests and giveaways.

Sales are expected to be high during peak summer season. It is anticipated that a regular and loyal customer base will be established within the local community to ensure a consistent positive cash flow during the slow season.

GROWTH STRATEGY

We wholeheartedly believe in the long–term viability of our business. This is due to the following factors:

- Visible, easily accessible location
- Lack of comparable competition
- Cigarette sales
- Attractive convenience store
- Cafe
- Friendly customer service

Courier Service

CORPORATE COURIER

8910 Greenleaf Blvd.
Williamsburg, Virginia 23081

Gerald Rekve

Matthew Park will be opening a courier service with a difference. The goals of the service will focus on catering to professional clients like doctors, lawyers, accountants, and large corporations. During the start-up we will hire twenty contract drivers. These drivers will then help start up and grow the business. Because this is a start-up courier service, we will need to win new clients. These clients can only be won with either word of mouth or by sales using our drivers to be our sales people. The drivers we will hire are older semi–retired or retired people who still want to be a part of the work force and make a few dollars while enjoying the being out with people every day.

EXECUTIVE SUMMARY

Mission

Our mission is to provide our clients with great service at competitive prices, while employing retired individuals who still want to contribute to the work force.

Management Summary

Our company will be a corporation that is owned by one person. Matthew Park's background is as a newspaper publisher. This background is quite different than the courier business, yet has many of the same qualities. The courier business is all about management of packages and publishing is all about management of packs of information. This will give Matthew a solid foundation for which to grow his business.

MARKET ANALYSIS

Our target market includes professional businesses like doctors, lawyers, accountants and so on; these clients demand the highest in service because, in most cases, they are sending information that is highly confidential.

Examples include sensitive medical information and legal notices, both of which must legally be kept confidential. Knowing this, we are certain that these sectors will adopt our company and be willing to pay extra to use our services.

Who are the customers? As indicated above, the main client base we will focus all our efforts on will be:

- Doctors
- Lawyers

- Accountants
- Engineers
- Medical labs
- Dental labs
- Medical offices
- Dentals offices
- X–ray offices
- Medical professional services
- Courts
- Police ticket delivery
- Architects offices
- Bank offices
- Realtors offices
- Real estate agents and their clients

Because we are a courier service, we will deliver *any item* up to a maximum of 60 pounds, in accordance with the local government's regulations on one person maximum lifting limits.

While the courier service is not new, our specialized market is unique and is willing to pay a higher price for the higher level of service we will provide to our clients. Further, this level of service will garner a high percent of the market. We aim to secure 15 percent of the market in the first year of business, an amount that is achievable and will provide significant income for our employees.

We will operate our main courier terminal in Williamsburg, Virginia. Our hours of operation will be from 8:00 am to 8:00 pm every day of the week. We will be set up as a sole ownership corporation and will employ 10 contract drivers. Each driver will meet a high level of security clearances.

Competition

All potential competitors are segmented into different areas of courier services, doing everything from truck loads of freight to envelope delivery. There are only two that will be offering the exact same services as ours—offering high–level package privacy and security demanded by doctors and lawyers for various reports and documents that require the highest level of discretion and protection.

FINANCIAL ANALYSIS

We will be able to operate our business using start up funds of $50,000. Of this total, there will be a loan request for $20,000 and the remaining $30,000 is being provided by the owner.

PRODUCTS & SERVICES

The biggest barrier to entry for us is to gain acceptance by our key clients. Having said this, our research indicates that potential clients will indeed use our services. We will provide service on a daily basis from 8:00 am to 8:00 pm every day of the week. Our company will provide courier service to our clients. We will offer pre–scheduled services as well as on–time or on–demand services. We will deliver and carry any item up to 60 pounds and delivery it either in a short schedule or normal delivery service.

All of our deliveries will be recorded by a new online delivery tracking service. Once a client's delivery destination signs for an item, the client will get an email indicating the package was delivered and all the important information will be included in the email, including who signed for it, the time it was delivered, etc.

MARKETING & SALES

Sales Strategy

Sales strategy will be managed by the owner. All of our drivers will act as our sales agents, keeping costs down and making sure we target all the markets we want to target. A sales bonus program will be offered to our drivers—for each new client they sign up, the driver will get 2 percent of every dollar that client spends with our service after the first 12 months the client has been with our company. This includes all businesses even though the driver may not personally make the deliveries. This is will be an incredible bonus and will keep our drivers motivated to stay with us for a long time.

Advertising

We intend to promote our business using various methods as outlined below.

- Word of mouth
- Alliances
- Customer service
- Telemarketing
- Advertising
- Direct mail
- Magazines
- Newspapers
- Phone book
- Signage
- Website
- Public relations
- Demonstrations/booths
- Flyers
- Newsletters
- Press releases
- Promotional products
- Sponsored events

Pricing Strategy

Because of the high level of privacy and protection for our service, we are going to be charging a higher fee than some of our competitors. This goes along with the need for our client's top secret service and on time delivery. Our prices are set higher than our competition because we are not a normal courier service.

Our Pricing

Below is a detailed breakdown of our prices, based on mileage and desired turn-around time. As noted, these may be higher than potential competitors, but they cannot compete with our level of privacy and customer service. Our customers will be willing to pay more for our services because of this.

Mileage	Quick (4.5 Hours)	Quicker (2.5 Hours)	Quickest (1.5 Hours)
0–5	$30.00	$35.00	$40.00
6–10	$35.00	$40.00	$45.00
11–15	$40.00	$45.00	$50.00
16–20	$45.00	$50.00	$55.00
21–25	$50.00	$55.00	$60.00
26–30	$55.00	$60.00	$65.00
31–35	$60.00	$65.00	$70.00
36–40	$65.00	$70.00	$75.00
41–45	$70.00	$75.00	$80.00
46–50	$75.00	$80.00	$85.00

Ethanol Fuel Production

Ontario Ethanol Supply

1700 Ottawa St.
Windsor, ON, Canada N8Y 1R8

Gerald Rekve

We are raising $500,000 to start an ethanol fuel production company. In the recent economy with increasing gas prices, ethanol production is both cost effective and a smart alternative to more traditional forms of fuel.

EXECUTIVE SUMMARY

With the growth of the ethanol industry along with the increasing gas prices, the timing could not be any better for a start up of an ethanol business. We are raising $500,000 in order to start this business. Once funding is in place, we will be driving sales in the first three months of operation. The long–term outlook is also very strong.

PRODUCT

Our product is simple. We will be selling ethanol fuel for consumer uses such as automobiles and other small engines like those used in lawn mowers, rototillers, and the like.

Because of the increase in fuel prices at the pump and the forecasted continued rise, consumers are looking for alternatives to gasoline. Our product will fill that need.

The technology available today allows for the ability for almost anyone to produce ethanol. We have decided to produce the product on a mass scale, large enough to corner a market in our region.

TARGET MARKET

Ethanol does not burn as clean as higher-end gasoline. Therefore, we will not be targeting the high-end cars and SUVs that require high octane gasoline. Furthermore, our product does not work in any motorcycles or mopeds, and we will therefore not be targeting those markets.

The type of vehicles that our product will work in:

- Trucks—Quarter, half, three–quater and 1 ton
- Vans—Half, three–quater and 1 ton
- Nissan

- GMC

- Chevy

- Ford

- Dodge

- Honda

- Hyundai

- Toyota

- All two and four cycle engines

- Garden trackers

Because of the way our product is produced, we will use a just–in–time type of ordering and delivery process for our product.

PRODUCTION AND TRAINING

We will use the following method to produce our product.

1. Wheat or corn kernels are ground in a hammermill to expose the starch.

2. The ground grain is mixed with water, cooked briefly, and enzymes are added to convert the starch to sugar using a chemical reaction called hydrolysis.

3. Yeast is added to ferment the sugars to ethanol.

4. The ethanol is separated from the mixture by distillation.

5. Water is removed from the mixture using dehydration.

A new process is under development for making ethanol from the cellulose and hemicellulose components of cheaper biomass feedstocks such as wood and agricultural residues. The method is similar to the traditional process that uses the starch component of grain or corn. However, this method is more difficult because these types of feedstock require more complex pre–treatment and hydrolysis steps that use acid or enzymes before the sugars can be fermented to ethanol.

We have already contracted with about twenty farmers in the region. Each month we will purchase from these farmers only the best corn. The farmers realize that we have high quality needs so they are taking extra care in the farming process in order to supply us with the best in their product. The farmers that accommodate us will make about four times per bushel then if they were to sell their corn to the regular distribution channels.

Training Staff

Because this is a newer, somewhat unusual product, some people may have questions about the product and its uses. We have created a list of common questions with appropriate responses to address these concerns. Some of these include:

Is ethanol a more powerful fuel than gasoline?

Yes, if the engine is designed for ethanol fuels. Gasoline actually has more heat content per gallon than ethanol (about 1.5 times as much), but ethanol contains oxygen. This means that you can burn about 1.6 times as much ethanol by volume as gasoline. You get more total heat and the engine is also cooled better. The net result is more power. The very high octane rating of ethanol (about 129) also means the engine can run a lot higher compression ratio, further increasing the horsepower potential.

How much higher is the octane with ethanol fuels?

The octane of pure ethanol is so high (about 113) that it cannot be measured in the same way as gasoline. Any amount of ethanol in gasoline raises the octane rating of the fuel. E–10 (10 percent ethanol/90 percent gasoline) has an octane about two to three points higher (typically around 93 octane for E–10).

Will ethanol damage a car's fuel system?

E–10 will not damage any parts of your car so long as it is a late model vehicle that specifies that it is E–10 compatible (refer to the owner's manual to be sure). In fact, E–10 fuels have been shown to promote cleaner fuel injectors and have a higher octane rating (less prone to knocking and run–on). With modern reformulated fuels, especially those containing ethanol, fuel injector clogging that was once a common problem is virtually nonexistent today. In order to run E85 (85 percent ethanol/10 percent gasoline), a car must be specifically designed for it. These are called "Flexible Fuel Vehicles" (FFVs) and are usually identified by a gas cap insignia and in the owner's manual.

If ethanol is so good, why aren't all gas stations carrying E–10 and E–85 fuels?

At the current rate of gasoline consumption, there simply isn't enough production capacity. However, this is rapidly changing. For example, the state of Indiana has only two operating ethanol production facilities, but has nine more under construction. You'll be seeing a lot more ethanol motor fuels as production capacity increases. New technologies are also improving the efficiency of production as well as opening up new raw materials that can be grown to produce ethanol.

Does ethanol make a car run cleaner?

Yes. As an effective oxygenate, ethanol promotes more complete combustion. Gasoline chemicals contain a lot of carbon resulting in emissions of carbon monoxide and carbon dioxide. Ethanol contains very little carbon and also contains oxygen, so it burns a lot cleaner.

Years ago, I heard about problems with "gasohol". Is E–10 just a new name for gasohol?

No. Gasohol was introduced in the late 1970's and really was just the existing gasolines of the time with ethanol added. New E–10 fuels are formulated in accordance with federal standards for lower sulphur content, detergency, controlled volatility, and many other factors that make it a much cleaner and better fuel.

Why will we be using more gasolines with ethanol in them?

There are a variety of reasons including those of economics, environmental issues, and even national security. Much of the ethanol made today uses corn and other renewable crops raised by our American farmers. This keeps more US dollars in America. Ethanol is environmentally friendly so we can enjoy cleaner air. Decreasing our dependence on foreign oil has also become a critical matter of national security. It is in our best interests to be as energy–independent as possible. Today, every domestic and foreign new car is E10 compatible and there are over two million E–85–comaptible "Flexible Fuel Vehicles" (FFVs) already on the road. By the end of this year 2006, there will be an additional 400,000 FFVs produced and sold.

BACKGROUND

Today, U.S. ethanol is primarily produced from starch– and sugar–based crops by dry–mill or wet–mill processing. Cellulose ethanol has not yet been produced commercially. However, several commercial cellulose ethanol production plants are under construction, and intensive research and development is rapidly advancing the state of cellulose ethanol technology.

Powering vehicles with ethanol across Canada

Ethanol is produced from the starch, or cellulose and hemicelluloses components of biomass. Ethanol can be blended with gasoline to produce an environmentally beneficial transportation fuel. The most common blend, which is composed of 10 percent ethanol and 90 percent gasoline, is known as E10. It can be burned in any car and is available at over 1,000 filling stations in 6 provinces across central and western Canada. In the future, a blend of 85 percent ethanol and 15 percent gasoline (E85) might become commercially available. Cars that are capable of burning any combination of ethanol/gasoline—up to 85 percent ethanol—are already available on the market for no, or insignificant, additional cost.

Bioenergy

Development Program Ethanol has many environmental advantages over gasoline—a major contributor to climate change. It is estimated that a litre of biomass ethanol used to replace a litre of gasoline reduces the accumulation of atmospheric carbon dioxide—a harmful greenhouse gas—by 70 percent. For the past two decades, Natural Resources Canada's CANMET Energy Technology Centre (CETC) has assisted Canadian firms in making ethanol from biomass a commercial reality.

The automotive industry's first investigation into fuel ethanol dates back to Henry Ford's original Model T design. While gasoline soon replaced ethanol as the fuel of choice, modern environmental concerns have revived interest in this green gasoline.

Until recently, environmental concerns were outstripped by the fact that gasoline was far cheaper and more accessible than ethanol. However, with heightened environmental awareness and a global commitment to reduce greenhouse gases, ethanol has emerged as an available option for consumers. 130 million litres of grain based fuel ethanol are produced in Canada each year. With the addition of new production plants currently under construction, this is expected to at least triple over the next few years. Grain ethanol, as an additive to transportation fuels, has now gained commercial acceptance. Over 950 retail outlets across Canada offer E–10 ethanol–blend fuels (10 percent ethanol, 90 percent gasoline).

Biomass Ethanol

Ethanol can be made from products other than grain. Major breakthroughs are being made to convert biomass products into ethanol. Currently, the focus of CETCs Bioenergy Development Program is on forestry wastes such as wood chips and sawdust, and agricultural wastes such as straw and chaff. Great strides are also being made to convert municipal wastes as well. There is enough wood waste in British Columbia alone to replace half of Canada's gasoline with E10.

Waste Ethanol

Based on the amount of waste currently available across the country, it is predicted that wastes alone could theoretically produce all of Canada's fuel ethanol needs. (3.8 billion litres/year or 10 percent blend in the 38 billion litres/year vehicle fuel demand projected for 2005). The challenge is that these wastes contain "lignocellulosic" or woody materials that require special treatment not required in traditional grain ethanol production.

At present, the production of alcohol from lignocellulosic feedstocks is a four stage process:

1. pre–treatment to expose the cellulose and hemicellulose components

2. converting the cellulose and hemicellulose components into sugars

3. fermenting the sugars to produce ethanol

4. recovering the ethanol

In 1974, it cost $2.50 to produce a litre of ethanol from wood. As a result of cooperative Research and Developement, the cost is now estimated at $0.30 to 0.35/litre. Within ten years, researchers expect production costs to drop to $0.22/litre.

Technology Advancement Innovative, high–tech systems are being developed to meet the specific requirements of producing ethanol from wastes. Basically, they all consist of four unit operations, each with it's own technical and economic barriers. Through our partnerships in research and development, we serve as a catalyst to remove these barriers and to make commercial implementation a reality.

1. pre–treatment: the pre–treatment of hard wood, soft wood and agricultural residues using steam or extrusion based processes has been optimized;

2. hydrolysis: specifically tailored acid or enzyme based processes have greatly improved the efficiency of conversion of the pre–treated feedstock to fermentable sugars;

3. fermentation: new genetically engineered strains of bacteria show promise for significantly improving ethanol production volumes; and

4. ethanol recovery: extractive fermentation and other new developments have greatly enhanced overall efficiency. As a result of some of these innovations, Canada's first demonstration plant to produce ethanol from agricultural and wood wastes is scheduled for construction in 1999.

START UP EXPENSES

Equipment—$15,000

Legal—$2,500

Business licence—$200

Corn for first month's production—$5,000

Other Ingredients—$3,000

Advertising—$2,000

Auto—$3,000

Miscellaneous—$3,300

Staff—$6,500

Lease hold improvements—$20,000

Lease—$3,400

COMPETITION

This is a very hot market and there is a lot of competition in both the region and the sector. We feel this will continue to grow, however the market size is tremendous and we feel our investment will not be affected by the competition.

MARKET ANALYSIS

With the ever-increasing demand for alternative fuels from around the world, the pressure on ethanol will continue to grow despite even its drawbacks. The author of this business plan has identified extensive data that will strongly support the investment in ethanol production.

Business Case for our Business Start up

Ontario corn farmers are big supporters of the expanded use of renewable fuels including ethanol–blended gasoline, and neat ethanol (fuels containing at least 85 percent ethanol). So, too, are a growing percentage of Canadian automobile owners.

Here's why:

- Biological renew ability. Ethanol is made from growing crops, not fossil energy sources. The sun is the source of most energy used to make fuel ethanol.

- Cleaner environment. When ethanol is used as an automotive fuel, either by itself or in an ethanol–gasoline blend, the result is less carbon monoxide, lower emissions of hydrocarbons into the air, and less dependence on toxic compounds used to increase the octane level of automotive fuels.

- Cleaner burning engines equals less carbon build–up.

- Lower net carbon dioxide emissions caused by the combustion of automotive fuels; this means less potential for global warming.

- Less dependence on imported light crude oil used, increasingly, for gasoline production in Canada.

- Expanded market opportunity for Canadian farmers, without hampering Canadian food production capabilities.

- Economic opportunities for rural Canada.

TIME LINE

Once we have access to the start up money, we will be in production within three months. We are hoping to raise $500,000 for this start–up, most of which will be used for operating expenses. Investors will be able to see return on their investment within 12 months of our start–up.

KEY STAFF

Bill Brown will be the Operations manager. Bill has over twenty years of management experience as a production manager.

Bob White will be the CFO; Bob has over ten years experience as a CFO for various business sectors.

Ben Black will be the procurement manager; he will in charge of all the buying of production products.

Dale Green will be the sales manager in charge of all aspects of selling the products.

Darren Winters and Karen Summer will be the two main shareholders of the company with an initial investment of $20,000 each. They are looking at raising $500,000 for the company. In the first year the sales target is $400,000 with an operating profit of $140,000.

Fantasy Book & Memorabilia Store

Wizard and Warlock Books

7100 Pinetree Bluffs
Cheyenne, Wyoming 82009

Gerald Rekve

Wizard and Warlock Books is a full–service retail operation selling hardcover books, magazines, specialty books, Japanese figurines and fantasy figurines related to the fantasy book market.

EXECUTIVE SUMMARY

Business Overview

Wizard and Warlock Books is a full–service retail operation selling hardcover books, magazines, specialty books, Japanese figurines and fantasy figurines related to the fantasy book market. Other book stock includes best–selling fiction and nonfiction and a lending library for children, which features books that fit school needs and are not necessarily purchased for home libraries. Hours are 10:00 am to 9:00 pm seven days a week.

Our target market are customers aged 12–20 who reside in the Cheyenne area, or within 25 miles of the store's location. Because of the demographics of the population, we feature many books that are teenage, fantasy, and Asian–themed; we are appealing to the mid– to high–income market segment.

Some of popular titles are: *Mango, Anime* magazines and books, as well *Figuring.* The goal of our company is to grow our business by appealing to clientele who currently purchase materials from the internet and other mail order places.

MARKET ANALYSIS

Cheyenne does not have any other stores that sell this type of product; we will be the only operation of this type. Even though Cheyenne only has a population of 60,000, we are very confident that our products will do well in such an area with limited population.

Based on our present statistics we have determined that there approximately 1,900 potential clients who buy the materials we will sell in our store. They purchase these items from the internet auction sites like Yahoo Auctions, Google search sales, and EBay auctions, but the pricing on these sites is comparable to the prices we will be able to offer. Therefore we will be able to sell our products and be very competitive with all the internet competitors. In fact, we will be able to offer better prices, if you factor the shipping fees in the online purchase price.

The growth of this business is mainly due to growth in computer software products that are on the market. The Asian artists seem to have started a cultural revolution about seven years ago in Japan. Today the products have made their way to North America and we are very confident that the products will continue to grow.

Marketing & Sales

Wizard and Warlock Books focuses largely on individuals and families whose incomes are such that they have the interest to purchase, as well as collect, some of the best art animation books in the industry. The retailer's basic discount is 45 percent for trade books and 29 percent for non–book merchandise. For the purpose of this business plan, the total cost of goods sold, after computing transportation costs, is 75 percent of gross sales.

Advertising

Using the recommendations of the American Booksellers Association (ABA), the owners intend to allocate a sum equal to two percent of annual sales for promotion and advertising in the following media:

- Regular newspaper ads in the *Wyoming Times*.

- Display ad in the Yellow Pages.

- Direct–mail advertising to regular book purchasers and to a list of prospective buyers who fill out in–store cards.

- Key word search on sites like Google, Yahoo!, and MSN.

- Library and school promotions during Library Week

- Special educational events.

FINANCIAL ANALYSIS

The owners of Wizard and Warlock Books started the business with their own equity investment of $50,000. To this sum, they are adding a second equity investment of $20,000, and will require an additional $50,000 as a business loan. These funds will be used for the following purposes, to build the business and to increase future sales:

- The addition of 1,200 square feet of store space, which is available directly adjacent to the present layout.

- Construction of new shelving and reorganization of existing shelves for the enhanced display of books.

- Redecorating the entire store with a new a fantasy theme, coinciding with the books we sell.

MANAGEMENT SUMMARY

We will be open seven days a week from 10:00AM to 9:00PM. We will hire six part–time and two full–time staff which includes one owner.

Salaries

Wages will be $12.00 per hour for part–time staff and $14.00 per hour for full–time staff. The owner will take a salary of $40,000 per year for the first year, then $45,000 per subsequent year, with a 33 percent share in net profits for every year thereafter. Each year the company meets expectations, the owner will get an additional 10 percent bonus to her salary.

START–UP COSTS

Start-up requirements

Start-up expenses

Cash purchases	$ 40,000
Utilities	$ 200
Repairs & maintenance	$ 1,000
Professional fees	$ 300
Insurance	$ 500
Rent	$ 1,100
Travel	$ 500
Telephone	$ 400
Postage	$ 100
Office equipment/supplies	$ 1,200
Marketing/advertising	$ 2,100
Freight	$ 5,000
Other	$ 1,500
Total Start-up expenses	**$ 53,900**

Start-up assets needed

Cash balance on starting date	$ 5,000
Start-up inventory	$ 40,000
Other current assets	$ 0
Total current assets	**$ 45,000**

Funding

Investor 1	$ 30,000
Investor 2	$ 20,000
Total investment	**$ 50,000**
Current liabilities	$ 40,000
Accounts payable	$ 10,000
Current borrowing	$ 60,000
Other current liabilities	$ 10,000
Total liabilities	**$120,000**

Food and Beverage Vending Company

PACO BELLO VENDING

79 Aspen Dr.
St. Louis, MO 63199

Gerald Rekve

Paco Bello Vending is a start–up business that specializes in placing vending machines and commercial food and beverage equipment. We desire to participate in the $11 billion food and beverage industry by supplying quality innovative equipment with national brand names like Coke, Pepsi, and Hershey's chocolate bars in our vending machines. We will penetrate the vending industry with innovative, first–to–market, high-quality vending machines. We will establish our own vending routes in the Southern and Central St. Louis region.

EXECUTIVE SUMMARY

Paco Bello Vending's mission is to lead the market in selling quality foods from quality vending machines in St. Louis's retail vending market. Placement of the vending machines will be in very specific buildings that meet the high–end demographic traffic we desire. This will allow us earn higher revenues and profits.

Paco Bello Vending is a privately owned corporation and maintains an office and a small warehouse in an area of central St. Louis. We maintain a showroom where we provide customers with product demonstrations; a warehouse where we keep an inventory of machines and supplies; and an administrative area to handle the business functions. Paco Bello Vending imports a variety of innovative products that serve the needs of special segments of the market. These machines all aim to expand existing sales and open new lines of sales for our customers.

All three of the investors in the company have full operational responsibility. Louis Galardi and Tomas Sheffield, the partners, have both entrepreneurial and industry experience. Henry Wilson brings operational management and financial skills to the operation.

Paco Bello Vending will sell most popular soft drinks available in the United States and snack foods like chips, chocolate bars, and other candy items. We will earn profit by selling one item through our vending machine at a time.

We will expand our products over time to include fresh sandwiches, pizza by the slice, milk, and non–food items in retail locations where staff can maintain the supply.

We are also pursuing supplier relationships with large nationally–branded juice and confectionary manufacturers to maximize the variety of products in our machines. This wide variety of products will insure more profit potential for both Paco Bello Vending and the locations where we supply the vending machines.

MARKET ANALYSIS

The total annual revenue from vending sales was $19.2 billion in 2006, an increase of 2 percent over 2007, according to *Vending Report* in March 2006. Small companies (those with sales of less than $1 million) accounted for 2.1 percent of the market and had projected sales for 2006 of $1.01 billion. About 67 percent of all vending operators are classified in the small category.

All of this indicates a fast–moving, innovative company that can introduce enhanced products to vending machines stand to gain a significant market share.

Paco Bello Vending will market its machines to market segments including: apartment building managers, large volume commercial buildings with office space and other business rental space; and, finally, wherever the machines can be placed in high traffic areas that show potential for good, solid revenue.

Buying Patterns

Both the food/beverage and vending industries are highly competitive. Price, return on investment (ROI), reliability, and customer service affect what products are bought and when.

There are many large name brand companies with vending machines in the market. We will focus on creating a niche market for our innovative machines to compete with larger, more recognizable names. We will need to educate our clients in areas where other machines are present.

Paco Bello Vending will achieve its sales targets through a combination of relationship building and aggressive pricing. Our initial targets will be medium–sized operators and distributors who have the capital to invest in our machines. We will continue to participate in industry trade shows and expand our advertising budget when the funds become available. Along with this strategy, we will establish relationships with larger brand name companies to become a supplier.

Paco Bello Vending's customers will derive immediate and lasting value from our products. Our vending machines will both expand existing markets and create new ones. The ROI exceeds the industry norm of 24–30 months. The quality of the products, as well as the attractive and distinctive design features, will work to satisfy existing customers and to attract new ones.

Paco Bello Vending will enjoy the traditional benefits of first–to–market. We will attempt to leverage this position to establish and solidify our brand in the market. As a small company looking to establish itself, we will be attentive and flexible in meeting our customer's demands.

Paco Bello's marketing strategy will emphasize the strengths of both our company and our products. We will position ourselves as a health food–focused company and an innovative company that supplies the market with new, high–quality products. We will position ourselves in trade shows, within industry publications, and other means to promote this strategy. Our brochures, letterhead, and business correspondence will further reinforce these concepts.

We also recognize that it costs more to attract a customer and almost nothing to retain one. To that end, we will operate under the principle that our best marketing is an exceedingly happy customer. While the industries we operate in are large, reputations play an important part.

TRADE SHOWS

Paco Bello Vending will participate each year in two sponsored trade shows. We will also attend a number of local and regional trade shows and distributor open houses to promote our product lines. During the year we will expand our advertising budget to allow us greater and higher quality exposure on the local newspapers. We are also positioned on the Internet to allow our company greater exposure and easier communication with our customers.

Placement Agreements

Paco Bello Vending will pursue placement agreements with large regional and national building owners and managers. Until these agreements are in place, we will sell directly to the small store or building owners in our market. We are also pursuing relationships with nationally–branded companies to supply them with machines for their locations.

FINANCIAL ANALYSIS

The company has an initial start–up cost of approximately $50,000. $25,000 of this cost will come from a ten–year Small Business Association loan. Short–term borrowing will provide us with an additional $15,000 and the rest will be provided by the owners as investment capital of $10,000.

Our monthly break–even will be roughly 20 vending units placed. The attractiveness of our innovative vending machines will provide us with a sales level far above this break–even point. We expect to generate $19,000 of net profit on $120,000 worth of sales in the first year.

Start–up

Our start–up costs, listed below, have been financed to date by the investment from its owners.

Start-up requirements

Start-up expenses

Cash purchases	$10,000
Utilities	$ 1,500
Repairs & maintenance	$ 5,000
Professional fees	$ 1,500
Insurance	$ 1,000
Rent	$ 1,500
Travel	$ 5,000
Inventory	$10,000
Telephone	$ 500
Postage	$ 100
Office equipment/Supplies	$ 1,500
Marketing/Advertising	$ 1,400
Freight	$ 5,000
Other	$ 1,000
Total start-up expenses	**$45,000**

Start-up assets needed

Cash balance on starting date	$ 5,000
Start-up Inventory	$10,000

Other current assets

Total current assets	$15,000
Total requirements	$60,000

Funding

Investment	
Investor 1	$20,000
Investor 2	$20,000
Investor 3	$20,000

OBJECTIVES

Paco Bello's primary objective in our first year of operation is to place 40 vending machines. For the following two years our growth objectives are:

- Grow our vending machine and equipment business by 44% each year.

- Grow revenues by 27% in our directly operated vending machines.

MISSION

Paco Bello Vending's mission is to form a company that has long–term sustainability based on providing our end users with products and services that meet or exceed their expectations. We will strive to provide easy accessibility to our machines and to keep the vending machines filled with merchandise.

Paco Bello strives to be the company that introduces innovative products to the market. To achieve this, we will search out the latest in food preparation in the vending and equipment business. As first to market, we currently enjoy a technological advantage over the competition.

As we increase our presence in the equipment business, we will continuously search out products to expand our existing line. A key component of this will be the feedback from our customer base.

Keys to Success

- Quality products

- Fresh and healthy products

- Growing our business, one client at a time

- Keeping our clients happy

BUSINESS OVERVIEW

Paco Bello Vending is a family–owned and operated import company. Located in Central St. Louis, our main investors have full operational responsibility. Paco Bello is a privately–held St. Louis corporation. Paco Bello Vending is owned by three of its key employees; the ownership breakdown is as follows:

- Louis Galardi—33%

- Tomas Sheffield—33%

- Henry Wilson—34%

PRODUCTS

Our vending products include:

- Dollar and Dash—This machine stores, in a refrigerated unit, up to 112 pre–packaged products that require refrigeration.

- Fresh Squeezie Juice—This machine delivers a chilled 9 oz. cup of fresh squeezed orange juice. In a refrigerated unit, the machine stores up to 190 lbs. of juice oranges. This will yield approximately 160 9–ounce cups. When an order is placed, the machine will dispense whole oranges that will be sliced in half; each half will then be pulverized for its juice. The juice will run through a filtering system to keep out the seeds and most of the pulp, to finally provide the customer with a 90 percent all natural cup of juice combined with 10 percent water in approximately 17 seconds.

- Quick Stop Machine—These versatile, low–cost, easy–to–maintain machines provide the end user with a variety of vending options, from phone cards to disposable cameras. Paco Bello is able to provide customers with machines that have three, four, or six product lines; this will provide flexibility to maximize unit revenue.

- Easy Expresso and Coffee—This high–quality espresso maker makes cups of delicious gourmet coffee from pre–packaged coffee packs. These pods provide great benefit to the owner by reducing the cost of measuring for each new order, and eliminating the waste associated with the traditional methods. This also allows for winter product sales where they tend to slow down due to the cold weather.

The cost of products in each type of machine is noted in the table below.

Machine	Cost
Snacks	$1–3, each item
Fresh JUICER	$2–4, each drink
Multi-line machines	$1–$20, each item
Other	$2–$5, each item
Espresso maker	$4–7, each drink
Juice machine	$1–4, each drink

COMPETITION

All of our vending machines will be the best in the market. We will only stock our machines with fresh product, which will allow us to grow our business based on our reputation—our users will know that each and every time they put money in one of our machines, they will get the freshest, best product available.

For juice drinks, the market only offers bottled or canned juices for a customer to purchase. Our Fresh Squeezie Juice machine will literally squeeze a fresh cup each and every vend transaction. The fact that the product is healthy is a huge competitive advantage over other machines.

There are a number of similar multi–line machines on the market today. We will offer the customer a quality product at prices below the existing prices for similar products. Our vending units also have a unique signage that will attract attention as compared to other competitors currently in the market.

GROWTH ANALYSIS

Within the industry, snacks and cold beverages are the largest product segments, representing 23 percent and 24 percent of the industry, respectively. These two segments are the driving force of the industry. The food category grew at a rate of 9 percent last year, according to *Vending Reports*. Cold storage machines grew at an even more impressive 35 percent in 2006, with this growth coming at the expense of shelf–stable products.

Broader economic and cultural trends are also positively impacting the industry. Food sales away from home have become a larger part of total food sales in the United States and Canada since the 1960s, according to the Department of Agriculture. The Department of Agriculture also reports an increase in demand for takeout meals. This has been proven with the extremely aggressive growth of the fast food restaurant chains like McDonalds, Burger King, etc. Fast food is here to stay for a while. The vending market has only way to go, and that is up.

Consumer preferences about taste, price, nutrition, convenience, and technology are changing. These changes flavor the vending industry, which now has the opportunity to spot these trends and develop their markets.

Sales Forecast

The following table reflects the forecasted sales for Paco Bello. We are forecasting sales growth of 20 percent a year for our vending and equipment sales, and 25 percent for the vending routes that we will establish and manage ourselves.

Unit placement—Sales forecast

Unit placement	FY 2004	FY 2005	FY 2006
JUICER machines	20	30	50
Snacks	20	30	50
Multi-line machines	20	30	50
Gums & chips	20	30	50
Cappuccino machine	20	30	50
Juice squeezer	20	30	50
Total unit sales	120	180	300
Unit prices	**FY 2004**	**FY 2005**	**FY 2006**
JUICER machines	$10,000 × 12	$15,000 × 12	$15,000 × 12
Snacks	$10,000 × 12	$15,000 × 12	$15,000 × 12
Multi-line machines	$10,000 × 12	$15,000 × 12	$15,000 × 12
Gum & chips	$10,000 × 12	$15,000 × 12	$15,000 × 12
Cappuccino machine	$10,000 × 12	$15,000 × 12	$15,000 × 12
Juice squeezer	$10,000 × 12	$15,000 × 12	$15,000 × 12
Sales			
JUICER machines	150,000	150,000	150,000
Snacks	150,000	150,000	150,000
Multi-line machines	150,000	150,000	150,000
Gum & chips	150,000	150,000	150,000
Cappuccino machine	150,000	150,000	150,000

Strategic Alliances

A leading objective of Paco Bello Vending is the development of key strategic alliances. We will pursue alliances with branded, national snack makers such as Hershey, Coke, Pepsi, and others to create greater market potential. We will also seek out strategic alliances with national juice brands, such as Tropicana, Sunkist, and others to increase the market potential for our Fresh Squeezie Juice machines.

Paco Bello Vending views the relationship between the company and our distributors as a strategic alliance. We will work closely with each distributor to co–market and promote our products and will work, wherever possible, in partnership to achieve desired market penetration.

The following Market Analysis table and chart are broken down by general market segments, versus the specifics listed above.

Market analysis

Potential customers	Growth	2005	2006	2007	2008	2009	CAGR
Cold beverage	3%	720	766	871	1,222	1,343	3.98%
Warm food	5%	1,530	1,665	1,784	1,878	1,980	5.01%
Hot coffee sales	5%	78	88	89	92	95	5.23%
Juice sales retail	4%	34	67	68	69	75	4.09%

Paco Bello Vending's initial strategy is to offer all of our products to all segments of the market. We will focus on the end user, as the strategy to secure accounts with the great high traffic locations will take some time to build. We will reach our target market by pursuing personalized relationships with contacts developed at business shows. The principle market need we will be addressing will be revenue. Each of our machines will act to expand existing profit for clients who place our machines, because we pay them either a percentage of sales or a fixed monthly fee. We will try to make sure it is a win–win for both us and the client who is allowing our machine on their site.

Growth rates in both the vending industry and fast food industry remain strong. This growth is fuelled by the changes in the workplace and workforce that are causing workers to consume more of their meals away from home. Away from home food sales are expected to increase by 59 percent, according to industry reports.

As more and more people eat away from home, the demand for higher quality is also growing. Vendors are now offering a full line of packaged frozen meals in their machines. Margins will increase as premium prices are being placed on branded, high–quality products. Demographic trends are affecting the industry. A large group of young adults, who mainly grew up on fast food, have emerged as an economic force.

Greenhouse and Flower Shop

LITTLE GREENIE SHOP

7 Pierson Rd.
Dunedin, Florida 34698

Gerald Rekve

Little Greenie Shop sells flowers and other greenhouse–related items to the local markets in both the retail and wholesale settings.

EXECUTIVE SUMMARY

Little Greenie Shop grows all types of flowers. These flowers are sold both in their own retail flower store and as wholesale flowers to regional small flower shops and food stores. The quality products grown at Little Greenie Shop are unique and exclusive. The target market is women of middle– to upper–income levels. Our competitive edge is that all of our products are all grown using state–of–the–art, environmentally friendly growing methods, rather than our competitors' more traditional methods requiring large amounts of insecticides and producing vast amounts of waste water.

The company plans to attract retailers to distribute our products by attending greenhouse trade shows in and around Clearwater. These trade shows are where suppliers' flowers and other greenhouse–related products are displayed and suppliers meet with buyers to arrange deals to sell the product.

Our projected sales is approximately $700,000 by the end of the first year of operation. Also during this year, we plan to open booths in three local farmers markets, all of which are within a 45 minute drive of our operation. Booths at farmers markets are easy to set up and normally last for only one to two days; the benefits of participating in them are twofold—we can sell extra products when they are in season and we can gain more exposure for our own retail store.

The Little Greenie Shop family will expand in 2009 with the addition of a second retail outlet. Every three years after this, we plan to add more retail stores as the market justifies and with the goal of always remaining profitable.

Little Greenie Shop headquarters are to be built at 7 Pierson Rd. in Dunedin at the founder's acreage. This area was recently rezoned for commercial operations. The greenhouse will be 15,000 square feet, with a 2,000 square–foot front for the retail store and offices.

Company Ownership

Little Greenie Shop is a privately–held corporation. Tabitha Westcott, founder and owner, is the sole owner of the greenhouse and retail outlet.

FINANCIAL ANALYSIS

Start–up Expenses

Start–up costs are approximated at $100,000 which primarily consists of building the first greenhouse and includes the cost of setting up the retail store.

Start-up expenses

Legal	$ 2,500
Insurance	$ 1,200
Monthly mortgage payment	$ 2,430
Other	$ 2,200
Total Start-up expenses	$ 8,330

Start-up assets

Cash balance on starting date	$200,000
Start-up inventory	$ 0
Other current assets	$ 0
Total current assets	$200,000

Long-term assets

	$ 0
Total assets	$200,000
Total requirements	$200,000

Investment

Investor 1	$100,000
Investor 2	$100,000
Total investment	$200,000

Current liabilities

Current borrowing	$100,000

Financial Goals

• Achieve sales of $700,000 by 2008

• Open first flower shop in front of greenhouse within first six months

• Expand to the wholesale business in first year by securing contracts with major food stores and other stores that sell flowers and plant items

BUSINESS STRATEGY

Mission

The mission of Little Greenie Shop is to become known for quality flower items and plant products that are priced at a competitive level. We will also be known for employing environmentally–friendly growing methods.

Growth Strategy

Little Greenie Shop focuses on providing high–quality products to consumers with outstanding customer service. Customization of orders and specialization of services will create a competitive advantage.

Little Greenie Shop is developing the organization by beginning with few employees to keep costs down; however, we will also hire local students in a work project through their school to secure the needed manpower at a significant savings.

The first year of service will be the most important, as Little Greenie Shop plans to establish strong relations with both suppliers and buyers. These relationships will help us to grow and evolve in this industry. Currently, the market for permanent floral products is rapidly expanding. According to 2002 statistics, the value of permanent floral products for the 2001 fiscal year was over $3.2 billion, and it still continues to grow. The greenhouse industry is also growing, as households headed by 25– to 59–year–olds are the biggest greenhouse purchasers.

In 2005, the average American household gave 5.8 percent of its total spending to flowers and home plants, a 0.3 percent increase from 2004. Households headed by 25– to 59–year–olds are the largest purchasers of house plants for both interior and exterior uses. These consumers spend an average of $296 per year on plants and seeds.

Households with incomes over $100,000 spend 32 percent more than average on greenhouse–related items. Households with incomes over $55,000 spent 27 percent more than average on greenhouse items. By the year 2011, it is estimated that households headed by 35– to 54–year–olds will account for 72 percent of the greenhouse sales market.

In the flowers and greenhouse industry, accumulated sales for flowers alone totalled more than $4.95 billion in 2002. This category still continues to grow.

SALES

Little Greenie Shop projects the gross margin to be approximately 32 percent. Sales projection for 2008 is at $700,000. Little Greenie Shop is looking for an investor who would invest $200,000 for a return of 15 percent over three years, 20 percent for two years and full payout of the original $200,000 in the fifth year. In addition, the investor will get 14 percent of gross profit over the next five years. Little Greenie Shop projects profits for every month of 2006 and on into both 2007 and 2008, in addition to positive growth margins for the same time periods.

	2007	2008
Sales	$700,000	$750,000
Expenses		
Sales and marketing	$130,000	$162,302
Depreciation	$ 3,200	$ 2,904
Utilities	$ 20,000	$ 25,000
Insurance	$ 2,500	$ 2,900
Mortgage	$ 20,000	$ 25,000
Payroll taxes	$ 15,300	$ 16,540

Building Blocks to Success

- High level of product quality

- Great customer service

- Keeping our costs in line with the market to insure profit

PRODUCTS AND GROWING SCHEDULES

Products

- House plants

- Bedding plants

- Annuals

- Flowers

- Trees and shrubs

- Water plants

- Garden rocks

- Fountains
- Ornaments
- Fertilizer
- Plant seeds
- Pots and planters
- Garden tools
- Wind chimes
- Lawn furniture
- Bird houses and feeders
- Gifts
- Gardening books

Product Growing Schedules

Month	Crop produced
January	spring bulbs, azalea, primula, cineraria, calceolaria, cyclamen
February	roses, spring bulbs, oxalis, cineraria, calceolaria, primula, cyclamen, azalea, lilies
March	hydrangea, kalanchoe, cineraria, calceolaria, primula, cyclamen, azalea, lilies, bedding plants
April	spring bulbs, azalea, lilies, gloxinia, heimalis begonia, bedding plants, flowering baskets
May	hydrangea, azalea, kalanchoe, lilies, gloxinia, potted roses, late flowering bulbs, geranium, new guinea impatiens, bedding plants, flowering baskets
June	gloxinia, heimalis, begonia, foliage, hibiscus, gerbera, potted bedding plants
July	gerbera, gloxinia, streptocarpus, heimalis begonia
August	hibiscus, azalea, heimalis begonia, foliage plants, field chrysanthemum
September	foliage plants, gloxinia, azalea, hibiscus, ornamental pepper, field chrysanthemum
October	hibiscus, foliage, flowering cabbage, flowering kale, cyclamen
November	poinsettia, cyclamen, Christmas cactus
December	poinsettia, Christmas cactus, cyclamen, heimalis begonia

Seasonal plant material produced for specific holidays is outlined below.

Occasion/season	Preferred type*	Plant material
Valentine's Day	cut	anything red, cut roses, potted tulips, azalea, cyclamen
Easter	potted	spring bulbs, Easter lily, hydrangea, chrysanthemum, azalea
Secretary's Day	both	cineraria, spring bulbs, potted chrysanthemum, primula
Mother's Day	both	roses, hydrangea, spring bulbs, azalea, potted chrysanthemum, gloxinia, African violet, early bedding plants, fuchsia
Memorial Day	potted	geranium
September	potted	foliage plants
Thanksgiving	cut	chrysanthemum
Christmas	potted	poinsettia, cyclamen, Christmas cactus

*The holidays are denoted as either 'cut' or 'potted' based on whether cut flowers or potted plants are the primary products sold.

Competition

All of our competitors sell a wide variety of products that will be the same or similar to ours. We will focus on quality and customer service to win our clients. We think this will be enough to earn 10 percent of the market in our first year.

CUSTOMER ANALYSIS

Below is an analysis of potential customers that will comprise our market. Wholesale clients will outweigh retail clients, but both will be instrumental to our success. In less than three years of operations, we anticipate sales of more than one million dollars.

Market analysis

Potential customers	2007	2008	2009	2010	CAGR
Wholesale clients	$500,000	$600,000	$ 650,000	$ 700,000	$ 750,000
Retail clients	$200,000	$300,000	$ 350,000	$ 400,000	$ 450,000
Other	$ 50,000	$ 50,000	$ 50,000	$ 50,000	$ 50,000
Total	**$750,000**	**$950,000**	**$1,050,000**	**$1,105,000**	**$1,250,000**

PERSONNEL

Only incremental growth in personnel costs are expected in the coming years. Planters, retail staff, and production workers comprise the biggest expense.

Personnel plan

	2007	2008	2009
Production	$120,000	$130,000	$140,000
Sales and marketing	$ 12,000	$ 14,000	$ 14,000
Administration	$ 20,000	$ 25,000	$ 35,000
Planters	$150,000	$170,000	$190,000
Retail staff	$120,000	$120,000	$120,000

Home Furnishing Manufacturer

CASTELLINI MANUFACTURING

6521 Hamilton St.
Allentown, PA 18101

Gerald Rekve

Castellini Manufacturing manufactures solid furniture for the home, which will make productive home environments with well–designed furniture that incorporates new technology into the classic home model, in which real people can live happily.

This yearly business plan calls for another two years of solid growth. Because our sales growth has brought some working capital pressures, we are carefully planning to manage growth and provide for steady cash flow. We also expect to be profitable these next two years at a higher level. In all, this plan is a healthy company with solid long-term prospects.

BUSINESS OVERVIEW

Castellini Manufacturing was established in 1971 by the Castellini Family when they immigrated into the United States. We were able to develop sales through distributors of home furniture that sell directly to home owners.

Objectives

- Increase sales beyond the half–million mark by 2009
- Maintain a gross margin close to 40 percent, despite the sales increase
- Increase the net profit to more than 12 percent of sales by 2009

Mission

Castellini Manufacturing manufactures solid furniture for the home, which will make productive home environments with well–designed furniture that incorporates new technology into the classic home model, in which real people can live happily. We are sensitive to the look and feel of good wood and fine furniture. We always provide the best possible value to our customers who care about quality home environments, and we want every dollar spent with us to be well spent. We also create and nurture a healthy, creative, respectful, and fun home environment, in which our employees are fairly compensated and encouraged to respect the customer and the quality of the product we produce. We seek fair and responsible profit, enough to keep the company financially healthy for the long-term and to fairly compensate owners and investors for their money and risk.

Keys to Success

- The highest in quality of the end product: quality wood, quality workmanship, quality design, quality of end result.

- Successful marketing: Our target market is a quality–conscious customer regardless of where they live, and with proper target marketing we will focus on the high–yield buyers.

- Almost–automatic assembly: we can't afford to ship fully–assembled furniture, but assembly must be so easy and automatic that it makes the customer feel better about the quality, not worse.

Company History

Castellini Manufacturing is a privately–owned specialty manufacturer of high–end home furniture for users who care about elegant home space. Our customers are in all levels of income that can afford very high quality home furniture.

Castellini Manufacturing is a Pennsylvania corporation, owned entirely by Tony and Tanya Castellini. It was created in 1971. At that time, the product line and industrial property rights (including trademarks) were purchased from the heirs to the Castellini family. Castellini Manufacturing had actually existed since 1971 as a small family manufacturer when the furniture line was inherited by Tony and Tanya Castellini. The Castellinis moved to Pennsylvania from New Jersey to take over the business as part of an inheritance.

Sales took a big jump in 1971, when we reached more effective channels of distribution. The key was winning a place in the National Furniture Distributors' home shows for Furniture Stores, which led to winning the interest of the national furniture distributors and display space in hundreds of retail stores.

Profitability was our major challenge during our past two years, but we now have better management of our costs.

Past performance

	2004	2005	2006
Sales	$2,300,000	$2,500,000	$2,700,000

OPERATIONS

Castellini Manufacturing is located in Allentown, Pennsylvania. The facility is a state of the art production facility with room to employ up to 500 production workers. The majority of the equipment has been installed in the last ten years. Over the course of the business life, the owners always believed in keeping up with current production methods. This allows for more profit potential.

Over the next ten years it will be determined if there is a need for a western seaboard location to manufacture the furniture. Right now the determination has been made to stay with one location and ship to wherever the need is greatest.

Our Pennsylvania location is a distinct advantage for local wood. We can buy higher quality oak and cherry than either of our competitors (one in Michigan, one in New Jersey). Since our sales increased over the last two years, we have been able to buy at better prices, because of higher volumes.

We work with several wood suppliers, some local. Allentown Oak supplies most of our oak and a bit of cherry and some other specialty woods. Allentown Oak has been in business for as long as we have, and has given us good service and good prices. This is a good, stable supplier. Wood Suppliers is a good second source, particularly for cherry and specialty woods. We've used Fantastic Wood as well, frequently, for filling in when either of our main two suppliers were short.

We also work with a number of specialty manufacturers for furniture fittings, drawer accessories, glass, shelving accessories, and related purchases.

Although we aren't a major player compared to the major furniture manufacturers, we are one of the biggest buyers of the custom materials we need. Most of our suppliers are selling through channels to hobbyists and carpenters, so they treat us as a major account.

Technology

We depend on our dominance of the latest in technology of ergonomics, combined with classic design elements of fine furniture. We must remain on top of new technologies in display, input and output, and communications.

Our assembly patents are an important competitive edge. No competitor can match the way we turn a drawback—having to assemble the product—into a feature. Our customer surveys confirm that customers take the interlocking assembly system as an enhancement to the sense of quality.

Products

Castellini Manufacturing offers very high–quality home furniture to the home owner who wants quality furniture in their home. The basis to our product is a classic style that incorporates the latest in production technology, yet looks very good in a high–end home. Our price lines are targeted to the middle and upper income levels. We will manufacture a wide range of products that gives us sales in all of areas of the home.

Our main lines are the bedroom set and the coffee table. They will be an elegant piece of home furniture designed to look good in executive homes. The bedroom set versions have similar production attributes as automakers use in their production cycle. The parts from one bedroom set can be used in another bedroom set.

We also make complementary pieces to fill out the home suite, including file cabinets and bookcases. These components are easy to change and manufacture as the design requirements change.

We also manufacture custom designs to fit exact measurements.

Competition

The main volume in the industry is now concentrated in four main brands, all of which compete for retail sales through major retail chain stores: Home Depot, Home Max, Staples, and others. These same four are also concentrating efforts in the major club discount stores. The growth of the home superstores made a few large brands dominant. Designs are similar and quite competitive, costs and cost control is critical, and channel management and channel marketing are the keys to this business's continued success. In mainstream home furniture, the rise of the home store channel has siphoned a lot of volume from the older and more traditional manufacturers. The channels that sold the more traditional lines are also suffering. What are left are smaller brands, smaller companies, and divisions of more traditional furniture companies. There are also some traditional manufacturers still making furniture lines focused mainly on home furnishings. Some of these have looked at times at our niche, and are competing for the same dollars.

Within our niche we have two significant competitors, Turner Furniture and Poole Manufacturing. Turner is a bigger company operating mainly in our same niche, but whose marketing is better than its product quality. Poole Manufacturing is a subsidiary of Wooden Furniture, a major furniture manufacturer, which has recently targeted our niche.

In general, however, our competition is not in our niche. We compete against generalized furniture manufacturers, cheaper traditional furniture, and the mainstream merchandise in the major furniture channels and home supply stores. It isn't that people choose our competitors instead of our product, it is that they choose lesser quality, mainstream materials instead of the higher quality furniture we offer. This was a major reason why we chose to remain in the high–end production of home furniture. Home owners after a while realize that they are buying a new couch every two years because the materials breakdown and do not stand up to our better materials. We know once a home owner buys our products, they will never switch back to the cheaper made items.

In the mainstream business, channels are critical to volume. The manufacturers with impact in the national sales are going to win display space in the store, and most buyers seem content to pick their product off the store floor. Price is critical, because the channels take significant margins. Buyers are willing to settle for laminated quality and serviceable design.

In direct sales to homes, price and volume is critical. The corporate buyer wants trouble–free buying in volume, at a great price. Reliable delivery is as important as reliable quality.

In the high–end specialty market, particularly in our niche, features are very important. Our target customer is not making selections based on price. The ergonomics, design, accommodation of the furniture features within the high–quality feel of good wood, is much more important than mere price. We are also seeing that assembly is critical to shipping and packing, but our customer doesn't accept any assembly problems. We need to make sure that the piece comes together almost like magic, and as it does; it presents a greater feel of quality than if it hadn't required assembly at all.

Key Competition

Turner Furniture. Turner has been operating since the middle 1950s, and grew up with traditional furniture. It was one of the first, certainly the first we are aware of, to develop Victorian traditional and market through advertising in fashion & home styles magazines. Today they are about twice our size. They have good relationships with two distributors. Their strengths include good marketing, strong advertising budget, good relationships with distributors, and strong direct sales. Their weaknesses include standardized products, lesser quality products, products with less sense of design, lack of quality materials, and lack of quality workmanship.

Poole Manufacturing. Poole Manufacturing is a division of Wooden Furniture, one of the largest manufacturers of mainstream home furnishings. Wooden bought Poole five years ago and is focusing on our niche. We see very good quality product and an excellent sense of design, but little movement in channels. Their strengths include financial backing and product quality. Their weaknesses include that they have not seemed to understand our niche, where to find the buyers, and how to market as a specialty niche instead of the more traditional furniture channels.

MARKETING & SALES

For 2009 we plan to develop a company online order catalogue, which would include all of our other products for the same target customers. The focus will be the executive home magazines, with furniture, lamps, and other accessories.

Our target market is people who want to have very fine furniture combined with an old fashioned sense of fine woods and fine woodworking.

Market Segmentation

Potential customers	Growth	2008	2009	2010	2011	2012
Eastern States	1%	2,407,000	2,727,000	2,057,250	2,577,003	2,000,071
Mid-States	4%	11,777,000	11,575,000	11,555,570	12,555,504	12,323,555
Northern States	10%	35,000,000	37,577,000	45,777,000	47,909,000	52,990,700
Western States	3%	1,000,000	1,030,000	1,050,900	1,092,727	1,125,509

Target Market Strategy

Our segment definition is of itself strategic. We are definitely out to address the needs of the high–end buyer, who is willing to pay more for quality.

In our particular market, we also seek the buyer who appreciates two attributes: the quality of furniture workmanship and the excellence of design, with an understanding of technology and ergonomics built in.

Market Analysis

Our market has finally grown to recognize the disparity between most of the standard home furniture sold through channels, and our own products. The development of high–end homes, home owners, and baby–boomer executive is an important trend for us.

The home furniture industry has undergone a great deal of change in this decade. The growth of the home superstores made a few large brands dominant. They produce relatively inexpensive furniture that make compromises in order to stay at the low price level. Makers of higher-quality furniture are in general shuffling for niches to hide in. Although Castellini Manufacturing was essentially developed around a niche, many of the more traditional furniture makers are looking for niches, trying to deal with declining sales as the main volume goes elsewhere.

Growth Strategy

According to *Furniture News Unlimited USA*, the market for home furniture is growing at 12 percent per year, and is projected to increase. With the aging of the baby boomers, this will allow for the long-term sustainable growth of our lines of high-end furniture. This market needs to have quality home furnishings versus the low-end particle board-type products that are low in quality and lack in design and construction and materials. Most important is the growth in home offices with personal furniture equipment. As the cost of the furniture goes down steadily, the number of home offices goes up. According to the same publication, this is about 35 million right now, growing at 15 percent per year. Households spent $12 billion last year on home furnishings.

Distribution Patterns

The six main manufacturers are selling direct to the home superstores and buying discount clubs. This accounts for the main volume of distribution. The home furniture customer seems to be growing steadily more comfortable with the retail buy in the chain store.

The major corporate purchases are still made directly with manufacturers. Although this is still a major channel for some of the more traditional manufacturers, it is essentially closed to new competition. The direct channel is dominated by two manufacturers and three distributors. The distributors will occasionally take on a new line—happily, this has helped Castellini Manufacturing—but the main growth is in retail.

Published research indicates that 43 percent of the total sales volume in the market goes through the retail channel, most of that to the major national chains. Another 27 percent goes through the direct sales channel, although in this case direct sales include sales by distributors who are buying from multiple manufacturers. Most of the remainder (20 percent) is sold directly to buyers by other means.

Business Strategy

We focus on a special kind of customer, the person who wants very high quality home furniture customized to work beautifully with modern lifestyles. What is important to the customer is elegance, fine workmanship, ease of use, ergonomics, and practicality. Our marketing strategy assumes that we need to go into niche areas to address our target customer's needs. The tie–in with the high–end quality magazines is perfect, because these magazines cater to our kind of customers. We position ourselves as the highest quality, offering status and prestige levels of purchase.

The product strategy is also based on quality; the intersection of technical understanding with very high quality woodworking and professional materials, and workmanship. Our most important competitive edge is our assembly strategy, which is based on interlocking wood pieces of such high quality that assembly is not only a pleasure for our customers; it is actually a feature that enhances the sense of quality.

Our main strategy at Castellini Manufacturing is to position ourselves at the top of the quality scale, featuring our combination of superb technology and fine old–fashioned woodworking, for the buyer who wants the best quality regardless of price. Tactics underneath that strategy include research and development related to new designs and new technology, choosing the right channels of distribution, and communicating our quality position to the market. Programs are mainly those listed in the milestones table, including new design programs, new equipment to keep up with design, channel development, channel marketing programs, our direct sales, and our continued presence in high–end magazines channels and new presence in the web.

Castellini Manufacturing offers the furniture buyer who wants design and quality furniture and quality of working environment a combination of the highest-quality furniture and latest technology. Our product is positioned very carefully: this is high–quality home furniture combining workmanship and ergonomics for the customer who understands quality, is a user of high technology equipment, and is willing to spend money on the best. Unlike the mainstream products, we do not use laminates or cheap manufacturing technology.

Our marketing strategy is based mainly on making the right information available to the right target customer. We can't afford to sell people on our expensive products, because most don't have the budget. What we really do is make sure that those who have the budget and appreciate the product know that it exists, and know where to find it.

The marketing has to convey the sense of quality in every picture, every promotion, and every publication. We can't afford to appear in second–rate magazines with poor illustrations that make the product look less than it is. We also need to leverage our presence using high–quality magazines and specialty distributors.

For discriminating personal furniture users who want to integrate their lifestyle with fine furniture, our family line offers exquisite workmanship and design combined with state–of–the–arts ergonomics and technology. Unlike the Poole line, Castellini Manufacturing makes no design compromises for standardization.

Sales Forecast

Our sales forecast assumes no change in costs or prices, which is a reasonable assumption for the last few years.

We are expecting to increase sales from $400,000 last year to $720,000 in the next year, which is almost doubling in size. The growth forecast is in line with our last year, and is relatively high for our industry because we are developing new channels. In 2007 and 2008 we expect growth closer to 50 percent per year, to a projected total of more than $1 million in 2009.

We are projecting significant change in the product line, or in the proportion between different lines. The key to our growth is the growth of the new channels.

Specific sales programs

- *Magazine Sales:* Develop placement with one additional magazine catering to the high–end home executive, paying for space and positioning. The budget is $20,000 for this program.

- *Distributor Sales:* We need to develop at least one new distributor, spending for co–promotion as required, and making direct sales calls.

- *Direct Sales:* We will do a mailing of new in–house magazines, developed by the marketing department, to add to our direct telephone sales. Tanya will be responsible, without a budget or a deadline because the magazines are a marketing program.

ADVERTISING

Our most important vehicle for sales promotion is the direct mail magazines published by the specialty retailer. Our advertising budget goes mainly for space in the specialty magazines. We also participate in major industry events, including both the spring and fall national furniture shows and the fall furniture show. Our total budget for events is $50,000, plus about half of the $44,000 travel budget. This year we will also promote our products with in–house magazines, including our own products plus related merchandise of interest to the same target market.

Our strategy focuses first on maintaining the identity with the high–end buyer who appreciates the best available quality, but is also very demanding regarding furniture systems and technology. We've been able to find these customers using a combination of direct mail magazines and direct sales to distributors.

For the next year we continue to focus on growing presence in the high–end direct mail magazines that find our specialty customer. We will work with speciality magazines more than ever, and we expect to gain position in the major airline magazines as well. Specialty retail is a new channel that could become important for us.

Our work with distributors has been promising. We hope to continue the relationship with distributors selling directly to larger homes, even though this takes working capital to support receivables.

Strategic Alliances

The accompanying table shows specific milestones, with responsibilities assigned, dates, and (in most cases) budgets. We are focusing in this plan on a few key milestones that should be accomplished.

Milestones

Milestone	Start Date	End Date	Budget	Manager	Department
Third magazines placement	5/15/2007	5/15/2007	$54,000	Jan	Ads
Second magazines	4/1/2007	5/13/2007	$55,000	Jan	Ads
First magazines	3/1/2007	4/13/2007	$97,000	Jan	Ads
New distributor	3/15/2007	4/30/2007	$ 5,000	Jan	Travel
New distributor	3/15/2007	4/30/2007	$ 3,000	Jan	Sales
Our in-house magazines plan	1/31/2007	2/12/2007	$ 0	Mike	Other
In-house magazines design	3/1/2007	4/1/2007	$ 2,000	Mike	Other
In-house magazines mailing	3/1/2007	5/1/2007	$ 5,000	Mike	Other
Design product test	7/15/2006	5/20/2007	$11,000	Ben	Other
Design product release	2/1/2007	10/15/2007	$14,000	Mike	PR
Spring trade show	1/1/2007	3/15/2007	$12,000	Mike	PR
Fall trade show	5/12/2007	2/15/2007	$ 4,000	Mike	PR
Fall trade show	5/12/2007	2/15/2007	$21,000	Mike	Events
Spring trade show	1/1/2007	5/23/2007	$10,000	Mike	Events
Spring trade show	1/5/2007	5/3/2007	$ 5,000	Mike	Travel
Fall trade show	5/15/2007	10/15/2007	$ 5,000	Mike	Travel
Totals					

MANAGEMENT SUMMARY

We are a small company owned and operated by Tony and Tanya Castellini, husband and wife, as a Subchapter S corporation. Tony is the developer and designer of the products, and Tanya manages the company as president.

The management style reflects the participation of the owners. The company respects its community of co–workers and treats all workers well. We attempt to develop and nurture the company as a community. We are not very hierarchical. The theory is that of the Japanese style where low level employees have a huge impact on how the production lines work and are managed.

Organizational Structure

- Tanya Castellini, President, is responsible for overall business management. Our managers of finance, marketing, and sales report directly to Tanya. Tanya had a successful career in retail before becoming half–owner of Castellini Manufacturing. She was an area manager of Trinkets and Things, a buyer for Youth Styles, and merchandising assistant for the Sports Store. She has a degree in Business from Penn State.

- Tony Castellini, Manager and Designer, is responsible for product design and development, assembly, and manufacturing. Our workshop manager reports directly to Tony. Tony designed furniture for Oaken Accents before becoming half owner of Castellini Manufacturing He was responsible for one of the first executive desks designed to include customized fittings for personal computers, and was one of the first to design the monitor inside the desk under glass. He has a Business Degree from Penn State.

As co–owners, Tony and Tanya jointly develop business strategy and long–term plans. Tony is strong on product know–how and technology, and Tanya is strong on management and business know–how.

Management Team Gaps

We depend on our professionals, our CPA, and our attorney for some key management help. We don't have a strong background in finance or business management.

As we grow we will need to develop more manufacturing technique and more mass production. Tanya grew up with the hand–made and custom furniture business, knows fine woodworking well, but admits a weakness in establishing standardized assembly.

Personnel Plan

The personnel table assumes slow growth in employees, and 10 percent per annum pay raises. We already have a strong benefits policy (with fully–paid medical, dental, and life insurance, plus a profit sharing and 401K plan) and very low turnover. Salaries are generally in line with market pay for the Pennsylvania area, although our benefits are above standard market level, so we ultimately pay a bit more for our people than what might be considered standard in our market. Allentown, however, is on average a lower wage location than most of the more developed business areas. As we grow, we expect to see steady increases in our personnel to match the increases in sales.

Personnel plan	2008	2009	2010
Workshop manager	$ 33,000	$ 40,000	$ 50,000
Assembly	$ 17,000	$ 17,000	$ 19,000
Marketing manager	$ 35,000	$ 40,000	$ 50,000
President	$ 55,000	$ 55,000	$ 75,000
Design	$ 13,000	$ 17,000	$ 20,000
Total payroll	**$153,000**	**$169,000**	**$214,000**

FINANCIAL ANALYSIS

The financial position is strong. We have not taken on a lot of debt, but with our sales increase we do expect to apply for a credit line with the bank, to a limit of $300,000. The credit line is easily supported by assets. The credit line will be used to support our growth curves as we start building momentum. Also the credit line is there to give our managers less pressure in times where receivables are not coming as they may normally.

We do expect to be able to take some money out as dividends. The owners don't take overly generous salaries, so some draw is appropriate.

Financial Assumptions

The accompanying table lists our main assumptions for developing our financial projections. The most sensitive assumption is the collection days. We would like to improve collection days to take pressure off of our working capital, but our increasing sales through channels makes the collection time a cost of doing business. We also expect to see a decline in our inventory turnover ratio, another unfortunate side effect of increasing sales through channel. We find ourselves having to buy earlier and hold more finished goods in order to deal with sales through the channel.

General assumptions	2008	2009	2010
Plan month	1	2	3
Current interest rate	7.00 percent	7.00 percent	7.00 percent
Long-term interest rate	7.00 percent	7.00 percent	7.00 percent
Tax rate	15.00 percent	19.00 percent	25.00 percent
Sales on credit percent	55.00 percent	55.00 percent	55.00 percent

Break–even Analysis

Our break–even analysis is based on running costs, the "burn–rate" costs we incur to keep the business running, not on theoretical fixed costs that would be relevant only if we were closing. Between payroll, rent, utilities, and basic marketing costs, we think $33,000 is a good estimate of fixed costs.

Our assumptions on average unit sales and average per–unit costs depend on averaging. We don't really need to calculate an exact average; this is close enough to help us understand what a real break–even point might be. The essential insight here is that our sales level seems to be running comfortably above break–even.

Break-even Analysis

Monthly units break-even	55
Monthly revenue break-even	$ 77,000

Assumptions

Average per-unit revenue	$1,100.00
Average per-unit variable cost	$ 500.00

We do expect a significant increase in profitability this year, and in the future, because we have learned how to deal with the increasing sales levels of selling through channels. Despite the lower profitability levels of recent years, we expect to pass 5 percent in 2007, and remain at that level through 2010.

Our higher sales volume has lowered our cost of goods and increased our gross margin. This increase in gross margin is important to profitability.

Pro Forma profit and loss	2008	2009	2010
Sales	$300,000	$400,000	$500,000
Direct costs of goods	$111,000	$175,000	$275,000
Production payroll	$ 50,000	$ 73,000	$170,000
Other	$ 3,110	$ 0	$ 0
Cost of goods sold	$147,595	$252,000	$444,000
Gross margin	$200,700	$400,900	$577,000
Operating expenses:			
Sales and marketing expenses			
Sales and marketing payroll	$ 44,000	$ 55,000	$ 77,000
Miscellaneous	$ 4,200	$ 2,200	$ 3,300
Advertising/Promotion	$ 50,000	$ 70,000	$ 75,000
Events	$ 5,550	$ 5,232	$ 7,112
Public relations	$ 720	$ 400	$ 400
Travel	$ 7,500	$ 7,000	$ 5,000
Total sales and marketing expenses	$150,200	$222,700	$244,100
General and administrative expenses:			
General and administrative payroll	$ 47,000	$ 75,000	$100,000
Depreciation	$ 1,400	$ 1,500	$ 1,200
Leased equipment	$ 4,500	$ 5,700	$ 11,900
Utilities	$ 2,500	$ 2,900	$ 4,900
Insurance	$ 1,200	$ 1,400	$ 1,500
Building lease—own	$ 9,000	$ 11,000	$ 12,000
Other	$ 1,200	$ 1,300	$ 1,400
Payroll taxes	$ 22,010	$ 30,000	$ 50,000

Projected Cash Flow

Although we expect to be more profitable in 2007, we still have drains on the cash flow. We need to invest $70,000 in new assembly and manufacturing equipment, plus $20,000 in new furniture equipment, and another $30,000 in miscellaneous short–term assets, including home furniture. Because of our increased sales through channels, and necessary increase in inventory levels, we need to increase working capital.

Pro Forma cash flow

	2008	2009	2010
Cash received			
Cash from operations			
Cash sales	$212,010	$233,000	$255,000
Cash from receivables	$270,000	$410,000	$720,100
Additional cash received			
New current borrowing	$ 25,000	$200,000	$200,000
New investment received	$ 50,000	$ 0	$ 0
Expenditures			
Expenditures from operations			
Cash spending	$127,052	$145,495	$214,495
Payment of accounts payable	$304,727	$457,294	$727,353
Additional cash spent			
Principal repayment of current borrowing	$ 10,000	$ 0	$ 0
Purchase long-term assets	$ 50,000	$ 20,000	$ 30,000

Projected Balance Sheet

Our projected balance sheet shows an increase in net worth to more than $660,000 in 2010, at which point we expect to be making 14 percent profit on sales of $1.6 million. With the present financial projections we will be careful in supporting our working capital credit line, and we are growing assets both because we want to— new equipment—and because we have to grow receivables and inventory to support growth in sales through channels.

Pro forma balance sheet

Assets

Current assets	2008	2009	2010
Cash	$ 77,134	$157,152	$313,044
Accounts receivable	$ 74,179	$113,752	$179,530
Inventory	$ 47,270	$ 73,704	$115,220
Other current assets	$ 2,375	$ 2,375	$ 2,375
Total current assets			
Long-term assets			
Long-term assets	$ 53,210	$ 73,210	$103,210
Accumulated depreciation	$ 2,720	$ 3,720	$ 5,020
Total long-term assets	**$ 50,490**	**$ 59,390**	**$ 97,190**
Liabilities and capital			
Current liabilities			
Accounts payable	$ 7,791	$ 9,977	$ 14,725
Current borrowing	$200,000	$200,000	$200,000
Other current liabilities	$ 1,703	$ 1,703	$ 1,703
Subtotal current liabilities			
Total liabilities	**$125,594**	**$175,791**	**$271,527**
Paid-in capital	$ 54,500	$ 54,500	$ 54,500
Retained earnings	$ 15,355	$ 71,354	$132,302
Earnings	**$ 27,709**	**$132,357**	**$176,170**
Total capital	**$137,754**	**$240,702**	**$427,931**
Total liabilities and capital	**$253,457**	**$417,593**	**$709,459**

Business Ratios

Our ratios look healthy and solid. Gross margin is projected to decline below 50 percent, return on assets getting to about 17 percent, and return on equity at 35 percent or better. Debt and liquidity ratios also look tough, with debt to net worth running at more than 1.4 to one. The projections, if we make them, are manageable.

Interior Renovation Company

Addams Interiors

431 Lyme Circle
St. Louis, Missouri 63101

Mary Green, Andrea Hibbeler, Bryan King, and Arilova Randrianasolo

We are a minority–owned general contractor and carpentry subcontractor, based in St. Louis, Missouri. We specialize in commercial interior renovations.

BUSINESS OVERVIEW

Until recently, workforce diversity was not a priority in the St. Louis construction industry. This changed when Governor Matt Blunt issued his 2005 Executive Order, establishing goals for minority business utilization. Unfortunately, many minority–owned businesses have taken advantage of this good–faith effort by entering the market with intentions only to turn a quick profit and not to create a sustainable company. As a result, finding reliable, minority–owned contractors has become a challenge within this industry.

Addams Interiors was created to satisfy this demand. We are a minority–owned general contractor and carpentry subcontractor, based in St. Louis, Missouri. We specialize in commercial interior renovations. Our customers will have the confidence that projects will be completed to their standards and in adherence to all safety requirements.

Although the economy has slowed, the revitalization efforts of downtown St. Louis have stabilized the market for interior renovations. According to the Downtown St. Louis Partnership, since a Development Action Plan was adopted in 1999, over $4.6 billion was spent or committed to projects, with over $900 million of these jobs currently in development.

Federal and city tax incentives are strong motivators for developers to utilize minority–owned contractors to complete their projects. In order to receive these benefits, developers must submit an approved subcontractor list to the proper officials. This increases the appeal of working with committed minority–owned contractors.

In our first year, Addams Interiors projects to reach $1 million in sales with positive growth in the years following. Maintaining low overhead costs enables us to achieve profitability starting in our first month of operation. Startup funding needs have already been met through personal savings of the owners and generous outside contributions.

We realize that in the construction industry, networking is vital to success, especially for an emerging company. We have already formed a valuable alliance with Rosen Contracting, who is mentoring us through the start–up phase and going to subcontract us our first job.

The purpose of this plan is to demonstrate our competence and present the opportunities in our industry. We have a solid understanding of our core competencies and are now looking to network with customers and industry professionals who share our values of commitment, integrity, and responsibility.

MISSION

Addams Interiors is committed to the customer in every job by providing the highest quality of work 100 percent of the time. Five years after its inception, Addams seeks to have 70 percent of its revenue earned from jobs the company wins as a general contractor, rather than from minority set–asides.

Core Values

- Commitment to safety and our work
- Integrity to treat our employees and customers equally
- Responsibility to give back to our community

BUSINESS STRATEGY

Four walls that set the foundation for Addams' success are the customer, quality, our work, and partnerships.

The Customer

Addams must always remember to focus on the needs of our customers, who lay at the heart of our business. We perform our best work for each customer so as to build long–lasting relationships within the construction world.

Quality

We must never lose sight of our central tool to success: the focus on performing the highest quality work within the industry. Addams Interiors does not believe in cutting corners or taking shortcuts. We intend to do everything in our power to provide the greatest degree of excellence and superiority in service to our customers, regardless of the size of the job.

Our Work is Our Own

Simply put, Addams must be able to take pride in the work we perform. We strive to positively imprint our name into the minds of every customer. Completing the projects we have been awarded with our own skilled team of employees will ensure high–quality work and satisfied customers.

Partnerships

Addams respects other firms in the industry as both honorable competitors and as valued clients. Our mutually beneficial relationships offer distinct interaction and teamwork between traditional competitors. At Addams, we consider our competitive partnerships to be a resource vital to the success of both companies.

SERVICES

Addams Interiors is a minority–owned interior general contractor and carpentry subcontractor, offering a comprehensive range of services for the commercial interior renovations market in the St. Louis Metropolitan area.

Our primary activities include pre–and post–construction services, which consist of demolition and clean–up of each job site; general construction services, which entail all interior components (i.e. ceilings, doors, drywall, insulation, millwork); and carpentry subcontracting, which allows the customer to choose specific duties they would like us to perform. Other services we offer include project management and supervision, which relieves the customer of project completion and on–site managerial responsibilities. An Addams project manager keeps in close contact with the client, offering progress updates as well as an outlet for questions and concerns the customer may have. We also take care of estimating and purchasing to ensure the right materials are selected and on site when needed, to avoid unnecessary delays.

Furthermore, we offer work order and purchase order management, which allows the customer several payment options with little or no paperwork, job cost reporting management to ensure there are no hidden fees or misspent money, and full accounting and administration services.

Not all of these services will be used during each job. Generally, larger jobs may require the use of more services due to the manpower necessary for a timely completion.

OPERATIONS

Field Work

Addams Interiors will employ its own construction teams, comprised of three equally important, union–supported employee groups:

- Carpenters—This principal field of Addams employees consists of skilled apprentices, journeymen, and foremen, finely trained through the Carpenters' Joint Apprenticeship Program (CJAP) by the Carpenters' District Council of Greater St. Louis and Vicinity. On our jobsites, carpenters are responsible for hanging drywall, insulation, and performing a variety of other installations.

- Laborers—Laborers belong to the Laborers' Union of St. Louis. They are responsible for initial demolition and post–job clean–up services.

- Tapers—Tapers are members of the Painters' District Council No. 2. After the carpenters have installed drywall, the tapers come through, sealing and finishing the joints between drywall wallboards, thus creating a finished wall or partition.

The Union

Union membership will provide Addams Interiors with many services that will help us attain our quality and service goals. The unions provide complete drug testing, superior training, and a comprehensive benefits package for employees, including health and dental care, retirement plans, and vacation stamps. At Addams, we believe that the satisfaction of our employees will transfer to the satisfaction of our customers. Belonging to the unions will help our business as a whole because customers tend to look to union businesses to fulfill their construction needs. Our specialized training and strict Occupational Safety and Health Administration (OSHA) compliance will give customers the confidence that their projects will be completed safely and in accordance with their standards. All of our carpenters, as a requirement, have graduated or are continuing their education with the Carpenters' Joint Apprenticeship Program (CJAP). This ensures that our employees are knowledgeable in their fields, enabling Addams to perform work of the highest quality.

OSHA Compliance

The Occupational Safety Hazard Association plays a significant role in the construction industry. The purpose of OSHA is to set and enforce guidelines in an effort to decrease workplace accidents and injuries through preventative measures. Following these measures closely will be one way Addams

Interiors can fulfill its promise of offering its customers a superior service. There are seven introductory steps for construction companies to follow to ensure compliance with OSHA regulations:

1. Review introduction to OSHA practices. The following practices and equipment fall under this category: Fall protection, Electrical, Stairways and ladders, Trenching and excavation, Scaffolding, Motor vehicle safety. All areas pertaining to an employee's work must be addressed. Each employee should be trained and provided with literature regarding safely conducting tasks falling under these categories.

2. Review secondary areas of construction. As with step one, any category that a company employee may encounter must be discussed, including: Personal Protective Equipment, Steel Erection, Hand and Power Tool, Fire Safety, Concrete or Masonry Products, Hazard Communication Standards, Welding, Cutting, Brazing, Cranes, Derricks, Hoists, Elevators, Conveyors, and Residential Construction.

3. Survey workplace for additional hazards.

4. Develop a jobsite safety and health program, which usually includes accident prevention seminars.

5. Train employees on the matters listed above and ensure that they are given appropriate literature.

6. Set up a system of record–keeping, reporting, and posting of injuries and illness.

7. Find additional compliance assistance information from the local OSHA representative.

Risk Factors

In order to provide the best quality construction, Addams Interiors has established and adheres to a set of constant guarantees geared towards minimizing common pain points in the industry. Listed below are the pain points, followed by Addams' means to alleviate them.

Lack of Performance

On–time Delivery: While our focus is not on completing jobs in record–time for our customers, we do guarantee that our work will be completed within schedule and in accordance with the standards of our customers. Addams will be able to ensure this through accurate bidding and detailed project management.

Finest Supplies: Addams realizes that the materials used in a job are just as important as the construction itself. High–quality, affordable materials and timely delivery from a reliable supplier are two major factors in our industry. Addams will be working closely with Moone Materials, Inc. in order to equip each job with the proper supplies.

Job–site Deliverance: On the actual job site, Addams guarantees a clean and safe work environment, in accordance with OSHA standards. Company–wide drug testing ensures substance–free job-sites. Noise awareness is a top priority for Addams, especially during the business hours of our customers.

Vision Partners: Whether Addams is searching for, establishing, or maintaining relationships within the industry, we will seek out only those who share the same commitment to quality and the customer.

Lack of Specialized Skills

Addams promises experienced craftsmanship and attention to detail on every job. As mentioned in this plan, the Union will provide the specialized education required of all our field workers.

Lack of Flexibility for Customer Inquiries

Point–person: There will be a project manager who knows the job intimately and sees each contract not as an agreement between a business and its consumer, but between partners striving towards a mutually–beneficial and long–term relationship. It is the job of this project manager to ensure the satisfaction of the customer. He or she will be accessible to the client at any time of the day, and will respond to missed calls in a maximum time of two hours.

Communication Modes: Personally attended office telephone lines with voice mail, Nextel mobile phones with two–way radio, text, and numeric messaging, as well as electronic mail accounts provide clients with various communication modes.

Undercapitalization: Addams has calculated the initial capital needs and is in the unique position to receive a total of $70,000 towards funding the company through the savings of the founders and contributions of friends and family. Should the need for capitalization grow, Addams has the option of negotiating an increase in the amount of outside contributions.

Cash Flow and Billing Problems

The prior experiences of Addams' founders and advisors in the construction and accounting fields give the company an advantage in cash flow supervision. Mandatory daily meetings of top management will also help Addams to monitor cash flow and billing periods. Detailed job cost reporting enables both Addams and the customer to track and review even the most specific elements of each project.

High Pricing: Addams will maintain relationships with a vast range of independent subcontractors and suppliers in order to offer competitive pricing.

To measure our performance and see where our efforts can improve, Addams will stay current with developments in the construction field, apply for quality and innovation awards, and continually solicit feedback from our customers.

The Construction Innovation Forum (CIF), founded in 1986, recognizes advances in construction technologies, processes, and projects by offering the NOVA Award, which is considered the "Nobel Prize for construction innovation" (http://www.cif.org). Addams will benefit from our commitment to quality through increased customer confidence and loyalty, improved reputation and word–of–mouth referrals, expanded networks, and company growth.

"Green" Movement

For the future, Addams Interiors is planning to join the "green" movement. Generally, "going green" means more efficient use of water, energy, and other resources, but in the construction industry every facet of the building process is impacted. This includes site selection, landscape preservation, use of recycled materials, efficient design (i.e. using natural light where available), reducing material waste, and installing low–flow water fixtures.

To be officially recognized as a green builder, a company must register with the U.S. Green Building Council (USGBC) and follow the Leadership in Energy and Environmental Design (LEED) standard for building excellence. LEED certification provides independent, third–party verification that a building project meets the highest environmental building and performance measures. All certified projects receive a LEED plaque, which is the nationally–recognized symbol demonstrating that a building is environmentally responsible, profitable and a healthy place to live and work.

Due to the expense of constructing and renovating LEED–certified buildings, we intend to gradually implement these practices. We expect that during our fourth year of operation we will be able to focus on completing projects that will fully meet LEED standards.

COMPETITION

The services provided by Addams Interiors may be common to other businesses in the industry, but the manner in which our services are performed is what that sets us apart. Addams seeks to be a major competitor in the interior general contracting segment, breaking the poor reputations and generally low achievement rates of minority–owned contractors. Minority business enterprises in the construction industry are frequently known for acting as "pass–throughs" for subcontracted work, simply putting their names on the jobs, taking a percentage of the revenues, and subcontracting the work out again. This practice is not in the spirit of the MBE goals and, unfortunately, has greatly hindered the respect of minority business owners who genuinely want to run legitimate businesses. We want our work to be our own in practice, not just on paper. If Addams is awarded a job that requires work which we are incapable of completing due to our specialized workforce or to time constraints, and it is in our client's best interest to subcontract the work, we will do so. We will not, however, act as a pass–through. Subcontractors will be chosen carefully to ensure our client's satisfaction and expectations are met and to maintain our quality standards.

Our tireless commitment to quality is demonstrated in the details of how we conduct our work. To us, quality is more than just a slogan. We understand that the customer defines quality. Due to the vast range of quality expectations from our customers, we realize that promising a 100 percent satisfaction guarantee is not feasible. Therefore, our promise is to work side–by–side with our customers and architects to identify the best way to serve each customer.

Our direct competition presents itself in two different forms. The first form is the competition Addams will have with other minority–owned interior contractors for carpentry subcontracting jobs in order to fulfill percentage goals. The only major competitor in this sector is Tubbs Subcontracting.

The second form of direct competition comes from other interior general contractors within the St. Louis Metropolitan area which are not minority–owned. The most dominant competitors in this sector are Rosen Contracting and Tubbs Construction.

The construction industry, as a whole, bases itself on fierce competition, which poses a potential long–term threat to Addams. In fact, companies must constantly compete against each other in order to win the bids for a majority of their projects. Providing the best services or low cost bidding are generally the two deciding factors for a customer. At Addams, we pride ourselves on offering the highest ranked quality and service, and therefore, will not always be able to offer the lowest costs. For this reason, the most likely source of direct competition for the company would be service–driven interior general contractors against whom we would bid for similar–sized jobs.

Jett Building has been in business for merely six years but has already landed several large jobs. As a union and minority–owned business, Jett Building offers services ranging from industrial and institutional design, advanced technology construction, new building construction, commercial and commercial–residential work, interior finish construction, and retail construction. Jett has built a portfolio of jobs with customers including First Bank, Wilson Tile and Roofing, Pharmaco Drug Store, and Trotter's Dance Club. Currently, Jett is working as a subcontractor for Pliff in the renovations of the district's elementary schools.

Rosen Contracting is also a young union, minority–owned business. Since its inception seven years ago, Rosen has offered services including demolition, rough carpentry, drywall, ceilings, insulation, concrete work, and foundations. Rosen works with customers such as Sandwich Shoppe, First Bank, and Speedy Taxi Company. In 2004, the company's fourth year of business, they were able to pull in revenues of $8 million. However, in year one, Rosen was only able to land a total of twelve projects. Due to our already growing networks, Addams anticipates landing forty–two projects of varying sizes the first year.

Tubbs Construction has experienced seventy years as an established minority–owned, union contractor. Current projects for Tubbs include several local restaurants and the local library branch. Tubbs prides itself in its ability to offer a vast array of capabilities. These services range from construction management to general contracting, design–build, build–to–suit, self–perform, and interior construction.

MBE Competitive Advantages

The medium–to large–sized general contractors in St. Louis are constantly searching for quality, minority–owned businesses to which they can subcontract work from large projects. This, however, has traditionally been a difficult task. Many minority–owned companies have been known for performing substandard work or subbing out jobs once they have been awarded. Addams looks to ease this pain for our customers by establishing itself as a quality–driven and trustworthy subcontractor. We will aid the customer in fulfilling its minority requirements and we will do so by reverting back to the traditional values of the construction industry: performing our own work and focusing on the customer.

If we are bidding against another minority–owned interior contractor for a subcontracting job, we will be able to differentiate ourselves by guaranteeing high–quality work that is our own. The only circumstance in which we will, in turn, subcontract out a portion of the work awarded to us is when the task is outside of our job scope (electrical, painting, etc), or current work is so busy that timeliness of job completion could be affected. It is also our guarantee that if we must subcontract out any work, Addams will only award the job to companies it feels can maintain the quality for the customer.

Non–MBE Competitors

Peters Brothers is a non–MBE that has been in business for over 25 years. With over 200 craftsmen on the payroll, Peters Brothers has completed many large projects throughout the Midwest. The company is divided into three divisions: Drywall Construction, Floor Covering/Ceramic Tile, and Tenant Finish. They employ only Union workers and subcontract to other Union companies who are managed and coordinated by Peters Brothers.

Potter Construction Services is one of the oldest family–owned businesses in St. Louis. They specialize in architectural salvage and historic site refurbishment, which makes them a major player in the St. Louis construction industry. Potter is also non–minority owned and utilizes Union contractors. Several projects Potter has completed include renovations at a hospice center, as well as original construction of a daycare center in St. Louis.

Non–MBE Competitive Advantages

If we are bidding against a well–established, interior general contractor who is not minority–owned, we can leverage the fact that since we are minority–owned already, we will not have to subcontract work to another company. This will ensure better quality work, control, and speed on our part. We also will pride ourselves on the quality of our work as a contractor, rather than just as an MBE subcontractor. Another advantage to be executed in the coming years will be our completion of "green" projects. This undertaking is relatively new among many contractors, and is especially rare for minority–owned businesses. The efficiency of green building is rising in demand, which is why we plan full implementation by our fourth year of business.

Although competition for Addams presents itself in two different forms, we feel we are entering the industry in a unique situation. By concentrating our work solely in the interior commercial sector and always striving for work of the highest–quality, Addams is able to focus all of our efforts on being the best at interior renovations. This is a contrast to our competitors, who offer a variety of services such as concrete work and new building construction in the commercial or non–commercial segment. This specialization will allow us to compete for jobs that do not require minority percentage work. In such a case, we will beat our competition through our commitment to quality, efficient work and accurate bid pricing. By specializing in one segment, the company is able to focus all of its attention on interior renovations, thereby improving quality and customer experience.

Competitive Partnerships

While Addams Interiors will be bidding against our competitors for our own jobs, as a carpentry subcontractor, these same competitors could also be our customers. Especially with the established companies being awarded large bids, Addams can offer its services if the job requires minority work or if special circumstances permit for a subcontractor. These circumstances include large jobs where the customer would be unable to finish it alone or times where the customer is especially busy with other projects and the timeliness of the job's completion would be affected.

This mutually beneficial relationship offers a distinct interaction and teamwork between traditional competitors. By working alongside these companies, Addams would be able to gain substantial industry knowledge. More importantly, these relationships would offer Addams a deeper source of networking which would communicate our top quality efforts to potential customers.

Presently, the best source of competitive partnerships is found in companies such as Peters Brothers. Peters Brothers began twenty–five years ago as a union commercial general contractor. Peters Brothers provides work similar to that of Addams, including demolition, architectural woodwork installation, doors and frames, gypsum wallboard, and acoustical ceilings. A business relationship has already been established with Peters Brothers. Peters Brothers boasts a job portfolio of well–known clients in our segment.

OBJECTIVES

Minority Business Enterprise

Because our Chief Executive Officer is a minority, Addams Interiors has decided to pursue official certification as a minority business enterprise (MBE) in the state of Missouri. As we grow, we will also obtain certification to operate as an MBE in the state of Illinois.

Certification Process

Once Addams Interiors is an operational business and registered with the Secretary of State, we can begin the process to become a certified MBE. This involves filling out a 16–page application and submitting resumes, a business plan, and a balance sheet to the Office of Supplier and Workforce Diversity. The process takes about 90 days to complete after the paperwork is properly submitted. Free workshops are held quarterly to familiarize new business owners with the program requirements and to help them compile their applications.

Minority Goals

In the construction industry, it is often hard for an upstart, minority–owned company to compete against the larger, more established firms. The state of Missouri, however, is taking many steps to alleviate some of these obstacles.

In 2004, Missouri Governor Matt Blunt, and the Office of Supplier and Workforce Diversity (OSWD), began to encourage the inclusion of these smaller companies by setting a goal that at least 10 percent of all government contracts valued at $100,000 or more be awarded to minority–owned businesses. The reason for instating such a goal was to increase workforce diversity and increase MBE participation in state contracts. This target goal is enforced primarily when awarding government contracts but all general contractors are highly encouraged to subcontract a minimum of 10 percent of large projects to minority–owned companies as well.

Many established St. Louis–based contractors, such as Rosen Contracting, who believe strongly in the purpose of these diversity efforts, subcontract as much as 25 or 30 percent of their own projects to disadvantaged firms. Private institutions, such as Saint Louis University (SLU) and Washington University, which are not required to utilize MBEs, do so in order to show diversity and good will. The recently constructed Edward A. Doisy Research Center at Saint Louis University, a $67 million project, had a 25 percent goal for MBE participation and the $80.5 million Chaifetz Arena project recently completed at SLU was heralded for reaching its minority participation goals. Fr. Lawrence Biondi, President of SLU and a strong proponent of revitalization efforts in midtown St. Louis, was awarded a lifetime achievement award from MOKAN, a regional organization dedicated to minority inclusion on construction projects (St. Louis Business Journal). The support of individuals and institutions that are committed to creating diverse working environments will provide Addams with a steady market.

Benefits

Addams can benefit in many ways by being classified as a Minority Business Enterprise. Being minority–owned makes us eligible to join associations that were created for the sole purpose of helping MBEs. In the initial stages of launching our business, these resources will offer excellent opportunities to expand our network. These organizations are discussed in detail in our marketing plan. While we will get our start from our MBE contracts, it is not our goal to be defined by this status, but rather by the quality of our work.

MARKET ANALYSIS

The sub–prime mortgage crisis that has devastated the residential construction industry has not had nearly the same negative impact on the nonresidential segment. While the residential construction industry has experienced a severe decrease in construction spending, dropping 16 percent in 2007, the nonresidential sector has seen an increase of 15 percent according to Bureau of Labor statistics for August 2007. Even with a declining economy, some industries are, for the most part, immune to macroeconomic activity. Accounting firms, law firms, educational institutions, and healthcare service providers are essential to the functionality of the general society and will continue to grow and will need renovation services for their facilities. Surges in the costs of material and labor inputs for construction services were a concern from 2004 to 2006, but the increases slowed in 2007. Recently the Associated General Contractors of America issued a warning that the input costs may again increase in 2008. This must be monitored and considered in bidding jobs to remain profitable.

Lower interest rates benefit the industry, as they will make construction more feasible and allow better building allowances on new office space. As a start–up business, Addams would be able to finance growth easier with lower interest rates.

We have set a plan to tackle a slowing economy. This plan includes:

- Diversifying within the commercial industry: Seeking jobs in a broader range of segments, including retail, hospitality, tenant finish, institutional, financial, and corporate.

- Cutting overhead costs: Being efficient with overhead spending.

- Improving jobs with existing customers: Guaranteeing customer satisfaction and the best quality we can give.

- Closely monitoring jobs and cash flow: Keeping satisfaction in terms of time and quality with current jobs.

- Improving margins on projects: Being financially efficient without sacrificing our core competency.

- Eliminating costly mistakes: Being aware of mistakes and how to avoid them.

- Billing and collecting aggressively: Keeping our Accounts Receivable in check.

- Targeting more stable industry segments: Focusing attention on companies that belong to industries that are less directly affected by macroeconomic activity.

We are also being especially mindful of our overhead expenses at start–up and keeping them at a minimum by working from a home office and setting low salaries for the founders until the company gains momentum.

Within the commercial interior industry, there are two facets of Addams Interiors. We seek to enter the market as both a commercial interior general contractor and as a commercial minority–owned sub-contractor.

Market Segment

Addams will target two segments:

1. New and growing organizations that use commercial buildings (including office, retail, hospitality, restaurant, financial, and institutional).

2. Large– or medium–sized construction companies looking to subcontract work to minority–owned companies to fulfill MBE percentage goals.

We anticipate entering the market with a fairly high acceptance rate from our clients because there is a need for quality, minority–owned interior contractors.

SWOT Analysis

Strengths

- One of the primary strengths of Addams is our classification as a minority–owned business. This places us in a coveted position with high demand by clients and other contractors who want to fulfill minority percentage goals. Additionally, this classification opens many opportunities for participation in mentoring and incubator programs in the St. Louis area.

- The management team of Addams has broad experiences that will give us a solid foundation from which to launch our business. Our team includes a union Journeyman, an accountant, and others with knowledge of the construction industry through prior employment and self–employment. The team has undergone training in construction project management to further add to their skill sets. While young, the managers are enthusiastic and aggressive, and are eager to put their talents to work.

- The owners of Rosen Contracting, veterans with over 45 years combined experience in the commercial interior construction industry, have offered their support and guidance as we proceed with this venture. Rosen has also agreed to provide us with our first job, guaranteeing us work from day one, and Rosen will continue to feed us subcontracted work. Having a vast network of current St. Louis–based contractors will further strengthen our marketing power and ability to generate leads and contracts in the beginning stages, propelling us through a quick start–up phase.

Weaknesses

- We currently have no workforce, but we will be able to hire from the union labor pool upon starting the company. We may experience a high turnover rate initially while we find a core group of quality employees.

- While being minority–owned is considered a strength in one sense, we are also entering a segment of the industry that has a reputation for producing low–quality work. This will be a challenge that our professional network will be able to help us overcome.

- Additionally, there are risks associated with starting a company with closely–related owners. Being part of a family–owned business already, the owners are aware of the inherent difficulties of working with this structure. Keeping business roles clearly defined will allow the owners to over-come these challenges. In Addams, Tabitha Addams will be serving as the CFO. As a CPA, she will perform all the tasks associated with the accounting side of the business. Bruno Palio, the CEO, will primarily be working as a project manager, bidding on jobs, managing the job sites, and interacting with our customers.

Opportunities

- Due to the percentage of contracts that must be fulfilled by disadvantage businesses, there is a high demand for minority–owned contractors. There is a severe shortage of interior contractors, as demonstrated in our competitive analysis, and this niche gives us the benefit of being a sought–after subcontractor.

Threats

- It is possible that the economic downturns which have disrupted the residential construction industry may also cause less spending on renovations in the commercial segment. Those in the industry, however, are optimistic about the future. They have affirmed that the commercial segment has not suffered as much as the residential segment and they expect it to recover within only a couple of years. Thomas McMaster, CEO of a successful development company based in St. Louis firmly believes that the economy should be out of its decline in two to three years.

- Competitive pressures from established general contractors may make winning large contracts on our own difficult at the beginning stages.

- Changes in government regulations, especially the overturning of percentage goals, could also lessen the appeal of one of our key selling points of being a MBE subcontractor, but would not impact our ability to bid for jobs as a prime contractor.

Affirmative Action

Ward Connerly, the founder and chairman of the American Civil Rights Institute, an organization opposed to racial and gender preferences, is currently promoting a ban of the affirmative action measures in Missouri. Connerly claims these initiatives to reach out to disadvantaged businesses are tantamount to racial discrimination, taking business from more qualified non–minorities and awarding the projects, instead, to undeserving DBEs. A similar ban was passed in California in 1996 under Connerly's leadership. This ban resulted in the women– and minority–owned share of State Department of Transportation contracts to drop from 27.7 percent to 8.2 percent. Industry leaders in St. Louis are optimistic, however, that this ban will not pass in Missouri and the directors of PRIDE of St. Louis, a local organization devoted to increasing efficiency by creating harmony between construction laborers and managers, speak against it, promoting instead the benefits of having a diverse workforce.

The implementation of mentor–programs, which pair an established company with an emerging one, is a positive step being taken in St. Louis to promote disadvantaged companies and to spur the construction industry and the economy at large. Rather than simply tracking minority participation statistics, the companies behind many large projects are taking a more proactive approach to increasing diversity on their jobsites. The Lambert Airport expansion was the pilot project for this initiative. Of the more than 550 companies and organizations involved in the $1.059 billion expansion project, about 100 were disadvantaged business enterprises. A project of this magnitude can severely hurt small companies, but through the mentor–program, the young companies were provided with many valuable benefits including free workshops, networking events, as well as the sharing of insight and wisdom from the established firms with which they were working.

The Busch Stadium project also integrated DBEs with a mentor–program. Eighty minority and women–owned firms were granted 130 contracts totaling $65 million of the $300 million project. The prime contractors were each required to mentor at least one DBE, many of which were small start–ups or companies inexperienced in working on large projects. The 23 participating protege firms received $21 million in contracts.

PRIDE is further promoting disadvantaged business enterprises through its incubator program, designed to mentor minority contractors to build strong businesses.

Tax Benefits

Additionally, general contractors who subcontract to MBEs are benefited by receiving tax abatements. Missouri is one of the more generous states in terms of tax credits for a variety of reasons. One reason being the attempt to salvage a vast number of historical properties. Specifically, the Missouri State Historic Tax Credit provides an incentive for developers to salvage these commercial and residential historic buildings. A second reason stems from the accelerated pace of the revitalization efforts of downtown St. Louis. Typically these changes occur over several decades, but St. Louis is seeing an incredible rate of transformation for these projects. One of the major tax benefit programs Addams will be dealing with is the *Tax Incremental Financing*, or *TIF*, which is designed as a financing tool encouraging the redevelopment in blighted districts. Under this program, a developer can underwrite the improvements and be reimbursed later for costs such as assembly, acquisition, demolition, financing, or renovation.

Developers can combine state building credits with federal historic tax credits. These credit programs allow developers to receive up to forty–five percent credit for renovation costs for commercial properties. The city also offers additional tax abatement programs to encourage the use of minority–owned companies in construction projects. In most cases, minority participation is required to receive the tax incentive. Both credit programs are highly utilized in the industry and drive the demand for quality minority–owned subcontractors.

GROWTH STRATEGY

Revitalization Efforts

St. Louis City provides a central location for institutions of higher learning and a wide variety of up–and–coming businesses. Downtown is already home to numerous buildings, apartments, condos, offices, shops, restaurants, sporting venues, convention centers, and entertainment centers. According to the St. Louis Regional Commerce and Growth Association, the Greater St. Louis Metropolitan area ranks 18th with a workforce larger than 1,450,000. The RGCA also reports that the *Site Selection* magazine issued in March 2008, lists the St. Louis region as #3 in the nation for attracting new and expanding corporate facilities. Validating these ranks is the number of new developments that are being planned, and the many more that are expected to come.

This downtown comeback continues to create new opportunities in the interior renovations industry. A renewed spirit in downtown revitalization efforts, tax incentives and lower interest rates contribute to a stronger industry for Addams. The Downtown St. Louis Partnership leads the way in the pursuit of a rejuvenated downtown. As a not–for–profit organization, the Downtown St. Louis Partnership provides funding for the revitalization efforts. After adopting the Downtown Development Action Plan in 1999, the partnership was able to focus on four main areas of downtown: the Washington Avenue Loft District, Post Office District, Riverfront and the Gateway Mall. Since the plan's inception, over $4.6 billion has been invested or committed with over $900 million currently in development downtown as a whole (www.downtownstl.org). This investment represents over $513 million in hotel development, $685 million in office expansion and renovation, and over 80 new shops, restaurants, and services since 2003. Through the partnership's help, new projects are still being announced at an astounding rate. Upcoming revitalization projects of downtown St. Louis include:

- *Ballpark Village:* Next to the current Busch Stadium, this 12–acre project will require much interior construction. The development will include 250,000 square feet of restaurants, shops, and entertainment venues, 450,000 square feet of office space, 400 residential units, and 1,900 parking spaces. Examples of the occupants are a St. Louis Cardinals Hall of Fame Museum and an aquarium. Renovation of the St. Louis Center Shopping Mall, spanning over 540,000 square feet, is also being considered.

- *Lyme Circle:* This has also been undergoing renovations over the past couple of years, and will continue to see improvements.

- *The Whittier Place:* Features the renovation of a five–story, 30,000 square foot building into a multi–purpose complex. It will feature loft apartments, office suites, 5,500 square feet of first–floor retail, and an underground parking lot.

- *Potter Place:* A seven–story, 66,800 square feet, multi–use building, with commercial projects as well as residential.

- *Circle Center Apartments:* This will feature 95 residential apartments and 10,000 square feet of street–level retail.

MARKETING & SALES

Our marketing strategy is to position Addams as the leading interior renovation contractor in the market through strong professional relationships.

Relationships with major area contractors and developers substantiate Addams' readiness for considerable growth and accomplishment in nonresidential interior construction services for the St. Louis area.

Jett Building, LLC, a minority–owned and union commercial general contractor, would also be an ideal competitive partner for Addams. Offering a variety of services including construction consulting, estimating, scheduling, budget and value analysis, and project management, Jett has proven to be a top competitor in the commercial segment. As a minority–owned business itself, Jett would be an exemplary business to model as well as a potential mentor for Addams. Diversifying our relationships within the industry remains a top priority for Addams. Whether this means seeking contacts in the field of carpentry, architecture, management, real estate, or any other sector, Addams believes an expanded portfolio of contacts will more effectively communicate our abilities to the construction industry. By fully committing to our customers today, we believe they will not only provide repeat business, but they will also recommend us in the future. Addams has already made the first step in initiating contact with a number of influential individuals established in St. Louis. A brief look at our network portfolio includes:

- Alicia Tweat, Executive Vice President of Tweat Properties,

- Phillip Fraeniser, Anchor Consulting,

- Michael Hubbard, a construction insurance consultant,

- Jackson Unkel, an attorney,

- Wyatt Stone, owner of the minority–certified Carpets and More in California,

- The previously mentioned Thomas McMaster.

Professional membership in organizations such as the Associated General Contractors and the St. Louis Minority Business Council will help us network. Each organization has regular meetings and networking opportunities to meet with prospective customers and competitive partners.

The key value behind networking for Addams will be the steps taken after initial contact is made. After obtaining these contacts through networking events and favorable introductions, we will look to establish and maintain long–term relationships with those who share our same values and commitment. Our reputation and the contacts we make are integral to the success of Addams. In the task of relationship building, we will be proactive in informing our potential partners about our capabilities, professionalism, and core values. In terms of relationships with our customers, our policy is to make follow–up contact with each customer and to request feedback from current and past clients to evaluate our performance and their overall satisfaction. Our goal at Addams is to create mutually beneficial relationships from the first day of contact.

MANAGEMENT SUMMARY

Our management team consists of seasoned managers and experts whose backgrounds and experiences make them ideally suited to their respective roles.

- Bruno Palio: Co–founder & CEO—Bruno has been training in the Carpenters' Joint Apprenticeship Program for the last three years where he has acquired the skills, knowledge and experience necessary to succeed in the construction industry. Before beginning his career in construction, Bruno worked five years as a certified air conditioning technician and building maintenance supervisor. Currently he is also enrolled in the construction supervisory program which will provide him with further project management education.

- Tabitha Addams: Co–founder & CFO—For the last three years, Tabitha has been attending Saint Louis University, working towards her degree in Accounting and Entrepreneurship, with a Spanish minor. Tabitha has an extensive interior construction background and has acquired invaluable experience within the commercial segment working with Jett for the last five years. Currently, Tabitha is taking a construction supervisory class with the Carpenter's Joint Apprenticeship Program in order to further her knowledge in project management.

- Matt Jones is double–majoring in Entrepreneurship and Spanish. Always drawn to entrepreneurship, he has been self–employed in various capacities for the past seven years, including running a house–painting business through College Works Painting that generated over $36,000 in sales in less than eight months. His interest in construction was fostered by this experience as well as many years of assisting his father with woodworking and home remodeling projects.

- Patrick Essen is also majoring in Entrepreneurship. He has 6 years experience between two different construction companies, and has become familiar with the technicalities of the industry. This background, paired with his management coursework, should make him an ample manager for Addams.

- Jane Dow is a senior at Saint Louis University with concentrations in International Business and Entrepreneurship. She has worked at Credit Unions of America, which has given her experience in the corporate world. The skills she acquired from the nearly four years she has studied at Saint Louis University combined with her work experience will prove to be a valuable asset for Addams.

Advisory Board

Addams' Board of Advisors is comprised of respected members of the St. Louis construction community. Such a team provides Addams with further industry experience and expertise.

- Peter Dewitt: President & Co–founder, Peters Brothers—With nearly thirty years of experience in the construction industry, Peter started his construction career as a carpenter so he has both knowledge of the field and office. As an active member of the industry, Peter serves on the board of the Associated General Contractors of St. Louis.

- Larry Twoell: CPA & Controller, Peters Brothers—Larry has acted as Controller for Peters Brothers for the last ten years. He semi–retired in July 2007 and now works on special projects and training within the company. Larry has utilized his proficiency in accounting to provide Peters Brothers with complete, reliable financials throughout his ten years with the company. With a degree in accounting and a Masters in finance, Larry was able to acquire many high profile positions. He was the Mid West Operations Manager for Putten Industries from 1987 through 1997 before coming to Peters Brothers. Larry also held the position of Accounting Manager for Rosen. He is currently pursuing an Associate's Degree in Architecture.

FINANCIAL ANALYSIS

Financial Assumptions

- Our fiscal year begins in January and ends in December.
- Our Income Statement is shown on a monthly basis.
- Our Balance Sheets and Cash Flow Statements are presented on a cumulative basis.
- For the first three years, we will be working out of the home of Bruno Palio and Tabitha Addams.

For all of our assumptions, we assume 4.33 weeks per month.

Revenue Assumptions

- Contract revenue is our main source of income.
- Revenue earned is equal to the amount billed each month.
- Contracts received are founded on projections based on our competitor's job mix and scaled to our company size.
- In year one, we receive a total of 42 jobs which, combined, total $1,105,300 in contract revenue.
- In year two, we receive 47 jobs totaling $1,572,500 in revenue.
- In year three, we receive 54 jobs worth $2,124,544 in revenue.
- We will be working up to three, five, and six jobs simultaneously in years one, two and three, respectively.
- Jobs classified as "other" do not apply to the first three years of projections.
- Our billings are set up so that we will receive contract payments 30 days after the billing date.
- Our first billing will be for 50 percent of the contract amount; our second for 40 percent; and our third for 10 percent of the contract amount.
- For the 10 percent retention payment, we use the late payment date to yield a conservative receipt date.
- For each job, we assume a 20 percent markup.

Cost Assumptions

- Employees are paid for a 40–hour work week period.
- Costs account for 87 percent of revenues earned.
- Labor cost for field employees is computed as 60 percent of the current contract billings.
- Materials cost is computed as 40 percent of the current contract billings.

- Our owners are paid an annual salary of $30,000 for the first three years.

- In year two, we acquire a third office employee at a rate of $12 per hour, amounting to $24,940.80 each year.

- We intend to offer health care to our office employees in year four.

- After year three, there will be a 3 percent raise to each office employee every year.

- We will have one company car in year one with an additional car in year two with a quoted monthly lease rate of $450.

- Our printer/copier/fax machine will be leased for $350 per month.

- Accounts payable per month is equal to the current direct materials plus equipment purchases.

Funding

Our start–up funding of $70,000 consists of a $50,000 interest–only note from Peter Dewitt and a $20,000 contribution from Bruno Palio and Tabitha Addams. Interest expense on the 25–year $50,000 note is amortized at a rate of 7.5 percent per month. At start–up, we will authorize 100 shares of $1 par value common stock, with 500 shares issued and outstanding, which will contribute a total of $500 in the company. Over the course of three years, we will require three lines of credit from the US Bank Cash Flow Manager reaching a total of $113,687.50, including interest payments at a rate of 6.25 percent. We will pay the line of credit off in the next month when our cash flow is sufficient to cover it.

Organic Grower and Supplier

GREAT LAKES ORGANICS

65129 Drake Rd.
Okemos, Michigan 48864

Adam Theurer, Alex Wander, John Benoist, and Gustavo Ramis

We are planning to be the first major organic, hydroponic grower in the Lansing area to target local grocers, markets and restaurants.

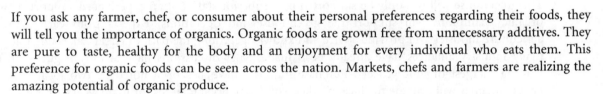

EXECUTIVE SUMMARY

If you ask any farmer, chef, or consumer about their personal preferences regarding their foods, they will tell you the importance of organics. Organic foods are grown free from unnecessary additives. They are pure to taste, healthy for the body and an enjoyment for every individual who eats them. This preference for organic foods can be seen across the nation. Markets, chefs and farmers are realizing the amazing potential of organic produce.

However, over the past several decades, farmers have realized the profitability of growing their foods with high efficiency. This entails applying dangerous chemicals to the soil, practicing hazardous tilling procedures and genetically altering seeds, among many other potentially harmful practices. Over the years, applying these techniques have damaged our soils and have made organic growing a time–consuming venture. Currently, modern farmers that till the soil are agitating natural processes that may have serious consequences.

Tillage practices degrade the fertility of soils, cause air and water pollution, intensify droughts, destroy wildlife habitats, waste energy, and contribute to global warming. These tillage methods are also draining tons of soil into the Gulf of Mexico each year and making America's breadbasket into an arid desert. Other farmers, in warm and tropical climates, have capitalized off of their year–round production and ship their herbs into the Lansing market daily. Importing herbs from warmer climates is an inefficient method. Importing produces excessive water and air pollution. Both of these practices are wearing on an already fragile environment.

Great Lakes Organics utilizes the concept of hydroponics to grow natural herbs, locally. We are planning to be the first major organic, hydroponic grower in the Lansing area to target local grocers, markets and restaurants. Growing locally will encourage the Lansing community to be involved in the process while encouraging sustainable practices in agriculture. Additionally, Great Lakes Organics will eliminate the high costs associated with shipping by growing locally all year round.

Currently, there are no year-round hydroponic herbal gardens in the Midwest that operate on a commercial scale. There are smaller, seasonal gardens located across the region but none use hydroponic technologies. There are also plenty of seasonal gardens located across the warmer regions of the

United States. In addition to these farms, there are large amounts of imported herbs from warmer climates. These competitors all have high-quality and organic products; however, they are far from our region. This leads to higher shipping costs and lowers efficiency. Great Lakes Organics specializes in supporting the local market, year–round. This local production helps our community, implements new techniques, and promotes efficiency and sustainability.

Creating our greenhouses in the Lansing area will not only help support local markets, grocers, and restaurants, but they will also help educate Midwest farmers about hydroponic technologies. The greenhouses at Great Lakes Organics will also help retail customers support their environmental values.

Greenhouse growing in Michigan:

- Eliminates the need for large shipping infrastructures

- Our techniques promote sustainability

- Organics are better for our bodies and environment

Customers are becoming increasingly aware about where and how their food is grown. Consumer uncertainty is a large factor when it comes to purchasing foods. Many imported foods are not monitored by USDA growing standards. In addition to where and how their food is grown, consumers like to be certain about quality and care measures associated with their foods. Pesticides, herbicides and insecticides are all potential carcinogens. This creates fear in the customer, and drives them closer to the organic markets.

The greenhouse will not only be supported by a superior staff, but an experienced support network of organic champions will support the greenhouse and operations. Experts from each area of the agriculture industry will provide advice and knowledge. Along the path of Great Lakes Organics origin, many industry alliances have already been made. Sales discussions have already begun with one of Lansing's largest organic grocers. Purchase inquiries have also been noted by two local chefs. Great Lakes Organics will provide the local market with fresh, organic herbs for many years. Our greenhouses are meant to multiply on our current location in Ann Arbor. There are also plans to expand across the Midwest, to support multiple cities with the ability to self–sustain. Many cities located in northern latitudes require greenhouses to grow locally and year–round.

Four critical elements are brought together under the glass roofs at Great Lakes Organics:

- Rich, organic compounds

- Experienced horticulturists

- High quality seeds

- Superior, year–round production

Below is the projected financial summary for Great Lakes Organics for the first four years.

	2009 Totals	2010 Totals	2011 Totals	2012 Totals
Gross sales	55,143	649,231	1,005,361	1,159,998
Total COGS	27,592	259,671	397,043	471,056
Gross margin	27,551	389,560	608,318	688,941
Operating expense	74,354	222,674	277,100	303,394
Dividends paid	0	26,745	66,244	77,110
Net income	(51,106)	129,289	254,939	301,072
Year ending cash balance	37,638	95,801	296,465	568,157

MISSION

Done

Great Lakes Organics provides Lansing with quality organic herbs at a fair price. We provide our customers with healthier options that are grown in an environment that fosters global sustainability.

Great Lakes Organics' mission is to produce the highest quality, locally grown organic herbs. With the utilization of hydroponics and safe, nutrient rich fertilizers, Great Lakes Organics will grow high quality herbs for the beneficial use of our customers. Only serving locally will allow us to ensure product quality. We will conduct operations prudently and strive to grow steadily, increasing profits, size, and market share. Great Lakes Organics shares the world's obligation to protect the environment and will carry out all operations accordingly.

Great Lakes Organics's Mantra

"Year–Round, Organic Quality"

The 4 Keys to Our Success

1. Reliable and year–round product delivery. This enables us to capture peak produce prices in the winter.

2. Promotion and use of hydroponics. This allows us to grow organically with scientific accuracy and efficiency.

3. Community involvement. By creating a friendly greenhouse environment and sharing our processes with the community, we promote sustainability and educate consumers.

4. Industry alliances and organizations. Fraternizing with our vendors, competitors, customers, and affiliations will create an ideal business environment.

OBJECTIVES

Done

As a local grower, Great Lakes Organics strives to provide the Lansing market with locally grown produce. Each year, companies around the world spend unnecessary funds on shipping produce from warmer climates, where the production takes place, to colder climates, where many of the buyers live. In addition to the money spent, energy and resources are wasted by the transfer of these products. Great Lakes Organics' goal is to ease the strain on our environment and on markets by producing food locally.

Local production of these goods will also ensure quality control. Any of our buyers or end–users can visit our grow houses, year–round. This will not only showcase our high quality methods and products, but it will also serve as an education tool for many Lansing families and schools. By educating the end user about our product we can reduce uncertainty factors about the production process of the herbs.

Providing our customers the best organic product is crucial for our success. Not only will we strive to make organic products, but the best. Many organic products lack quality due to prolonged shipping methods, premature harvesting, and too much handling. Our locally grown goods will not be subject to any of their methods and, therefore, none of the repercussions.

Great Lakes Organics will sell high–demand herbs that include basil, mint and chives, in the Lansing area, where the market for organic produce has not yet reached its full potential. The final system will be composed of five greenhouses, located south of Lansing, that will use modern hydroponics to increase quality control and crop yields. Through automation of the greenhouse and hydroponic systems, the amount of labor required (which is the largest expense in operating a greenhouse) will be reduced (USDA).

Great Lakes Organics will serve the Lansing area with consistent and reliable service. Our products will be recognized as local and organic; this will show our customers that we have higher level of quality control, and give them an opportunity to see it firsthand. We plan to be the first large scale organic greenhouse to serve the Lansing area.

Hydroponics

As mentioned above, we will use a hydroponics system to grow our produce. Hydroponics is the method of growing plants in nutrient rich water, instead of soil. Plants can be grown with their roots directly in this solution or in an inert medium like gravel.

More hydroponics greenhouses in the United States are becoming certified as organic. Aiding this increase are companies like Water Aid that offer hydroponic packages that are certifiable and other certified operations that act as a precedent.

To meet the UDSA standards we will be required to use fertilizer that is not synthetic and contains no refined elements. In other words, the fertilizer will need to be composed of 100 percent organic materials. In the past, these types of fertilizers were difficult to find; however, more companies are producing products that meet these requirements. These companies include Friendly Fertilizer, which makes an organic hydroponic fertilizer, and Hydroponics Inc., which has several products for hydroponics that are 100 percent organic.

The hydroponics system utilized at Great Lakes Organics will make the most of limited greenhouse space. The system used in our greenhouses is the Great Lakes Vertical System. The system is designed so one can stack growing pots on top of each other to obtain the maximum plants per square foot. The stackable pots are manufactured with high density polystyrene foam that will help insulate roots during both hot and cold weather. The stacks of pots are able to be rotated, which allows uniform light absorption for each plant. Rotation also allows for easy harvesting and planting. The Vertical System's direct watering system reduces the amount of water and fertilizers that are required. Vertical System claims that fertilizers and water usage can be reduced by up to 80 percent when compared to other conventional systems. Also, because there is no soil used, there is no chance for soil born diseases. There will be less harm caused by insects and no need for weeding or herbicides. The cost to equip each greenhouse with the hydroponic system will be $6,000.

The Vertical System will increase our growing space within the greenhouse. Because the Vertical System stacks pots vertically, more plants can be grown per square foot than traditional greenhouse growing. "Grow strawberries, lettuce, herbs and many other crops vertically in 80 percent less space." (Vertical System's marketing material).

Growing hydroponically and vertically will help us grow more plants per square foot, conserve energy and water, and control pests.

OPERATIONS

Location

Our location will be in Lansing. The reason this site as chosen is because it is owned by the parents of the owner and will be used rent free. The tract we will use is in a field on top of a hill. We will have access to a well for water and power lines are less than 100 yards away. Gaining access to this site will be done with ease since there is an existing road that goes to the location. This location also has good access to roads. We are in close proximity to I-96 and US-23.

Because of our location, we expect to need little security. It is located off the main road in an area where people do not lock their doors. If security does become a problem, a chain link fence will be purchased for an estimated $5,500, and some of the greenhouse lights will be lit at night as a deterrent. Additional precautions may be taken if necessary (i.e. cameras and guards).

Greenhouses

The greenhouses that will be used at Great Lakes Organics will be purchased from York greenhouse manufacturing. These greenhouses offer many options that will allow Great Lakes Organics to design a greenhouse that best fits our needs. The model that will be used is the Great Greenhouse because it offers the most square feet per dollar. This greenhouse has a total of 3,264 square feet and will cost around $13,000 for a per square foot cost of $4.

The greenhouses will be equipped with modern equipment that will reduce labor and increase control of the environment. Some of the features include: automatic vents, temperature controls that will be linked to the furnace and cooling fans, and, among other things, insulated wall ends.

The purchase price for each greenhouse will break down as follows:

Frame	6,345
Plastic	included
Doors	510
Vents	2,515
Wallends	2,150
Gear box	430
Roll up side vents	490
Automated vent control	600
Total	**13,040**

Using a Corn Stove as a Heat Source

In using a corn stove, we will not only be saving money by burning a less expensive fuel, but will also be burning a renewable resource that will add to our image of being green. It was calculated that in the coldest part of winter we will need the ability to produce 2 million BTUs per hour, with a yearly total of 1 billion BTU hours. Our estimated heating expense for using different energy sources is as follows:

		Annual Cost
Wood	$120 per cord	$ 7,930
Corn	$4 per bushel	$13,600
Wood pellets	$200 per ton	$16,640
Electric	8 cents per kilowatt hour	$23,440
Fuel oil	$3.50 per gallon	$31,251
Propane	$2.66 per gallon	$36,140

The reason corn was chosen over wood is because a wood stove requires more around the clock attention than a corn stove does. Using corn will allow for more control over the price of fuel. With fuels like electricity and propane, you are limited on who you can purchase from. However, with the numerous farming contacts near the greenhouse location, Great Lakes Organics can likely purchase fuel at a discounted and more consistent rate.

Using an external corn stove will allow for low cost per BTU and will reduce the labor required to feed the stove when compared to a wood stove.

Lighting

In order to maintain consistent production rates, we plan to supplement light in order to maintain a minimum of 12 hours of light a day. On the shortest day of the year, the winter solstice, 3.5 hours of light will be supplemented. Supplemental lighting also gives us more control in the quantity produced. If demand shrinks, we can cut back on the quantity of light to slow growth.

The lamp we chose is a metal halide. Metal halide lamps provide a full light spectrum and are more comfortable to work under than other lamps. They are the best lamp for promoting plant growth. This color of light promotes plant growth and is excellent for green leafy growth. The average lifespan of a bulb is about 10,000 hours so a bulb will last for years.

Lights will be hung 4–6 feet above plants for optimal lighting. Each 1000 watt bulb will light 140 square feet. A total of 23 lights will be needed per greenhouse at a purchase price of $300 per fixture. Bulb replacement cost will be around $60. The expected electric expense for operating 5 greenhouses, at a kilowatt hour costing $0.10, will be $12,000. The cost for equipping each greenhouse will be $8,000.

Using Metal halide bulbs will encourage plant growth and provide pleasant working conditions for employees.

Propagtion

Through the year some plants will inevitably die. Therefore we will have a propagation system that will allow us to take cuttings from existing plants and grow them into actual plants. Through propagation from plant cuttings instead of from seeds, a plant will be able to be harvested in about half the time. A propagation system can be as simple as a tray of moist sand. Plants can be grown from cuttings instead of seeds which saves time.

Typical Work Day

In going through the day: the day will begin with a 10 minute meeting to discuss any current and potential problems, as well as give praise and feedback for positive items. The meeting will also be used to motivate employees and try to help their job from being monotonous. Employees will have a 15 minute break midmorning, and a half hour lunch. They will be given the option of working through lunch if they desire. This option will not be encouraged because we want to develop community in employees and social times like a lunch break together will help this. Mornings at the greenhouse will consist of harvesting and packaging in order to allow same day deliveries. Afternoons will be used to propagate plants, and perform any maintenance on the operational systems.

Also, since there is only so much that can be done in a greenhouse, employees will be able to leave early if they accomplish their required jobs. We will not allow this option to be abused, but will allow some leeway because employees will get limited time off during holidays.

Legal Structure

Great Lakes Organics will be structured as a Limited Liability Company. There are several advantages of forming an LLC. First of all, Great Lakes will have limited liability protection. This will not only be good for the company, but also the owners. We will also be a pass through entity that allows Great Lakes Organics to pass the tax on profits to the owners; this will be helpful, especially during the startup phase. Other advantages of an LLC include flexibility in operations and no ownership restrictions. In Michigan, becoming an LLC is very easy and inexpensive.

ADVERTISING

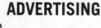 Packaging

Labels and clamshells will be purchased in bulk in order to reduce the per unit cost. Labels will be purchased online. If we purchase 10,000 at a time, labels will cost 1.5 cents each. Clamshells will be purchased from a company called Jones Specifications. The one ounce packing clamshell we will purchase will cost 10 cents each. Several companies make appropriate packing bags that cost 2 cents each. The yearly total for packaging supplies per greenhouse will be around $20,000. Purchasing packing supplies will reduce the per unit cost.

Dove ✔

BUSINESS STRATEGY

There are three unique features of Great Lakes Organics that will aid in becoming an organic competitor in the Lansing market.

The first unique feature of Great Lakes Organics is that the produce will be grown in a greenhouse. This will allow for year–round production that will offer a stable revenue stream as well as provide customers with consistent service and produce. Year round production has a two–fold effect. Not only will we be receiving year round profits, but market price on herbs can increase during the winter months. Additionally, the control of production will increase with the use of a hydroponics system. Further benefits from the greenhouse and hydroponics approach include providing a sanitary environment for product growth, temperature and fertility control, elimination of soil–borne diseases, and availability of technical assistance for the hydroponics system.

The second feature is the locality factor of our business, will provide a competitive advantage over more commercialized, non–local companies. In 2007, 43 percent of consumers typically sought out food grown by local producers whether they were organic or not. Last year the number one word added to the Webster dictionary was locavore (Webster). This is defined as a person who is committed to eating only locally grown and produced food. Great Lakes Organics will cater to the needs and desires of consumers by promoting our product in the local market, involving the community, and offering the freshest organic produce. Currently, 47 percent of consumers worry that more commercialized, non–local organic companies are not following the production regulations as laid out by the USDA. Concern about the production standards of other companies is a legitimate concern. Several "organic" producers have had pesticides found on their farms (likely being transferred from a nearby farm by the wind). There have also been reports of companies buying nonorganic produce and packaging it as organic. The community–centered nature of Great Lakes Organics could alleviate many of these concerns. By holding greenhouse visitations, other community events, and offering more information for consumers on our production standards and techniques, we can establish a more loyal and committed relationship with the community. Through public awareness we will increase sales of our product and taxable revenue within the community. Being a local grower would also create more job opportunities for the community and, in so doing so, add to the local economy. Another advantage of the locality feature exists in the reduction of transportation costs. Less money is required for shipping since Great Lakes Organics does not ship our products cross–country. The distance a product travels from the farm to its destination and its impact on fuel costs and global warming is a growing concern among consumers.

The third advantage arises from the positive attitudes consumers hold toward organics. For instance, 48 percent of consumers believe organic foods are more nutritious than non–organic, while 30 percent of consumers say that organic food tastes better. Many people are concerned with maintaining a healthy lifestyle. Another benefit for the health–minded consumer is that organic food is not grown using any harmful, potentially cancer–causing chemicals, including pesticides, herbicides, and fungicides. Avoidance of these chemicals is especially important during the pre–natal and early development stages of children. Due to their sensitive systems, small children, pregnant women and consumers with allergies who are especially vulnerable will benefit most from the avoidance of pesticide and chemical use. By switching to organic products, children can lower their pesticide levels in only five days, making for a healthier development process. In addition to growing organics free of chemicals known to be harmful, they also contain no Genetically Modified Organisms, or "GMOs", of which 56 percent of all consumers are concerned about digesting.

Risk Factors

One of the largest threats to the organic food market is the perishable quality of our produce. The inability to sell all of our finished products due to the fact that produce only stays fresh for a short period of time, could lead to lost profits. Organic food is labor intensive and as a result, organic produce costs more than non–organic. This is significant because 67 percent of consumers say they would buy more organics if the cost was less. Therefore, monitoring price and understanding our consumer becomes invaluable as the high price of organics proves to be a barrier for the consumer.

One way around limitation of perishability is value–added activities. These activities can include dehydrating herbs and selling to a packaging company or creating soup or dip packages.

Due to the high margins that can be associated with selling organic food, the USDA published organic regulations in October of 2002 in order to try and regulate the market. Among the most pertinent prohibited materials and practices include the avoidance of genetically engineered seeds and materials, the mandatory waiting period when applying proper composting techniques, and the banning of irradiation and sewage sludge. Complying with these USDA standards can be time consuming and expensive, and claiming to be better than a competitor can be a difficult task with the uniform standards.

We realize that this segment of business can fluctuate and make it difficult to compete. Because of the system Great Lakes Organics will use, there is the option to change what is grown. The existing hydroponics system can be used to grow other products like tomatoes, lettuce and even flowers. Or the hydroponics system can be moved out and replaced with materials that are for growing mushrooms or potted plants.

MARKET ANALYSIS

Popularity of organic foods continues to grow within the continental United States. In fact, the sales of this segment increased nationwide 115 percent at current prices, or 89 percent after adjusting for inflation, from 2002–2007. Sales are expected to continue increasing for future periods, which makes it an ideal opportunity to enter the market.

There is a continuous increase in sales of organic food. The constant increase in growth supports the premise that organic foods are becoming more acceptable—and more in demand by consumers looking for foods they consider to be more healthful. With this trend, the industry continues to grow at a rapid pace, as demand for organically grown food in local markets is also likely to rise, indicating encouraging trends.

Agricultural trends also point to the organic produce market as being one of the fastest growing segments of US agriculture. The organic food industry is in the growth stage. Additionally, there seems to be a trend towards eating healthier in the United States, which includes organic foods. Rising nutritional awareness and a preference for a produce–rich diet across the nation has a positive effect on demand for fruit and vegetables generally, including those grown under cover. A general concern for well–being boosts the market for healthy foods such as organic fruits and vegetables.

In 2000, the organic food industry hit a milestone when traditional supermarkets became the primary venue for organic foods. An organic product reaching the shelves of places such as Schnucks, Dierbergs, Wal–Mart, and other large grocers represents an important step for organics. It signifies that the growth of a product and the demand for the product is still increasing. Large retailers such as Wal–Mart have started to stock organic foods to regain and retain many customers siphoned away by retailers such as Whole Foods. In 2006, retail giant Wal–Mart announced it will increase the variety of organic food in its stores, which is expected to lead to a faster adoption of organic farming.

Through mainstream retailers seeking to stock organic foods, the industry becomes self–promoting. Retailers will respond to a rise in demand by increasing their orders. Therefore, those growers who are able to provide year–round service can reap the benefits of the grocery stores and larger retailers' increasing need for inventory.

Competition   Done   ✓

Local competition from large–scale organic greenhouses in Michigan is limited. The current herb industry is located primarily in California, Florida, Colorado, Arizona, Ohio, Texas, Pennsylvania as well as Mexico, Canada, Holland, and Israel. The lack of large regional competitors will reduce the chance of more established companies driving Great Lakes Organics out during our introduction to the market. We will establish a niche market characterized by our locally–grown, year–round products in order to compete with organic growers who may not use a greenhouse but have established themselves in the Michigan market and supply to grocery retailers.

In order to obtain local supply and demand data for the Lansing produce industry, we interviewed the store manager of a prominent grocery store in the area. However, he could not supply exact figures because they were considered confidential. He said that the sales of organic food varied greatly within the city and that consistent suppliers are hard to come by.

Not only is the demand for local produce increasing, produce prices are increasing across the board. This is largely due to the fact that fuel prices have increased substantially over the past decade and that there is a higher demand internationally.

Industry Trends   Done   ✓

Currently the organic produce industry is experiencing high growth in all sectors; locally, nationally, and globally. Not only are there higher standards being set by shoppers, but higher standards are also being set by governments. Regulations on USDA organics have been around for a long time; however, new restrictions on pesticide sprays, irrigation practices, and fungicides have been mounting on the industry.

The most important industry trend is driven by our consumers. Each year the demand for organic produce increases. Studies are increasingly showing grocery shoppers the benefits of eating organic foods, and they are willing to pay the premium. Online polls, grocery store surveys and industry reports are all pointing in the same direction. Organic foods are important to consumers and will be in the foreseeable future.

Organic farming is practiced in approximately 100 countries throughout the world, with more than 24 million hectares (59 million acres) now under organic management. Australia leads with approximately 10 million hectares (24.6 million acres), followed by Argentina, with approximately 3 million hectares (7.4 million acres); both have extensive grazing lands. Latin America has approximately 5.8 million hectares (14.3 million acres) under organic management, Europe has more than 5.5 million hectares (13.5 million acres), and North America has nearly 1.5 million hectares (3.7 million acres).

Organic is a niche, but a very profitable niche. Give consumers what they truly want/need and they will dig deeply into their pockets. Organic is here to stay, not a fad marching by in the night. Others will likely get involved. Whether you opt in or not, it certainly is a category worth watching. It gives us one more window into the minds of consumers.

CUSTOMERS   Done   ✓   ✓

Everyone deserves and enjoys high quality produce; however Great Lakes Organics will focus on the early majority and late majority adopters. Our efforts will also be focused on higher end stores. We are selling our products at local groceries stores which will include Whole Foods, Schnucks, and Dierbergs. We will also focus on smaller, local markets. Most of these grocers buy in smaller increments, fitting for our first year. Many markets and grocers are facing higher demand, due to elevated demand on organic products. This makes it easier for our product to be recognized around the community and our end–user. Placing our products in high–end community supermarkets will facilitate our opportunity to expand quickly. Launching our products to higher–end consumers is vital since they have more disposable income to spend on quality products. As the local community becomes aware of our product, it will be easier for us to expand to other grocery markets that will be attracted in selling our product.

We plan to target areas that have customers who purchase organic food on a regular basis. Many of these areas are easy to find because the stores already exist. Stores like Whole Foods, Trader Joe's,. draw in a certain demographic. The main two are income and ethnicity. Middle and upper class people purchase the majority of organic food, likely because of the higher price tag that is associated with it. Also, people of Asian ethnicity purchase the largest amount of organic products per capita.

Each business and individual's adoption processes has an affect on our business. Even though Great Lakes Organics does not sell directly to the retail consumer, their preferences still impact our business. Out of adopters the early majority and innovators are going to be our primary end–users. The early adopters and innovators are consumers who want to buy local products. These are the consumers who desire to eat locally to promote local economic development and reduce the externalities caused by importing goods and shipping goods across the country.

Shoppers who are interested in our products will typically shop at stores that stock organic products. These customers will be interested in locality, organic quality, and price. The main grocers serving these customers are as follows.

• Whole Foods

• Jones and Peters

• Trader Joe's

• Several smaller, local stores

Each of our adopters takes on a different process for perceiving and purchasing new goods. In the case of Great Lakes Organics, we want to know where these adopters are, even though we are not selling directly to them. By understanding the purchasing and adoption habit of the end user, we will be able to better understand the following:

• Where they will go to purchase new/trendy goods

• How much they are looking to spend on organic goods

• And, exactly what kinds of goods they are looking for

Economic Factors

Organic food is one of the fastest growing agricultural markets in the U.S. With a growing presence in supermarkets and satisfied consumer, organic food is an expanding market. Food quality, freshness, and food safety is what makes organic food more demanding.

Each year, the demand for organic foods increases. However, farmers are not increasing their organic production rate at the same rate of the increasing demand. This means a lot for our business. As the demand for organic goods rises, grocers will be struggling to meet demand needs.

We are currently facing a slowing economy, where disposable income is thinning. Our organic produce can be up to ten times the price of normal produce. Knowing that our economy is slowing and budgets are tightening, we will focus on the middle and upper class, and their grocers. We are targeting higher income consumers who are able to spend more on a higher–end product. International consumers spend around 14 percent of their income on quality food, compared to U.S. consumers which spend around 7 percent. Grocery shoppers that are cost consumers will not be our targets. Most of these shoppers purchase goods at Wal–Mart, Costco, and Sam's Club.

One positive aspect of the economic hard times is that it will add protection from foreign competition as the dollar becomes weak. As the dollar weakens, it could become less profitable for foreign companies to export to the United States.

MARKETING & SALES

Our sales and marketing strategy will rely primarily on personal sales abilities as well as market situations. Most of our sales positioning and pricing will be in response to the markets. Our distribution methods will be unique to Great Lakes Organics and our approach to advertising will be a cold call sales tactic, relying on personal selling capabilities.

Informing, Persuasion, and Reminding

The process of *informing* will revolve around defining the technology of hydroponics in simple terms. Most have a general idea of what "organic" entails but we have a responsibility to make sure we educate ourselves as well as our customers when the terminology is vague or unclear. We must also reassure the organic buying customers that our version of hydroponics produce is just as natural, safe, and as organic as soil grown fruits and vegetables. Assuring product quality will also be an important aspect of informing. If our products do not own up to the best organic competitors, they will reject the hydroponics method.

Organic agriculture is an ecological production management system that promotes and enhances biodiversity, biological cycles and soil biological activity. It is based on minimal use of off–farm inputs and on management practices that restore, maintain and enhance ecological harmony.

Not only are we trying to grow a healthy food but also a food that is safer for the consumer and the environment. Although this is a business, we will show that we care about the environment and our production of organic goods will reflect our dedication.

Persuasion of organic products comes naturally, derived from the sale of organic foods, and their continuance to flourish throughout the various lines. The sale of organic foods continues to flourish throughout the various lines. "Products labeled as natural or organic have seen double–digit sales growth in recent years and now represent close to $21 billion annually." Currently, in the Lansing market, stores like Whole Foods cannot buy enough produce to stock their shelves.

We will continue to *remind* our customers and the retail buyers about the benefits of organic foods (more nutrients, less harmful to humans and the environment, etc.) We also must remind our customers of the environmental advantages of locally grown produce and hydroponics produce. These characteristics use less energy to distribute and are less harmful to the land. We will also remind them that fruits and vegetables grown organically show significantly higher levels of cancer–fighting anti-oxidants than conventionally grown foods.

Advertising

Our main sources of advertising will come through local newspapers with strong editorial columns pertaining to food (*Sauce Magazine*, Trader Joe's and Whole Foods newspapers/letters, supermarket newspapers) as well as Internet capabilities (online clubs, newsletters, etc).

- *Sauce Magazine*
- Whole Foods' Newsletters

- Lansing newspapers

- Local radio and television shows

Sales Strategy

Positioning

We will position our product against others as being locally produced and of high, organic quality. There are very few distinguishable differences with herbs. Most of our customers will be seeing the same products offered, at similar prices. Great Lakes Organics will sell to grocers and restaurants by positioning ourselves against the competition as a local provider. This characteristic will help us stand out in terms of sustainability. We will also us it to show how shipping our products 30 miles to our customers will give way to better products. Local products will not be subjected to days of unnatural shipping methods, or border crossing. Producing herbs locally, as mentioned, during the winter and colder months will be a competitive advantage.

Another positioning method against wholesale distributors and other sellers is that we will be local and have dependable service. Many of our competitors will depend on distributors to ship their product across the country. This process can be disrupted by weather, infrastructure, and contamination. By providing a local product, Great Lakes Organics will not be at the mercy of conditions around the country. This will let us boast about our unique, dependable service.

Pricing

The price of our product will fluctuate with the supply and demand of the market. In the summer time the market supplied with additional locally produced herbs. Because of this, prices will drop and people will buy more. In the winter, when supply is not as abundant, prices go up. However, if we are able to establish brand recognition, we could likely charge a higher price year round. Selling directly to Michigan chefs and restaurants could pose a lucrative pricing opportunity. Typically, restaurants are much more particular about their products, but they will pay a much higher price. During the winter months, some restaurants will pay up to eight times the summer market price for high quality produce.

Personal Selling

We must make it clear that we are well educated in what we produce and how it is done in order to ensure that our clients and potential clients can confidently purchase our products. We will cold call in order to set up appointments. Setting up appointments, giving free samples, and demonstrating the hydroponic method will be the objective for many of our appointments. Through writing this plan, Great Lakes has made several contacts that could be potential buyers. Between the founders, over fifteen years of sales experience has been accumulated. We will rely on this heavily for our establishment in the organic food markets. Initially we will court our existing contacts. Throughout our research, the founders of Great Lakes Organics have established over ten reputable industry contacts. This will be our base for sales. Our plan will be to establish territories, then split them up and place personal cold calls. Salespersons will earn a base salary of $500 per month plus 7 percent of gross margin.

Indirect Sales/Distribution

We plan to be a selective seller and sell directly to grocers and markets. There is a chance that we could partner with a company like Whole Foods and supply them exclusively. But we may not want to limit ourselves in such a manner. If we grow an excess we could sell to a wholesaler, however they may demand we sell it at a lower price because they become the middle man.

In the winter months we will sell 70 percent of goods to retailers and 30 percent to restaurants. In the summer when there is more local competition, 55 percent will be sold to retailers, 30 percent to restaurants, and 15 percent will be sold wholesale or will participate in value–added activities.

COMPETITION

Great Lakes Organics will only have a handful of competitors in a market seeking an increasing supply. Additionally, our unique advantages will help us stand out amongst this small group of local growers.

Primary Competitors

We currently have a few primary competitors. They are all somewhat local and are producers of organic produce. Several currently have multiple farms and greenhouses all within 150 miles of Lansing. Their ability to produce locally cuts down on their costs, and is more appealing to locavores. They also operate out of greenhouses in the winter months, allowing them the ability to reap the high profits from winter months.

Secondary Competitors

We have two different types of secondary competitors: Local, but not organic and Organic, but not local. These competitors come from a wide range of locations and operations. Secondary competitors also represent all imports from other countries. Countries such as Poland, Italy, and China have organic farms in place and provide fresh organic goods to their respective regions. Due to their location, lengthy shipping and unknown practices of shipping these goods, international organic goods only represents a small number of producers that will concern our business. Nevertheless, these producers should still be taken into account as we assess the competitive environment surrounding our business.

We will deal with this competition by targeting smaller retail locations during the summer and selling our products as higher quality than those exposed to the unnatural elements found on outdoor farms and nonorganic produce.

Unique Competitors

We will also be dealing with unique competitors. These competitors either grow different products, pose an opportunity to partner, or operate under a different business model. The People's Farm, for instance, is located in the heart of Saginaw, Michigan. They grow organic produce of all sorts, year round, but under the model of a CSA (Community Supported Agriculture). CSAs will collect funds and labor from a neighborhood and provide fresh fruits, vegetables, herbs, and meat for a small community. This CSA will not be seen as a threat to our business, but an opportunity to advertise, give back to the community, and promote Great Lakes Organics.

Competitive Advantages

Great Lakes Organics' competitive advantages can be summarized in four concise bullets:

*   *Greenhouse Growing*—By growing our foods in a greenhouse, we obtain a clear competitive advantage over our competitors. Growing indoors allows us to grow our foods year–round. We will be able to take advantage of higher market prices. Greenhouse growing also allows us to control our environment and therefore our quality. We will not be subject to the elements; floods, high winds, drought, etc. The threat offered by insects and animals can be greatly reduced in using a greenhouse. And lastly, we control our outputs. Conventional farms destroy native environments with water and chemical runoff and organic matter. We will not partake in destructive practices but will focus on sustainability.

*   *Organic Produce*—Growing organic produce is the obvious advantage. With prices up to ten times as much as modern produce, organics will increase our profit margins while keeping our customers healthy.

*   *Grow System*—Using a hydroponic system allows more control over production. It eliminates the need for pesticides, herbicides and soil borne diseases. It also provides higher production and requires less time required per unit produced. The growing medium, perlite, holds water content

and is an excellent vehicle for delivering nutrients to plants. Using automated greenhouses allows for labor savings and year round production reliability.

- *Local*—Being a local provider will cut our costs significantly. We will not have to pay any tariffs or fuel costs for shipping. We will also become more attractive to our customers, more dependable, and environmentally sound.

MANAGEMENT SUMMARY

- *Thomas Graham*—Thomas graduated from Southern Illinois University with honors and a BSBA with a concentration in entrepreneurship. He established his first LLC at the age of 19 and purchased a piece of investment property while a freshmen in college. Thomas has worked in construction since he was 13 and qualified for the advanced placement plumbing apprentice program while still in high school. Much of his family are farmers and he grew up on a plot of land where his chores included maintaining a garden, and tending to small livestock.

- *Alice Wearen*—Alice recently graduated from Central Michigan University. She received a BSBA, with a concentration in entrepreneurship. Alice studied environmental science as well, taking courses focusing on global sustainability and environmental issues. At Central Michigan University, she served as a board member of the Collegiate Entrepreneurs' Organization. For the past 3 years, she has focused on marketing efforts at a local cancer treatment center and office supply company.

- *Erik Clive*—Erik recently graduated from Michigan State University where he received a BSBA with concentrations in Marketing and International Business and a supporting concentration in Entrepreneurship. Erik worked as a Leasing Agent for a local real estate company learning valuable personal selling and interpersonal communication skills.

- *Pilar Christopher*—Pilar recently graduated from Michigan State University where she received a BSBA, with a concentration in entrepreneurship. She gained many interpersonal and human relation skills through her experiences in her previous positions working at local banks. Being naturally from Puerto Rico, her language skills in English as well as in Spanish have helped her excel in the business world. In addition, her strong background in business throughout the years have helped her acquire the experience needed to succeed in this changing and competitive field.

Job Descriptions

The horticulturist's primary job is to monitor the system and make any necessary adjustments to nutrient level, Ph level, lights, and temperature. This portion of his job should become routine because of the automated control systems that will be installed. The horticulturist will also be in charge of ordering materials, such as packing materials, seeds, fertilizers and other regularly needed materials. The horticulturist will also be in charge of supervising the laborers. He/she will need to give laborers direction, make any changes, and keep other employees motivated. The horticulturist will report to the owner and inform about any problems with personnel, production, etc. With the automation of the greenhouse, day–to–day tasks should not have a great deal of variation.

Laborers will have the job of harvesting, packing, and propagating plants, as well as any maintenance on the system the horticulturist sees needed. They will also have the task of record keeping that will be reported to the book keeper and owner. We are looking to have tours (to qualify for educational grants) on Friday afternoons; the laborers will be in charge of conducting the tours and answering any questions.

At the beginning, the owner will make deliveries to restaurants and retailers. Most deliveries will be made in the late morning, and early afternoon. The owner will be at the greenhouse much of the time and will be able to monitor the operation and help things run smoothly.

Strategic Alliances

LSSf All Inc· Non plof.

We have the ability to join groups and organizations throughout the United States. Though joining various organizations we will form a network with those who have similar businesses to ours and offer sound advice in an effort to efficiently run our business.

- *State–Level Organic Association:* Shows our desire to help educate Michiganders on the benefits of organically grown foods.

- *Organic Co–op:* A co–op that offers grants and other funding to help start–up organic growers fund their projects in order to start their businesses.

- *Ecological Farming Association:* Shares concerns about the duties as agriculturalists to protect the earth and provide an economically practical quality product.

- *World Wide Opportunities on Organic Farms (WWOOF–USA):* Started by the EFA in an effort to spread global awareness about the benefits of organically grown foods. Organization places volunteers at organic farms to assist in the daily operations. In return, the volunteers receive education about living the organic lifestyle and its benefits for the world.

- *Organic Trade Association:* Offers free business listings in its group sites and reduced advertisement costs on it website(s) to those who sign up for membership.

- *All Things Organic (Trade Show):* Sponsored by OTA and held in Chicago, IL, this would be an event to consider attending (if held beyond the upcoming show) in order to move our business to a national level and increase brand recognition.

Mentors and Support Network

From ↓ AM

Through developing this plan we have made several contacts that will aid Great Lakes Organics in the future. Some of these contacts include:

- *Marc Ford:* Marc believes in the benefits of organic food and wants to develop the market of organic food. Marc is working to develop a co–op that will provide people with locally grown and organic food.

- *Gina Spivey:* Gina works at the intellectual property office at the University of Michigan. She previously worked for NASA and has an understanding and interest in hydroponics.

- *York Greenhouses:* York is the company who we are purchasing greenhouses from. They offer a good product with a wide range of options that will allow up to chose the exact options we want for what we are growing. York also offers support information during the construction stage and any maintenance issues that will arise in the future.

- *Henry Wallabee:* Henry is the produce forager for the local Whole Foods Market. He has worked in agricultural business his entire life and has been a valuable mentor for the Great Lakes Organics development team. She has offered her advice for business planning, business development and strategic positioning. She has also helped in networking across Lansing's organic industry.

FINANCIAL ANALYSIS

Additional Revenue Streams

There are several options that will allow for value added activities for any goods that are not able to be sold. We are looking into activities like dehydrating and selling to organic dry herb packagers. We are also considering selling to a salsa or sauce manufacturer or even creating dehydrated soup packages. Value–added activities will protect Great Lakes Organics from lost revenue.

Start–Up Expenses

In order to start business, a first investment will be secured. A total of $180,000 will be needed to cover expenses incurred during that startup phase. Currently there is $65,000 available in the owner's equity provided by the founders. An additional $30,000 has been pledged from the family of one of the owners. A loan of $70,000 will be secured, likely through Whole Foods who has a loan program to aid local growers become established. Even though this loan is through a grocer, it does not limit us in who we sell to, but requires us to supply Whole Foods for at least 3 years. The $15,000 difference in funding will come from grants for the promotion and education of sustainable agriculture or a line of credit secured by one of the owners.

Annual income summary

	2009 Totals	2010 Totals	2011 Totals	2012 Totals
Gross sales	55,143	649,231	1,005,361	1,159,998
Total COGS	27,592	259,671	397,043	471,056
Gross margin	27,551	389,560	608,318	688,941
Operating expense	74,354	222,674	277,100	303,394
Dividends paid	0	26,745	66,244	77,110
Net income	(51,106)	129,289	254,939	301,072

Income statement

	Jan	Feb	Mar	Apr	May	Jun	Jul	Aug	Sep	Oct	Nov	Dec	Totals
Gross sales	38,096	38,096	38,096	38,096	35,662	53,493	53,493	52,586	71,885	76,576	76,576	76,576	649,231
COGS													
Labor	10,586	10,586	10,586	10,586	10,586	15,879	15,879	15,879	21,171	21,171	21,171	21,171	185,249
Growing material	802	802	802	802	802	1,151	1,151	1,151	1,501	1,501	1,501	1,501	13,468
Packing material	3,483	3,483	3,483	3,483	3,483	5,225	5,225	5,225	6,966	6,966	6,966	6,966	60,953
Total	14,871	14,871	14,871	14,871	14,871	22,255	22,255	22,255	29,638	29,638	29,638	29,638	259,671
Gross margin	23,225	23,225	23,225	23,225	20,792	31,239	31,239	30,331	42,246	46,938	46,938	46,938	389,560
Operating expenses													
Salaries	10,453	10,453	10,453	10,453	11,924	13,559	13,559	13,486	15,239	15,617	15,617	15,617	156,430
Depreciation	877	877	877	877	877	1,062	1,062	1,062	1,247	1,247	1,247	1,247	12,562
Other expenses	6,107	5,283	4,641	3,511	2,501	2,511	2,551	2,551	3,987	5,203	6,519	7,815	53,682
Total operating expenses	17,438	16,614	15,972	14,842	15,302	17,132	17,172	17,099	20,473	22,067	23,383	24,679	222,674
Operating income	5,787	6,611	7,253	8,383	5,489	14,106	14,066	13,232	21,773	24,871	23,555	22,259	166,885
Dividends paid	1,157	1,322	1,451	1,677	0	0	0	2,646	4,355	4,974	4,711	4,452	26,745
Interest expense	716	871	857	1,007	989	971	953	935	916	898	879	860	10,851
Net income	3,914	4,418	4,946	5,700	4,500	13,135	13,113	9,651	16,502	18,999	17,965	16,946	129,289

For the year ended December 31st 2010

Cash flow summary

change

	2009	2010	2011	2012
Beginning cash	180,000	37,638	95,801	296,465
Net income (loss)	(51,106)	129,789	254,939	301,072
Depreciation expense	3,887	12,562	15,707	17,187
Cash flow from operations	132,781	179,989	366,447	614,723
Less, capital investments	81,551	42,851	21,425	0
Cash flow from investing	110,000	0	0	0
Long term borrowing	70,000	0	0	0
Principal paid	14,092	41,337	48,557	46,566
Year ending cash	37,638	95,801	296,465	568,157

Break even analysis

Not that this is not needed

	2009			2010			2011			2012		
	Basil	Mint	Chives	Basil	Mint	Chives	Basil	Mint	Chives	Basil	Mint	Chives
Total units in ounces	41,244	16,498	16,498	481,179	192,472	192,472	714,894	285,958	285,958	824,878	329,951	329,951
Unit price	0.90	0.60	0.90	0.90	0.60	0.90	0.90	0.60	0.90	0.90	0.60	0.90
Gross sales	35,160	10,579	9,404	388,535	153,384	107,311	616,025	229,696	159,640	710,061	265,860	184,077
COGS	16,555	5,518	5,518	155,803	51,934	51,934	238,226	79,409	79,409	282,634	94,211	94,211
Gross margin	18,605	5,061	3,885	232,732	101,450	55,377	377,799	150,287	80,231	427,427	171,649	89,865
Gross margin/unit	0.45	0.31	0.24	0.48	0.53	0.29	0.53	0.53	0.28	0.52	0.52	0.27
Operating expenses	44,612	14,871	14,871	133,605	44,535	44,535	166,260	55,420	55,420	182,036	60,679	60,679
Breakeven units needed	98,897	48,479	63,146	276,230	84,492	154,787	314,607	105,450	197,526	351,306	116,639	222,789
Surplus (shortage)	(57,653)	(31,981)	(46,648)	204,949	107,980	37,684	400,288	180,508	88,432	473,572	213,312	107,162

Dec / Jan No School
May - Aug No School

Pet Sitting Service

PET CARE PEOPLE

31 First St.
Lampasas, Texas 76550

Gerald Rekve

Pet Care People is a company that will provide pets with companionship and exercise within their home environment.

EXECUTIVE SUMMARY

Thema Ritter is a lover of pets. She has extensive experience in both the retail and therapeutic aspects of pet care, having worked in pet stores and veterinarian's offices as a veterinarian technician. For many years she thought about the possibility of starting her own business that catered to pets. One day, after reading an article on pet services, Thema saw her opportunity to run a business that accommodates pets and that will provide enough income for her to support herself.

Based in Lampasas, Texas, Thema will operate Pet Care People. This will not be a traditional pet hotel; instead, all the care for the clients' animals will take place at the clients' homes. The main reason for this is to ease the stress that is caused to the family pet when they are taken to unknown and unfamiliar surroundings. With our service, the pet will be in its natural surroundings and be able to remain stress–free. Lack of companionship and exercise for long periods of time can also cause stress to family pets; personal care and attention from a loving companion during their owner's absence can also ease their anxiety and helps ensure a happy, healthy pet.

Mission
Our mission is to provide all of our pets with companionship and exercise in a stress–free environment, while at the same time earning a decent living for ourselves.

MARKET ANALYSIS

Our market will be Lampasas, Texas and the surrounding community. While this is a small city, it does have a large pet population that we are confident will sustain the products and services we offer.

Customers
Customer Demographics

- Our clients are mainly between ages 24 and 55 and work on a full–time basis.

- Clients also include people who are going on holidays for the weekend or for more extended vacations.

- The income levels of our clients range from $40,000 to $300,000 per year. We do get clients outside of these income levels, but they are relatively few in numbers.

Growth Analysis

At this moment we have seen a rise in people who have pets and who no longer want to take them to pet hotels because the of the stress the pets get from being removed from their homes and being left in these unfamiliar places. Increased risk of disease transmission at traditional pet hotels is another factor that discourages people from using their services. Even though all pets need to get the shots before attending to these pet hotels, there are always a small percentage of pets that get very ill and end up costing the owner a lot of money in subsequent veterinarian bills. In some cases, the illness can be fatal.

The unique services we provide address the need for family pets to get the exercise and companionship they need while also doing so in a safe, familiar and stress–free way. We are the only provider that offers these services, and thus our opportunity for success and continued growth is great.

Although there are no signs of any competitors at this time, we want to start operating as soon as possible to ensure we gain the advantage of being the only service of our kind available.

SERVICES

We are not a pet hotel. We are a pet walking and pet care service company, providing service to the market of Lampasas, Texas and the surrounding community. Traditionally, pet care service has been restricted to care of family cats and dogs. We will offer services to these pets, but will also care for other types of pets as well. A list of pets for which care can be provided includes:

- Dogs
- Cats
- Hamsters
- Gerbils
- Guinea pigs
- Rats
- Rabbits
- Fish
- Turtles
- Hermit crabs
- Lizards
- Ferrets
- Chinchillas
- Birds
- Snakes
- Frogs

Basic Services

- We will take care of your pet on a daily, weekly or monthly basis
- Each home visit will last a minimum of 45 minutes

- If desired, we can make multiple visits to your home per day

- Pet care will happen in your home, eliminating your transportation time and reducing stress on your pet

- While at your home, we may offer additional services as requested including watering plants, checking security, etc.

- Other requests for our services can be handled on an as–needed basis

Pricing

We charge based on what services we are providing. All prices listed below are for pets within one household with the same owner.

- Pet companionship and exercise for one pet, once per day—$20

- Pet companionship and exercise for two pets, once per day—$35

- Pet companionship and exercise for three pets, once per day—$50

- Pet companionship and exercise for four pets, once per day—$60

- Pet companionship and exercise for one pet, twice per day—$30

- Pet companionship and exercise for two pets, twice per day—$45

- Pet companionship and exercise for three pets, twice per day—$60

- Pet companionship and exercise for four pets, twice per day—$70

Additional pet–related services include:

- Taking your pet to the veterinarian—$60 plus mileage

- Taking your pet anywhere that requires the use of our vehicle—$60 plus mileage

- Grooming—fee varies based on pet

- Drop–in service where we quickly check up on your pets—fee varies based on travel time and number of pets

- Status reports on your pet's health and well–being when we are with them, either via phone or text messages—fee to be determined

We can also attend to other tasks in your home while spending time with your animals. Additional services while in your home include:

- Watering plants—$10

- Watering the lawn—$15

- Open/close blinds or curtains—$10

- Turn lights on or off—$5

- Mowing the lawn—fee varies based on size of lawn

- Bringing in the mail, newspapers, and signing for packages—$10

- Pet waste removal—fee varies based on pet

FINANCIAL ANALYSIS

Start—Up Expenses

Start up requirements	**$10,000**
Start-up expenses	
Legal	$ 500
Stationery etc.	$ 200
Rent	$ 1,400
Expensed equipment	$ 2,300
Other	$ 600
Total start-up expense	**$ 5,000**
Start-up assets	
Cash balance on starting date	$ 1,000
Start-up inventory	$ 4,000
Total short-term assets	**$ 5,000**
Funding	
Investment	
Owner/founder	$10,000
Total investment	**$10,000**

Monthly Expenses

Advertising (Newspaper)	$ 100.00
Advertising (Yellow Pages)	$ 100.00
Advertising (Truck signage)	$ 30.00
Fuel	$ 500.00
Repairs	$ 100.00
Insurance	$ 100.00
Office supplies	$ 50.00
Misc.	$ 100.00
Accountant	$ 50.00
Bank fees	$ 50.00
Business fees	$ 50.00
Parking fee's	$ 100.00
Park permits	$ 50.00
Other	$ 100.00
Staff	$2,000.00 (Varies based on how many clients we have)
Monthly van lease	$ 500.00

OPERATIONS

Equipment

We will lease a 2007 Dodge Commercial Window Van because of the room it offers as well as its safety record. We will also hire a local carpenter to install cages in the van to keep pets safe during transportation.

Hours of Operation

We will be open 7 days a week, from 10AM to 10PM. We will be available for additional fees for major holidays like Thanksgiving and Christmas.

Residential and Commercial Painting Service

COLOR MY WORLD, INC.

90 Dunes Blvd.
San Mateo, CA 94401

Gerald Rekve

Color My World's team of painters will provide top–quality interior and exterior residential and commercial painting services to the local area. The owner of Color My World believes that most companies can be profitable and successful if they focus on maintaining customer satisfaction.

EXECUTIVE SUMMARY

Business Overview

Color My World is a start–up company that will be incorporated. Color My World will be a sole ownership corporation. The owner will be investing significant amounts of his own capital into Color My World and will also be seeking a loan of $15,000 to cover start–up costs and future growth. Finally, Color My World will ask the bank for a $25,000 line of credit that will be used if necessary to cover unforeseen expenses.

Color My World will be located in a business mall in San Mateo, California. The facilities will include a reception area where clients can come in and buy paint and various paint tools such as brushes, rollers, etc. There will be storage area for inventory, an employee coffee room, and an office for the owner.

SERVICES

Color My World offers a full line of services primarily focused on interior and exterior residential and commercial painting. The firm also provides such services as drywall plastering, acoustical ceilings, pressure washing, and others. The idea is to provide clients with a broad range of related services that will minimize their need to employ a variety of different contractors. Color My World will focus on each job's cost while insuring quality.

Initially, Color My World will focus on residential and commercial customers in the San Mateo area. However, by the end of the first year, Color My World expects to be serving the entire San Diego area.

OBJECTIVES

The objectives for Color My World are:

- Achieve sales revenues of approximately $600,000 by year end.

- Achieve a good mix of commercial and residential paint contracts in our first year.

- Expand operations to include all the Greater San Diego area.

Mission

The mission of Color My World is to provide top–quality interior and exterior residential and commercial painting services. Color My World will seek to provide these services in a way that is profitable for Color My World and makes the homeowners happy. In addition, we will strive to be environmentally friendly and reduce waste.

Philosophy

Color My World will seek to provide its painting services based on when they were booked. The owner sees each contract as a partnership between two parties with mutual needs, one being the homeowner who needs something painted, and the contractor who wants to maintain a long–term successful business relationship. With this approach we are hoping to get repeat business and many referrals.

Color My World will set up the following guidelines to reach its goals:

- Have one person assigned as the job planner and responsible for booking the time and date for each job.

- Assign one person at each job to be the person responsible to make sure the job is done right the first time and to deal with all client issues.

- Start a program for profit sharing for all employees. This will insure all employees are on board and committed to each job and each client.

FINANCIAL ANALYSIS

Start–Up Expenses

Start-up expenses

Legal	$ 1,200
Stationery	$ 600
Brochures	$ 800
Consultants	$ 4,200
Insurance	$ 1,200
Rent	$ 1,000
Expensed equipment	$10,000
Other	$ 1,000
Total start-up expenses	**$20,000**

Start-up assets

Cash required	$20,000
Start-up inventory	$10,000
Total requirements	**$50,000**

We will be buying all new equipment as listed below.

4 Commercial paint spraying machines ($2,500 each)	$ 10,000
200 each of the high grade paint brushes of various sizes	$ 1,000
1,000 rollers of various sizes (along with all the paint trays and equipment)	$ 2,000
2 Floor sanders ($3,000 each)	$ 6,000
Miscellaneous paint equipment	$ 5,000
Scaffolding	$ 5,000
Inventory for store front	$ 10,000
First and Last months rent	$ 1,700
Telephone setup fee	$ 120
Legal	$ 600
Business cards/stationary	$ 500
Office furniture and fixtures	$ 2,500
Computers and office equipment	$ 2,000
Advertising	$ 1,000
Paint supplies	$ 1,000
Clothing and uniforms	$ 500
Gas and power	$ 250
Accounting set up	$ 500
Business software	$ 1,200
Total	**$ 50,870**

MONTHLY OPERATING EXPENSES

Rent	$ 850
Telephone	$ 50
Phone book advertising	$ 75
Office materials	$ 100
Inventory (based on sales)	$ 2,000
Internet	$ 50
Advertising	$ 200
Paint supplies	$ 1,000
Cleaning clothing & uniforms	$ 50
Gas & power to store/office	$ 250
Accounting set up	$ 125
Gas & fuel for truck	$ 250
Salary for owner	$ 4,000
Average salary for painters ($1,200 each for 4 painters)	$ 4,800
Total	**$13,800**

PRODUCTS & SERVICES

Color My World will sell paint products by the gallon and in five–gallon containers, along with stains and other painting products. We will also offer comprehensive interior and exterior painting services for both the residential and commercial markets.

Color My World services include:

- Full prep work
- Dry wall installing
- Fine detailing
- Complete carpentry work
- Specialty wall coatings (wallpaper and textured ceilings)
- Refinishing and touch up

- Stipple and smooth ceilings

- Wall pressure washing

- Wallpaper install and removal

- Deck and fence staining

- Special ceiling applications

Each project is based on the job and what is required. Prices are determined by the job, materials needed, etc.

COMPETITION

The painting market is very competitive, but we are entering the market with unique services. The barriers to entry and exit in this market are very low, making this an industry with a large number of competing painting companies with high turnover rates.

Color My World believes that it can improve on the quality of services in this industry by using a different approach to the job. While all we *really do* is paint, in the end painting can be very different from one provider to another provider. We will provide high–end service and quality workmanship— that is the key to our success.

There are a lot of competitors for Color My World. The phone book contains listings for more than 40 painters and another 20 painters run ads in the local newspaper. This seems to indicate there is little room in the market for another painting company.

However, several factors are in our favor. A survey of all of these paint companies indicated that approximately 90% had a wait time of at least four weeks. This wait time indicates a strong need for the services and plenty of work available for all companies.

In addition, many of the painting companies—especially those who advertise in the newspaper—are not bonded or registered with the local Better Business Bureau. Because of this, many potential customers will refrain from using them and are thus these companies are not true competitors.

MARKET ANALYSIS

Color My World will focus on two markets within the industry: the residential segment which includes condos, home renovation, and new home building; and the commercial segment, which includes buildings used for professional purposes.

It is the goal of Color My World to eventually have approximately one–third of all business coming from the commercial segment. This market requires the shortest amount of time to complete projects and usually requires the least amount of specialized work. Since our projects impinge upon a business's profitability, it is absolutely crucial for our project manager to maintain tight time frames and keep the building owners informed of the job's progress.

Although the above is also true for the residential owner, time is not as critical to this market segment. Rather, quality and meeting the needs and wants of the client come first in the residential segment. The client is often willing to wait a little longer to have the project done to his or her specifications. The site manager must be willing to be more flexible and willing to meet the specific needs of the client.

Market analysis

Potential customers	Growth	2004	2005	2006	2007	2008	CAGR
Commercial buildings	4%	300,000	320,000	360,000	400,000	420,000	3.50%
Residential buildings	3%	300,000	320,000	360,000	400,000	420,000	2.50%
Total							2.68%

This sector is highly seasonal. The busiest times are during the summer months when it is easy for a company to become so busy that it must turn down jobs. The down turn in the winter months has led Color My World to focus on building business in other areas that are connected to the renovation market. To that end, Color My World will also sell pre–made kitchen wall covering. These are one–piece units that cover whole areas of the kitchen. Color My World will make these in the shop and install them at the customer site as needed. These are profitable, especially in the winter months. In the summer, Color My World will focus on its mainline business—painting.

MARKETING & SALES

Advertising

Color My World will price each project based on time, material, and a flat 5–10 percent profit margin, depending on the segment. In the first year or two, depending on sales, Color My World will focus more on establishing contracts than on maintaining its pricing structure. Therefore, profit margin may be a little low for the first couple of years.

Color My World will start an advertising plan that includes mailers and phone solicitation to get exposure to our market. With the end goal being market penetration, we will use all our resources to target the market that is willing to pay extra for quality workmanship.

Sales

Our sales forecast is based on the existing client base of the owner of Color My World and his hired painter subcontractors. Our reputation had led to these potential projects with little advertising or sales work involved.

Sales forecast

Sales	2006	2007	2008
Commercial buildings	300,000	320,000	340,000
Residential buildings	300,000	320,000	340,000

Personnel plan

Production personnel	2006	2007	2008
Forman #1	$20,000	$24,000	$28,000
Forman #2	$20,000	$24,000	$28,000
Painter	$14,000	$14,000	$14,000
Painter	$14,000	$14,000	$14,000
Painter	$14,000	$14,000	$14,000
Painter	$14,000	$14,000	$14,000
Painter	$14,000	$14,000	$14,000
Painter	$14,000	$14,000	$14,000
Painter	$14,000	$14,000	$14,000
Painter	$14,000	$14,000	$14,000

MANAGEMENT SUMMARY

Management consists of one person, Elliot Geran, who has extensive experience in the painting contractors industry. He has a long history of contacts in the market and a solid reputation with general contractors and the public in the area.

Each job will be assigned a lead painter; this painter then is responsible to the owner of Color My World. The lead painter does the job quote and then forecasts the profit for the job. When the job is done, the lead painter will be given a percentage of the profit of the job.

Shoe Store

THOMASSON SHOES

10 Ritter Rd.
Boston, Massachusetts 02101

Gerald Rekve

We will sell shoes to mid–market customers in the Boston area.

EXECUTIVE SUMMARY

We are going into a market where there is a good opportunity to sell a lot of medium–priced shoes to both men and women.

Mission

Our mission is to provide our clients with comfortable shoes that are economically priced, yet provide the owners of the shoe store with an annual profit that makes this business viable for the long term.

Competition

Our competitors range from high–end to low–end sellers of shoes for men, women, and children.

Other competitors like Wal–Mart and Target also sell a lot of shoes to our clients but, like most stores, these stores lack good customer service, especially service dedicated to the department and knowledgeable in the product line. This is where we will excel and set ourselves apart from the competition.

OPERATIONS

Location and Facilities

We will lease 1,800 square feet in the downtown core to set up our shoe store. The reason we have chosen the downtown core is because our product is destination purchased and not an impulse purchase. The downtown core is where you will find all the need–to–go–to type stores. Our clients will search us out and drop into our store. Finally, three of our largest independent competitors are operating out of a downtown location.

We will lease the location for the simple reason that it will cost us roughly 40 percent less in monthly costs as compared to purchasing the location. This being so, we would opt to lease the property even if the location was up for sale.

FINANCIAL ANALYSIS

Start–up budget

- Advertising—$5,000

- Inventory—$150,000

- Leasehold improvements—$20,000

- Staffing—$10,000

- Miscellaneous items—$5,000

- Legal—$1,500

- Accounting—$1,500

- Office supplies—$500

- Office equipment—$2,000

- Office furniture—$2,000

- Power/Utilities—$1,000

- Auto—$1,000

- Fuel—$500

- Meals—$500

- Phone book ads—$1,200

- Lease first and last months rent—$2,400

- Salary–management—$5,000

- Salary–staff—$12,000

The owner's investment is $100,000; the remaining balance of $80,000 will be secured from the bank as an operating line of credit.

Major Suppliers

- Alisida SA (GREECE)

- Alpargatas s.a.i.c. (ARGENTINA)

- B.B. Walker Company (UNITED STATES)

- Barry (R.G.) Corporation (UNITED STATES)

- Bata India Limited (INDIA)

- Bata Shoe of Thailand Public Company Limited (THAILAND)

- CEPS PLC (UNITED KINGDOM)

- Chausseria (FRANCE)

- Crocs, Inc. (UNITED STATES)

- Deckers Outdoor Corporation (UNITED STATES)

- FGI Group Inc. (UNITED STATES)

- The Fashion House Holdings, Inc. (UNITED STATES)

- Feng Tay Enterprise (TAIWAN)

- Grendene SA (BRAZIL)

- Grimoldi S.A. (ARGENTINA)

- K–Swiss Inc. (UNITED STATES)

- KTP Holdings Limited (HONG KONG)

- King's Safetywear Ltd (SINGAPORE)

- Kingmaker Footwear Holdings Limited (HONG KONG)

- LaCrosse Footwear, Inc. (UNITED STATES)

- Lambert Howarth Group p.l.c. (UNITED KINGDOM)

- Merchant House International Limited (AUSTRALIA)

- Nike Inc. (UNITED STATES)

- PT Fortune Mate Indonesia Terbuka (INDONESIA)

- PT Sepatu Bata (INDONESIA)

- PT Surya Intrindo Makmur Terbuka (INDONESIA)

- Pan Asia Footwear Public Company Limited (THAILAND)

- Pegasus International Holdings Limited (HONG KONG)

- Pou Chen Corporation (TAIWAN)

- Prime Success International Group Limited (HONG KONG)

- Puma Aktiengesellschaft Rudolf Dassler Sport (GERMANY)

- Regal Corporation (JAPAN)

- Rocky Brands, Inc. (UNITED STATES)

- Salamander Aktiengesellschaft (GERMANY)

- Sang Lim Leather Co., Ltd. (KOREA (SOUTH))

- Skechers U.S.A. Incorporated (UNITED STATES)

- Skins Inc. (UNITED STATES)

- Stephane Kelian (FRANCE)

- Sunny Global Holdings Ltd. (HONG KONG)

- Symphony Holdings Limited (HONG KONG)

- TOD'S SPA (ITALY)

- The Timberland Company (UNITED STATES)

- Unichem Company Limited (KOREA (SOUTH))

- Union Footwear Public Company Limited (THAILAND)

- Vulcabras SA (BRAZIL)

- Wellco Enterprises, Inc. (UNITED STATES)

- Weyco Group, Inc. (UNITED STATES)

- Wolverine World Wide, Inc (UNITED STATES)

- Yue Yuen Industrial Holdings Limited (HONG KONG)

MANAGEMENT SUMMARY

The shoe store will be managed by Tony Thomasson who has over seven years of experience in shoe store management and sales. Tony will hire three full–time staff and two part–time staff to help run the shoe store. All the staff will be trained in all areas of shoe sales, including the health portion for orthopaedics.

All the staff will be paid a salary that averages 25 percent higher than the competitors; this will create a positive draw and allow us to hire only the best, most motivated staff available.

MARKETING & SALES

Our marketing plan includes several facets to help increase sales. We will set up the store with signage that contains quick facts on shoe styles and the various health reasons are shoes are superior to other shoes on the market. In addition, we will run both sustaining ads and sale ads in the local newspaper and radio station that also delineates the benefits of our products. Because radio tends to have a better return for the advertising dollar invested, we will devote more of our budget to the radio advertising than newspaper advertising.

Advertising

Advertising Budget

- Radio—$12,000 annually

- Newspaper—$6,000 annually

- Flyers—$1,500 annually

Customers

We will focus on selling our shoes to mid–market customers. This is the market that Wal–Mart targets, however Wal–Mart also targets the lower end of the sales ratio. We will not sell in the low end market. Even though Wal–Mart sells in our market, we are very confident that our customer service skills will help us sell more products. In the end all clients want is customer service. When our clients go to large retailers most often the client can never get an employee to answer any questions or give advice about the product. Our staff will give this advice and be there to offer the level of service our clients demand.

SWOT ANALYSIS

Business Feasibility & SWOT Analysis

- *Strengths:* We will be competitively priced, yet we will offer sound advice to our clients about the medical needs

- *Weaknesses:* We may not be able to be priced lower than large retailers

- *Opportunities:* We can grow the market where clients want advice and excellent customer service

- *Threats:* Other independents or chains that educate their staff the way we will and offer excellent customer service

Smoothie and Juice Shop

SUZIE'S SMOOTHIES

690 LaSalle St.
Ann Arbor, Michigan 48103

Gerald Rekve

Suzie Cronin has been in the restaurant and food industries for over twenty years, in both ownership and management. This is a key factor why Suzie decided to open a healthy type of restaurant—she sees the need and potential success for serving all healthy food products in a market that has very few restaurants willing or able to do so.

The products will all be produced based on the new health craze, and will include various forms of smoothies and juice drinks. Health drinks like this are made from all natural products like bananas, oranges, pineapples, grapes, mangos, pears, ice, and others. In addition, we will offer meals that are low in fat, high on vitamins, and low on calories.

EXECUTIVE SUMMARY

Suzie Cronin has owned a restaurant for the past four years, and recently sold it after Suzie realized that the long hours and the need for a lot of staff where taking a toll on her. Suzie sold the restaurant with the goal to open another smaller, fast food operation that only served healthy choices for meals and drinks. The Smoothie business model matches all of Suzie's requirements. It is a small restaurant, only requires a few staff members to operate, and sells healthy products.

Mission

Suzie's Smoothies will sell healthy food choices for drinks and meals that are high in nutrition and low in fat and calories. Our goal is to gain market share in an even and steady pace, allowing us to enjoy our sales growth.

Our success will be based on our ability it produce products that give our customers healthy food that tastes great. Our mission is to assist our clients in reducing calories and fat intake and to live healthier lives by offering them easy, convenient ways to get healthy, nutritious meals in a hurry.

BUSINESS STRATEGY

After reviewing all of the franchises that are on the market, it was decided that Suzie's Smoothies would be independent. Suzie made this decision based her needs to operate a small shop—something simple without all the red tape and paperwork that is required of a franchise. By doing this, Suzie understood she would need to develop her own drinks, meals and so on without the help of a corporate model, but she knew her background in restaurant ownership would give her a solid base from which to operate.

Market Analysis

The target market for Suzie's Smoothies will be the entire city of Ann Arbor, Michigan. Our customers are mainly in the age group of 12 to 35; however, there is a growing trend for the 35 to 46 age group to adopt the healthy life style for food products.

Growth in popularity for smoothie products over the past five years has shown that, once the customer has used this product, they tend to stick with it and tell their friends about it. Healthy food choices are not expensive compared to other food choices. It is just a matter of educating the customer to understand that our food tastes great.

Competition

The current opportunity is greatest right now for our kind of restaurant simply because competing restaurants in the area provide little or no health food choices. Furthermore, even if they were to start offering healthy choices, the branding of their products has been so entrenched in the local market that it will be difficult for restaurants to re–brand themselves as proprietors of healthy options. Our foods as well as drinks will be on average lower priced than our competitors.

The future of our business looks bright as long as we open soon enough in order to garner market share. If we have a true competitor open before us, we will lose the ability to get market share. There are no signs of any competitors opening in the near future and we are prepared to open in a very timely fashion.

FINANCIAL ANALYSIS

Here is a breakdown of our financial needs and projected outcomes.

Total amount of funds sought for venture: $40,000

Total amount of estimated startup costs: $20,000

Total amount of projected average monthly expenses: $50,000

Total amount of projected average monthly revenue: $42,000

Start–up Expenses

A chart explaining our needed start–up expenses is included below.

Start-up requirements

Start-up expenses

Legal	$ 1,500
Stationery etc.	$ 200
Rent	$ 2,600
Expensed equipment	$13,700
Other	$ 2,000
Total start-up expense	**$20,000**

Start-up assets needed

Cash balance on starting date	$10,000
Start-up inventory	$10,000
Total short-term assets	**$20,000**

Investment

Owner/founder	$40,000
Total investment	**$40,000**

MARKET ANALYSIS

Juice and Smoothie Bars in the U.S., 2005 edition

U.S. foodservice industry share of retail dollars by segment 2002–2005 (p)

Segment	2002	2003	2004	2005(P)
Eating & Drinking	72.6%	73.3%	73.0%	70.7%
Juice & Smoothie Bars*	0.3%	0.4%	0.4%	0.5%
All others	72.3%	72.9%	72.6%	70.3%
Food contractors	6.6%	6.8%	6.7%	6.9%
Other commercial**	12.5%	12.2%	12.3%	13.9%
Subtotal commercial	**91.7%**	**92.3%**	**92.0%**	**91.5%**
All other†	8.3%	7.7%	8.0%	8.5%
Total	**100.0%**	**100.0%**	**100.0%**	**100.0%**

(P) Preliminary
*Includes juice and smoothie retail stores, frozen desert retail stores and smoothie mixes.
**Includes lodging, vending, mobile caterers, non-store retailers and recreation and sports venues.
†Includes military and other institutional foodservice.

SOURCE: Beverage Marketing Corporation; Juice Gallery Multimedia; National Restaurant Association.

Growth Strategy

The US smoothie market has grown rapidly over the last five years, driven mostly by the consumption habits of Americans who skip meals and often depend on snack foods as a substitute. Since smoothies offer healthier treat than other snack options, but also taste good and offer convenience and portability, the market is expected to grow at a rate of 10 to 13 percent in the next five years.

The smoothie market has lower barriers of entry because of lower capital investment. But in order to grow, what is required is the quality of the product and brand awareness. Drink Den, the leader in the US smoothie market, has clearly taken a lead over its competitors in terms of market share and, most important, brand awareness.

As a result of tremendous growth, many food chains, quick service restaurants and beverage companies are entering the smoothie segment by opening new stores. The growing interest of large beverage companies in this segment is mostly driven by the declining sales of soft drinks in the United States. There is a possibility of consolidation of the smoothie market, particularly resulting from the inevitable fallout of smoothie brands which will happen as the market starts to settle.

MARKETING & SALES

Advertising

We will utilize various forms of promotion, including:

Word of mouth

- Alliances

- Customer service

- Telemarketing

Advertising

- Billboards

- Direct mail

- Magazines

- Newspapers

- Phone book

Public Relations

- Demonstrations/booths

- Flyers

- Newsletters

- Press releases

- Promotional products

- Event sponsors

Point of Sale

- Signage

- Web site

OPERATIONS

- We will operate our business at 690 LaSalle St. in Ann Arbor, Michigan.

- We will be open 7 days a week, from 11 am to 7 pm daily.

- We will be closed for major holidays like Thanksgiving and Christmas.

- We will be a corporation with one owner.

- We will employ 10 full– and part–time staff, including one part–time manager to manager the restaurant when the owner is away. The owner will only work a 40 hour week.

In order to operate efficiently, a number of lease hold improvement items and equipment is needed. These items include:

- Convection ovens

- Electric ovens

- Fryers

- Gas ovens

- Griddle top range

- Microwave ovens

- Walk–In refrigerator

- Walk–In freezer

- Tables

- Booths

- Chairs

- Highchairs and booster seats

- Stools

Other items are needed for food preparation as well, including:

- Aprons
- Blenders
- Can openers
- Chef knives
- Cooking utensils
- Food warmers
- Gloves
- Heat lamps
- Measuring cups
- Storage containers
- Toaster
- Trays
- Work tables
- 20–quart mixers
- Condiment bottles
- Condiment pump

Needed office supplies include:

- Clipboards
- Desks
- Dispenser tape
- Files and filing supplies
- Message pad
- Money bags
- Mounting tape
- Office tape
- Receiving record book
- Safe
- Time clock and time cards

Necessary pots and pans include:

- Sauce pots
- Stock pots
- Pans
- Bread pans
- Cake pans
- Saute pans
- Fry pans

To adequately have dine–in service, we need the following tableware:

- Bread and butter plates
- Cloth napkins
- Cloth tablecloths
- Cutlery
- Paper napkins
- Napkin dispensers
- Salt and Pepper shakers

Glassware and beverage essentials include:

- Ice machine–cube
- Ice machine–flaker
- Ice machine–nugget
- Coffee maker
- Coffee filters
- Beverage dispensing systems
- Syrup dispenser
- Tea dispenser
- Glassware
- Plastic cups
- Pitchers
- Straws

Cleaning supplies and equipment we need are:

- Automatic hand dryer
- Compact brooms, mops and wringers
- Under counter cleaning supplies
- Dust mops
- Worktop dusting supplies
- Paper towel dispenser and paper towels
- Soap and soap dispensers
- Sponges
- Trash cans and liners
- Toilet Paper

Other necessary equipment:

- Label dispenser and labels
- Freezer merchandisers

- Signs
- Wet and dry vacuum
- Ice cream case
- First aid supplies

Tattoo & Body Piercing
CHAPEL HILL TATTOO

410 Mountainview Rd.
Chapel Hill, North Carolina 27517

Gerald Rekve

Chapel Hill Tattoo's mission is to provide top quality tattoos and body piercing using state–of–the–art equipment and highly trained staff, thus ensuring all safety methods are followed to guarantee the well–being of both clients and staff.

EXECUTIVE SUMMARY

Business Strategy

Mike Hunter along with his wife, Geri Hunter, will open a new state–of–the–art tattoo and body piercing store located in Chapel Hill, North Carolina. The business will be a partnership between Mike Hunter and Geri Hunter, with each partner retaining fifty percent responsibility and ownership. We will provide body tattoos and body piercing to everyone with a minimum age of 18, as required by law. With the couple's extensive background in the industry, they will be able to provide clients with a safe and exceptional place to get their tattoos and body piercing. In the past, clients for these services have traditionally been young men of lower income levels; however, the past ten years have seen the popularity of body art expand to include female clients and clients of almost every age and socioeconomic level. The result of this change means a much larger base of clientele for businesses of this type.

The owners of this body art store have extensive education and training in art and have considerable experience in designing and applying tattoos as well as administering a wide array of available body piercing. Furthermore, they have extensive training in all aspects of safety and taking the necessary precautions to ensure the well–being of their clients.

We intend to capitalize on the demand for tattoos and body piercing by offering a clean, safe environment in which clients can be assured they will receive quality tattoos and hygienic piercing using state–of–the–art equipment. All this will be achieved without compromising the artistic value of their chosen body art.

Mission

Our mission is to provide top quality tattoos and body piercing using state–of–the–art equipment and highly trained staff, thus ensuring all safety methods are followed to guarantee the well–being of both clients and staff.

Customers

Chapel Hill, North Carolina is a strong market for our products. While there is a lot of competition in the market we are very confident that our skills in the trade will be sought after by clients who see our work. Because of our extensive experience in the field, we expect to get a significant number of referrals and repeat customers.

There are over 400,000 people in our core target market. Research has shown that, at any given time, approximately 10 percent of the total population is contemplating getting a tattoo or piercing, or is actively seeking a place to do so. This means that about 40,000 potential clients live within a 30 minute drive of our shop. Accounting for the 10 other competitors in the area, our potential market is roughly 4,000 clients at any given time.

The average amount being spent on a tattoo for one person is $200.00; piercing typically runs $100.00. Using the number of clients as predicted above, the amount of annual revenue potential for our shop is enough to sustain both the owners and possibly another two staff.

PRODUCTS & SERVICES

Types of Tattoos

American symbols	Fantasy tattoos	Love symbols
Animals	Flames	Moons, Stars and Sun
Arabic symbols	Flowers	Music symbols
Armband tattoos	Grim reaper tattoos	Names
Biomechanical symbols	Harley Davidson	Native American
Black and white tattoos	tattoos	symbols
Celtic knots	Irish tattoos	People
Chinese symbols	Japanese symbols	Photos
Christian symbols	Kanji tattoos	Tribal symbols

Tattoo Styles

- "New School" Style Tattoos—These are modern versions of the old sailor style of tattoos such as anchors and swallows. They are much brighter and more animated than their predecessors which look very flat in comparison. A lot of people—especially females—are asking for tattoos of swallows and anchors on their neck.

- Japanese Kanji Tattoos—Japanese style tattoos are popular among females who are going for "full sleeve" style tattoos depicting Japanese characters such as koi or carp fish.

- Floral and Love Heart Chest Tattoos—This style has a certain timeless look harkening back to the days of the 1950s.

- Star Tattoos—These have always been popular but more people are getting them done on visible places such as wrists and on the lower legs. Unsurprisingly, Hollywood stars are lining up for the tattooist's chair and demanding tattoos that reflect their lives.

- Tribal Tattoos—Tribal tattoo designs have been around for hundreds of years but are becoming more and more complex and constantly evolving and morphing into what has become known as neo tribal tattoo styles. Tribal styles can be traditional "black work" covering the arms or more colorful styles characterized by the "Modern Primitive" look covering the entire body.

Piercing

Jewellery

Sometimes the jewellery is combined in the price, other times you have to pay extra on top of a price depending on what jewellery you want. For example—getting pierced with gold will be more expensive than getting pierced with titanium and getting pierced with titanium will be more expensive than getting pierced with stainless steel. Piercing almost always cost a little less if you intend on getting pierced with a ring, rather than a barbell.

Piercing Costs

Here is a rough guide to regular piercing prices (surgical stainless steel jewellery included):

Ears

- Earlobes—$20
- Pena—$20
- Triages—$60

Nose

- Septum—$75
- Nostril—$20
- Bridge—$75

Other facial piercing

- Madonna—$60
- Eyebrow—$60
- Labret—$60
- Tongue—$25
- Cheek—$75

Body Piercing

- Navel—$50
- Nipple—$75
- Back—$75
- Nape—$75
- Web of hand—$75

Multiple piercing discounts are also available.

We will also offer the service of tattoo removal; this is an area where all of our competitors lack service and is a nice complement to our service line.

MARKETING & SALES

We will use the following methods to promote our store.

- Yellow pages
- Newspaper
- Radio
- Flyers
- Trade shows

Our main focus will be to have a Yellow Page ad the same size as our largest competitor. We will also run weekly ads in our local newspaper, and sustaining ads in two local niche fringe–type newspapers that cater to our market. Radio advertising will be employed to promote our grand opening; additional usage of this media will be determined at a later date based on the response we get from the grand opening specials we offer on the radio ads. If the response is significant and justifies the cost, we may plan to use radio advertising on an ongoing basis.

Flyers will be used on an ongoing basis. We also plan to attend "lifestyle" trade shows that cater to our markets.

All of our promotions will focus on quality and services and not on prices. Our profession is that like a dentist; we offer quality in service and products providing our clients with healthy services. Pricing will play a factor when our clients are deciding what product to buy, but will not be the reason why our clients come to our shop in the first place.

OPERATIONS

Location

We have already been in discussions with a strip mall positioned in a central location in Chapel Hill; it is also a mere two blocks from one of the major shopping malls in the area.

The location is 1,200 square feet. It is larger than our current needs, but the quoted rent we are paying is equivalent to other, smaller locations available on the market. The extra space afforded with this site will allow us to easily expand to a hair salon or tanning studio if we decide to at some future date.

Insurance

We will purchase enough insurance to protect ourselves from the issues we may face as a business operating in our industry.

Training and Education Requirements

Both Mike and Geri Hunter are professionally educated and trained in tattooing and piercing. Mike spent seven years working with one of Boston's largest tattoo shops. During this time Mike was accredited with tattooing certification for all aspects of tattooing and piercing.

Geri also worked with Mike at Boston's largest tattoo shop. She focused mainly on the piercing side of the business. Geri has taken some courses in tattooing but, for this business start–up, Geri will focus her efforts on piercing.

The goal will be to hire two extra staff to assist in tattooing. Both additional staff members must be accredited.

GROWTH ANALYSIS

Business Feasibility & SWOT Analysis

Strengths	Our staff will be the highest trained with the most credentials.
Weaknesses	Because of the training our staff has, we will be charging higher rates; this could have a impact on our budget-minded clients.
Opportunities	We have decided to open this location because there is more demand for healthier services for our business.
Threats	Competitors getting the required training.

Viability and Long Range Plans

Research indicates that the body art industry is on a long–term growth pattern. Over the past 50 years, there has been incremental growth and acceptance in the market, expanding the potential clientele to include women and people from all socioeconomic backgrounds.

FINANCIAL ANALYSIS

Start–Up Costs

Purchase of business	**60,000.00**
Equipment and inventory	16,500.00
Equipment	7,000.00
Plumbing	4,000.00
Interior needs	11,000.00
Retail displays	4,000.00
Storefront and artwork	5,000.00
Advertising	7,000.00
6 months rent in savings	**20,000.00**
20% personal investment	
To be financed	
25% private investor–owners	30,0000.00
Financial Institute	100,000.00
Structural needs	7,000.00
Piercing equipment	18,000.00
$10,000 Bond for store	10,000.00
State license	300.00
Text, mannequin, classroom supplies	3,000.00
Printing costs	3,000.00
Office equipment	3,000.00
Computer software	2,590.00
Hardware in clinic	1,825.00
Retail inventory	10,000.00
Phone expenses	925.00
Misc.	1,963.00

Used Clothing, Furniture, and Antique Store

REBECCA'S SHOPPE

59 Brookstone Dr.
Bangor, Maine 04401

Gerald Rekve

Rebecca's is a used clothing, furniture, housewares, and antique store. The main products will be those donated by local residents; we will not buy any inventory for resale. Instead, we will contract with local charities and pay them a percentage of the sales we incur as a monetary donation.

EXECUTIVE SUMMARY

This is a used clothing, furniture, housewares, and antique store. The main products will be those donated by local residents; we will not buy any inventory for resale. Instead, we will contract with local charities and pay them a percentage of the sales we incur as a monetary donation. People will be more willing to donate to a store they know will be recycling and reusing items while at the same time helping to fund worthy charities. This will give us an edge up on any competition as well help fuel our inventory.

Our immediate goal is to have this business up and running in six months. Our long–term ambition is to expand to a second location within 24 months. Once we prove this concept to be successful, we plan to branch out and sell conditional franchises to other cities in the area.

Business Strategy

The concept of our business is very simple. In order to keep inventory costs down, we will get our entire inventory by means of donations. We will use local radio to get our message out to the public and use the charities we partner with to be the messenger. This will allow us to remain in the background while the charity takes all the attention. By doing the promotion this way, we will increase our credibility to our market. People will be more trusting in donating their gently used and new, unused items to us. The more this happens, the more we will get product for our store.

Because we are selling donated items, our real inventory cost is zero. This complete lack of inventory overhead will allow us to use our available funds to lease a 10,000 square foot location in a major highway or business retail location. Inventorying this large of a location can be challenging; however, we are confident that we will be able to have enough stock in place on opening day. One of our major competitors for both donations and retail sales may be the Salvation Army. To combat this, we have decided to donate a percentage of our sales to the Salvation Army in

121

addition to the other charities we will partner with; this will ensure the market accepts our business model for both donations and retail sales and does not see us as a threat to other, more established charities.

The store layout is going to be similar to other stores. We will use new merchandise racks to display and sell all of the clothing. Used clothing will be washed and inspected prior to being displayed. All furniture and kitchen items will also be cleaned and inspected prior to resale. The key will be to sell products that look and smell clean and fresh. This will garner higher prices, which will mean more profit for our charities as well more profit for us.

OPERATIONS

We will lease a 10,000 square foot retail location that previously housed a retail outlet. The size is appropriate for our needs and the store is still in relatively good shape. The only immediate need is a repaint job, which must be completed prior to opening. The store has a great deal of parking and is located on a major roadway. Our major expenses for the start–up will be the store fixtures as well as displays. In addition, we will need to fund staffing costs until we begin to earn sales.

Organization

We will employ a total of twenty full– and part–time staff. We will also ask our charities to offer volunteers; this will keep our employee costs down and will also allow our charities to take a more direct role in our business model. Furthermore, having representatives from the various charities present in the store will reinforce, or in some cases introduce, our business model to customers; hence, they may be more willing to donate items to our store or continue to shop there, knowing the revenues will help the charities and are not all profit for a nameless corporation.

We will hire all age groups for staff; this will allow us to have a good representation of the demographics in the city we operate.

We will be open seven days a week from 9 am to 9 pm. Here is the proposed staff work schedule:

Monday—12 hours, 4 full time/4 part time

Tuesday—12 hours, 4 full time/4 part time

Wednesday—12 hours, 4 full time/4 part time

Thursday—12 hours, 4 full time/4 part time

Friday—12 hours, 4 full time/4 part time

Saturday—12 hours, 4 full time/4 part time

Sunday—12 hours, 4 full time/4 part time

We will pay our full–time staff $12 per hour and our part–time staff $8 per hour. All staff will be given the option to work either part–time or full–time. The goal is to make our workplace very employee–friendly and as flexible as possible.

Management Summary

Matt Flowers will be the sole owner of the business and has over twenty years experience working for Costco. During his time at this major retailer, Matt worked in every department. When he decided to leave, he was the assistant store manager. Matt's background in retail sales is extensive—he will use all the skills he learned at Costco to ensure his own business is successful.

During Matt's career at Costco, he worked in seven new store start–ups. This experience has given him the perfect foundation to operate a business like the re–sale of previously owned items. Matt understands inventory flows, seasonal changes and how they affect inventory, as so on.

Two of the most important parts of the success of a retail store are the management team and the products that are sold. In this case, we excel at both.

MARKET ANALYSIS

Our products are used clothing, furniture, kitchen and household times. We will also accept tools, garden furniture, and yard furniture. If something is donated to us and it is working condition, we will re–sell the item. Our market niche is that we reuse products instead of throwing them away.

We also understand that some of our products may be collector's items. Knowing this, we will have one assistant manager dedicated to researching and pricing items appropriately. This will ensure we sell our products for what they worth. If cannot identify an item, then we will price it at approximately 30 percent of the retail cost.

With the increases in housing and living expenses, as well gas prices, we know our products will be attractive to people who do not want to spend a lot of money on new products when they can buy used items that are just as good as new for a fraction of the price. Low income or simply environmental–thinking people will be attracted to our products. Over the last two years the world went from the wars around the world to the need to take care of the world we live in. This is a very strong directional change with everyone now doing things to save the planet, and our business will be seen as green–friendly business.

Customers

We will have two types of clients—the person or business donating products to us and the customer who buys those products from us.

The donating clients will be looking for a credible place to donate their items; they will need to see that we are a good community of citizens. They will need to see that we are paying a percentage of our sales to the charity we say we are. The donations these customers see must be placed in the store within a short time period and be priced fairly. This will ensure these customers will be happy that their donations are going to good use and will convince them that we are a good, trustworthy business.

Our clients will come all walks of life; however, the major group of clients will come from the 18 to 36 age group, of which about 65 percent will be female and 35 percent will be male. The yearly income levels will primarily be in the $20,000–$45,000 range. Having said this, there will also be clients from other age and income groups.

Success Factors

The main reason our business will succeed is this—our entire inventory is free, and our only two major expenses are staffing and the lease to our location. Both of these are fixed so we can easily budget. Once the leasehold improvements are made and we open up, our business will produce pre–tax profits in the 44 percent range; this is about 27 percent higher than traditional retail businesses that sell similar products.

Competition

Our competitors are retail stores that sell similar products; however, theirs will be new, where ours are used. There are two stores in our market right now that sell similar products.

MARKETING & SALES

Sales

General merchandise store sales increased 4.9 percent in January after falling the previous two months. Overall, general merchandise stores have seen their sales remain essentially flat throughout 2004. Within the general merchandise sector, department store sales picked up in January, after two months of declines. Sales in department stores jumped 6.1 percent in January, a rise partly attributed to new store openings in the last week of the month but also to stronger consumer spending after a weak holiday season. Other general merchandise stores also enjoyed rising sales in January (+3.6 percent), after two consecutive monthly declines.

Food and beverage retailers posted a 3.0 percent sales gain in January, canceling out the 2.4 percent drop in December. Beer, wine and liquor stores (+12.5 percent) enjoyed by far the largest sales gain of the sector, partly making up for the lost ground in the previous three months, when sales fell 16.0 percent over the period. Supermarkets (+1.5 percent) also saw their sales rise in January, following a 0.7 percent decline in December. In general, sales in the food and beverage sector have been increasing rapidly since the beginning of 2004.

Pharmacies and personal care stores experienced a 2.6 percent sales gain in January, following a decline of similar size in December (-2.4 percent). December's lower sales were the first monthly decline in five months in these stores.

Consumer spending in furniture, home furnishings and electronics stores increased 2.5 percent in January, reflecting gains in three of the four store categories included in this sector. Furniture stores (+5.5 percent) posted by far the largest increase in sales, after experiencing two consecutive monthly declines. For their part, home electronics and appliance stores (+1.5 percent) and computer and software stores (+1.5 percent) enjoyed their second straight monthly sales gain in January. Sales in the overall sector have regained some strength since the summer of 2004, after remaining essentially flat in the first half of the year.

Sales advanced 2.4 percent in building and outdoor home supplies stores in January, after falling 1.6 percent in December. Despite January's sizable gain, these retailers have seen little change in their monthly sales since last August. Retailers in the automotive sector saw their sales rise for the first time in three months in January (+0.5 percent). The 1.3 percent sales gain observed at new car dealers was partially offset by a 2.5 percent decline at used and recreational motor vehicle and parts dealers. While new car dealers' sales seem exceptionally strong (+9.9 percent) compared with January 2003, they were only 1.1 percent above those observed in the same month two years ago. Except for the sharp declines seen in the second half of 2003, sales at new car dealers have remained more or less steady over the past three years.

FINANCIAL ANALYSIS

Location

The location we have chosen to lease will be an old retail store location. We will be spending about $50,000. This money will mostly go to the painting of the store's inside and outside walls, along with a new tile floor to be installed. All of the colors to be painted on the walls will be light, which will make the store bright and cheery.

The major advantage to leasing will be the fact that we will not need to spend a lot of money to buy a location. While the location we are leasing is going to be expensive, we will save the money we would have used to buy the building to instead to use it to manage the cash flows of our business.

Start'up Expenses

Rent	$ 3,500
Improvements/build-out	$50,000
Salaries/wages	$40,000
Payroll expenses	$25,000
Equipment leases (copiers, fax machines, telephone system, computer)	$10,000
Furniture	$ 5,000
Supplies	$ 2,000
Inventory	$ 1,000
Advertising	$15,000
Utilities	$ 5,000
Licenses/permits	$ 2,000
Insurance	$ 2,500
Accountant's fees	$ 1,500
Attorney's fees	$ 2,500
Other expenses	$ 2,400

Budget

Budget January 1 to December 31

Category	Actual	Budget	Difference
Inflows			
Net sales	385,400	300,000	85,400
Cost of goods			
Merchandise inventory, January 1	160,000	160,000	0
Purchases	120,000	90,000	30,000
Freight charges	2,500	2,000	500
Total merchandise handled	**282,500**	**252,000**	**30,500**
Less inventory, December 31	100,000	120,000	(20,000)
Cost of goods sold	**182,500**	**132,000**	**50,500**
Gross profit	**202,900**	**168,000**	**34,900**
Interest income	500	700	(200)
Total income	**202,500**	**168,700**	**33,800**
Expenses			
Salaries	68,250	45,000	23,250
Utilities	5,800	4,500	1,300
Rent	23,000	23,000	0
Office supplies	2,250	3,000	(750)
Insurance	3,900	3,900	0
Advertising	2,550	2,900	(350)
Telephone	8,650	8,250	400
Travel and entertainment	2,700	2,000	700
Dues & subscriptions	1,100	1,000	100
Interest paid	2,140	2,500	(360)
Repairs & maintenance	1,250	1,000	250
Taxes & licenses	11,700	10,000	1,700
Total expenses	**133,290**	**106,850**	**26,440**
Net income	$ 69,210	$ 61,850	$ 7,360

Investment

The total investment required for this retail store includes $100,000 from the owner, Matt Flowers, and another $300,000 from four private investors. With the start up equity in place, Matt Flowers will put the business plan in place, secure the location, and secure the partnerships with charities. It is planned that the store will be up and running within three months.

Water Purification System Distributor

Fresh Faucet Distribution

570 Turnberry Dr.
Tulsa, Oklahoma 74101

Christopher Lee Aubuchon, Ryan Franklin, Justin Gimotea, and Elliot Smith

The need for clean water in the developing world is a large and growing concern. Today, over one billion people do not have reliable access to clean drinking water. To help alleviate this suffering, Fresh Faucet Distribution will operate as a micro–franchisor for water purification systems in the developing world. We will partner with local microfinance institutions in India to provide simple water purification systems that can be operated locally. We will provide knowledge, training, and support for local entrepreneurs in building and operating their own small water filtration and distribution businesses. We will utilize the existing infrastructure and resources available through our microfinance partner institutions to gain access to underserved markets and to reach local entrepreneurs. By coupling the power of microfinance with proven business systems we can scale the distribution of clean drinking water faster and more efficiently than traditional charity organizations, create job opportunities, and share business knowledge with aspiring small entrepreneurs in the developing world.

PRODUCTS & SERVICES

Fresh Faucet Distribution is a Microfranchise Institution that will provide an integrated service and product to small entrepreneurs in Bangalore, India. This integrated service and product features three components. First, Fresh Faucet Distribution will connect small entrepreneurs to the Industrial Credit and Investment Corporation of India, a leading Microfinance Institution. Second, Fresh Faucet will enable these small entrepreneurs, now equipped with capital to invest in a water filtration system produced by Filtration Systems Ltd. Finally, after connecting Bangalorean entrepreneurs to capital and equipment necessary for them to operate a small enterprise, Fresh Faucet will provide them with a training system that will educate them on how to effectively operate their water filtration systems and how to effectively run their small enterprise. In order to provide this integrated product and service and in accord with the typical structure of a franchise business on a micro–scale, Fresh Faucet will charge royalties on profits.

Fresh Faucet will connect local entrepreneurs in Bangalore with local Microfinance Institutions (MFIs) in order to aid their purchase of water filtration systems, essentially enabling their potential as micro–franchisees. For initial entry into India, Fresh Faucet will utilize the infrastructure of one of India's largest and most successful MFIs, Industrial Credit and Investment Corporation of India (ICICI).

ICICI operates with the critical understanding that universal financial inclusion requires a systematic understanding of the markets, people and the local economies. With this critical understanding, ICICI's mission is to address the needs of the poorest of the poor and vulnerable populations across the country and to provide funding support to institutions that address critical resource gaps. ICICI concentrates on the most vulnerable geographies and sections of society that get excluded by other initiatives thereby enabling Fresh Faucet to connect more small entrepreneurs to the lifeline of micro–finance. More particularly, Fresh Faucet's partnership with ICICI will enable small entrepreneurs in Bangalore to purchase water filtration systems that will serve as a key element of their small enterprise.

Filtration Systems Ltd.

Fresh Faucet Distribution will connect Bangalorean entrepreneurs to Filtration Systems Ltd., producers of a solar powered UV light based filtration system capable of turning nearly any well, creek, river or other water source into clean and safe drinking water. The three step filtration process involves: sediment pre–filter, a Carbon Block Polishing Filter, and an ultraviolet light. The sediment filter removes dirt and large debris. The Polishing filter removes herbicides, pesticides, chemicals, odor, color, and bad tastes. The UV light removes Bacteria and Viruses, including Typhoid Fever, Dysentery, Cholera, Jaundice, Hepatitis, Influenza, E–coli, and other unwanted microorganisms to a 99.999 percent purity.

The system's effectiveness and value is confirmed in the way that it is currently used by Rotary International, Medical Missions, relief groups, missionary organizations as well as the Red Cross, UNICEF and the UN. It will produce about 3 gallons per minute and 500 gallons of water per day. This system is very easy to install. It can be set up in under one hour and is very simple to operate. It is a turn–key system with everything pre–assembled. The system plugs straight into the water source and can be mounted to any flat surface. It comes pre–assembled, and is simple to operate. Maintenance is typically needed once per year. The solar power means that is can be used in any village, even without electricity. The system can produce over 500 gallons per day, making it helpful to larger communities as well.

Our product runs on solar panels and does not need electricity. Not only does this make our product available to a larger market, but it also means that there is no energy cost for operating the machine. In addition, the machine requires little maintenance. Our unique "business in a box" package includes training and support in addition to the water purification.

Entrepreneurial Training

Training is unique in the fact that it goes beyond maintenance of the water filter; it will feature an intensive entrepreneurial workshop, equipping our clientele with comprehensive skills to run a successful business. The following delineates the details of the two–part training system:

Product Training:

Product maintenance and repair

How to diagnose problems with the machine

How to order replacement parts and filters

Entrepreneurial Training:

Competitive Pricing Technique

Networks and referral marketing

Customer Service Training

Small Scale Distribution

Ethical Business Practices

Bookkeeping and Financial Practices

Long–Term Planning

RISK FACTORS

Already established multinationals have barred entry into the water distribution market through buyouts and exploitation of huge water reservoirs. We do not plan to attempt competition with these corporations, but they also should not affect operations based on the fact that their services are primarily bottled water distribution. There are minimal hurdles during due process of business establishment, but bureaucratic backlog may hinder initial growth of the business. There is a concern and evidence that the poverty level is so low in some areas that people may choose to drink contaminated water rather than pay for clean water. Given this concern, Fresh Faucet Distribution has engaged in intensive market research prior to entry.

OBJECTIVES

Fresh Faucet is currently exploring the idea stage. This feasibility study is to examine our potential in the global water market, and more specifically India's water market. Fresh Faucet expects to be ready for launch by the beginning of 2009. Within that year we expect to accomplish the following:

- Complete feasibility study: May 5th 2008

- Begin and complete business plan: August 1st 2008

- Pursue and Receive start up capital: August 1st 2008

- Assess applicant pool: December 31st 2008

- Beginning Due Process: August 31st 2008

- End Due Process: September 4th 2008

- Start sales within India: January 1st 2009

OPERATIONS

Legal Restrictions and Rights

Fresh Faucet will operate as a non–for–profit organization. This is to ensure the lowest possible tax rate on any profits due to the low revenue nature of the business. Fresh Faucet will be comprised of a four–member board of trustees who will be responsible for planning and implementing board made decisions and who will be responsible for day to day activities. All revenues that are generated will be put back into the organization barring a small salary for the board and their subordinates. We will operate as a four-member board. Each member will be assigned to specialize in either product knowledge or training. There are few legal restrictions in India that would serve as an impediment to growth.

Insurance Requirements

Although not required Fresh Faucet has decided to implement the following insurances to alleviate some of the liability burdened to the board of trustees:

- *Property insurance*—will insure the organization in the event of damage or loss to the business property.

- *Liability Insurance*—to insure against a employee or customer being injured in a situation where Fresh Faucet would be the liable party.

BUSINESS OVERVIEW

Micro–financing entails the extension of financial services to those living in poverty and without access to traditional mainstream credit markets or sources of capital. Micro–credit is a term which refers to loans made out to individuals, most often with no collateral, in the developing world through Micro–Finance Institutions (MFIs). These MFIs are a broad array of non–government organizations, credit unions, co–ops, private banks, and commercial banks which increasingly offer an array of financial options to the world's poorest who have little or no access to capital. These MFIs provide a diverse range of small business loans, savings, education/mentoring opportunities, and insurance to the world's poorest.

"Microcredit, or microfinance, is banking the unbankables, bringing credit, savings and other essential financial services within the reach of millions of people who are too poor to be served by regular banks..." (Gert van Maanen, Microcredit: Sound Business or Development Instrument, Oikocredit, 2004)

Micro–financing is a unique tool which offers those in the developing world a chance to actively engage in lifting themselves out of poverty. It supplements and improves upon traditional charity models by providing a means of sustained economic growth for the world's poorest without sustained subsidies. MFIs have proven themselves to be profitable and sustainable, and often provide valuable business skills and financial literacy to the developing world's budding entrepreneurs.

"For a microentrepreneur, the cost of a microcredit loan represents a small proportion of total business costs. Studies conducted in India, Kenya and the Philippines found that the average annual return on investments by microbusinesses ranged from 117 percent to 847 percent." (International Year of Microcredit, United Nations, 2005)

It's estimated that total market demand for micro–financing totals above $300 billion worldwide, yet less than 18 percent of the world's poorest households have access to financial services totaling just over $25 billion today. The micro–finance industry is comprised of over 10,000 MFIs worldwide. As the industry matures, a process of consolidation has begun to occur, with professional industry leaders (the top 10 percent) expanding their acquisition of smaller firms and implementing best practices. Also, leading MFIs have begun to mature both financially and operationally, in some cases transforming into banks, and integrate into the financial sector. The industry has begun to take on the skin of the more traditional financial sector with ground–breaking securitizations of micro–loans and local bond issues. This is occurring at a time when many new entrants are also entering the industry, most notably, large commercial banks. The confluence of these trends, coupled with increased acceptance of micro–credit and online vehicles for individual investors (such as Kiva.com and MicroPlace.com) suggest a rapid closing of the supply–demand gap for global micro–credit in the years ahead.

MARKET ANALYSIS

Micro–franchising represents the very latest innovation in enterprise social development and serves as a natural complement to the micro–finance industry. Micro–franchises are broadly defined as small businesses that can easily be replicated by following proven marketing and operational concepts. This is an industry that is in its infancy and is an outgrowth of the micro–finance industry model.

The underlying premise of the micro–franchise concept is that, in addition to underutilization of labor, there exists in the developing world an underinvestment in human capital (the knowledge, skills, and abilities necessary for success). In addition to all the hurdles faced by small business owners in the developed world, micro–entrepreneurs operating in the informal sector in the developing world must face low and uncertain wages, and little–to–no social welfare or security. They are not registered and cannot benefit from many support programs initiated by the government including training, financial assistance, tax incentives, etc.

Microfinance provides its clients with working capital loans for self–employment, but often does not offer the business skills, training, or technical assistance necessary for the owner to run a successful business. Micro–franchising fills this gap by offering proven business models, technical training, supervision, quality control or marketing expertise, and resource distribution scheme. The existing network capacity of microfinance institutions is still the most powerful tool for reaching a large number of the world's poorest. Integration of these two powerful concepts is beneficial because microfinance can provide the capital needed for self–employment while micro–franchise opportunities provide the capacity to develop businesses strong enough to generate continuous growth in sales, jobs and profits. One of the underlying problems with micro–financing as a poverty reduction tool has been the inability of many local entrepreneurs to scale their businesses beyond what a single person can sell, produce, and/or transport in a day. Micro–franchising can address this problem by providing simplified and proven systems for scaling businesses on the local level, thereby providing added job growth, wealth creation, and knowledge transfer.

Trends in Governmental Support

In 2000, as part of the United Nations' Millennium Declaration, International Heads of State pledged to reduce by half the number of people who lack accessible and affordable drinking water by 2015. This pledge also includes ending unsustainable exploitation of water resources and the development of integrated water resource management and efficiency plans. Fresh Faucet will benefit from this UN–sanctioned governmental support and will enable it to realize its goals with greater expediency and success.

The efforts of the Global Water Partnership (GWP) will ease Fresh Faucet's entry into the Indian market. GWP is a working partnership among all those involved in water management: government agencies, private companies, professional organizations, multilateral development agencies and others committed to meeting international goals related to water and sanitation. The GWP's particular contribution to the U.N. Decade includes working within countries, and with the community of international organizations, in order to assist countries in developing integrated water resources management and water efficiency.

Current State of Water Industry in India

Currently over 1 billion people, or 20 percent of the world's population does not have reliable access to safe drinking water. Contaminated water is one of the single largest sources of disease and death in our world. Worldwide, 250 million people suffer from water–related diseases each year. These cases of sickness and death take a great toll on the economy of developing nations, costing untold billions of dollars in lost economic output. About 226 million Indian people lack access to safe water and over 46 percent of India's people are living on less than a $1 U.S. dollar per day. In India alone, over 450,000 people die annually of diarrhea, an affliction whose leading contributor is a lack of access to clean water and the total number of children who die of water–related diseases each year is 1.5 million. Large multinationals such as GE India have begun to pay attention to this problem, and have responded by marketing water purifiers, mostly on an industrial scale. Even in this category, market penetration is a mere 2.5 percent and use of personal or village purification systems in rural areas is negligible. During the 1990s, India's access to clean tap water in both urban and rural areas actually declined, and greater use of groundwater sources ensued. Over half of the rural population now relies on groundwater and dependence on open wells (25.8 percent) continues to be high. The declining quality of groundwater due to pollution is posing health problems for people in India.

Current Microfinance Industry in India

The market potential for this industry in India is tremendous. The water market in India is a $2 billon industry and is growing at a rate of 15 percent–20 percent annually. According to data from India's

National Sample Survey Organization, only 70 percent of urban and 18.7 percent of rural households have access to piped tap water supply in India. This represents a net decrease from 72.1 percent in 1988 for urban areas and only a marginal increase in rural areas. This leaves a large proportion of the population without access to water infrastructure and dependent on increasingly polluted groundwater. Moreover, as India's population and water demand increases, these groundwater sources are becoming increasingly polluted. All this occurs alongside rapid economic growth within the country and increasing per–capita income, which creates a huge potential market for local water purification.

Market Potential for Microfinance in India

- Among its varied MF providers, India has nearly all the ingredients for CMF: demand, infrastructure, human capital, management capacity, wide outreach, commercial viability

- Credit potential estimated at $6–$8 billion

- Average annual Gross National Income growth from 1990–2003: 5.8 percent

Current Microfinance Industry in India

- 1,000 private MFIs; only 1 has 200,000 clients & only very few have 100,000. Most have 500–1,500 clients.

- 90 MFIs rated by Micro–Credit Ratings International Ltd. in 2003 had, in aggregate, loans of $US 52 million & reached 1.9 million clients

- Presence of many highly educated people; some Commercial Microfinance experts with high technical capacity

- Already existing vast banking infrastructure

- Considerable financial liberalization

- High diversity of MF providers, and a new dynamic of experiments & ideas

Current Microfinance Providers in India

- Commercial banks (priority sector loans)

- SHG–Bank Linkage program

- Regional Rural Banks (RRBs) (owned by GOI, sponsor banks, & State Governments)

- Cooperative Banks

- MFIs (NGOs, Non–banking Finance Companies, & cooperatives)

- Postal banks (savings)

- Others (wholesale, retail, & some that are both)

We will be using Industrial Credit and Investment Corporation of India. They have great qualifications:

- ICICI, a private sector bank, is India's second largest bank

- Network of 955 branches in India & presence in 18 countries

- ICICI Bank reports recent presence in rural & microfinance markets, with outreach to over 500,000 rural and poor households

- Interested in scaling up, reaching underserved markets, & developing innovations for MFI

- Partnerships with MFIs; buys MFI portfolios; & has retail CMF pilots

- Internet Service provider partnerships to finance 1,500 village–level Internet kiosks; franchised distribution of ICICI products

- ICICI Bank Social Initiative Group:studies of international CMF best practices, action–research on CMF, working papers, etc.

- A promising example of building toward CMF future.

COMPETITION

Our competitive advantage is the package of products and services we offer. It is the efficiency associated with specialized training and product knowledge, offered by our company. The solar powered Filtration Systems Limited water filtration system was chosen because, unlike most other purification systems, it is not limited by water type or electricity. Whereas other systems remove bacteria or sediment, our system effectively and efficiently removes both. The Fresh Faucet filtration system provides the most cost–efficient and effective water filtration system available. This system has few, if any, limitations, as it was designed specifically for our purposes. This system also fits our budget. With a small wholesale price of $1,700, the system can pay for itself within one year and fits the criteria for issuance of micro–credit.

Another competitor, Matt Fritz, has created a water filtration system. This system is similar to Filtration Systems' products in some respects. The system filters wastes through an evaporation mechanism and can even filter sewage waste products into potable water. This system is offered as a micro-franchise opportunity similar to our own. The system has begun an initial trial run with local entrepreneurs in Bangladesh. Though the system has features which ours does not, such as the ability to produce excess electricity and filter raw sewage, there is a considerable cost differential. Initially the product cost $100,000 to produce. The cost has been reduced to just over $3,000 for the entire system, however, this still represents an exorbitant cost to local entrepreneurs who might benefit from the system.

Fresh Faucet plans to open in India. There are three sources of competition: bottled water companies, tap water/purification companies, and public water. There are nearly 200 bottled water companies, nearly 80 percent of which are local brands. Larger, foreign companies include Nestle, PepsiCo's Aquafina, and Coca–Cola's Dasani. Some of these larger companies, such as Coca–Cola, have been accused of causing water shortages in more than 50 surrounding villages. Another problem with bottled water companies is that approximately 90 percent of bottles are used just once, and then thrown away. It takes 1,000 years for a bottle to biodegrade. Recycling is not a strong program in India. Pesticides and other toxins are still common in bottled water.

Tap water companies are less common. They allow locals to fill containers at a price based on volume. There are many problems that stem from this. Industrial commercial businesses rarely get enough profit to stay afloat. One of the few commercialized businesses with a model similar to our own has 60 locations, including one in Bangalore. They are, however, limited in location because they are a joint venture with local governments and are under private ownership. Despite these impediments, it is estimated that on a hot summer day, Bangalore slum dwellers buy anything between three to four thousand liters of canned water. This is besides the volume of drinking water that residents get from public sources and numerous borewells.

Public tap sources of clean water are not widely available and are subject to rationing, while past attempts to teach locals how to maintain the public sanitation process have fallen by the wayside. Locals want water controlled by the people, yet the people have been shown not to have enough incentive to maintain public well systems in the past. In Bangalore, slum dwellers have access to clean tap water through public tap sources; however, they are severely limited by rationing of water and are forced to stand in line for hours to fill their water needs. Also, public water sources are only available during certain times of the day, require a long travel time for most users, and are subject to frequent breakdowns/backlogs/or contaminations.

Another company has begun selling a bromide–based water purification system for use by individual families. It is a table–top device which requires no electricity and is being sold locally door–to–door in Bangalore. The purifiers, however, cost $68 U.S. apiece. Furthermore, the system requires replacement filters approximately every 4–6 months which cost an additional $10 U.S. This is a considerable capital cost for families living on less than $1 per day, making the units unaffordable for those needing them most.

Fresh Faucet provides a low cost, no waste operation that stays in the hands of the local people. It provides monetary incentive to keep the business going, and the costs are low enough that it can be open to a larger variety of villages and towns.

CUSTOMERS

1.1 billion people in the world do not have access to safe water, 2.6 billion people do not have access to adequate sanitation, 1.8 million children die every year as a result of diseases caused by unclean water and poor sanitation—this equates to 5,000 deaths a day.

The lack of clean water has fatal ramifications on all age groups. 90 percent of deaths from diarrhoeal disease occur in children ages 0 to 4 years. The World Health Organization reports that "Improved drinking water and sanitation services and better hygiene behavior especially by mothers are crucial in cutting child mortality." Children in Africa and Asia, especially girls, ages 5 to 14 years, miss school because of lack of adequate drinking water and sanitation in their homes and schools. This decrease in school attendance exacerbates the cycle of poverty. For people ages 15 to 59, improved drinking water and sanitation services through the efforts of community projects bring economic returns far greater than the capital investment and recurrent costs. People aged 60 years and over comprise an increasingly large proportion of the population, and in the way that they are more susceptible to diseases spread by unclean water, it is imperative that they also be considered in water and sanitation programs.

In particular, the water crisis in India is threatening economic prosperity. Lack of clean water in agricultural regions could stem massive migration of rural farmers into urban centers. This population influx into congested urban areas will put enormous pressure on existing infrastructure. Experts suggest several directives:

*   Public education of wealthy farmers on water conservation

*   Improvement of water management and waste facilities

*   An increase in technological innovation through further advances in desalinization, water recycling, deeper drilling, and water transportation techniques

Fresh Faucet's microfranchise efforts can serve as a timely and valuable solution to this crisis.

India has the largest growing bottled water consumption rate in the world. There has been an increase of over 57 percent during the last five years. One reason for this is the scarcity of clean drinking water which forces many to drink from the same water source that others use to bathe and wash clothes.

Fresh Faucet's typical customer would be a person with low income in a rural area. Towns and villages with easy access to a water source would allow costs to be at a low. These are places where Fresh Faucet can be most effective for the people in that town.

The specified region within India for Fresh Faucet's initial entry is Bangalore. It is one of India's fastest growing cities, with a growth rate of 38 percent over 10 years. Almost 20 percent of its 6.5 million residents are packed into informal settlement areas, better known as slums.

Most of the people living in these areas do not have access to safe drinking water or household toilets. In Bangalore, people living in the slums typically collect water from a water tanker or from a polluted stream that can be as many as two miles from their homes. There are some public water connections, but the water is only available for a few hours each day. Often, the water collected is not enough to meet the most basic needs of the households. In order to get water from the water tanker, community members (mainly women and children) wait in long lines for a city water truck.

Providing access to safe water and sanitation facilities in the home and providing health education will transform the daily lives of thousands of people, enhance security and reduce the causes of communicable diseases.

ADVERTISING

Fresh Faucet's market penetration plan stems from local citizens starting their own business. There is no need to spend significant amounts of money on advertising. Word of mouth is the most powerful form of advertising, so the local entrepreneur will begin spreading the word with people he/she already knows (per our networking training). Most of the traffic in the towns we will operate will be on foot, so many people will pass the business daily and continue spreading the word. An easily accessible location and word of mouth will be the main way that the company expands the business. As each location nears operating capacity, additional locations will be considered.

A website will be created in order to raise awareness for Fresh Faucet. It will teach people significance of the impact of clean water, and show them what they can do to help.

GROWTH STRATEGY

Fresh Faucet is committed to bringing clean water to those in the developing and impoverished world. Our company structure is designed to help us grow quickly, since we are not limited by charitable donations. This fact, coupled with our dedication to the cause, means that our focus for the future is to change as many lives as possible.

In order to affect the greatest number of lives, we must first start with awareness. In the long term, a comprehensive marketing strategy will be ideal, but an initial step in raising awareness is the web as it is an inexpensive way to accomplish this. One way we can continually foster awareness is through the use of link sharing. Fresh Faucet will place links for other socially just causes on our website in exchange for a link on their site. Facebook is another way to spread awareness very quickly. As part of our future plan, we must constantly be looking for ways to spread our name, and the web is a great tool for that.

Secondly, we must seek more entrepreneurs within various parts of Bangalore. While each system can make up to 500 gallons per day, there are more than 1.3 million people living in the Bangalore slums. While not every person will be in the market, Fresh Faucet still faces enormous growth potential from Bangalore alone. In the way that there are countless other areas within India with vast numbers of people in need of clean water, there are tremendous possibilities of growth.

While Fresh Faucet wants to take advantage of economies of scale in regards to training and support, we do not want to be limited by the locations in which we grow. Fresh Faucet will also be seeking to expand into locations beyond India to make clean water sources a global possibility.

With new locations, Fresh Faucet will have to seek alternative MFIs beyond ICICI. By developing a diverse group of MFIs, Fresh Faucet will be able to keep MFIs competitive and create more safety measures in the event that MFI funds become more difficult to obtain. While ICICI does have a vast infrastructure in India as wall as in 18 other countries, Fresh Faucet will be looking to create business relationships with as many credible MFIs as possible to expand its reach further.

Website Designer

Portal Code, Inc.

6190 Lakeview Blvd.
Walla Walla, Washington 99362

Gerald Rekve

Portal Code, Inc. will sell website design and hosting services for businesses and residential clients.

EXECUTIVE SUMMARY

Portal Code, Inc. has been established to sell website design and hosting services with the following sale channels:

- Door–to–door sales for both businesses and residential clients

- Internet sales via our own websites

The owner, Pat Newman, has extensive sales experience and has worked for a couple different types of door–to–door sales companies. While there, he quickly realized what it takes to succeed in sales. This allowed him to rise to the top of his field and he remained the top income–earner for seven years in a row.

While working hard in his sales positions, Pat also worked on his hobby of creating websites for friends and then hosting them on his own server. Eventually he was managing an average of 21 websites a week, just by word of mouth. Pat realized the revenue from his hobby was greater than that for his position in sales. Therefore, he decided to quit his sales job and founded Portal Code, Inc.

MARKET ANALYSIS

Of the 20,000 business in the area, only 15 percent have a website and, of this 15 percent, it is estimated that only 4 percent have spent more than $1,000 on their site. This has resulted in a lot of websites that need some professional attention and redesign. We are estimating that in the next 12 months we are going to capture 10 percent of this market, which will result in rebuilding existing sites and designing new sites.

Competition

There are five web design firms listed in the local yellow pages with large ads that will the sell the same type of service for design and hosting that we plan to provide. This seems excessive simply because of the cost to advertise in this medium and the lack of quality websites published to date. We checked the competing companies's sites and called each with a list of questions. Here are our direct competitors and their prices:

- Tomas Web Design—$3,500 starting price

- Pitter Patter Webs—$3,200 starting price

- United Web Company—$2,600 starting price

- Wilson Web Services—$1,600 starting price

- Brown and Hill Internet Sites—$800 starting price

We will position our starting price in the mid–level range of $2,900. Our hosting will range from $75 per month to $500 per month based on the requirements of the client.

OPERATIONS

Staff

We will employ the following staff:

- 2 web designers, including the owner and one hired designer.

- 3 sales staff. These sales staff will be outside sales staff to call on the business market.

- 1 telemarketer. This telemarketer will sell websites to the home market via cold calls on the phone and scan the internet, for prospects etc. This person will also answer the phone and provide client services.

- 1 accountant, part–time. The owner's wife will manage this area. She will also continue to work at her day job as a sales associate for a major retailer, and manage the accounting functions of Portal Code, Inc. in the evening. This will allow for a steady stream of income coming into the household.

Equipment

The equipment required to start this business includes:

- 6 IBM desktop computers

- 2 Apple notebook computers

- ZED Website design software

- Paypilta Art software

- Photoshop Professional software

- MSN Office Suite software

- ACCPAC Accounting software

- Norton Anti–Virus and Firewall software

- 4 desks and chairs

- 2 fax machines

- 1 wireless router

- 1 server

In addition, we will require traditional office products necessary to running an office such as pens, paperclips, etc.

MARKETING & SALES

Sales Staff

Compensation

Our sales staff will follow the following sales strategy:

We will be the first web design firm to sell websites door to door. We will hire seasoned sales staff that will make cold calls on prospective clients.

The key to this strategy is simple; we will divide the region into territories, with each one being equal. Each sales rep will be given a sales quota; this quota is going to be fair but must be met each month. We have set the quota higher than what we need to succeed, so in the event we come in at 30 percent below budget, we will still make money and the sales staff will still earn a good income.

Sales staff can expect the following compensation:

- Base salary of $200 per week

- Car allowance of $100 per week

- Cell phone allowance of $50 per week

Each sales person will be required to supply their own notebook computer. The reason for this is to prevent the staff from handling our equipment or increasing our costs for equipment.

We will offer the sales staff the following commission structure:

- Based on a quota of $15,000 per month of 6 websites per month, we will give the rep a 20 percent commission over and above their salary.

- We will give the sales rep a $500 quarterly bonus if they meet their sales budget.

- We will give the sales rep a 5 percent bonus if they find a lead in another sale representative's territory and hand over the lead. This will insure great team work, as well focus the sales staff on performance verses in–fighting which is common with highly productive sales staff.

The reason the earning for the sales staff seems high is simply because we strongly feel the only way to grow sales for a new firm is to attack the market aggressively. We will start out slowly, however, and only hire 1 sales staff for the first 3 months. We will then add staff as we continue to grow and expand.

Responsibilities

The sales rep will be expected to go out and make cold calls on local businesses on a daily basis. This will be done by sitting down with the owners of the business and show them how we could increase as well improve their web presence and the positive results of having increased web awareness.

The sales rep will also be expected to network with a variety of business associations, like the local Chamber of Commerce, national business networks, and small business administrations.

Finally, because our main focus for sales will be direct and door–to–door, we will only run a small advertisement in the Yellow Pages. At the end of the day, the success of our company will be based on our sales staff.

One of the main keys to our sales success will be understanding our clients and their needs. We will find a coach in the target business area, whose role will be to act as a guide for this sale. We will have at least one coach per industry. The coach will provide information and interpret statistics about the industry outlook, buying influences, and other important factors.

Strategic Selling

We will employ the method of strategic selling. This means we will strive to achieve the following benchmarks for each and every potential sale.

- Position yourself with the real decision makers

- Spot key client needs

- Ask for the order

- Listen 80 percent of the time, talk only 20 percent of the time and no more

- Always treat old clients like new clients

- Always ask for referrals; make it a habit to get two referrals for every sale you make.

- Do not stop until all your client's needs are taken care of

- Always follow up on your sales to make sure the client is still satisfied

Sales Projections

Quite simply, we will focus our efforts into sales and marketing. Our office will be set up in a simple, inexpensive location that is centrally located with free parking so all the sales staff have easy access to the office.

FINANCIAL ANALYSIS

Start–up Expenses

We will focus solely on revenue growth of our firm and as we move along, we will establish a good client base. The key to our success will be to "keep it simple." We will invest $20,000 on computer equipment and office equipment. This will allow us to also have money for cash flows.

Start–up Expenses

- Leasehold improvements—$2,000

- Advertising—$2,000

- Rent—$1,500

- Office supplies—$500

- Accountant—$600

- Legal—$600

- Power—$400

- Telephone—$500

- Computers—$10,000

- Miscellaneous—$500

Wooden Furniture Manufacturer and Supplier

NASHVILLE FURNITURE

61 Main St.
Nashville, Indiana 47448

Gerald Rekve

Nashville Furniture strives to be the best manufacturer of fine furniture, partnering with our craftsmen and making them a key component to our business. The owners will build state–of–the–art furniture for the local, as well as national, market in the United States. All the craftsmen that will be hired to build this furniture will be at the top of their field, allowing us to be the best provider of furniture in America.

EXECUTIVE SUMMARY

Business Strategy

Nashville Furniture will be formed as a furniture company that focuses on fine workmanship for home owners who want the best in handcrafted products. The owners have extensive experience in the furniture industry. Nashville Furniture will be a part of the Nashville Furnishing Group and operate as its own division.

With the baby boomer generation maturing, the growth in the fine furniture is exploding. To take advantage of this new opportunity, Nashville Furniture is going to expand into this area. In doing so, we will require extra staff, equipment and facilities to run this business.

Objectives

- To be a top fine furniture supplier to home owners both locally and nationally

- To become a top ten supplier

- To hire the best craftsmen for fine furniture construction

- To buy the best wood from every country that sells it

- To buy the rights to rebuild like furniture from the Chippendale collection

Mission

Nashville Furniture strives to be the best manufacturer of fine furniture, partnering with our craftsmen and making them a key component to our business. We want to give our customer base the best quality on the market today.

MARKET ANALYSIS

Start–up Summary

Budget January 1 to December 31

Category	Actual	Budget	Difference
Inflows			
Net Sales	385,400	300,000	85,400
Cost of Goods			
Merchandise Inventory, January 1	160,000	160,000	0
Purchases	120,000	90,000	30,000
Freight Charges	2,500	2,000	500
Total Merchandise	**282,500**	**252,000**	**30,500**
Handled Less Inventory, December 31	100,000	120,000	(20,000)
Cost of Goods Sold	**182,500**	**132,000**	**50,500**
Gross Profit	**202,900**	**168,000**	**34,900**
Interest Income	500	700	(200)
Total Income	**202,500**	**168,700**	**33,800**
Expenses			
Salaries	68,250	45,000	23,250
Utilities	5,800	4,500	1,300
Rent	23,000	23,000	0
Office Supplies	2,250	3,000	(750)
Insurance	3,900	3,900	0
Advertising	2,550	9,000	(350)
Telephone	8,650	2,300	400
Travel and Entertainment	2,700	2,000	550
Dues & Subscriptions	1,100	1,000	100
Interest Paid	2,140	2,500	(360)
Repairs & Maintenance	1,250	1,000	250
Taxes & Licenses	11,700	10,000	1,700
Total Expenses	**133,290**	**106,850**	**26,440**
Net Income	$69,210	$61,850	$7,360

Nashville Furniture will build their client base by targeting the retail stores that sell high–end furniture; this will allow Nashville to quickly get a foothold in the market with already established distribution channels.

International Marketplace

In 1999, the world production of furniture amounted to $62.4 billion dollars. The top of the list of leading producers includes: Italy and Germany, closely followed by the United States, Japan, the United Kingdom, France, Sweden, Canada and other Asian countries near the Pacific.

China can be considered by itself—it is estimated that by the end of the 21st century, China will become the second leading producer of furniture in the world. Furthermore, the People's Republic of China is currently one of the five most desired markets.

World sales in furniture amount to about $3 billion US dollars. On the other hand, the market is somewhat varied, with consumers preferring a wide variety of styles, designs, quality and prices. In terms of consumption, the most important market is surely the United States, representing 27 percent of the market, followed by Japan with 15 percent and Germany with 11 percent.

Import/ Export

Italy and Germany are the biggest furniture exporters in the world. However, some Asian countries, such as China and Taiwan, are beginning to take advantage of low labor costs, which translates to strong growth prospects.

The furniture sector in the United States has been able to reap the benefits of the boom in the economy in the last few years. The statistics indicate that sales dropped in the early 1990s, while they picked up in the second half of the decade.

China

Furniture sales in China in the last six years have increased by 8.5 percent. This increase is the result of several factors, including: low cost, unrecognized brands, and buyers being unaware of where the product was made.

In 1996, the Chinese purchased furniture totaling $8.2 billion US dollars. Three percent of this figure included products that were imported and 90 percent accounts for low-quality furniture made by local craftsmen. Only 7 percent of purchases were local industrial production. China seems to be a market that has yet to be discovered!

Target Market Segment

Nashville Furniture will be focusing on securing the distribution channel from high-end retailers, some of whom are national chains like Sears.

Across the United States there are a number of high-end furniture retailers who specialize in the sale of quality furniture. We know it will take time to build relationships with all the retailers, so we will focus on small retailers to begin with, while getting our systems and processes in place. By the time we are able to break in to the larger retail store business, we will have all the bugs worked out and will be ready to tackle the increased production demands.

Industry Snapshot

The wholesale distribution of the furniture industry is subdivided into two categories: establishments engaged primarily in the sale of household and lawn furniture, and establishments primarily engaged in the sale of office and business furniture. According to statistics compiled by the U.S. Census Bureau, 29,920 establishments were listed in this classification in 2001. Combined sales totaled $23.1 billion in 2003. There were 278,231 people employed within this industry, with an annual payroll of $7.5 million. The average establishment generated $2.7 million in sales. California, Florida, and New York controlled 32 percent of the market.

CUSTOMERS

This industry is affected by interest rates and the housing market. When these economic indicators are stable and strong, the furniture industry generally has higher retail sales. *Barron's* reported that the furniture industry experienced a slump from 1988 until mid-1992 when a "stop-and-start" recovery process began. Conditions within the furniture industry reflected the nation's general economy as consumers postponed purchases. As a result, when the economy began to improve, there was a pent-up demand for industry products, and the American Furniture Manufacturers Association (AFMA) predicted an increase in furniture shipments.

Following a slump in the early 1990s, the International Wholesale Furniture Association found more than 90 percent of survey respondents reported their sales increased in 1993. Sales continued to climb in 1994 and 1995. Throughout 1995, monthly sales for furniture and home furnishings were between $3.1

and $3.4 million. AFMA also predicted an increase in the value of shipments of 7.6 percent in 1999, and a smaller increase of 2.1 percent for 2000. Consumer demand was expected to increase by 5.5 percent and 4.5 percent for 1999 and 2000, respectively.

Housing starts were forecasted to increase by 2.9 percent in 1999, followed by only 0.3 percent in 2000. In the late 1990s, much of this industry's strength came from the industrial (offices, hotels, restaurants) side of the market. The office furniture market was estimated at $12 billion. Some analysts predicted that 50 million families were to occupy a home office.

Current Conditions

The largest type of customer—furniture stores—represented 69.4 percent of sales. Other types of customers included rental dealers with 19.2 percent of sales, manufactured homes with 4.9 percent, specialty stores with 2.5 percent, interior designers with 1.4 percent and institutional buyers with 0.5 percent. The two largest product categories—living room/upholstered and bedroom—accounted for half of the sales.

Customary distribution channels within the industry, however, have changed. To reduce costs and improve efficiency, many manufacturers have increased their direct sales to retailers and rental dealers. As a result, wholesalers faced a shrinking number of traditional customers, and innovative wholesale concepts, such as warehouse clubs and electronic shopping networks, emerged. Wholesalers are also being threatened by large discount department stores.

The Business and Institutional Furniture Manufacturers Association (BIFMA) International announced that furniture shipments climbed 5.6 percent in 2004, up from a 4.7 percent drop in 2003. Office furniture also declined 20 percent nationally in 2002. However, according to Furniture Today, furniture spending would increase 23 percent by 2011.

COMPETITION

There are a few main types of furniture suppliers in the industry, including:

- High volume manufactures who skimp on quality in order to get volume. You can see these easily by looking at the product—for example, they have molded patterns where the ancient masters would have hand–carved them.

- Low volume manufactures who build great furniture but have low sales volume because they cannot produce enough product for increased sales.

Nashville Furniture has put together an assembly line product system that will be unmatched in the industry. We will be able to turn out complete products in about 35 percent of the time it would take a master woodworker to do the same. This means we will be able to produce enough of these units to make a great profit and have a lot of happy clients.

At the moment, there is no one in the market that can produce these furniture items in the time it takes us to produce them. This means we will be a leader in the market.

In the late 1990s, industry leaders included Value City Furniture Division of Ohio, Office Depot Incorporated Business Services Division of California, and TAB Products Company, also of California. In 2003, industry leaders were Furniture Brands International Inc. of St. Louis, Missouri, La–Z–Boy Inc. of Monroe, MI, and Hon Industries, Inc. In the second half of 2003, demand for commercial furniture began to stabilize and, in December, both shipments and orders grew for the first time in three years.

Largest furniture makers by value of shipments, 2001

In millions of dollars

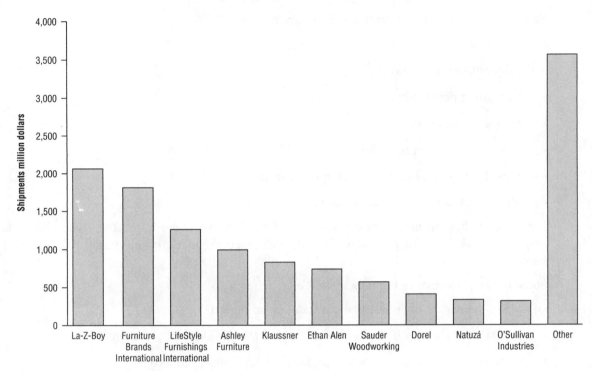

SOURCE: Market Share Reporter, 2004.

OPERATIONS

Our sales strategy is to sell our products to retailers in the United States. These retailers already have a client base, so all we will be doing is putting our products in their stores. This will reduce any costs we have in marketing and sales.

Production Facilities

We will manufacture all of our furniture from a 10,000 square foot production facility located just 20 minutes north of downtown Nashville. This warehouse was used to produce other tangibles products, so all the mechanical needs are already in place. We will only need to do some small upgrades and some wiring moves to handle the 240 volt equipment we will be installing in the building.

All the equipment will be installed about four weeks prior to us having our staff in place, so we will be able to train once we bring in the staff.

Management Summary

Tory Toseat will act as President. Tory has 24 years of manufacturing experience, from auto making to plastics, as well four years with the largest medium–price furniture manufacturer in the United States.

Harriet Wallace will serve as Vice President. Harriet has 19 years of experience in the area of accounting and finance. Most of her career has been spent as an accountant and finance manager in a variety of different business sectors.

While both career paths are unique, they add an extremely strong experience background for the company which will be very helpful as the company grows or runs into issues later on.

We have already hired a foreman to manage our production of our furniture. He has over 15 years experience in the same role with a large furniture manufacturer. He will be able to hire the top quality tradespeople we will require in order to operate our business.

Some of the traits these craftsmen will require are listed below.

- Eye for detail

- Skills with all shop tools

- Easy going personality

- Enjoys the business

- Always wants to learn, never stops

- Must have good references or samples of work

- May do a test build on site at our plant

We will pay these furniture makers anywhere from $25 to $50 per hour. There will also be bonuses in place for our furniture makers; this will help keep them motivated and will insure they work harder.

Some of the performance bonuses we will offer are as follows:

- $25.00 bonus for each unit that is produced on budget

- $50.00 weekly bonus if the department makes their weekly units–produced goal

- $200.00 if department makes budget for monthly units–produced

- $20.00 bonus for each percentage over budget we are in number of units produced

- $25.00 reduction for each unit that fails to make inspection for quality

This table shows salaries for the entire company. Salary increases are kept to a minimum to help ensure the growth of the company. An administrative assistant will be hired later in the year.

Personnel plan	2007	2008	2009
Owner 1	50,000	50,000	50,000
Owner 2	50,000	50,000	50,000
Carpenters	550,000	600,000	700,000
Total payroll	**650,000**	**700,000**	**800,000**
Total headcount	**15**	**15**	**19**

Financial Analysis

Initial financial goals

- Obtain an operating line of credit from a financial institution.

- Finance growth through retained earnings.

- Operate on a 25–30 percent gross margin.

Annual sales goals

- Year one–$900,000

- Year two–$1,200,000

- Year three–$1,500,000

PRODUCTS & SERVICES

Production Process

We will use the blueprints provided to us by Chippendale which include the all the original designs.

Our furniture will be built by highly–trained craftsmen. We realize that the time it takes to make a quality hand–built piece of furniture is about three times longer than to make a mass produced piece.

Because the price range for our furniture pieces will vary from $500 up to $40,000 each, a large portion of the population will not be interested in our products. This will result in a small piece of the overall market.

Some of the items we will be manufacturing are:

- Kitchen tables
- End tables
- Hutches
- Bedroom sets
- Dressers
- Armoires
- Couches
- Rocking chairs
- Coffee tables

Materials and woods we will be using include:

- Amboyna Burl #1 Grade
- Amboyna Burl #2 Grade
- Banksia Pods/Nuts
- Beefwood
- Birch Burl (eyes)
- Box Elder Burl (pink)
- Buckeye Burl
- Camphor
- Chechen Burl
- Curly Maple 'A'
- Curly Maple 'AA'
- Curly Maple 'AAA'
- English Walnut
- Figured She Oak
- Firelace She Oak
- Golden Amboyna Burl
- Goldfield Burls "SALE"
- Grass Tree Root

- Jarrah Burl
- Jarrah, Figured
- Jarrah, Plain
- Jarrah, Table tops
- Madrone Burl
- Magnolia
- Mallee Chunks
- Mallee Root
- Manzanita
- Maple Burl
- Maple Burl, Big Leaf
- Maple Burl, Premium
- Maple, Quilted
- Marri
- Mesquite, Texas
- Myrtle Burl
- Narra
- PNG Walnut
- Ramone Burl
- Redwood Burl
- Rosewood, Brazilian
- She Oak
- Sumac Logs–dry
- Thuya Burl #1 Grade
- Thuya Burl #2 Grade
- Walnut Burl/Stump
- Walnut, Claro figured
- Willow Burl

SALES & MARKETING

We will hire two full–time sales consultants whose job it will be to secure contracts with various retailers across the United States and Canada with the goal to sell our products in these stores. At the beginning of our business venture we will not use the traditional distribution network to sell our products. The reason for this is simple—we need to get feedback about our products, and better know the clients' likes and dislikes regarding our furniture.

Each sales consultant will be assigned to either the western or eastern half of the United States. They will both travel to all the tradeshows for furniture retailers and assist in managing the booth at these trade shows. Management will also work these booths because we will need as much feedback as possible in order for us to build a very strong company.

As we are building our client list, we will also focus on training of our sales staff. It will be very important for our sales staff to completely understand our products, so when they are being challenged by competitors, they can respond to our clients knowing that what they are saying is accurate and realistic. In the end, this will help our sales staff win more contracts.

We are going to pay our sales staff with a combination of salary and commission. We realize that when sales staff members are dependent solely on commission and not producing well, they will say almost anything to win the contract. In understanding this, we do not want to be in a position where a client is promised something we cannot deliver. Therefore we will give our sales staff a salary as a base. This salary will be about 70 percent of the average for sales reps in similar fields. The commission plan will add approximately another 70 percent to the potential the sales rep can make. In total, the average our sales consultants can make is going to be around $150,000 to $200,000 per year. This is about $75,000 higher than the average representative makes now. We are very confident this will attract top notch sales staff.

Business Plan Template

USING THIS TEMPLATE

A business plan carefully spells out a company's projected course of action over a period of time, usually the first two to three years after the start-up. In addition, banks, lenders, and other investors examine the information and financial documentation before deciding whether or not to finance a new business venture. Therefore, a business plan is an essential tool in obtaining financing and should describe the business itself in detail as well as all important factors influencing the company, including the market, industry, competition, operations and management policies, problem solving strategies, financial resources and needs, and other vital information. The plan enables the business owner to anticipate costs, plan for difficulties, and take advantage of opportunities, as well as design and implement strategies that keep the company running as smoothly as possible.

This template has been provided as a model to help you construct your own business plan. Please keep in mind that there is no single acceptable format for a business plan, and that this template is in no way comprehensive, but serves as an example.

The business plans provided in this section are fictional and have been used by small business agencies as models for clients to use in compiling their own business plans.

GENERIC BUSINESS PLAN

Main headings included below are topics that should be covered in a comprehensive business plan. They include:

Business Summary

Purpose
Provides a brief overview of your business, succinctly highlighting the main ideas of your plan.

Includes

- Name and Type of Business
- Description of Product/Service
- Business History and Development
- Location
- Market
- Competition
- Management
- Financial Information
- Business Strengths and Weaknesses
- Business Growth

Table of Contents

Purpose
Organized in an Outline Format, the Table of Contents illustrates the selection and arrangement of information contained in your plan.

Includes
- Topic Headings and Subheadings
- Page Number References

Business History and Industry Outlook

Purpose

Examines the conception and subsequent development of your business within an industry specific context.

Includes
- Start-up Information
- Owner/Key Personnel Experience
- Location
- Development Problems and Solutions
- Investment/Funding Information
- Future Plans and Goals

- Market Trends and Statistics
- Major Competitors
- Product/Service Advantages
- National, Regional, and Local Economic Impact

Product/Service

Purpose

Introduces, defines, and details the product and/or service that inspired the information of your business.

Includes
- Unique Features
- Niche Served
- Market Comparison
- Stage of Product/Service Development
- Production

- Facilities, Equipment, and Labor
- Financial Requirements
- Product/Service Life Cycle
- Future Growth

Market Examination

Purpose

Assessment of product/service applications in relation to consumer buying cycles.

Includes
- Target Market
- Consumer Buying Habits
- Product/Service Applications
- Consumer Reactions
- Market Factors and Trends

- Penetration of the Market
- Market Share
- Research and Studies
- Cost
- Sales Volume and Goals

Competition

Purpose

Analysis of Competitors in the Marketplace.

Includes
- Competitor Information
- Product/Service Comparison
- Market Niche

- Product/Service Strengths and Weaknesses
- Future Product/Service Development

Marketing

Purpose

Identifies promotion and sales strategies for your product/service.

Includes

- Product/Service Sales Appeal
- Special and Unique Features
- Identification of Customers
- Sales and Marketing Staff
- Sales Cycles
- Type of Advertising/Promotion
- Pricing
- Competition
- Customer Services

Operations

Purpose

Traces product/service development from production/inception to the market environment.

Includes

- Cost Effective Production Methods
- Facility
- Location
- Equipment
- Labor
- Future Expansion

Administration and Management

Purpose

Offers a statement of your management philosophy with an in-depth focus on processes and procedures.

Includes

- Management Philosophy
- Structure of Organization
- Reporting System
- Methods of Communication
- Employee Skills and Training
- Employee Needs and Compensation
- Work Environment
- Management Policies and Procedures
- Roles and Responsibilities

Key Personnel

Purpose

Describes the unique backgrounds of principle employees involved in business.

Includes

- Owner(s)/Employee Education and Experience
- Positions and Roles
- Benefits and Salary
- Duties and Responsibilities
- Objectives and Goals

Potential Problems and Solutions

Purpose

Discussion of problem solving strategies that change issues into opportunities.

Includes

- Risks
- Litigation
- Future Competition
- Economic Impact
- Problem Solving Skills

Financial Information

Purpose

Secures needed funding and assistance through worksheets and projections detailing financial plans, methods of repayment, and future growth opportunities.

Includes

- Financial Statements
- Bank Loans
- Methods of Repayment
- Tax Returns
- Start-up Costs
- Projected Income (3 years)
- Projected Cash Flow (3 Years)
- Projected Balance Statements (3 years)

Appendices

Purpose

Supporting documents used to enhance your business proposal.

Includes

- Photographs of product, equipment, facilities, etc.
- Copyright/Trademark Documents
- Legal Agreements
- Marketing Materials
- Research and or Studies
- Operation Schedules
- Organizational Charts
- Job Descriptions
- Resumes
- Additional Financial Documentation

Fictional Food Distributor

Commercial Foods, Inc.

This plan demonstrates how a partnership can have a positive impact on a new business. It demonstrates how two individuals can carve a niche in the specialty foods market by offering gourmet foods to upscale restaurants and fine hotels. This plan is fictional and has not been used to gain funding from a bank or other lending institution.

3003 Avondale Ave.
Knoxville, TN, 37920

STATEMENT OF PURPOSE

Commercial Foods, Inc. seeks a loan of $75,000 to establish a new business. This sum, together with $5,000 equity investment by the principals, will be used as follows:

- Merchandise inventory $25,000
- Office fixture/equipment $12,000
- Warehouse equipment $14,000
- One delivery truck $10,000
- Working capital $39,000
- Total $100,000

DESCRIPTION OF THE BUSINESS

Commercial Foods, Inc. will be a distributor of specialty food service products to hotels and upscale restaurants in the geographical area of a 50 mile radius of Knoxville. Richard Roberts will direct the sales effort and John Williams will manage the warehouse operation and the office. One delivery truck will be used initially with a second truck added in the third year. We expect to begin operation of the business within 30 days after securing the requested financing.

MANAGEMENT

A. Richard Roberts is a native of Memphis, Tennessee. He is a graduate of Memphis State University with a Bachelor's degree from the School of Business. After graduation, he worked for a major manufacturer of specialty food service products as a detail sales person for five years, and, for the past three years, he has served as a product sales manager for this firm.

B. John Williams is a native of Nashville, Tennessee. He holds a B.S. Degree in Food Technology from the University of Tennessee. His career includes five years as a product development chemist in gourmet food products and five years as operations manager for a food service distributor.

Both men are healthy and energetic. Their backgrounds complement each other, which will ensure the success of Commercial Foods, Inc. They will set policies together and personnel decisions will be made jointly. Initial salaries for the owners will be $1,000 per month for the first few years. The spouses of both principals are successful in the business world and earn enough to support the families.

They have engaged the services of Foster Jones, CPA, and William Hale, Attorney, to assist them in an advisory capacity.

PERSONNEL

The firm will employ one delivery truck driver at a wage of $8.00 per hour. One office worker will be employed at $7.50 per hour. One part-time employee will be used in the office at $5.00 per hour. The driver will load and unload his own trucks. Mr. Williams will assist in the warehouse operation as needed to assist one stock person at $7.00 per hour. An additional delivery truck and driver will be added the third year.

LOCATION

The firm will lease a 20,000 square foot building at 3003 Avondale Ave., in Knoxville, which contains warehouse and office areas equipped with two-door truck docks. The annual rental is $9,000. The building was previously used as a food service warehouse and very little modification to the building will be required.

PRODUCTS AND SERVICES

The firm will offer specialty food service products such as soup bases, dessert mixes, sauce bases, pastry mixes, spices, and flavors, normally used by upscale restaurants and nice hotels. We are going after a niche in the market with high quality gourmet products. There is much less competition in this market than in standard run of the mill food service products. Through their work experiences, the principals have contacts with supply sources and with local chefs.

THE MARKET

We know from our market survey that there are over 200 hotels and upscale restaurants in the area we plan to serve. Customers will be attracted by a direct sales approach. We will offer samples of our products and product application data on use of our products in the finished prepared foods. We will cultivate the chefs in these establishments. The technical background of John Williams will be especially useful here.

COMPETITION

We find that we will be only distributor in the area offering a full line of gourmet food service products. Other foodservice distributors offer only a few such items in conjunction with their standard product line. Our survey shows that many of the chefs are ordering products from Atlanta and Memphis because of a lack of adequate local supply.

SUMMARY

Commercial Foods, Inc. will be established as a foodservice distributor of specialty food in Knoxville. The principals, with excellent experience in the industry, are seeking a $75,000 loan to establish the business. The principals are investing $25,000 as equity capital.

The business will be set up as an S Corporation with each principal owning 50% of the common stock in the corporation.

Fictional Hardware Store

Oshkosh Hardware, Inc.

The following plan outlines how a small hardware store can survive competition from large discount chains by offering products and providing expert advice in the use of any product it sells. This plan is fictional and has not been used to gain funding from a bank or other lending institution.

123 Main St.
Oshkosh, WI, 54901

EXECUTIVE SUMMARY

Oshkosh Hardware, Inc. is a new corporation that is going to establish a retail hardware store in a strip mall in Oshkosh, Wisconsin. The store will sell hardware of all kinds, quality tools, paint, and housewares. The business will make revenue and a profit by servicing its customers not only with needed hardware but also with expert advice in the use of any product it sells.

Oshkosh Hardware, Inc. will be operated by its sole shareholder, James Smith. The company will have a total of four employees. It will sell its products in the local market. Customers will buy our products because we will provide free advice on the use of all of our products and will also furnish a full refund warranty.

Oshkosh Hardware, Inc. will sell its products in the Oshkosh store staffed by three sales representatives. No additional employees will be needed to achieve its short and long range goals. The primary short range goal is to open the store by October 1, 1994. In order to achieve this goal a lease must be signed by July 1, 1994 and the complete inventory ordered by August 1, 1994.

Mr. James Smith will invest $30,000 in the business. In addition, the company will have to borrow $150,000 during the first year to cover the investment in inventory, accounts receivable, and furniture and equipment. The company will be profitable after six months of operation and should be able to start repayment of the loan in the second year.

THE BUSINESS

The business will sell hardware of all kinds, quality tools, paint, and housewares. We will purchase our products from three large wholesale buying groups.

In general our customers are homeowners who do their own repair and maintenance, hobbyists, and housewives. Our business is unique in that we will have a complete line of all hardware items and will be able to get special orders by overnight delivery. The business makes revenue and profits by servicing our customers not only with needed hardware but also with expert advice in the use of any product we sell. Our major costs for bringing our products to market are cost of merchandise of 36%, salaries of $45,000, and occupancy costs of $60,000.

Oshkosh Hardware, Inc.'s retail outlet will be located at 1524 Frontage Road, which is in a newly developed retail center of Oshkosh. Our location helps facilitate accessibility from all parts of town and reduces our delivery costs. The store will occupy 7500 square feet of space. The major equipment involved in our business is counters and shelving, a computer, a paint mixing machine, and a truck.

THE MARKET

Oshkosh Hardware, Inc. will operate in the local market. There are 15,000 potential customers in this market area. We have three competitors who control approximately 98% of the market at present. We feel we can capture 25% of the market within the next four years. Our major reason for believing this is that our staff is technically competent to advise our customers in the correct use of all products we sell.

After a careful market analysis, we have determined that approximately 60% of our customers are men and 40% are women. The percentage of customers that fall into the following age categories are:

Under 16: 0%
17-21: 5%
22-30: 30%
31-40: 30%
41-50: 20%
51-60: 10%
61-70: 5%
Over 70: 0%

The reasons our customers prefer our products is our complete knowledge of their use and our full refund warranty.

We get our information about what products our customers want by talking to existing customers. There seems to be an increasing demand for our product. The demand for our product is increasing in size based on the change in population characteristics.

SALES

At Oshkosh Hardware, Inc. we will employ three sales people and will not need any additional personnel to achieve our sales goals. These salespeople will need several years experience in home repair and power tool usage. We expect to attract 30% of our customers from newspaper ads, 5% of our customers from local directories, 5% of our customers from the yellow pages, 10% of our customers from family and friends, and 50% of our customers from current customers. The most cost effect source will be current customers. In general our industry is growing.

MANAGEMENT

We would evaluate the quality of our management staff as being excellent. Our manager is experienced and very motivated to achieve the various sales and quality assurance objectives we have set. We will use a management information system that produces key inventory, quality assurance, and sales data on a weekly basis. All data is compared to previously established goals for that week, and deviations are the primary focus of the management staff.

GOALS IMPLEMENTATION

The short term goals of our business are:

1. Open the store by October 1, 1994
2. Reach our breakeven point in two months
3. Have sales of $100,000 in the first six months

In order to achieve our first short term goal we must:

1. Sign the lease by July 1, 1994
2. Order a complete inventory by August 1, 1994

In order to achieve our second short term goal we must:

1. Advertise extensively in Sept. and Oct.
2. Keep expenses to a minimum

In order to achieve our third short term goal we must:

1. Promote power tool sales for the Christmas season
2. Keep good customer traffic in Jan. and Feb.

The long term goals for our business are:

1. Obtain sales volume of $600,000 in three years
2. Become the largest hardware dealer in the city
3. Open a second store in Fond du Lac

The most important thing we must do in order to achieve the long term goals for our business is to develop a highly profitable business with excellent cash flow.

FINANCE

Oshkosh Hardware, Inc. Faces some potential threats or risks to our business. They are discount house competition. We believe we can avoid or compensate for this by providing quality products complimented by quality advice on the use of every product we sell. The financial projections we have prepared are located at the end of this document.

JOB DESCRIPTION-GENERAL MANAGER

The General Manager of the business of the corporation will be the president of the corporation. He will be responsible for the complete operation of the retail hardware store which is owned by the corporation. A detailed description of his duties and responsibilities is as follows.

Sales

Train and supervise the three sales people. Develop programs to motivate and compensate these employees. Coordinate advertising and sales promotion effects to achieve sales totals as outlined in budget. Oversee purchasing function and inventory control procedures to insure adequate merchandise at all times at a reasonable cost.

Finance

Prepare monthly and annual budgets. Secure adequate line of credit from local banks. Supervise office personnel to insure timely preparation of records, statements, all government reports, control of receivables and payables, and monthly financial statements.

Administration

Perform duties as required in the areas of personnel, building leasing and maintenance, licenses and permits, and public relations.

Organizations, Agencies, & Consultants

A listing of Associations and Consultants of interest to entrepreneurs, followed by the ten Small Business Administration Regional Offices, Small Business Development Centers, Service Corps of Retired Executives offices, and Venture Capital and Finance Companies.

Associations

This section contains a listing of associations and other agencies of interest to the small business owner. Entries are listed alphabetically by organization name.

American Business Women's Association
9100 Ward Pkwy.
PO Box 8728
Kansas City, MO 64114-0728
(800)228-0007
E-mail: abwa@abwa.org
Website: http://www.abwa.org
Jeanne Banks, National President

American Franchisee Association
53 W Jackson Blvd., Ste. 1157
Chicago, IL 60604
(312)431-0545
E-mail: info@franchisee.org
Website: http://www.franchisee.org
Susan P. Kezios, President

American Independent Business Alliance
222 S Black Ave.
Bozeman, MT 59715
(406)582-1255
E-mail: info@amiba.net
Website: http://www.amiba.net
Jennifer Rockne, Director

American Small Businesses Association
206 E College St., Ste. 201
Grapevine, TX 76051
800-942-2722
E-mail: info@asbaonline.org
Website: http://www.asbaonline.org/

American Women's Economic Development Corporation
216 East 45th St., 10th Floor
New York, NY 10017

(917)368-6100
Fax: (212)986-7114
E-mail: info@awed.org
Website: http://www.awed.org
Roseanne Antonucci, Exec. Dir.

Association for Enterprise Opportunity
1601 N Kent St., Ste. 1101
Arlington, VA 22209
(703)841-7760
Fax: (703)841-7748
E-mail: aeo@assoceo.org
Website: http://www.microenterpriseworks.org
Bill Edwards, Exec.Dir.

Association of Small Business Development Centers
c/o Don Wilson
8990 Burke Lake Rd.
Burke, VA 22015
(703)764-9850
Fax: (703)764-1234
E-mail: info@asbdc-us.org
Website: http://www.asbdc-us.org
Don Wilson, Pres./CEO

BEST Employers Association
2505 McCabe Way
Irvine, CA 92614
(949)253-4080
800-433-0088
Fax: (714)553-0883
E-mail: info@bestlife.com
Website: http://www.bestlife.com
Donald R. Lawrenz, CEO

Center for Family Business
PO Box 24219
Cleveland, OH 44124
(440)460-5409
E-mail: grummi@aol.com
Dr. Leon A. Danco, Chm.

Coalition for Government Procurement
1990 M St. NW, Ste. 400
Washington, DC 20036
(202)331-0975
E-mail: info@thecgp.org
Website: http://www.coalgovpro.org
Paul Caggiano, Pres.

Employers of America
PO Box 1874
Mason City, IA 50402-1874
(641)424-3187
800-728-3187
Fax: (641)424-1673
E-mail: employer@employerhelp.org
Website: http://www.employerhelp.org
Jim Collison, Pres.

Family Firm Institute
200 Lincoln St., Ste. 201
Boston, MA 02111
(617)482-3045
Fax: (617)482-3049
E-mail: ffi@ffi.org
Website: http://www.ffi.org
Judy L. Green, Ph.D., Exec.Dir.

Independent Visually Impaired Enterprisers
500 S 3rd St., Apt. H
Burbank, CA 91502
(818)238-9321
E-mail: abazyn@bazyncommunications.com
http://www.acb.org/affiliates
Adris Bazyn, Pres.

International Association for Business Organizations
3 Woodthorn Ct., Ste. 12
Owings Mills, MD 21117
(410)581-1373
E-mail: nahbb@msn.com
Rudolph Lewis, Exec. Officer

International Council for Small Business
The George Washington University School of Business and Public Management
2115 G St. NW, Ste. 403
Washington, DC 20052
(202)994-0704
Fax: (202)994-4930
E-mail: icsb@gwu.edu
Website: http://www.icsb.org
Susan G. Duffy. Admin.

International Small Business Consortium
3309 Windjammer St.
Norman, OK 73072
E-mail: sb@isbc.com
Website: http://www.isbc.com

Kauffman Center for Entrepreneurial Leadership
4801 Rockhill Rd.
Kansas City, MO 64110-2046
(816)932-1000
E-mail: info@kauffman.org
Website: http://www.entreworld.org

National Alliance for Fair Competition
3 Bethesda Metro Center, Ste. 1100
Bethesda, MD 20814
(410)235-7116
Fax: (410)235-7116
E-mail: ampesq@aol.com
Tony Ponticelli, Exec.Dir.

National Association for the Self-Employed
PO Box 612067
DFW Airport
Dallas, TX 75261-2067
(800)232-6273
E-mail: mpetron@nase.org
Website: http://www.nase.org
Robert Hughes, Pres.

National Association of Business Leaders
4132 Shoreline Dr., Ste. J & H
Earth City, MO 63045
Fax: (314)298-9110
E-mail: nabl@nabl.com
Website: http://www.nabl.com/
Gene Blumenthal, Contact

National Association of Private Enterprise
PO Box 15550
Long Beach, CA 90815
888-224-0953

Fax: (714)844-4942
Website: http://www.napeonline.net
Laura Squiers, Exec.Dir.

National Association of Small Business Investment Companies
666 11th St. NW, Ste. 750
Washington, DC 20001
(202)628-5055
Fax: (202)628-5080
E-mail: nasbic@nasbic.org
Website: http://www.nasbic.org
Lee W. Mercer, Pres.

National Business Association
PO Box 700728
5151 Beltline Rd., Ste. 1150
Dallas, TX 75370
(972)458-0900
800-456-0440
Fax: (972)960-9149
E-mail: info@nationalbusiness.org
Website: http://www.nationalbusiness.org
Raj Nisankarao, Pres.

National Business Owners Association
PO Box 111
Stuart, VA 24171
(276)251-7500
(866)251-7505
Fax: (276)251-2217
E-mail: membershipservices@nboa.org
Website: http://www.rvmdb.com.nboa
Paul LaBarr, Pres.

National Center for Fair Competition
PO Box 220
Annandale, VA 22003
(703)280-4622
Fax: (703)280-0942
E-mail: kentonp1@aol.com
Kenton Pattie, Pres.

National Family Business Council
1640 W. Kennedy Rd.
Lake Forest, IL 60045
(847)295-1040
Fax: (847)295-1898
E-mail: lmsnfbc@email.msn.com
Jogn E. Messervey, Pres.

National Federation of Independent Business
53 Century Blvd., Ste. 250
Nashville, TN 37214
(615)872-5800
800-NFIBNOW
Fax: (615)872-5353
Website: http://www.nfib.org
Jack Faris, Pres. and CEO

National Small Business Association
1156 15th St. NW, Ste. 1100
Washington, DC 20005
(202)293-8830
800-345-6728
Fax: (202)872-8543
E-mail: press@nsba.biz
Website: http://www.nsba.biz
Rob Yunich, Dir. of Communications

PUSH Commercial Division
930 E 50th St.
Chicago, IL 60615-2702
(773)373-3366
Fax: (773)373-3571
E-mail: info@rainbowpush.org
Website: http://www.rainbowpush.org
Rev. Willie T. Barrow, Co-Chm.

Research Institute for Small and Emerging Business
722 12th St. NW
Washington, DC 20005
(202)628-8382
Fax: (202)628-8392
E-mail: info@riseb.org
Website: http://www.riseb.org
Allan Neece, Jr., Chm.

Sales Professionals USA
PO Box 149
Arvada, CO 80001
(303)534-4937
888-736-7767
E-mail: salespro@salesprofessionals-usa.com
Website: http://www.salesprofessionals-usa.com
Sharon Herbert, Natl. Pres.

Score Association - Service Corps of Retired Executives
409 3rd St. SW, 6th Fl.
Washington, DC 20024
(202)205-6762
800-634-0245
Fax: (202)205-7636
E-mail: media@score.org
Website: http://www.score.org
W. Kenneth Yancey, Jr., CEO

Small Business and Entrepreneurship Council
1920 L St. NW, Ste. 200
Washington, DC 20036
(202)785-0238
Fax: (202)822-8118
E-mail: membership@sbec.org
Website: http://www.sbecouncil.org
Karen Kerrigan, Pres./CEO

Small Business in
Telecommunications
1331 H St. NW, Ste. 500
Washington, DC 20005
(202)347-4511
Fax: (202)347-8607
E-mail: sbt@sbthome.org
Website: http://www.sbthome.org
Lonnie Danchik, Chm.

Small Business Legislative Council
1010 Massachusetts Ave. NW, Ste. 540
Washington, DC 20005
(202)639-8500
Fax: (202)296-5333
E-mail: email@sblc.org
Website: http://www.sblc.org
John Satagaj, Pres.

Small Business Service Bureau
554 Main St.
PO Box 15014
Worcester, MA 01615-0014
(508)756-3513
800-343-0939
Fax: (508)770-0528
E-mail: membership@sbsb.com
Website: http://www.sbsb.com
Francis R. Carroll, Pres.

Small Publishers Association of North
America
1618 W COlorado Ave.
Colorado Springs, CO 80904
(719)475-1726
Fax: (719)471-2182
E-mail: span@spannet.org
Website: http://www.spannet.orgScott
Flora, Exec. Dir.

SOHO America
PO Box 941
Hurst, TX 76053-0941
800-495-SOHO
E-mail: soho@1sas.com
Website: http://www.soho.org

Structured Employment Economic
Development Corporation
915 Broadway, 17th Fl.
New York, NY 10010
(212)473-0255
Fax: (212)473-0357
E-mail: info@seedco.org
Website: http://www.seedco.org
William Grinker, CEO

Support Services Alliance
107 Prospect St.
Schoharie, NY 12157

800-836-4772
E-mail: info@ssamembers.com
Website: http://www.ssainfo.com
Steve COle, Pres.

United States Association for Small
Business and Entrepreneurship
975 University Ave., No. 3260
Madison, WI 53706
(608)262-9982
Fax: (608)263-0818
E-mail: jgillman@wisc.edu
Website: http://www.ususbe.org
Joan Gillman, Exec. Dir.

Consultants

This section contains a listing of consultants specializing in small business development. It is arranged alphabetically by country, then by state or province, then by city, then by firm name.

Canada

Alberta

Common Sense Solutions
3405 16A Ave.
Edmonton, AB, Canada
(403)465-7330
Fax: (403)465-7380
E-mail: gcoulson@comsensesolutions.com
Website: http://www.comsensesolutions.com

Varsity Consulting Group
School of Business
University of Alberta
Edmonton, AB, Canada T6G 2R6
(780)492-2994
Fax: (780)492-5400
Website: http://www.bus.ualberta.ca/vcg

Viro Hospital Consulting
42 Commonwealth Bldg., 9912 - 106 St. NW
Edmonton, AB, Canada T5K 1C5
(403)425-3871
Fax: (403)425-3871
E-mail: rpb@freenet.edmonton.ab.ca

British Columbia

SRI Strategic Resources Inc.
4330 Kingsway, Ste. 1600
Burnaby, BC, Canada V5H 4G7
(604)435-0627
Fax: (604)435-2782
E-mail: inquiry@sri.bc.ca
Website: http://www.sri.com

Andrew R. De Boda Consulting
1523 Milford Ave.
Coquitlam, BC, Canada V3J 2V9
(604)936-4527
Fax: (604)936-4527
E-mail: deboda@intergate.bc.ca
Website: http://www.ourworld.
compuserve.com/homepages/deboda

The Sage Group Ltd.
980 - 355 Burrard St.
744 W Haistings, Ste. 410
Vancouver, BC, Canada V6C 1A5
(604)669-9269
Fax: (604)669-6622

Tikkanen-Bradley
1345 Nelson St., Ste. 202
Vancouver, BC, Canada V6E 1J8
(604)669-0583
E-mail: webmaster@tikkanenbradley.com
Website: http://www.tikkanenbradley.com

Ontario

The Cynton Co.
17 Massey St.
Brampton, ON, Canada L6S 2V6
(905)792-7769
Fax: (905)792-8116
E-mail: cynton@home.com
Website: http://www.cynton.com

Begley & Associates
RR 6
Cambridge, ON, Canada N1R 5S7
(519)740-3629
Fax: (519)740-3629
E-mail: begley@in.on.ca
Website: http://www.in.on.ca/~begley/
index.htm

CRO Engineering Ltd.
1895 William Hodgins Ln.
Carp, ON, Canada K0A 1L0
(613)839-1108
Fax: (613)839-1406
E-mail: J.Grefford@ieee.ca
Website: http://www.geocities.com/
WallStreet/District/7401/

Task Enterprises
Box 69, RR 2 Hamilton
Flamborough, ON, Canada L8N 2Z7
(905)659-0153
Fax: (905)659-0861

HST Group Ltd.
430 Gilmour St.
Ottawa, ON, Canada K2P 0R8
(613)236-7303
Fax: (613)236-9893

Harrison Associates
BCE Pl.
181 Bay St., Ste. 3740
PO Box 798
Toronto, ON, Canada M5J 2T3
(416)364-5441
Fax: (416)364-2875

TCI Convergence Ltd. Management Consultants
99 Crown's Ln.
Toronto, ON, Canada M5R 3P4
(416)515-4146
Fax: (416)515-2097
E-mail: tci@inforamp.net
Website: http://tciconverge.com/
index.1.html

Ken Wyman & Associates Inc.
64B Shuter St., Ste. 200
Toronto, ON, Canada M5B 1B1
(416)362-2926
Fax: (416)362-3039
E-mail: kenwyman@compuserve.com

JPL Business Consultants
82705 Metter Rd.
Wellandport, ON, Canada L0R 2J0
(905)386-7450
Fax: (905)386-7450
E-mail: plamarch@freenet.npiec.on.ca

Quebec

The Zimmar Consulting Partnership Inc.
Westmount
PO Box 98
Montreal, QC, Canada H3Z 2T1
(514)484-1459
Fax: (514)484-3063

Saskatchewan

Trimension Group
No. 104-110 Research Dr.
Innovation Place, SK, Canada S7N 3R3
(306)668-2560
Fax: (306)975-1156
E-mail: trimension@trimension.ca
Website: http://www.trimension.ca

Corporate Management Consultants
PO Box 7570 Station Main
Saskatoon, SK, Canada, S7K 4L4
(306)343-8415
Fax: (650)618-2742
E-mail: cmccorporatemanagement
@shaw.ca
Website: http://www.Corporate
managementconsultants.com
Gerald Rekve

United states

Alabama

Business Planning Inc.
300 Office Park Dr.
Birmingham, AL 35223-2474
(205)870-7090
Fax: (205)870-7103

Tradebank of Eastern Alabama
546 Broad St., Ste. 3
Gadsden, AL 35901
(205)547-8700
Fax: (205)547-8718
E-mail: mansion@webex.com
Website: http://www.webex.com/~tea

Alaska

AK Business Development Center
3335 Arctic Blvd., Ste. 203
Anchorage, AK 99503
(907)562-0335
Free: 800-478-3474
Fax: (907)562-6988
E-mail: abdc@gci.net
Website: http://www.abdc.org

Business Matters
PO Box 287
Fairbanks, AK 99707
(907)452-5650

Arizona

Carefree Direct Marketing Corp.
8001 E Serene St.
PO Box 3737
Carefree, AZ 85377-3737
(480)488-4227
Fax: (480)488-2841

Trans Energy Corp.
1739 W 7th Ave.
Mesa, AZ 85202
(480)827-7915
Fax: (480)967-6601
E-mail: aha@clean-air.org
Website: http://www.clean-air.org

CMAS
5125 N 16th St.
Phoenix, AZ 85016
(602)395-1001
Fax: (602)604-8180

Comgate Telemanagement Ltd.
706 E Bell Rd., Ste. 105
Phoenix, AZ 85022
(602)485-5708

Fax: (602)485-5709
E-mail: comgate@netzone.com
Website: http://www.comgate.com

Moneysoft Inc.
1 E Camelback Rd. #550
Phoenix, AZ 85012
Free: 800-966-7797
E-mail: mbray@moneysoft.com

Harvey C. Skoog
PO Box 26439
Prescott Valley, AZ 86312
(520)772-1714
Fax: (520)772-2814

LMC Services
8711 E Pinnacle Peak Rd., No. 340
Scottsdale, AZ 85255-3555
(602)585-7177
Fax: (602)585-5880
E-mail: louws@earthlink.com

Sauerbrun Technology Group Ltd.
7979 E Princess Dr., Ste. 5
Scottsdale, AZ 85255-5878
(602)502-4950
Fax: (602)502-4292
E-mail: info@sauerbrun.com
Website: http://www.sauerbrun.com

Gary L. McLeod
PO Box 230
Sonoita, AZ 85637
Fax: (602)455-5661

Van Cleve Associates
6932 E 2nd St.
Tucson, AZ 85710
(520)296-2587
Fax: (520)296-3358

California

Acumen Group Inc.
(650)949-9349
Fax: (650)949-4845
E-mail: acumen-g@ix.netcom.com
Website: http://pw2.netcom.com/
~janed/acumen.html

On-line Career and Management Consulting
420 Central Ave., No. 314
Alameda, CA 94501
(510)864-0336
Fax: (510)864-0336
E-mail: career@dnai.com
Website: http://www.dnai.com/
~career

Career Paths-Thomas E. Church & Associates Inc.
PO Box 2439
Aptos, CA 95001
(408)662-7950
Fax: (408)662-7955
E-mail: church@ix.netcom.com
Website: http://www.careerpaths-tom.com

Keck & Co. Business Consultants
410 Walsh Rd.
Atherton, CA 94027
(650)854-9588
Fax: (650)854-7240
E-mail: info@keckco.com
Website: http://www.keckco.com

Ben W. Laverty III, PhD, REA, CEI
4909 Stockdale Hwy., Ste. 132
Bakersfield, CA 93309
(661)283-8300
Free: 800-833-0373
Fax: (661)283-8313
E-mail: cstc@cstcsafety.com
Website: http://www.cstcsafety.com/cstc

Lindquist Consultants-Venture Planning
225 Arlington Ave.
Berkeley, CA 94707
(510)524-6685
Fax: (510)527-6604

Larson Associates
PO Box 9005
Brea, CA 92822
(714)529-4121
Fax: (714)572-3606
E-mail: ray@consultlarson.com
Website: http://www.consultlarson.com

Kremer Management Consulting
PO Box 500
Carmel, CA 93921
(408)626-8311
Fax: (408)624-2663
E-mail: ddkremer@aol.com

W and J PARTNERSHIP
PO Box 2499
18876 Edwin Markham Dr.
Castro Valley, CA 94546
(510)583-7751
Fax: (510)583-7645
E-mail: wamorgan@wjpartnership.com
Website: http://www.wjpartnership.com

JB Associates
21118 Gardena Dr.
Cupertino, CA 95014
(408)257-0214

Fax: (408)257-0216
E-mail: semarang@sirius.com
PO Box 1615
Davis, CA 95617-1615
(916)753-3361
Fax: (916)753-0464
E-mail: infoag@houseag.com
Website: http://www.houseag.com/

3C Systems Co.
16161 Ventura Blvd., Ste. 815
Encino, CA 91436
(818)907-1302
Fax: (818)907-1357
E-mail: mark@3CSysCo.com
Website: http://www.3CSysCo.com

Technical Management Consultants
3624 Westfall Dr.
Encino, CA 91436-4154
(818)784-0626
Fax: (818)501-5575
E-mail: tmcrs@aol.com

RAINWATER-GISH & Associates, Business Finance & Development
317 3rd St., Ste. 3
Eureka, CA 95501
(707)443-0030
Fax: (707)443-5683

Global Tradelinks
451 Pebble Beach Pl.
Fullerton, CA 92835
(714)441-2280
Fax: (714)441-2281
E-mail: info@globaltradelinks.com
Website: http://www.globaltradelinks.com

Strategic Business Group
800 Cienaga Dr.
Fullerton, CA 92835-1248
(714)449-1040
Fax: (714)525-1631

Burnes Consulting
20537 Wolf Creek Rd.
Grass Valley, CA 95949
(530)346-8188
Free: 800-949-9021
Fax: (530)346-7704
E-mail: kent@burnesconsulting.com
Website: http://www.burnesconsulting.com

Pioneer Business Consultants
9042 Garfield Ave., Ste. 312
Huntington Beach, CA 92646
(714)964-7600

Beblie, Brandt & Jacobs Inc.
16 Technology, Ste. 164
Irvine, CA 92618

(714)450-8790
Fax: (714)450-8799
E-mail: darcy@bbjinc.com
Website: http://198.147.90.26

Fluor Daniel Inc.
3353 Michelson Dr.
Irvine, CA 92612-0650
(949)975-2000
Fax: (949)975-5271
E-mail: sales.consulting@fluordaniel.com
Website: http://www.fluordanielconsulting.com

MCS Associates
18300 Von Karman, Ste. 710
Irvine, CA 92612
(949)263-8700
Fax: (949)263-0770
E-mail: info@mcsassociates.com
Website: http://www.mcsassociates.com

Inspired Arts Inc.
4225 Executive Sq., Ste. 1160
La Jolla, CA 92037
(619)623-3525
Free: 800-851-4394
Fax: (619)623-3534
E-mail: info@inspiredarts.com
Website: http://www.inspiredarts.com

The Laresis Companies
PO Box 3284
La Jolla, CA 92038
(619)452-2720
Fax: (619)452-8744

RCL & Co.
PO Box 1143
737 Pearl St., Ste. 201
La Jolla, CA 92038
(619)454-8883
Fax: (619)454-8880

Comprehensive Business Services
3201 Lucas Cir.
Lafayette, CA 94549
(925)283-8272
Fax: (925)283-8272

The Ribble Group
27601 Forbes Rd., Ste. 52
Laguna Niguel, CA 92677
(714)582-1085
Fax: (714)582-6420
E-mail: ribble@deltanet.com

Norris Bernstein, CMC
9309 Marina Pacifica Dr. N
Long Beach, CA 90803
(562)493-5458

Fax: (562)493-5459
E-mail: norris@ctecomputer.com
Website: http://foodconsultants.com/
bernstein/

Horizon Consulting Services
1315 Garthwick Dr.
Los Altos, CA 94024
(415)967-0906
Fax: (415)967-0906

Brincko Associates Inc.
1801 Avenue of the Stars, Ste. 1054
Los Angeles, CA 90067
(310)553-4523
Fax: (310)553-6782

**Rubenstein/Justman Management
Consultants**
2049 Century Park E, 24th Fl.
Los Angeles, CA 90067
(310)282-0800
Fax: (310)282-0400
E-mail: info@rjmc.net
Website: http://www.rjmc.net

F.J. Schroeder & Associates
1926 Westholme Ave.
Los Angeles, CA 90025
(310)470-2655
Fax: (310)470-6378
E-mail: fjsacons@aol.com
Website: http://www.mcninet.com/
GlobalLook/Fjschroe.html

Western Management Associates
5959 W Century Blvd., Ste. 565
Los Angeles, CA 90045-6506
(310)645-1091
Free: (888)788-6534
Fax: (310)645-1092
E-mail: gene@cfoforrent.com
Website: http://www.cfoforrent.com

Darrell Sell and Associates
Los Gatos, CA 95030
(408)354-7794
E-mail: darrell@netcom.com

Leslie J. Zambo
3355 Michael Dr.
Marina, CA 93933
(408)384-7086
Fax: (408)647-4199
E-mail: 104776.1552@compuserve.com

Marketing Services Management
PO Box 1377
Martinez, CA 94553
(510)370-8527

Fax: (510)370-8527
E-mail: markserve@biotechnet.com

William M. Shine Consulting Service
PO Box 127
Moraga, CA 94556-0127
(510)376-6516

Palo Alto Management Group Inc.
2672 Bayshore Pky., Ste. 701
Mountain View, CA 94043
(415)968-4374
Fax: (415)968-4245
E-mail: mburwen@pamg.com

BizplanSource
1048 Irvine Ave., Ste. 621
Newport Beach, CA 92660
Free: 888-253-0974
Fax: 800-859-8254
E-mail: info@bizplansource.com
Website: http://www.bizplansource.com
Adam Greengrass, President

The Market Connection
4020 Birch St., Ste. 203
Newport Beach, CA 92660
(714)731-6273
Fax: (714)833-0253

Muller Associates
PO Box 7264
Newport Beach, CA 92658
(714)646-1169
Fax: (714)646-1169

International Health Resources
PO Box 329
North San Juan, CA 95960-0329
(530)292-1266
Fax: (530)292-1243
Website: http://www.futureofhealthcare.com

NEXUS - Consultants to Management
PO Box 1531
Novato, CA 94948
(415)897-4400
Fax: (415)898-2252
E-mail: jimnexus@aol.com

Aerospcace.Org
PO Box 28831
Oakland, CA 94604-8831
(510)530-9169
Fax: (510)530-3411
Website: http://www.aerospace.org

Intelequest Corp.
722 Gailen Ave.
Palo Alto, CA 94303
(415)968-3443

Fax: (415)493-6954
E-mail: frits@iqix.com

McLaughlin & Associates
66 San Marino Cir.
Rancho Mirage, CA 92270
(760)321-2932
Fax: (760)328-2474
E-mail: jackmcla@msn.com

**Carrera Consulting Group, a division of
Maximus**
2110 21st St., Ste. 400
Sacramento, CA 95818
(916)456-3300
Fax: (916)456-3306
E-mail: central@carreraconsulting.com
Website: http://www.carreraconsulting.com

**Bay Area Tax Consultants and Bayhill
Financial Consultants**
1150 Bayhill Dr., Ste. 1150
San Bruno, CA 94066-3004
(415)952-8786
Fax: (415)588-4524
E-mail: baytax@compuserve.com
Website: http://www.baytax.com/

AdCon Services, LLC
8871 Hillery Dr.
Dan Diego, CA 92126
(858)433-1411
E-mail: adam@adconservices.com
Website: http://www.adconservices.com
Adam Greengrass

California Business Incubation Network
101 W Broadway, No. 480
San Diego, CA 92101
(619)237-0559
Fax: (619)237-0521

G.R. Gordetsky Consultants Inc.
11414 Windy Summit Pl.
San Diego, CA 92127
(619)487-4939
Fax: (619)487-5587
E-mail: gordet@pacbell.net

Freeman, Sullivan & Co.
131 Steuart St., Ste. 500
San Francisco, CA 94105
(415)777-0707
Free: 800-777-0737
Fax: (415)777-2420
Website: http://www.fsc-research.com

Ideas Unlimited
2151 California St., Ste. 7
San Francisco, CA 94115
(415)931-0641
Fax: (415)931-0880

Russell Miller Inc.
300 Montgomery St., Ste. 900
San Francisco, CA 94104
(415)956-7474
Fax: (415)398-0620
E-mail: rmi@pacbell.net
Website: http://www.rmisf.com

PKF Consulting
425 California St., Ste. 1650
San Francisco, CA 94104
(415)421-5378
Fax: (415)956-7708
E-mail: callahan@pkfc.com
Website: http://www.pkfonline.com

Welling & Woodard Inc.
1067 Broadway
San Francisco, CA 94133
(415)776-4500
Fax: (415)776-5067

Highland Associates
16174 Highland Dr.
San Jose, CA 95127
(408)272-7008
Fax: (408)272-4040

ORDIS Inc.
6815 Trinidad Dr.
San Jose, CA 95120-2056
(408)268-3321
Free: 800-446-7347
Fax: (408)268-3582
E-mail: ordis@ordis.com
Website: http://www.ordis.com

Stanford Resources Inc.
20 Great Oaks Blvd., Ste. 200
San Jose, CA 95119
(408)360-8400
Fax: (408)360-8410
E-mail: sales@stanfordsources.com
Website: http://www. stanfordresources.com

Technology Properties Ltd. Inc.
PO Box 20250
San Jose, CA 95160
(408)243-9898
Fax: (408)296-6637
E-mail: sanjose@tplnet.com

Helfert Associates
1777 Borel Pl., Ste. 508
San Mateo, CA 94402-3514
(650)377-0540
Fax: (650)377-0472

Mykytyn Consulting Group Inc.
185 N Redwood Dr., Ste. 200
San Rafael, CA 94903

(415)491-1770
Fax: (415)491-1251
E-mail: info@mcgi.com
Website: http://www.mcgi.com

Omega Management Systems Inc.
3 Mount Darwin Ct.
San Rafael, CA 94903-1109
(415)499-1300
Fax: (415)492-9490
E-mail: omegamgt@ix.netcom.com

The Information Group Inc.
4675 Stevens Creek Blvd., Ste. 100
Santa Clara, CA 95051
(408)985-7877
Fax: (408)985-2945
E-mail: dvincent@tig-usa.com
Website: http://www.tig-usa.com

Cast Management Consultants
1620 26th St., Ste. 2040N
Santa Monica, CA 90404
(310)828-7511
Fax: (310)453-6831

Cuma Consulting Management
Box 724
Santa Rosa, CA 95402
(707)785-2477
Fax: (707)785-2478

The E-Myth Academy
131B Stony Cir., Ste. 2000
Santa Rosa, CA 95401
(707)569-5600
Free: 800-221-0266
Fax: (707)569-5700
E-mail: info@e-myth.com
Website: http://www.e-myth.com

Reilly, Connors & Ray
1743 Canyon Rd.
Spring Valley, CA 91977
(619)698-4808
Fax: (619)460-3892
E-mail: davidray@adnc.com

Management Consultants
Sunnyvale, CA 94087-4700
(408)773-0321

RJR Associates
1639 Lewiston Dr.
Sunnyvale, CA 94087
(408)737-7720
E-mail: bobroy@rjrassoc.com
Website: http://www.rjrassoc.com

Schwafel Associates
333 Cobalt Way, Ste. 21
Sunnyvale, CA 94085

(408)720-0649
Fax: (408)720-1796
E-mail: schwafel@ricochet.net
Website: http://www.patca.org

Staubs Business Services
23320 S Vermont Ave.
Torrance, CA 90502-2940
(310)830-9128
Fax: (310)830-9128
E-mail: Harry_L_Staubs@Lamg.com

Out of Your Mind...and Into the Marketplace
13381 White Sands Dr.
Tustin, CA 92780-4565
(714)544-0248
Free: 800-419-1513
Fax: (714)730-1414
E-mail: lpinson@aol.com
Website: http://www.business-plan.com

Independent Research Services
PO Box 2426
Van Nuys, CA 91404-2426
(818)993-3622

Ingman Company Inc.
7949 Woodley Ave., Ste. 120
Van Nuys, CA 91406-1232
(818)375-5027
Fax: (818)894-5001

Innovative Technology Associates
3639 E Harbor Blvd., Ste. 203E
Ventura, CA 93001
(805)650-9353

Grid Technology Associates
20404 Tufts Cir.
Walnut, CA 91789
(909)444-0922
Fax: (909)444-0922
E-mail: grid_technology@msn.com

Ridge Consultants Inc.
100 Pringle Ave., Ste. 580
Walnut Creek, CA 94596
(925)274-1990
Fax: (510)274-1956
E-mail: info@ridgecon.com
Website: http://www.ridgecon.com

Bell Springs Publishing
PO Box 1240
Willits, CA 95490
(707)459-6372
E-mail: bellsprings@sabernet
Website: http://www.bellsprings.com

Hutchinson Consulting and Appraisal
23245 Sylvan St., Ste. 103
Woodland Hills, CA 91367
(818)888-8175
Free: 800-977-7548
Fax: (818)888-8220
E-mail: r.f.hutchinson-cpa@worldnet.att.net

Colorado

Sam Boyer & Associates
4255 S Buckley Rd., No. 136
Aurora, CO 80013
Free: 800-785-0485
Fax: (303)766-8740
E-mail: samboyer@samboyer.com
Website: http://www.samboyer.com/

Ameriwest Business Consultants Inc.
PO Box 26266
Colorado Springs, CO 80936
(719)380-7096
Fax: (719)380-7096
E-mail: email@abchelp.com
Website: http://www.abchelp.com

GVNW Consulting Inc.
2270 La Montana Way
Colorado Springs, CO 80936
(719)594-5800
Fax: (719)594-5803
Website: http://www.gvnw.com

M-Squared Inc.
755 San Gabriel Pl.
Colorado Springs, CO 80906
(719)576-2554
Fax: (719)576-2554

Thornton Financial FNIC
1024 Centre Ave., Bldg. E
Fort Collins, CO 80526-1849
(970)221-2089
Fax: (970)484-5206

TenEyck Associates
1760 Cherryville Rd.
Greenwood Village, CO 80121-1503
(303)758-6129
Fax: (303)761-8286

Associated Enterprises Ltd.
13050 W Ceder Dr., Unit 11
Lakewood, CO 80228
(303)988-6695
Fax: (303)988-6739
E-mail: ael1@classic.msn.com

The Vincent Company Inc.
200 Union Blvd., Ste. 210
Lakewood, CO 80228

(303)989-7271
Free: 800-274-0733
Fax: (303)989-7570
E-mail: vincent@vincentco.com
Website: http://www.vincentco.com

Johnson & West Management Consultants Inc.
7612 S Logan Dr.
Littleton, CO 80122
(303)730-2810
Fax: (303)730-3219

Western Capital Holdings Inc.
10050 E Applwood Dr.
Parker, CO 80138
(303)841-1022
Fax: (303)770-1945

Connecticut

Stratman Group Inc.
40 Tower Ln.
Avon, CT 06001-4222
(860)677-2898
Free: 800-551-0499
Fax: (860)677-8210

Cowherd Consulting Group Inc.
106 Stephen Mather Rd.
Darien, CT 06820
(203)655-2150
Fax: (203)655-6427

Greenwich Associates
8 Greenwich Office Park
Greenwich, CT 06831-5149
(203)629-1200
Fax: (203)629-1229
E-mail: lisa@greenwich.com
Website: http://www.greenwich.com

Follow-up News
185 Pine St., Ste. 818
Manchester, CT 06040
(860)647-7542
Free: 800-708-0696
Fax: (860)646-6544
E-mail: Followupnews@aol.com

Lovins & Associates Consulting
309 Edwards St.
New Haven, CT 06511
(203)787-3367
Fax: (203)624-7599
E-mail: Alovinsphd@aol.com
Website: http://www.lovinsgroup.com

JC Ventures Inc.
4 Arnold St.
Old Greenwich, CT 06870-1203

(203)698-1990
Free: 800-698-1997
Fax: (203)698-2638

Charles L. Hornung Associates
52 Ned's Mountain Rd.
Ridgefield, CT 06877
(203)431-0297

Manus
100 Prospect St., S Tower
Stamford, CT 06901
(203)326-3880
Free: 800-445-0942
Fax: (203)326-3890
E-mail: manus1@aol.com
Website: http://www.RightManus.com

RealBusinessPlans.com
156 Westport Rd.
Wilton, CT 06897
(914)837-2886
E-mail: ct@realbusinessplans.com
Website: http://www.RealBusiness
Plans.com
Tony Tecce

Delaware

Focus Marketing
61-7 Habor Dr.
Claymont, DE 19703
(302)793-3064

Daedalus Ventures Ltd.
PO Box 1474
Hockessin, DE 19707
(302)239-6758
Fax: (302)239-9991
E-mail: daedalus@mail.del.net

The Formula Group
PO Box 866
Hockessin, DE 19707
(302)456-0952
Fax: (302)456-1354
E-mail: formula@netaxs.com

Selden Enterprises Inc.
2502 Silverside Rd., Ste. 1
Wilmington, DE 19810-3740
(302)529-7113
Fax: (302)529-7442
E-mail: selden2@bellatlantic.net
Website: http://www.seldenenterprises.com

District of Columbia

Bruce W. McGee and Associates
7826 Eastern Ave. NW, Ste. 30
Washington, DC 20012

(202)726-7272
Fax: (202)726-2946

McManis Associates Inc.
1900 K St. NW, Ste. 700
Washington, DC 20006
(202)466-7680
Fax: (202)872-1898
Website: http://www.mcmanis-mmi.com

Smith, Dawson & Andrews Inc.
1000 Connecticut Ave., Ste. 302
Washington, DC 20036
(202)835-0740
Fax: (202)775-8526
E-mail: webmaster@sda-inc.com
Website: http://www.sda-inc.com

Florida

BackBone, Inc.
20404 Hacienda Court
Boca Raton, FL 33498
(561)470-0965
Fax: 516-908-4038
E-mail: BPlans@backboneinc.com
Website: http://www.backboneinc.com
Charles Epstein, President

Whalen & Associates Inc.
4255 Northwest 26 Ct.
Boca Raton, FL 33434
(561)241-5950
Fax: (561)241-7414
E-mail: drwhalen@ix.netcom.com

E.N. Rysso & Associates
180 Bermuda Petrel Ct.
Daytona Beach, FL 32119
(386)760-3028
E-mail: erysso@aol.com

Virtual Technocrats LLC
560 Lavers Circle, #146
Delray Beach, FL 33444
(561)265-3509
E-mail: josh@virtualtechnocrats.com;
info@virtualtechnocrats.com
Website: http://www.virtualtechnocrats.com
Josh Eikov, Managing Director

Eric Sands Consulting Services
6193 Rock Island Rd., Ste. 412
Fort Lauderdale, FL 33319
(954)721-4767
Fax: (954)720-2815
E-mail: easands@aol.com
Website: http://www.ericsandsconsultig.com

Professional Planning Associates, Inc.
1975 E. Sunrise Blvd. Suite 607
Fort Lauderdale, FL 33304
(954)764-5204
Fax: 954-463-4172
E-mail: Mgoldstein@proplana.com
Website: http://proplana.com
Michael Goldstein, President

Host Media Corp.
3948 S 3rd St., Ste. 191
Jacksonville Beach, FL 32250
(904)285-3239
Fax: (904)285-5618
E-mail: msconsulting@compuserve.com
Website: http://www.mediaservicesgroup.com

William V. Hall
1925 Brickell, Ste. D-701
Miami, FL 33129
(305)856-9622
Fax: (305)856-4113
E-mail: williamvhall@compuserve.com

F.A. McGee Inc.
800 Claughton Island Dr., Ste. 401
Miami, FL 33131
(305)377-9123

Taxplan Inc.
Mirasol International Ctr.
2699 Collins Ave.
Miami Beach, FL 33140
(305)538-3303

T.C. Brown & Associates
8415 Excalibur Cir., Apt. B1
Naples, FL 34108
(941)594-1949
Fax: (941)594-0611
E-mail: tcater@naples.net.com

RLA International Consulting
713 Lagoon Dr.
North Palm Beach, FL 33408
(407)626-4258
Fax: (407)626-5772

Comprehensive Franchising Inc.
2465 Ridgecrest Ave.
Orange Park, FL 32065
(904)272-6567
Free: 800-321-6567
Fax: (904)272-6750
E-mail: theimp@cris.com
Website: http://www.franchise411.com

Hunter G. Jackson Jr. - Consulting Environmental Physicist
PO Box 618272
Orlando, FL 32861-8272

(407)295-4188
E-mail: hunterjackson@juno.com

F. Newton Parks
210 El Brillo Way
Palm Beach, FL 33480
(561)833-1727
Fax: (561)833-4541

Avery Business Development Services
2506 St. Michel Ct.
Ponte Vedra Beach, FL 32082
(904)285-6033
Fax: (904)285-6033

Strategic Business Planning Co.
PO Box 821006
South Florida, FL 33082-1006
(954)704-9100
Fax: (954)438-7333
E-mail: info@bizplan.com
Website: http://www.bizplan.com

Dufresne Consulting Group Inc.
10014 N Dale Mabry, Ste. 101
Tampa, FL 33618-4426
(813)264-4775
Fax: (813)264-9300
Website: http://www.dcgconsult.com

Agrippa Enterprises Inc.
PO Box 175
Venice, FL 34284-0175
(941)355-7876
E-mail: webservices@agrippa.com
Website: http://www.agrippa.com

Center for Simplified Strategic Planning Inc.
PO Box 3324
Vero Beach, FL 32964-3324
(561)231-3636
Fax: (561)231-1099
Website: http://www.cssp.com

Georgia

Marketing Spectrum Inc.
115 Perimeter Pl., Ste. 440
Atlanta, GA 30346
(770)395-7244
Fax: (770)393-4071

Business Ventures Corp.
1650 Oakbrook Dr., Ste. 405
Norcross, GA 30093
(770)729-8000
Fax: (770)729-8028

Informed Decisions Inc.
100 Falling Cheek
Sautee Nacoochee, GA 30571

(706)878-1905
Fax: (706)878-1802
E-mail: skylake@compuserve.com

Tom C. Davis & Associates, P.C.
3189 Perimeter Rd.
Valdosta, GA 31602
(912)247-9801
Fax: (912)244-7704
E-mail: mail@tcdcpa.com
Website: http://www.tcdcpa.com/

Illinois

TWD and Associates
431 S Patton
Arlington Heights, IL 60005
(847)398-6410
Fax: (847)255-5095
E-mail: tdoo@aol.com

Management Planning Associates Inc.
2275 Half Day Rd., Ste. 350
Bannockburn, IL 60015-1277
(847)945-2421
Fax: (847)945-2425

Phil Faris Associates
86 Old Mill Ct.
Barrington, IL 60010
(847)382-4888
Fax: (847)382-4890
E-mail: pfaris@meginsnet.net

Seven Continents Technology
787 Stonebridge
Buffalo Grove, IL 60089
(708)577-9653
Fax: (708)870-1220

Grubb & Blue Inc.
2404 Windsor Pl.
Champaign, IL 61820
(217)366-0052
Fax: (217)356-0117

ACE Accounting Service Inc.
3128 N Bernard St.
Chicago, IL 60618
(773)463-7854
Fax: (773)463-7854

AON Consulting Worldwide
200 E Randolph St., 10th Fl.
Chicago, IL 60601
(312)381-4800
Free: 800-438-6487
Fax: (312)381-0240
Website: http://www.aon.com

FMS Consultants
5801 N Sheridan Rd., Ste. 3D
Chicago, IL 60660
(773)561-7362
Fax: (773)561-6274

Grant Thornton
800 1 Prudential Plz.
130 E Randolph St.
Chicago, IL 60601
(312)856-0001
Fax: (312)861-1340
E-mail: gtinfo@gt.com
Website: http://www.grantthornton.com

Kingsbury International Ltd.
5341 N Glenwood Ave.
Chicago, IL 60640
(773)271-3030
Fax: (773)728-7080
E-mail: jetlag@mcs.com
Website: http://www.kingbiz.com

MacDougall & Blake Inc.
1414 N Wells St., Ste. 311
Chicago, IL 60610-1306
(312)587-3330
Fax: (312)587-3699
E-mail: jblake@compuserve.com

James C. Osburn Ltd.
6445 N. Western Ave., Ste. 304
Chicago, IL 60645
(773)262-4428
Fax: (773)262-6755
E-mail: osburnltd@aol.com

Tarifero & Tazewell Inc.
211 S Clark
Chicago, IL 60690
(312)665-9714
Fax: (312)665-9716

Human Energy Design Systems
620 Roosevelt Dr.
Edwardsville, IL 62025
(618)692-0258
Fax: (618)692-0819

China Business Consultants Group
931 Dakota Cir.
Naperville, IL 60563
(630)778-7992
Fax: (630)778-7915
E-mail: cbcq@aol.com

Center for Workforce Effectiveness
500 Skokie Blvd., Ste. 222
Northbrook, IL 60062
(847)559-8777
Fax: (847)559-8778

E-mail: office@cwelink.com
Website: http://www.cwelink.com

Smith Associates
1320 White Mountain Dr.
Northbrook, IL 60062
(847)480-7200
Fax: (847)480-9828

Francorp Inc.
20200 Governors Dr.
Olympia Fields, IL 60461
(708)481-2900
Free: 800-372-6244
Fax: (708)481-5885
E-mail: francorp@aol.com
Website: http://www.francorpinc.com

Camber Business Strategy Consultants
1010 S Plum Tree Ct
Palatine, IL 60078-0986
(847)202-0101
Fax: (847)705-7510
E-mail: camber@ameritech.net

Partec Enterprise Group
5202 Keith Dr.
Richton Park, IL 60471
(708)503-4047
Fax: (708)503-9468

Rockford Consulting Group Ltd.
Century Plz., Ste. 206
7210 E State St.
Rockford, IL 61108
(815)229-2900
Free: 800-667-7495
Fax: (815)229-2612
E-mail: rligus@RockfordConsulting.com
Website: http://www.Rockford
Consulting.com

RSM McGladrey Inc.
1699 E Woodfield Rd., Ste. 300
Schaumburg, IL 60173-4969
(847)413-6900
Fax: (847)517-7067
Website: http://www.rsmmcgladrey.com

A.D. Star Consulting
320 Euclid
Winnetka, IL 60093
(847)446-7827
Fax: (847)446-7827
E-mail: startwo@worldnet.att.net

Indiana

Modular Consultants Inc.
3109 Crabtree Ln.
Elkhart, IN 46514

(219)264-5761
Fax: (219)264-5761
E-mail: sasabo5313@aol.com

Midwest Marketing Research
PO Box 1077
Goshen, IN 46527
(219)533-0548
Fax: (219)533-0540
E-mail: 103365.654@compuserve

Ketchum Consulting Group
8021 Knue Rd., Ste. 112
Indianapolis, IN 46250
(317)845-5411
Fax: (317)842-9941

MDI Management Consulting
1519 Park Dr.
Munster, IN 46321
(219)838-7909
Fax: (219)838-7909

Iowa

McCord Consulting Group Inc.
4533 Pine View Dr. NE
PO Box 11024
Cedar Rapids, IA 52410
(319)378-0077
Fax: (319)378-1577
E-mail: smmccord@hom.com
Website: http://www.mccordgroup.com

Management Solutions L.C.
3815 Lincoln Pl. Dr.
Des Moines, IA 50312
(515)277-6408
Fax: (515)277-3506
E-mail: wasunimers@uswest.net

Grandview Marketing
15 Red Bridge Dr.
Sioux City, IA 51104
(712)239-3122
Fax: (712)258-7578
E-mail: eandrews@pionet.net

Kansas

Assessments in Action
513A N Mur-Len
Olathe, KS 66062
(913)764-6270
Free: (888)548-1504
Fax: (913)764-6495
E-mail: lowdene@qni.com
Website: http://www.assessments-in-action.com

Maine

Edgemont Enterprises
PO Box 8354
Portland, ME 04104
(207)871-8964
Fax: (207)871-8964

Pan Atlantic Consultants
5 Milk St.
Portland, ME 04101
(207)871-8622
Fax: (207)772-4842
E-mail: pmurphy@maine.rr.com
Website: http://www.panatlantic.net

Maryland

Clemons & Associates Inc.
5024-R Campbell Blvd.
Baltimore, MD 21236
(410)931-8100
Fax: (410)931-8111
E-mail: info@clemonsmgmt.com
Website: http://www.clemonsmgmt.com

Imperial Group Ltd.
305 Washington Ave., Ste. 204
Baltimore, MD 21204-6009
(410)337-8500
Fax: (410)337-7641

Leadership Institute
3831 Yolando Rd.
Baltimore, MD 21218
(410)366-9111
Fax: (410)243-8478
E-mail: behconsult@aol.com

Burdeshaw Associates Ltd.
4701 Sangamore Rd.
Bethesda, MD 20816-2508
(301)229-5800
Fax: (301)229-5045
E-mail: jstacy@burdeshaw.com
Website: http://www.burdeshaw.com

Michael E. Cohen
5225 Pooks Hill Rd., Ste. 1119 S
Bethesda, MD 20814
(301)530-5738
Fax: (301)530-2988
E-mail: mecohen@crosslink.net

World Development Group Inc.
5272 River Rd., Ste. 650
Bethesda, MD 20816-1405
(301)652-1818
Fax: (301)652-1250
E-mail: wdg@has.com
Website: http://www.worlddg.com

Swartz Consulting
PO Box 4301
Crofton, MD 21114-4301
(301)262-6728

Software Solutions International Inc.
9633 Duffer Way
Gaithersburg, MD 20886
(301)330-4136
Fax: (301)330-4136

Strategies Inc.
8 Park Center Ct., Ste. 200
Owings Mills, MD 21117
(410)363-6669
Fax: (410)363-1231
E-mail: strategies@strat1.com
Website: http://www.strat1.com

Hammer Marketing Resources
179 Inverness Rd.
Severna Park, MD 21146
(410)544-9191
Fax: (305)675-3277
E-mail: info@gohammer.com
Website: http://www.gohammer.com

Andrew Sussman & Associates
13731 Kretsinger
Smithsburg, MD 21783
(301)824-2943
Fax: (301)824-2943

Massachusetts

Geibel Marketing and Public Relations
PO Box 611
Belmont, MA 02478-0005
(617)484-8285
Fax: (617)489-3567
E-mail: jgeibel@geibelpr.com
Website: http://www.geibelpr.com

Bain & Co.
2 Copley Pl.
Boston, MA 02116
(617)572-2000
Fax: (617)572-2427
E-mail: corporate.inquiries@bain.com
Website: http://www.bain.com

Mehr & Co.
62 Kinnaird St.
Cambridge, MA 02139
(617)876-3311
Fax: (617)876-3023
E-mail: mehrco@aol.com

Monitor Company Inc.
2 Canal Park
Cambridge, MA 02141

(617)252-2000
Fax: (617)252-2100
Website: http://www.monitor.com

Information & Research Associates
PO Box 3121
Framingham, MA 01701
(508)788-0784

Walden Consultants Ltd.
252 Pond St.
Hopkinton, MA 01748
(508)435-4882
Fax: (508)435-3971
Website: http://www.waldenconsultants.com

Jeffrey D. Marshall
102 Mitchell Rd.
Ipswich, MA 01938-1219
(508)356-1113
Fax: (508)356-2989

Consulting Resources Corp.
6 Northbrook Park
Lexington, MA 02420
(781)863-1222
Fax: (781)863-1441
E-mail: res@consultingresources.net
Website: http://www.consultingresources.net

Planning Technologies Group L.L.C.
92 Hayden Ave.
Lexington, MA 02421
(781)778-4678
Fax: (781)861-1099
E-mail: ptg@plantech.com
Website: http://www.plantech.com

Kalba International Inc.
23 Sandy Pond Rd.
Lincoln, MA 01773
(781)259-9589
Fax: (781)259-1460
E-mail: info@kalbainternational.com
Website: http://www.kalbainternational.com

VMB Associates Inc.
115 Ashland St.
Melrose, MA 02176
(781)665-0623
Fax: (425)732-7142
E-mail: vmbinc@aol.com

The Company Doctor
14 Pudding Stone Ln.
Mendon, MA 01756
(508)478-1747
Fax: (508)478-0520

Data and Strategies Group Inc.
190 N Main St.
Natick, MA 01760
(508)653-9990

Fax: (508)653-7799
E-mail: dsginc@dsggroup.com
Website: http://www.dsggroup.com

The Enterprise Group
73 Parker Rd.
Needham, MA 02494
(617)444-6631
Fax: (617)433-9991
E-mail: lsacco@world.std.com
Website: http://www.enterprise-group.com

PSMJ Resources Inc.
10 Midland Ave.
Newton, MA 02458
(617)965-0055
Free: 800-537-7765
Fax: (617)965-5152
E-mail: psmj@tiac.net
Website: http://www.psmj.com

Scheur Management Group Inc.
255 Washington St., Ste. 100
Newton, MA 02458-1611
(617)969-7500
Fax: (617)969-7508
E-mail: smgnow@scheur.com
Website: http://www.scheur.com

I.E.E.E., Boston Section
240 Bear Hill Rd., 202B
Waltham, MA 02451-1017
(781)890-5294
Fax: (781)890-5290

Business Planning and Consulting Services
20 Beechwood Ter.
Wellesley, MA 02482
(617)237-9151
Fax: (617)237-9151

Michigan

Walter Frederick Consulting
1719 South Blvd.
Ann Arbor, MI 48104
(313)662-4336
Fax: (313)769-7505

Fox Enterprises
6220 W Freeland Rd.
Freeland, MI 48623
(517)695-9170
Fax: (517)695-9174
E-mail: foxjw@concentric.net
Website: http://www.cris.com/~foxjw

G.G.W. and Associates
1213 Hampton
Jackson, MI 49203

(517)782-2255
Fax: (517)782-2255

Altamar Group Ltd.
6810 S Cedar, Ste. 2-B
Lansing, MI 48911
(517)694-0910
Free: 800-443-2627
Fax: (517)694-1377

Sheffieck Consultants Inc.
23610 Greening Dr.
Novi, MI 48375-3130
(248)347-3545
Fax: (248)347-3530
E-mail: cfsheff@concentric.net

Rehmann, Robson PC
5800 Gratiot
Saginaw, MI 48605
(517)799-9580
Fax: (517)799-0227
Website: http://www.rrpc.com

Francis & Co.
17200 W 10 Mile Rd., Ste. 207
Southfield, MI 48075
(248)559-7600
Fax: (248)559-5249

Private Ventures Inc.
16000 W 9 Mile Rd., Ste. 504
Southfield, MI 48075
(248)569-1977
Free: 800-448-7614
Fax: (248)569-1838
E-mail: pventuresi@aol.com

JGK Associates
14464 Kerner Dr.
Sterling Heights, MI 48313
(810)247-9055
Fax: (248)822-4977
E-mail: kozlowski@home.com

Minnesota

Health Fitness Corp.
3500 W 80th St., Ste. 130
Bloomington, MN 55431
(612)831-6830
Fax: (612)831-7264

Consatech Inc.
PO Box 1047
Burnsville, MN 55337
(612)953-1088
Fax: (612)435-2966

Robert F. Knotek
14960 Ironwood Ct.
Eden Prairie, MN 55346
(612)949-2875

DRI Consulting
7715 Stonewood Ct.
Edina, MN 55439
(612)941-9656
Fax: (612)941-2693
E-mail: dric@dric.com
Website: http://www.dric.com

Markin Consulting
12072 87th Pl. N
Maple Grove, MN 55369
(612)493-3568
Fax: (612)493-5744
E-mail: markin@markinconsulting.com
Website: http://www.markinconsulting.com

Minnesota Cooperation Office for Small Business & Job Creation Inc.
5001 W 80th St., Ste. 825
Minneapolis, MN 55437
(612)830-1230
Fax: (612)830-1232
E-mail: mncoop@msn.com
Website: http://www.mnco.org

Enterprise Consulting Inc.
PO Box 1111
Minnetonka, MN 55345
(612)949-5909
Fax: (612)906-3965

Amdahl International
724 1st Ave. SW
Rochester, MN 55902
(507)252-0402
Fax: (507)252-0402
E-mail: amdahl@best-service.com
Website: http://www.wp.com/amdahl_int

Power Systems Research
1365 Corporate Center Curve, 2nd Fl.
St. Paul, MN 55121
(612)905-8400
Free: (888)625-8612
Fax: (612)454-0760
E-mail: Barb@Powersys.com
Website: http://www.powersys.com

Missouri

Business Planning and Development Corp.
4030 Charlotte St.
Kansas City, MO 64110

(816)753-0495
E-mail: humph@bpdev.demon.co.uk
Website: http://www.bpdev.demon.co.uk

CFO Service
10336 Donoho
St. Louis, MO 63131
(314)750-2940
E-mail: jskae@cfoservice.com
Website: http://www.cfoservice.com

Nebraska

International Management Consulting Group Inc.
1309 Harlan Dr., Ste. 205
Bellevue, NE 68005
(402)291-4545
Free: 800-665-IMCG
Fax: (402)291-4343
E-mail: imcg@neonramp.com
Website: http://www.mgtconsulting.com

Heartland Management Consulting Group
1904 Barrington Pky.
Papillion, NE 68046
(402)339-2387
Fax: (402)339-1319

Nevada

The DuBois Group
865 Tahoe Blvd., Ste. 108
Incline Village, NV 89451
(775)832-0550
Free: 800-375-2935
Fax: (775)832-0556
E-mail: DuBoisGrp@aol.com

New Hampshire

Wolff Consultants
10 Buck Rd.
Hanover, NH 03755
(603)643-6015

BPT Consulting Associates Ltd.
12 Parmenter Rd., Ste. B-6
Londonderry, NH 03053
(603)437-8484
Free: (888)278-0030
Fax: (603)434-5388
E-mail: bptcons@tiac.net
Website: http://www.bptconsulting.com

New Jersey

Bedminster Group Inc.
1170 Rte. 22 E
Bridgewater, NJ 08807

(908)500-4155
Fax: (908)766-0780
E-mail: info@bedminstergroup.com
Website: http://www.bedminstergroup.com
Fax: (202)806-1777
Terry Strong, Acting Regional Dir.

Delta Planning Inc.
PO Box 425
Denville, NJ 07834
(913)625-1742
Free: 800-672-0762
Fax: (973)625-3531
E-mail: DeltaP@worldnet.att.net
Website: http://deltaplanning.com

Kumar Associates Inc.
1004 Cumbermeade Rd.
Fort Lee, NJ 07024
(201)224-9480
Fax: (201)585-2343
E-mail: mail@kumarassociates.com
Website: http://kumarassociates.com

John Hall & Company Inc.
PO Box 187
Glen Ridge, NJ 07028
(973)680-4449
Fax: (973)680-4581
E-mail: jhcompany@aol.com

Market Focus
PO Box 402
Maplewood, NJ 07040
(973)378-2470
Fax: (973)378-2470
E-mail: mcss66@marketfocus.com

Vanguard Communications Corp.
100 American Rd.
Morris Plains, NJ 07950
(973)605-8000
Fax: (973)605-8329
Website: http://www.vanguard.net/

ConMar International Ltd.
1901 US Hwy. 130
North Brunswick, NJ 08902
(732)940-8347
Fax: (732)274-1199

KLW New Products
156 Cedar Dr.
Old Tappan, NJ 07675
(201)358-1300
Fax: (201)664-2594
E-mail: lrlarsen@usa.net
Website: http://www.klwnewproducts.com

PA Consulting Group
315A Enterprise Dr.
Plainsboro, NJ 08536
(609)936-8300
Fax: (609)936-8811
E-mail: info@paconsulting.com
Website: http://www.pa-consulting.com

Aurora Marketing Management Inc.
66 Witherspoon St., Ste. 600
Princeton, NJ 08542
(908)904-1125
Fax: (908)359-1108
E-mail: aurora2@voicenet.com
Website: http://www.auroramarketing.net

Smart Business Supersite
88 Orchard Rd., CN-5219
Princeton, NJ 08543
(908)321-1924
Fax: (908)321-5156
E-mail: irv@smartbiz.com
Website: http://www.smartbiz.com

Tracelin Associates
1171 Main St., Ste. 6K
Rahway, NJ 07065
(732)381-3288

Schkeeper Inc.
130-6 Bodman Pl.
Red Bank, NJ 07701
(732)219-1965
Fax: (732)530-3703

Henry Branch Associates
2502 Harmon Cove Twr.
Secaucus, NJ 07094
(201)866-2008
Fax: (201)601-0101
E-mail: hbranch161@home.com

Robert Gibbons & Company Inc.
46 Knoll Rd.
Tenafly, NJ 07670-1050
(201)871-3933
Fax: (201)871-2173
E-mail: crisisbob@aol.com

PMC Management Consultants Inc.
6 Thistle Ln.
Three Bridges, NJ 08887-0332
(908)788-1014
Free: 800-PMC-0250
Fax: (908)806-7287
E-mail: int@pmc-management.com
Website: http://www.pmc-management.com

R.W. Bankart & Associates
20 Valley Ave., Ste. D-2
Westwood, NJ 07675-3607
(201)664-7672

New Mexico

Vondle & Associates Inc.
4926 Calle de Tierra, NE
Albuquerque, NM 87111
(505)292-8961
Fax: (505)296-2790
E-mail: vondle@aol.com

InfoNewMexico
2207 Black Hills Rd., NE
Rio Rancho, NM 87124
(505)891-2462
Fax: (505)896-8971

New York

Powers Research and Training Institute
PO Box 78
Bayville, NY 11709
(516)628-2250
Fax: (516)628-2252
E-mail: powercocch@compuserve.com
Website: http://www.nancypowers.com

Consortium House
296 Wittenberg Rd.
Bearsville, NY 12409
(845)679-8867
Fax: (845)679-9248
E-mail: eugenegs@aol.com
Website: http://www.chpub.com

Progressive Finance Corp.
3549 Tiemann Ave.
Bronx, NY 10469
(718)405-9029
Free: 800-225-8381
Fax: (718)405-1170

Wave Hill Associates Inc.
2621 Palisade Ave., Ste. 15-C
Bronx, NY 10463
(718)549-7368
Fax: (718)601-9670
E-mail: pepper@compuserve.com

Management Insight
96 Arlington Rd.
Buffalo, NY 14221
(716)631-3319
Fax: (716)631-0203
E-mail:
michalski@foodserviceinsight.com
Website: http://www.foodserviceinsight.
com

**Samani International Enterprises,
Marions Panyaught Consultancy**
2028 Parsons
Flushing, NY 11357-3436

(917)287-8087
Fax: 800-873-8939
E-mail: vjp2@biostrategist.com
Website: http://www.biostrategist.com

Marketing Resources Group
71-58 Austin St.
Forest Hills, NY 11375
(718)261-8882

**Mangabay Business Plans &
Development**
Subsidiary of Innis Asset Allocation
125-10 Queens Blvd., Ste. 2202
Kew Gardens, NY 11415
 (905)527-1947
Fax: 509-472-1935
E-mail: mangabay@mangabay.com
Website: http://www.mangabay.com
Lee Toh, Managing Partner

ComputerEase Co.
1301 Monmouth Ave.
Lakewood, NY 08701
(212)406-9464
Fax: (914)277-5317
E-mail: crawfordc@juno.com

Boice Dunham Group
30 W 13th St.
New York, NY 10011
(212)924-2200
Fax: (212)924-1108

Elizabeth Capen
27 E 95th St.
New York, NY 10128
(212)427-7654
Fax: (212)876-3190

Haver Analytics
60 E 42nd St., Ste. 2424
New York, NY 10017
(212)986-9300
Fax: (212)986-5857
E-mail: data@haver.com
Website: http://www.haver.com

The Jordan, Edmiston Group Inc.
150 E 52nd Ave., 18th Fl.
New York, NY 10022
(212)754-0710
Fax: (212)754-0337

KPMG International
345 Park Ave.
New York, NY 10154-0102
(212)758-9700
Fax: (212)758-9819
Website: http://www.kpmg.com

Mahoney Cohen Consulting Corp.
111 W 40th St., 12th Fl.
New York, NY 10018
(212)490-8000
Fax: (212)790-5913

Management Practice Inc.
342 Madison Ave.
New York, NY 10173-1230
(212)867-7948
Fax: (212)972-5188
Website: http://www.mpiweb.com

Moseley Associates Inc.
342 Madison Ave., Ste. 1414
New York, NY 10016
(212)213-6673
Fax: (212)687-1520

Practice Development Counsel
60 Sutton Pl. S
New York, NY 10022
(212)593-1549
Fax: (212)980-7940
E-mail: pwhaserot@pdcounsel.com
Website: http://www.pdcounsel.com

Unique Value International Inc.
575 Madison Ave., 10th Fl.
New York, NY 10022-1304
(212)605-0590
Fax: (212)605-0589

The Van Tulleken Co.
126 E 56th St.
New York, NY 10022
(212)355-1390
Fax: (212)755-3061
E-mail: newyork@vantulleken.com

Vencon Management Inc.
301 W 53rd St.
New York, NY 10019
(212)581-8787
Fax: (212)397-4126
Website: http://www.venconinc.com

Werner International Inc.
55 E 52nd, 29th Fl.
New York, NY 10055
(212)909-1260
Fax: (212)909-1273
E-mail: richard.downing@rgh.com
Website: http://www.wernertex.com

Zimmerman Business Consulting Inc.
44 E 92nd St., Ste. 5-B
New York, NY 10128
(212)860-3107
Fax: (212)860-7730

E-mail: ljzzbci@aol.com
Website: http://www.zbcinc.com

Overton Financial
7 Allen Rd.
Peekskill, NY 10566
(914)737-4649
Fax: (914)737-4696

Stromberg Consulting
2500 Westchester Ave.
Purchase, NY 10577
(914)251-1515
Fax: (914)251-1562
E-mail: strategy@stromberg_consulting.
com
Website: http://www.stromberg_
consulting.com

Innovation Management Consulting Inc.
209 Dewitt Rd.
Syracuse, NY 13214-2006
(315)425-5144
Fax: (315)445-8989
E-mail: missonneb@axess.net

M. Clifford Agress
891 Fulton St.
Valley Stream, NY 11580
(516)825-8955
Fax: (516)825-8955

Destiny Kinal Marketing Consultancy
105 Chemung St.
Waverly, NY 14892
(607)565-8317
Fax: (607)565-4083

Valutis Consulting Inc.
5350 Main St., Ste. 7
Williamsville, NY 14221-5338
(716)634-2553
Fax: (716)634-2554
E-mail: valutis@localnet.com
Website: http://www.valutisconsulting.com

North Carolina

Best Practices L.L.C.
6320 Quadrangle Dr., Ste. 200
Chapel Hill, NC 27514
(919)403-0251
Fax: (919)403-0144
E-mail: best@best:in/class
Website: http://www.best-in-class.com

Norelli & Co.
Bank of America Corporate Ctr.
100 N Tyron St., Ste. 5160
Charlotte, NC 28202-4000
(704)376-5484

Fax: (704)376-5485
E-mail: consult@norelli.com
Website: http://www.norelli.com

North Dakota

Center for Innovation
4300 Dartmouth Dr.
PO Box 8372
Grand Forks, ND 58202
(701)777-3132
Fax: (701)777-2339
E-mail: bruce@innovators.net
Website: http://www.innovators.net

Ohio

Transportation Technology Services
208 Harmon Rd.
Aurora, OH 44202
(330)562-3596

Empro Systems Inc.
4777 Red Bank Expy., Ste. 1
Cincinnati, OH 45227-1542
(513)271-2042
Fax: (513)271-2042

Alliance Management International Ltd.
1440 Windrow Ln.
Cleveland, OH 44147-3200
(440)838-1922
Fax: (440)838-0979
E-mail: bgruss@amiltd.com
Website: http://www.amiltd.com

Bozell Kamstra Public Relations
1301 E 9th St., Ste. 3400
Cleveland, OH 44114
(216)623-1511
Fax: (216)623-1501
E-mail: jfeniger@cleveland.
bozellkamstra.com
Website: http://www.bozellkamstra.com

Cory Dillon Associates
111 Schreyer Pl. E
Columbus, OH 43214
(614)262-8211
Fax: (614)262-3806

Holcomb Gallagher Adams
300 Marconi, Ste. 303
Columbus, OH 43215
(614)221-3343
Fax: (614)221-3367
E-mail: riadams@acme.freenet.oh.us

Young & Associates
PO Box 711
Kent, OH 44240

(330)678-0524
Free: 800-525-9775
Fax: (330)678-6219
E-mail: online@younginc.com
Website: http://www.younginc.com

Robert A. Westman & Associates
8981 Inversary Dr. SE
Warren, OH 44484-2551
(330)856-4149
Fax: (330)856-2564

Oklahoma

Innovative Partners L.L.C.
4900 Richmond Sq., Ste. 100
Oklahoma City, OK 73118
(405)840-0033
Fax: (405)843-8359
E-mail: ipartners@juno.com

Oregon

INTERCON - The International Converting Institute
5200 Badger Rd.
Crooked River Ranch, OR 97760
(541)548-1447
Fax: (541)548-1618
E-mail: johnbowler@crookedriverranch.com

Talbott ARM
HC 60, Box 5620
Lakeview, OR 97630
(541)635-8587
Fax: (503)947-3482

Management Technology Associates Ltd.
2768 SW Sherwood Dr, Ste. 105
Portland, OR 97201-2251
(503)224-5220
Fax: (503)224-5334
E-mail: lcuster@mta-ltd.com
Website: http://www.mgmt-tech.com

Pennsylvania

Healthscope Inc.
400 Lancaster Ave.
Devon, PA 19333
(610)687-6199
Fax: (610)687-6376
E-mail: health@voicenet.com
Website: http://www.healthscope.net/

Elayne Howard & Associates Inc.
3501 Masons Mill Rd., Ste. 501
Huntingdon Valley, PA 19006-3509
(215)657-9550

GRA Inc.
115 West Ave., Ste. 201
Jenkintown, PA 19046
(215)884-7500
Fax: (215)884-1385
E-mail: gramail@gra-inc.com
Website: http://www.gra-inc.com

Mifflin County Industrial Development Corp.
Mifflin County Industrial Plz.
6395 SR 103 N
Bldg. 50
Lewistown, PA 17044
(717)242-0393
Fax: (717)242-1842
E-mail: mcide@acsworld.net

Autech Products
1289 Revere Rd.
Morrisville, PA 19067
(215)493-3759
Fax: (215)493-9791
E-mail: autech4@yahoo.com

Advantage Associates
434 Avon Dr.
Pittsburgh, PA 15228
(412)343-1558
Fax: (412)362-1684
E-mail: ecocba1@aol.com

Regis J. Sheehan & Associates
Pittsburgh, PA 15220
(412)279-1207

James W. Davidson Company Inc.
23 Forest View Rd.
Wallingford, PA 19086
(610)566-1462

Puerto Rico

Diego Chevere & Co.
Metro Parque 7, Ste. 204
Metro Office
Caparra Heights, PR 00920
(787)774-9595
Fax: (787)774-9566
E-mail: dcco@coqui.net

Manuel L. Porrata and Associates
898 Munoz Rivera Ave., Ste. 201
San Juan, PR 00927
(787)765-2140
Fax: (787)754-3285
E-mail: m_porrata@manuelporrata.com
Website: http://manualporrata.com

South Carolina

Aquafood Business Associates
PO Box 13267
Charleston, SC 29422
(843)795-9506
Fax: (843)795-9477
E-mail: rraba@aol.com

Profit Associates Inc.
PO Box 38026
Charleston, SC 29414
(803)763-5718
Fax: (803)763-5719
E-mail: bobrog@awod.com
Website: http://www.awod.com/gallery/business/proasc

Strategic Innovations International
12 Executive Ct.
Lake Wylie, SC 29710
(803)831-1225
Fax: (803)831-1177
E-mail: stratinnov@aol.com
Website: http://www. strategicinnovations.com

Minus Stage
Box 4436
Rock Hill, SC 29731
(803)328-0705
Fax: (803)329-9948

Tennessee

Daniel Petchers & Associates
8820 Fernwood CV
Germantown, TN 38138
(901)755-9896

Business Choices
1114 Forest Harbor, Ste. 300
Hendersonville, TN 37075-9646
(615)822-8692
Free: 800-737-8382
Fax: (615)822-8692
E-mail: bz-ch@juno.com

RCFA Healthcare Management Services L.L.C.
9648 Kingston Pke., Ste. 8
Knoxville, TN 37922
(865)531-0176
Free: 800-635-4040
Fax: (865)531-0722
E-mail: info@rcfa.com
Website: http://www.rcfa.com

Growth Consultants of America
3917 Trimble Rd.
Nashville, TN 37215

(615)383-0550
Fax: (615)269-8940
E-mail: 70244.451@compuserve.com

Texas

Integrated Cost Management Systems Inc.
2261 Brookhollow Plz. Dr., Ste. 104
Arlington, TX 76006
(817)633-2873
Fax: (817)633-3781
E-mail: abm@icms.net
Website: http://www.icms.net

Lori Williams
1000 Leslie Ct.
Arlington, TX 76012
(817)459-3934
Fax: (817)459-3934

Business Resource Software Inc.
2013 Wells Branch Pky., Ste. 305
Austin, TX 78728
Free: 800-423-1228
Fax: (512)251-4401
E-mail: info@brs-inc.com
Website: http://www.brs-inc.com

Erisa Adminstrative Services Inc.
12325 Hymeadow Dr., Bldg. 4
Austin, TX 78750-1847
(512)250-9020
Fax: (512)250-9487
Website: http://www.cserisa.com

R. Miller Hicks & Co.
1011 W 11th St.
Austin, TX 78703
(512)477-7000
Fax: (512)477-9697
E-mail: millerhicks@rmhicks.com
Website: http://www.rmhicks.com

Pragmatic Tactics Inc.
3303 Westchester Ave.
College Station, TX 77845
(409)696-5294
Free: 800-570-5294
Fax: (409)696-4994
E-mail: ptactics@aol.com
Website: http://www.ptatics.com

Perot Systems
12404 Park Central Dr.
Dallas, TX 75251
(972)340-5000
Free: 800-688-4333
Fax: (972)455-4100
E-mail: corp.comm@ps.net
Website: http://www.perotsystems.com

ReGENERATION Partners
3838 Oak Lawn Ave.
Dallas, TX 75219
(214)559-3999
Free: 800-406-1112
E-mail: info@regeneration-partner.com
Website: http://www.regeneration-partners.com

High Technology Associates - Division of Global Technologies Inc.
1775 St. James Pl., Ste. 105
Houston, TX 77056
(713)963-9300
Fax: (713)963-8341
E-mail: hta@infohwy.com

MasterCOM
103 Thunder Rd.
Kerrville, TX 78028
(830)895-7990
Fax: (830)443-3428
E-mail: jmstubblefield@mastertraining.com
Website: http://www.mastertraining.com

PROTEC
4607 Linden Pl.
Pearland, TX 77584
(281)997-9872
Fax: (281)997-9895
E-mail: p.oman@ix.netcom.com

Alpha Quadrant Inc.
10618 Auldine
San Antonio, TX 78230
(210)344-3330
Fax: (210)344-8151
E-mail: mbussone@sbcglobal.net
Website:http://www.a-quadrant.com
Michele Bussone

Bastian Public Relations
614 San Dizier
San Antonio, TX 78232
(210)404-1839
E-mail: lisa@bastianpr.com
Website: http://www.bastianpr.com
Lisa Bastian CBC

Business Strategy Development Consultants
PO Box 690365
San Antonio, TX 78269
(210)696-8000
Free: 800-927-BSDC
Fax: (210)696-8000

Tom Welch, CPC
6900 San Pedro Ave., Ste. 147
San Antonio, TX 78216-6207

(210)737-7022
Fax: (210)737-7022
E-mail: bplan@iamerica.net
Website: http://www.moneywords.com

Utah

Business Management Resource
PO Box 521125
Salt Lake City, UT 84152-1125
(801)272-4668
Fax: (801)277-3290
E-mail: pingfong@worldnet.att.net

Virginia

Tindell Associates
209 Oxford Ave.
Alexandria, VA 22301
(703)683-0109
Fax: 703-783-0219
E-mail: scott@tindell.net
Website: http://www.tindell.net
Scott Lockett, President

Elliott B. Jaffa
2530-B S Walter Reed Dr.
Arlington, VA 22206
(703)931-0040
E-mail: thetrainingdoctor@excite.com
Website: http://www.tregistry.com/jaffa.htm

Koach Enterprises - USA
5529 N 18th St.
Arlington, VA 22205
(703)241-8361
Fax: (703)241-8623

Federal Market Development
5650 Chapel Run Ct.
Centreville, VA 20120-3601
(703)502-8930
Free: 800-821-5003
Fax: (703)502-8929

Huff, Stuart & Carlton
2107 Graves Mills Rd., Ste. C
Forest, VA 24551
(804)316-9356
Free: (888)316-9356
Fax: (804)316-9357
Website: http://www.wealthmgt.net

AMX International Inc.
1420 Spring Hill Rd. , Ste. 600
McLean, VA 22102-3006
(703)690-4100
Fax: (703)643-1279
E-mail: amxmail@amxi.com
Website: http://www.amxi.com

Charles Scott Pugh (Investor)
4101 Pittaway Dr.
Richmond, VA 23235-1022
(804)560-0979
Fax: (804)560-4670

John C. Randall and Associates Inc.
PO Box 15127
Richmond, VA 23227
(804)746-4450
Fax: (804)730-8933
E-mail: randalljcx@aol.com
Website: http://www.johncrandall.com

McLeod & Co.
410 1st St.
Roanoke, VA 24011
(540)342-6911
Fax: (540)344-6367
Website: http://www.mcleodco.com/

Salzinger & Company Inc.
8000 Towers Crescent Dr., Ste. 1350
Vienna, VA 22182
(703)442-5200
Fax: (703)442-5205
E-mail: info@salzinger.com
Website: http://www.salzinger.com

The Small Business Counselor
12423 Hedges Run Dr., Ste. 153
Woodbridge, VA 22192
(703)490-6755
Fax: (703)490-1356

Washington

Burlington Consultants
10900 NE 8th St., Ste. 900
Bellevue, WA 98004
(425)688-3060
Fax: (425)454-4383
E-mail: partners@burlington
consultants.com
Website: http://www.burlington
consultants.com

Perry L. Smith Consulting
800 Bellevue Way NE, Ste. 400
Bellevue, WA 98004-4208
(425)462-2072
Fax: (425)462-5638

St. Charles Consulting Group
1420 NW Gilman Blvd.
Issaquah, WA 98027
(425)557-8708
Fax: (425)557-8731
E-mail: info@stcharlesconsulting.com
Website: http://www.stcharles
consulting.com

Independent Automotive Training Services
PO Box 334
Kirkland, WA 98083
(425)822-5715
E-mail: ltunney@autosvccon.com
Website: http://www.autosvccon.com

Kahle Associate Inc.
6203 204th Dr. NE
Redmond, WA 98053
(425)836-8763
Fax: (425)868-3770
E-mail: randykahle@kahleassociates.com
Website: http://www.kahleassociates.com

Dan Collin
3419 Wallingord Ave N, No. 2
Seattle, WA 98103
(206)634-9469
E-mail: dc@dancollin.com
Website: http://members.home.net/
dcollin/

ECG Management Consultants Inc.
1111 3rd Ave., Ste. 2700
Seattle, WA 98101-3201
(206)689-2200
Fax: (206)689-2209
E-mail: ecg@ecgmc.com
Website: http://www.ecgmc.com

Northwest Trade Adjustment Assistance Center
900 4th Ave., Ste. 2430
Seattle, WA 98164-1001
(206)622-2730
Free: 800-667-8087
Fax: (206)622-1105
E-mail: matchingfunds@nwtaac.org
Website: http://www.taacenters.org

Business Planning Consultants
S 3510 Ridgeview Dr.
Spokane, WA 99206
(509)928-0332
Fax: (509)921-0842
E-mail: bpci@nextdim.com

West Virginia

**Stanley & Associates Inc./
BusinessandMarketingPlans.com**
1687 Robert C. Byrd Dr.
Beckley, WV 25801
(304)252-0324
Free: 888-752-6720
Fax: (304)252-0470
E-mail: cclay@charterinternet.com

Website: http://www.Businessand
MarketingPlans.com
Christopher Clay

Wisconsin

White & Associates Inc.
5349 Somerset Ln. S
Greenfield, WI 53221
(414)281-7373
Fax: (414)281-7006
E-mail: wnaconsult@aol.com

Small business administration regional offices

This section contains a listing of Small Business Administration offices arranged numerically by region. Service areas are provided. Contact the appropriate office for a referral to the nearest field office, or visit the Small Business Administration online at www.sba.gov.

Region 1

U.S. Small Business Administration
Region I Office
10 Causeway St., Ste. 812
Boston, MA 02222-1093
Phone: (617)565-8415
Fax: (617)565-8420
Serves Connecticut, Maine, Massachusetts, New Hampshire, Rhode Island, and Vermont.

Region 2

U.S. Small Business Administration
Region II Office
26 Federal Plaza, Ste. 3108
New York, NY 10278
Phone: (212)264-1450
Fax: (212)264-0038
Serves New Jersey, New York, Puerto Rico, and the Virgin Islands.

Region 3

U.S. Small Business Administration
Region III Office
Robert N C Nix Sr. Federal Building
900 Market St., 5th Fl.
Philadelphia, PA 19107
(215)580-2807
Serves Delaware, the District of Columbia, Maryland, Pennsylvania, Virginia, and West Virginia.

Region 4

U.S. Small Business Administration
Region IV Office
233 Peachtree St. NE
Harris Tower 1800
Atlanta, GA 30303
Phone: (404)331-4999
Fax: (404)331-2354
Serves Alabama, Florida, Georgia, Kentucky, Mississippi, North Carolina, South Carolina, and Tennessee.

Region 5

U.S. Small Business Administration
Region V Office
500 W. Madison St.
Citicorp Center, Ste. 1240
Chicago, IL 60661-2511
Phone: (312)353-0357
Fax: (312)353-3426
Serves Illinois, Indiana, Michigan, Minnesota, Ohio, and Wisconsin.

Region 6

U.S. Small Business Administration
Region VI Office
4300 Amon Carter Blvd., Ste. 108
Fort Worth, TX 76155
Phone: (817)684-5581
Fax: (817)684-5588
Serves Arkansas, Louisiana, New Mexico, Oklahoma, and Texas.

Region 7

U.S. Small Business Administration
Region VII Office
323 W. 8th St., Ste. 307
Kansas City, MO 64105-1500
Phone: (816)374-6380
Fax: (816)374-6339
Serves Iowa, Kansas, Missouri, and Nebraska.

Region 8

U.S. Small Business Administration
Region VIII Office
721 19th St., Ste. 400
Denver, CO 80202
Phone: (303)844-0500
Fax: (303)844-0506
Serves Colorado, Montana, North Dakota, South Dakota, Utah, and Wyoming.

Region 9

U.S. Small Business Administration
Region IX Office
330 N Brand Blvd., Ste. 1270
Glendale, CA 91203-2304
Phone: (818)552-3434
Fax: (818)552-3440
Serves American Samoa, Arizona, California, Guam, Hawaii, Nevada, and the Trust Territory of the Pacific Islands.

Region 10

U.S. Small Business Administration
Region X Office
2401 Fourth Ave., Ste. 400
Seattle, WA 98121
Phone: (206)553-5676
Fax: (206)553-4155
Serves Alaska, Idaho, Oregon, and Washington.

Small business development centers

This section contains a listing of all Small Business Development Centers, organized alphabetically by state/U.S. territory, then by city, then by agency name.

Alabama

Alabama SBDC
UNIVERSITY OF ALABAMA
2800 Milan Court Suite 124
Birmingham, AL 35211-6908
Phone: 205-943-6750
Fax: 205-943-6752
E-Mail: wcampbell@provost.uab.edu
Website: http://www.asbdc.org
Mr. William Campbell Jr, State Director

Alaska

Alaska SBDC
UNIVERSITY OF ALASKA - ANCHORAGE
430 West Seventh Avenue, Suite 110
Anchorage, AK 99501
Phone: 907-274 -7232
Fax: 907-274-9524
E-Mail: anerw@uaa.alaska.edu
Website: http://www.aksbdc.org
Ms. Jean R. Wall, State Director

American Samoa

American Samoa SBDC
AMERICAN SAMOA COMMUNITY COLLEGE
P.O. Box 2609
Pago Pago, American Samoa 96799
Phone: 011-684-699-4830
Fax: 011-684-699-6132
E-Mail: htalex@att.net
Mr. Herbert Thweatt, Director

Arizona

Arizona SBDC
MARICOPA COUNTY COMMUNITY COLLEGE
2411 West 14th Street, Suite 132
Tempe, AZ 85281
Phone: 480-731-8720
Fax: 480-731-8729
E-Mail: mike.york@domail.maricopa.edu
Website: http://www.dist.maricopa.edu.sbdc
Mr. Michael York, State Director

Arkansas

Arkansas SBDC
UNIVERSITY OF ARKANSAS
2801 South University Avenue
Little Rock, AR 72204
Phone: 501-324-9043
Fax: 501-324-9049
E-Mail: jmroderick@ualr.edu
Website: http://asbdc.ualr.edu
Ms. Janet M. Roderick, State Director

California

California - San Francisco SBDC
Northern California SBDC Lead Center
HUMBOLDT STATE UNIVERSITY
Office of Economic Development
1 Harpst Street 2006A, Siemens Hall
Arcata, CA, 95521
Phone: 707-826-3922
Fax: 707-826-3206
E-Mail: gainer@humboldt.edu
Ms. Margaret A. Gainer, Regional Director

California - Sacramento SBDC

CALIFORNIA STATE UNIVERSITY - CHICO

Chico, CA 95929-0765

Phone: 530-898-4598

Fax: 530-898-4734

E-Mail: dripke@csuchico.edu

Website: http://gsbdc.csuchico.edu

Mr. Dan Ripke, Interim Regional Director

California - San Diego SBDC

SOUTHWESTERN COMMUNITY COLLEGE DISTRICT

900 Otey Lakes Road

Chula Vista, CA 91910

Phone: 619-482-6388

Fax: 619-482-6402

E-Mail: dtrujillo@swc.cc.ca.us

Website: http://www.sbditc.org

Ms. Debbie P. Trujillo, Regional Director

California - Fresno SBDC

UC Merced Lead Center

UNIVERSITY OF CALIFORNIA - MERCED

550 East Shaw, Suite 105A

Fresno, CA 93710

Phone: 559-241-6590

Fax: 559-241-7422

E-Mail: crosander@ucmerced.edu

Website: http://sbdc.ucmerced.edu

Mr. Chris Rosander, State Director

California - Santa Ana SBDC

Tri-County Lead SBDC

CALIFORNIA STATE UNIVERSITY - FULLERTON

800 North State College Boulevard, LH640

Fullerton, CA 92834

Phone: 714-278-2719

Fax: 714-278-7858

E-Mail: vpham@fullerton.edu

Website: http://www.leadsbdc.org

Ms. Vi Pham, Lead Center Director

California - Los Angeles Region SBDC

LONG BEACH COMMUNITY COLLEGE DISTRICT

3950 Paramount Boulevard, Ste 101

Lakewood, CA 90712

Phone: 562-938-5004

Fax: 562-938-5030

E-Mail: ssloan@lbcc.edu

Ms. Sheneui Sloan, Interim Lead Center Director

Colorado

Colorado SBDC

OFFICE OF ECONOMIC DEVELOPMENT

1625 Broadway, Suite 170

Denver, CO 80202

Phone: 303-892-3864

Fax: 303-892-3848

E-Mail: Kelly.Manning@state.co.us

Website: http://www.state.co.us/oed/sbdc

Ms. Kelly Manning, State Director

Connecticut

Connecticut SBDC

UNIVERSITY OF CONNECTICUT

1376 Storrs Road, Unit 4094

Storrs, CT 06269-1094

Phone: 860-870-6370

Fax: 860-870-6374

E-Mail: richard.cheney@uconn.edu

Website: http://www.sbdc.uconn.edu

Mr. Richard Cheney, Interim State Director

Delaware

Delaware SBDC

DELAWARE TECHNOLOGY PARK

1 Innovation Way, Suite 301

Newark, DE 19711

Phone: 302-831-2747

Fax: 302-831-1423

E-Mail: Clinton.tymes@mvs.udel.edu

Website: http://www.delawaresbdc.org

Mr. Clinton Tymes, State Director

District of Columbia

District of Columbia SBDC

HOWARD UNIVERSITY

2600 6th Street, NW Room 128

Washington, DC 20059

Phone: 202-806-1550

Fax: 202-806-1777

E-Mail: hturner@howard.edu

Website: http://www.dcsbdc.com/

Mr. Henry Turner, Executive Director

Florida

Florida SBDC

UNIVERSITY OF WEST FLORIDA

401 East Chase Street, Suite 100

Pensacola, FL 32502

Phone: 850-473-7800

Fax: 850-473-7813

E-Mail: jcartwri@uwf.edu

Website: http://www.floridasbdc.com

Mr. Jerry Cartwright, State Director

Georgia

Georgia SBDC

UNIVERSITY OF GEORGIA

1180 East Broad Street

Athens, GA 30602

Phone: 706-542-6762

Fax: 706-542-6776

E-mail: aadams@sbdc.uga.edu

Website: http://www.sbdc.uga.edu

Mr. Allan Adams, Interim State Director

Guam

Guam Small Business Development Center

UNIVERSITY OF GUAM

Pacific Islands SBDC

P.O. Box 5014 - U.O.G. Station

Mangilao, GU 96923

Phone: 671-735-2590

Fax: 671-734-2002

E-mail: casey@pacificsbdc.com

Website: http://www.uog.edu/sbdc

Mr. Casey Jeszenka, Director

Hawaii

Hawaii SBDC

UNIVERSITY OF HAWAII - HILO

308 Kamehameha Avenue, Suite 201

Hilo, HI 96720

Phone: 808-974-7515

Fax: 808-974-7683

E-Mail: darrylm@interpac.net

Website: http://www.hawaii-sbdc.org

Mr. Darryl Mleynek, State Director

Idaho

Idaho SBDC

BOISE STATE UNIVERSITY

1910 University Drive

Boise, ID 83725

Phone: 208-426-3799

Fax: 208-426-3877

E-mail: jhogge@boisestate.edu

Website: http://www.idahosbdc.org

Mr. Jim Hogge, State Director

Illinois

Illinois SBDC

DEPARTMENT OF COMMERCE AND ECONOMIC OPPORTUNITY

620 E. Adams, S-4

Springfield, IL 62701

Phone: 217-524-5700

Fax: 217-524-0171

E-mail: mpatrilli@ildceo.net

Website: http://www.ilsbdc.biz
Mr. Mark Petrilli, State Director

Indiana

Indiana SBDC
INDIANA ECONOMIC DEVELOPMENT CORPORATION
One North Capitol, Suite 900
Indianapolis, IN 46204
Phone: 317-234-8872
Fax: 317-232-8874
E-mail: dtrocha@isbdc.org
Website: http://www.isbdc.org
Ms. Debbie Bishop Trocha, State Director

Iowa

Iowa SBDC
IOWA STATE UNIVERSITY
340 Gerdin Business Bldg.
Ames, IA 50011-1350
Phone: 515-294-2037
Fax: 515-294-6522
E-mail: jonryan@iastate.edu
Website: http://www.iabusnet.org
Mr. Jon Ryan, State Director

Kansas

Kansas SBDC
FORT HAYS STATE UNIVERSITY
214 SW Sixth Street, Suite 301
Topeka, KS 66603
Phone: 785-296-6514
Fax: 785-291-3261
E-mail: ksbdc.wkearns@fhsu.edu
Website: http://www.fhsu.edu/ksbdc
Mr. Wally Kearns, State Director

Kentucky

Kentucky SBDC
UNIVERSITY OF KENTUCKY
225 Gatton College of Business
Economics Building
Lexington, KY 40506-0034
Phone: 859-257-7668
Fax: 859-323-1907
E-mail: lrnaug0@pop.uky.edu
Website: http://www.ksbdc.org
Ms. Becky Naugle, State Director

Louisiana

Louisiana SBDC
UNIVERSITY OF LOUISIANA - MONROE
College of Business Administration
700 University Avenue
Monroe, LA 71209

Phone: 318-342-5506
Fax: 318-342-5510
E-mail: wilkerson@ulm.edu
Website: http://www.lsbdc.org
Ms. Mary Lynn Wilkerson, State Director

Maine

Maine SBDC
UNIVERSITY OF SOUTHERN MAINE
96 Falmouth Street P.O. Box 9300
Portland, ME 04103
Phone: 207-780-4420
Fax: 207-780-4810
E-mail: jrmassaua@maine.edu
Website: http://www.mainesbdc.org
Mr. John Massaua, State Director

Maryland

Maryland SBDC
UNIVERSITY OF MARYLAND
7100 Baltimore Avenue, Suite 401
College Park, MD 20742
Phone: 301-403-8300
Fax: 301-403-8303
E-mail: rsprow@mdsbdc.umd.edu
Website: http://www.mdsbdc.umd.edu
Ms. Renee Sprow, State Director

Massachusetts

Massachusetts SBDC
UNIVERSITY OF MASSACHUSETTS
School of Management, Room 205
Amherst, MA 01003-4935
Phone: 413-545-6301
Fax: 413-545-1273
E-mail: gep@msbdc.umass.edu
Website: http://msbdc.som.umass.edu
Ms. Georgianna Parkin, State Director

Michigan

Michigan SBTDC
GRAND VALLEY STATE UNIVERSITY
510 West Fulton Avenue
Grand Rapids, MI 49504
Phone: 616-331-7485
Fax: 616-331-7389
E-mail: lopuckic@gvsu.edu
Website: http://www.misbtdc.org
Ms. Carol Lopucki, State Director

Minnesota

Minnesota SBDC
MINNESOTA SMALL BUSINESS DEVELOPMENT CENTER
1st National Bank Building
332 Minnesota Street, Suite E200

St. Paul, MN 55101-1351
Phone: 651-297-5773
Fax: 651-296-5287
E-mail: michael.myhre@state.mn.us
Website: http://www.mnsbdc.com
Mr. Michael Myhre, State Director

Mississippi

Mississippi SBDC
UNIVERSITY OF MISSISSIPPI
B-19 Jeanette Phillips Drive
P.O. Box 1848
University, MS 38677
Phone: 662-915-5001
Fax: 662-915-5650
E-mail: wgurley@olemiss.edu
Website: http://www.olemiss.edu/depts/mssbdc
Mr. Doug Gurley, Jr., State Director

Missouri

Missouri SBDC
UNIVERSITY OF MISSOURI
1205 University Avenue, Suite 300
Columbia, MO 65211
Phone: 573-882-1348
Fax: 573-884-4297
E-mail: summersm@missouri.edu
Website: http://www.mo-sbdc.org/index.shtml
Mr. Max Summers, State Director

Montana

Montana SBDC
DEPARTMENT OF COMMERCE
301 South Park Avenue, Room 114 / P.O. Box 200505
Helena, MT 59620
Phone: 406-841-2746
Fax: 406-444-1872
E-mail: adesch@state.mt.us
Website: http://commerce.state.mt.us/brd/BRD_SBDC.html
Ms. Ann Desch, State Director

Nebraska

Nebraska SBDC
UNIVERSITY OF NEBRASKA - OMAHA
60th & Dodge Street, CBA Room 407
Omaha, NE 68182
Phone: 402-554-2521
Fax: 402-554-3473
E-mail: rbernier@unomaha.edu
Website: http://nbdc.unomaha.edu
Mr. Robert Bernier, State Director

Nevada

Nevada SBDC
UNIVERSITY OF NEVADA - RENO
Reno College of Business
Administration, Room 411
Reno, NV 89557-0100
Phone: 775-784-1717
Fax: 775-784-4337
E-mail: males@unr.edu
Website: http://www.nsbdc.org
Mr. Sam Males, State Director

New Hampshire

New Hampshire SBDC
UNIVERSITY OF NEW HAMPSHIRE
108 McConnell Hall
Durham, NH 03824-3593
Phone: 603-862-4879
Fax: 603-862-4876
E-mail: Mary.Collins@unh.edu
Website: http://www.nhsbdc.org
Ms. Mary Collins, State Director

New Jersey

New Jersey SBDC
RUTGERS UNIVERSITY
49 Bleeker Street
Newark, NJ 07102-1993
Phone: 973-353-5950
Fax: 973-353-1110
E-mail: bhopper@njsbdc.com
Website: http://www.njsbdc.com/home
Ms. Brenda Hopper, State Director

New Mexico

New Mexico SBDC
SANTA FE COMMUNITY COLLEGE
6401 Richards Avenue
Santa Fe, NM 87505
Phone: 505-428-1362
Fax: 505-471-9469
E-mail: rmiller@santa-fe.cc.nm.us
Website: http://www.nmsbdc.org
Mr. Roy Miller, State Director

New York

New York SBDC
STATE UNIVERSITY OF NEW YORK
SUNY Plaza, S-523
Albany, NY 12246
Phone: 518-443-5398
Fax: 518-443-5275
E-mail: j.king@nyssbdc.org
Website: http://www.nyssbdc.org
Mr. Jim King, State Director

North Carolina

North Carolina SBDTC
UNIVERSITY OF NORTH CAROLINA
5 West Hargett Street, Suite 600
Raleigh, NC 27601
Phone: 919-715-7272
Fax: 919-715-7777
E-mail: sdaugherty@sbtdc.org
Website: http://www.sbtdc.org
Mr. Scott Daugherty, State Director

North Dakota

North Dakota SBDC
UNIVERSITY OF NORTH DAKOTA
1600 E. Century Avenue, Suite 2
Bismarck, ND 58503
Phone: 701-328-5375
Fax: 701-328-5320
E-mail: christine.martin@und.
nodak.edu
Website: http://www.ndsbdc.org
Ms. Christine Martin-Goldman, State
Director

Ohio

Ohio SBDC
**OHIO DEPARTMENT OF
DEVELOPMENT**
77 South High Street
Columbus, OH 43216
Phone: 614-466-5102
Fax: 614-466-0829
E-mail: mabraham@odod.state.oh.us
Website: http://www.ohiosbdc.org
Ms. Michele Abraham, State Director

Oklahoma

Oklahoma SBDC
**SOUTHEAST OKLAHOMA STATE
UNIVERSITY**
517 University, Box 2584, Station A
Durant, OK 74701
Phone: 580-745-7577
Fax: 580-745-7471
E-mail: gpennington@sosu.edu
Website: http://www.osbdc.org
Mr. Grady Pennington, State Director

Oregon

Oregon SBDC
LANE COMMUNITY COLLEGE
99 West Tenth Avenue, Suite 390
Eugene, OR 97401-3021
Phone: 541-463-5250
Fax: 541-345-6006

E-mail: carterb@lanecc.edu
Website: http://www.bizcenter.org
Mr. William Carter, State Director

Pennsylvania

Pennsylvania SBDC
UNIVERSITY OF PENNSYLVANIA
The Wharton School
3733 Spruce Street
Philadelphia, PA 19104-6374
Phone: 215-898-1219
Fax: 215-573-2135
E-mail: ghiggins@wharton.upenn.edu
Website: http://pasbdc.org
Mr. Gregory Higgins, State Director

Puerto Rico

Puerto Rico SBDC
**INTER-AMERICAN UNIVERSITY OF
PUERTO RICO**
416 Ponce de Leon Avenue, Union Plaza,
Seventh Floor
Hato Rey, PR 00918
Phone: 787-763-6811
Fax: 787-763-4629
E-mail: cmarti@prsbdc.org
Website: http://www.prsbdc.org
Ms. Carmen Marti, Executive Director

Rhode Island

Rhode Island SBDC
BRYANT UNIVERSITY
1150 Douglas Pike
Smithfield, RI 02917
Phone: 401-232-6923
Fax: 401-232-6933
E-mail: adawson@bryant.edu
Website: http://www.risbdc.org
Ms. Diane Fournaris, Interim State
Director

South Carolina

South Carolina SBDC
**UNIVERSITY OF SOUTH
CAROLINA**
College of Business
Administration
1710 College Street
Columbia, SC 29208
Phone: 803-777-4907
Fax: 803-777-4403
E-mail: lenti@moore.sc.edu
Website: http://scsbdc.moore.sc.edu
Mr. John Lenti, State Director

South Dakota

South Dakota SBDC

UNIVERSITY OF SOUTH DAKOTA

414 East Clark Street, Patterson Hall
Vermillion, SD 57069
Phone: 605-677-6256
Fax: 605-677-5427
E-mail: jshemmin@usd.edu
Website: http://www.sdsbdc.org
Mr. John S. Hemmingstad, State
Director

Tennessee

Tennessee SBDC

TENNESSEE BOARD OF REGENTS

1415 Murfressboro Road, Suite 540
Nashville, TN 37217-2833
Phone: 615-898-2745
Fax: 615-893-7089
E-mail: pgeho@mail.tsbdc.org
Website: http://www.tsbdc.org
Mr. Patrick Geho, State Director

Texas

Texas-North SBDC

DALLAS COUNTY COMMUNITY COLLEGE

1402 Corinth Street
Dallas, TX 75215
Phone: 214-860-5835
Fax: 214-860-5813
E-mail: emk9402@dcccd.edu
Website: http://www.ntsbdc.org
Ms. Liz Klimback, Region Director

Texas-Houston SBDC

UNIVERSITY OF HOUSTON

2302 Fannin, Suite 200
Houston, TX 77002
Phone: 713-752-8425
Fax: 713-756-1500
E-mail: fyoung@uh.edu
Website: http://sbdcnetwork.uh.edu
Mr. Mike Young, Executive Director

Texas-NW SBDC

TEXAS TECH UNIVERSITY

2579 South Loop 289, Suite 114
Lubbock, TX 79423
Phone: 806-745-3973
Fax: 806-745-6207
E-mail: c.bean@nwtsbdc.org
Website: http://www.nwtsbdc.org
Mr. Craig Bean, Executive Director

Texas-South-West Texas Border Region SBDC

UNIVERSITY OF TEXAS - SAN ANTONIO

501 West Durango Boulevard
San Antonio, TX 78207-4415
Phone: 210-458-2742
Fax: 210-458-2464
E-mail: albert.salgado@utsa.edu
Website: http://www.iedtexas.org
Mr. Alberto Salgado, Region Director

Utah

Utah SBDC

SALT LAKE COMMUNITY COLLEGE

9750 South 300 West
Sandy, UT 84070
Phone: 801-957-3493
Fax: 801-957-3488
E-mail: Greg.Panichello@slcc.edu
Website:http://www.slcc.edu/sbdc
Mr. Greg Panichello, State Director

Vermont

Vermont SBDC

VERMONT TECHNICAL COLLEGE

PO Box 188, 1 Main Street
Randolph Center, VT 05061-0188
Phone: 802-728-9101
Fax: 802-728-3026
E-mail: lquillen@vtc.edu
Website: http://www.vtsbdc.org
Ms. Lenae Quillen-Blume, State Director

Virgin Islands

Virgin Islands SBDC
UNIVERSITY OF THE VIRGIN ISLANDS

8000 Nisky Center, Suite 720
St. Thomas, VI 00802-5804
Phone: 340-776-3206
Fax: 340-775-3756
E-mail: wbush@webmail.uvi.edu
Website: http://rps.uvi.edu/SBDC
Mr. Warren Bush, State Director

Virginia

Virginia SBDC
GEORGE MASON UNIVERSITY

4031 University Drive, Suite 200
Fairfax, VA 22030-3409
Phone: 703-277-7727
Fax: 703-352-8515
E-mail: jkeenan@gmu.edu
Website: http://www.virginiasbdc.org
Ms. Jody Keenan, Director

Washington

Washington SBDC

WASHINGTON STATE UNIVERSITY

534 E. Trent Avenue
P.O. Box 1495
Spokane, WA 99210-1495
Phone: 509-358-7765
Fax: 509-358-7764
E-mail: barogers@wsu.edu
Website: http://www.wsbdc.org
Mr. Brett Rogers, State Director

West Virginia

West Virginia SBDC

WEST VIRGINIA DEVELOPMENT OFFICE

Capital Complex, Building 6, Room 652
Charleston, WV 25301
Phone: 304-558-2960
Fax: 304-558-0127
E-mail: csalyer@wvsbdc.org
Website: http://www.wvsbdc.org
Mr. Conley Salyor, State Director

Wisconsin

Wisconsin SBDC

UNIVERSITY OF WISCONSIN

432 North Lake Street, Room 423
Madison, WI 53706
Phone: 608-263-7794
Fax: 608-263-7830
E-mail: erica.kauten@uwex.edu
Website: http://www.wisconsinsbdc.org
Ms. Erica Kauten, State Director

Wyoming

Wyoming SBDC

UNIVERSITY OF WYOMING

P.O. Box 3922
Laramie, WY 82071-3922
Phone: 307-766-3505
Fax: 307-766-3406
E-mail: DDW@uwyo.edu
Website: http://www.uwyo.edu/sbdc
Ms. Debbie Popp, Acting State Director

Service corps of retired executives (score) offices

This section contains a listing of all SCORE offices organized alphabetically by state/U.S. territory, then by city, then by agency name.

Alabama

SCORE Office (Northeast Alabama)
1330 Quintard Ave.
Anniston, AL 36202
(256)237-3536

SCORE Office (North Alabama)
901 South 15th St, Rm. 201
Birmingham, AL 35294-2060
(205)934-6868
Fax: (205)934-0538

SCORE Office (Baldwin County)
29750 Larry Dee Cawyer Dr.
Daphne, AL 36526
(334)928-5838

SCORE Office (Shoals)
612 S. COurt
Florence, AL 35630
(256)764-4661
Fax: (256)766-9017
E-mail: shoals@shoalschamber.com

SCORE Office (Mobile)
600 S Court St.
Mobile, AL 36104
(334)240-6868
Fax: (334)240-6869

SCORE Office (Alabama Capitol City)
600 S. Court St.
Montgomery, AL 36104
(334)240-6868
Fax: (334)240-6869

SCORE Office (East Alabama)
601 Ave. A
Opelika, AL 36801
(334)745-4861
E-mail: score636@hotmail.com
Website: http://www.angelfire.com/sc/
score636/

SCORE Office (Tuscaloosa)
2200 University Blvd.
Tuscaloosa, AL 35402
(205)758-7588

Alaska

SCORE Office (Anchorage)
510 L St., Ste. 310
Anchorage, AK 99501
(907)271-4022
Fax: (907)271-4545

Arizona

SCORE Office (Lake Havasu)
10 S. Acoma Blvd.
Lake Havasu City, AZ 86403

(520)453-5951
E-mail: SCORE@ctaz.com
Website: http://www.scorearizona.org/
lake_havasu/

SCORE Office (East Valley)
Federal Bldg., Rm. 104
26 N. MacDonald St.
Mesa, AZ 85201
(602)379-3100
Fax: (602)379-3143
E-mail: 402@aol.com
Website: http://www.scorearizona.org/
mesa/

SCORE Office (Phoenix)
2828 N. Central Ave., Ste. 800
Central & One Thomas
Phoenix, AZ 85004
(602)640-2329
Fax: (602)640-2360
E-mail: e-mail@SCORE-phoenix.org
Website: http://www.score-phoenix.org/

SCORE Office (Prescott Arizona)
1228 Willow Creek Rd., Ste. 2
Prescott, AZ 86301
(520)778-7438
Fax: (520)778-0812
E-mail: score@northlink.com
Website: http://www.scorearizona.org/
prescott/

SCORE Office (Tucson)
110 E. Pennington St.
Tucson, AZ 85702
(520)670-5008
Fax: (520)670-5011
E-mail: score@azstarnet.com
Website: http://www.scorearizona.org/
tucson/

SCORE Office (Yuma)
281 W. 24th St., Ste. 116
Yuma, AZ 85364
(520)314-0480
E-mail: score@C2i2.com
Website: http://www.scorearizona.org/
yuma

Arkansas

SCORE Office (South Central)
201 N. Jackson Ave.
El Dorado, AR 71730-5803
(870)863-6113
Fax: (870)863-6115

SCORE Office (Ozark)
Fayetteville, AR 72701
(501)442-7619

SCORE Office (Northwest Arkansas)
Glenn Haven Dr., No. 4
Ft. Smith, AR 72901
(501)783-3556

SCORE Office (Garland County)
Grand & Ouachita
PO Box 6012
Hot Springs Village, AR 71902
(501)321-1700

SCORE Office (Little Rock)
2120 Riverfront Dr., Rm. 100
Little Rock, AR 72202-1747
(501)324-5893
Fax: (501)324-5199

SCORE Office (Southeast Arkansas)
121 W. 6th
Pine Bluff, AR 71601
(870)535-7189
Fax: (870)535-1643

California

SCORE Office (Golden Empire)
1706 Chester Ave., No. 200
Bakersfield, CA 93301
(805)322-5881
Fax: (805)322-5663

SCORE Office (Greater Chico Area)
1324 Mangrove St., Ste. 114
Chico, CA 95926
(916)342-8932
Fax: (916)342-8932

SCORE Office (Concord)
2151-A Salvio St., Ste. B
Concord, CA 94520
(510)685-1181
Fax: (510)685-5623

SCORE Office (Covina)
935 W. Badillo St.
Covina, CA 91723
(818)967-4191
Fax: (818)966-9660

SCORE Office (Rancho Cucamonga)
8280 Utica, Ste. 160
Cucamonga, CA 91730
(909)987-1012
Fax: (909)987-5917

SCORE Office (Culver City)
PO Box 707
Culver City, CA 90232-0707
(310)287-3850
Fax: (310)287-1350

SCORE Office (Danville)
380 Diablo Rd., Ste. 103
Danville, CA 94526
(510)837-4400

SCORE Office (Downey)
11131 Brookshire Ave.
Downey, CA 90241
(310)923-2191
Fax: (310)864-0461

SCORE Office (El Cajon)
109 Rea Ave.
El Cajon, CA 92020
(619)444-1327
Fax: (619)440-6164

SCORE Office (El Centro)
1100 Main St.
El Centro, CA 92243
(619)352-3681
Fax: (619)352-3246

SCORE Office (Escondido)
720 N. Broadway
Escondido, CA 92025
(619)745-2125
Fax: (619)745-1183

SCORE Office (Fairfield)
1111 Webster St.
Fairfield, CA 94533
(707)425-4625
Fax: (707)425-0826

SCORE Office (Fontana)
17009 Valley Blvd., Ste. B
Fontana, CA 92335
(909)822-4433
Fax: (909)822-6238

SCORE Office (Foster City)
1125 E. Hillsdale Blvd.
Foster City, CA 94404
(415)573-7600
Fax: (415)573-5201

SCORE Office (Fremont)
2201 Walnut Ave., Ste. 110
Fremont, CA 94538
(510)795-2244
Fax: (510)795-2240

SCORE Office (Central California)
2719 N. Air Fresno Dr., Ste. 200
Fresno, CA 93727-1547
(559)487-5605
Fax: (559)487-5636

SCORE Office (Gardena)
1204 W. Gardena Blvd.
Gardena, CA 90247

(310)532-9905
Fax: (310)515-4893

SCORE Office (Lompoc)
330 N. Brand Blvd., Ste. 190
Glendale, CA 91203-2304
(818)552-3206
Fax: (818)552-3323

SCORE Office (Los Angeles)
330 N. Brand Blvd., Ste. 190
Glendale, CA 91203-2304
(818)552-3206
Fax: (818)552-3323

SCORE Office (Glendora)
131 E. Foothill Blvd.
Glendora, CA 91740
(818)963-4128
Fax: (818)914-4822

SCORE Office (Grover Beach)
177 S. 8th St.
Grover Beach, CA 93433
(805)489-9091
Fax: (805)489-9091

SCORE Office (Hawthorne)
12477 Hawthorne Blvd.
Hawthorne, CA 90250
(310)676-1163
Fax: (310)676-7661

SCORE Office (Hayward)
22300 Foothill Blvd., Ste. 303
Hayward, CA 94541
(510)537-2424

SCORE Office (Hemet)
1700 E. Florida Ave.
Hemet, CA 92544-4679
(909)652-4390
Fax: (909)929-8543

SCORE Office (Hesperia)
16367 Main St.
PO Box 403656
Hesperia, CA 92340
(619)244-2135

SCORE Office (Holloster)
321 San Felipe Rd., No. 11
Hollister, CA 95023

SCORE Office (Hollywood)
7018 Hollywood Blvd.
Hollywood, CA 90028
(213)469-8311
Fax: (213)469-2805

SCORE Office (Indio)
82503 Hwy. 111
PO Drawer TTT

Indio, CA 92202
(619)347-0676

SCORE Office (Inglewood)
330 Queen St.
Inglewood, CA 90301
(818)552-3206

SCORE Office (La Puente)
218 N. Grendanda St. D.
La Puente, CA 91744
(818)330-3216
Fax: (818)330-9524

SCORE Office (La Verne)
2078 Bonita Ave.
La Verne, CA 91750
(909)593-5265
Fax: (714)929-8475

SCORE Office (Lake Elsinore)
132 W. Graham Ave.
Lake Elsinore, CA 92530
(909)674-2577

SCORE Office (Lakeport)
PO Box 295
Lakeport, CA 95453
(707)263-5092

SCORE Office (Lakewood)
5445 E. Del Amo Blvd., Ste. 2
Lakewood, CA 90714
(213)920-7737

SCORE Office (Long Beach)
1 World Trade Center
Long Beach, CA 90831

SCORE Office (Los Alamitos)
901 W. Civic Center Dr., Ste. 160
Los Alamitos, CA 90720

SCORE Office (Los Altos)
321 University Ave.
Los Altos, CA 94022
(415)948-1455

SCORE Office (Manhattan Beach)
PO Box 3007
Manhattan Beach, CA 90266
(310)545-5313
Fax: (310)545-7203

SCORE Office (Merced)
1632 N. St.
Merced, CA 95340
(209)725-3800
Fax: (209)383-4959

SCORE Office (Milpitas)
75 S. Milpitas Blvd., Ste. 205
Milpitas, CA 95035

(408)262-2613
Fax: (408)262-2823

SCORE Office (Yosemite)
1012 11th St., Ste. 300
Modesto, CA 95354
(209)521-9333

SCORE Office (Montclair)
5220 Benito Ave.
Montclair, CA 91763

SCORE Office (Monterey Bay)
380 Alvarado St.
PO Box 1770
Monterey, CA 93940-1770
(408)649-1770

SCORE Office (Moreno Valley)
25480 Alessandro
Moreno Valley, CA 92553

SCORE Office (Morgan Hill)
25 W. 1st St.
PO Box 786
Morgan Hill, CA 95038
(408)779-9444
Fax: (408)778-1786

SCORE Office (Morro Bay)
880 Main St.
Morro Bay, CA 93442
(805)772-4467

SCORE Office (Mountain View)
580 Castro St.
Mountain View, CA 94041
(415)968-8378
Fax: (415)968-5668

SCORE Office (Napa)
1556 1st St.
Napa, CA 94559
(707)226-7455
Fax: (707)226-1171

SCORE Office (North Hollywood)
5019 Lankershim Blvd.
North Hollywood, CA 91601
(818)552-3206

SCORE Office (Northridge)
8801 Reseda Blvd.
Northridge, CA 91324
(818)349-5676

SCORE Office (Novato)
807 De Long Ave.
Novato, CA 94945
(415)897-1164
Fax: (415)898-9097

SCORE Office (East Bay)
519 17th St.
Oakland, CA 94612
(510)273-6611
Fax: (510)273-6015
E-mail: webmaster@eastbayscore.org
Website: http://www.eastbayscore.org

SCORE Office (Oceanside)
928 N. Coast Hwy.
Oceanside, CA 92054
(619)722-1534

SCORE Office (Ontario)
121 West B. St.
Ontario, CA 91762
Fax: (714)984-6439

SCORE Office (Oxnard)
PO Box 867
Oxnard, CA 93032
(805)385-8860
Fax: (805)487-1763

SCORE Office (Pacifica)
450 Dundee Way, Ste. 2
Pacifica, CA 94044
(415)355-4122

SCORE Office (Palm Desert)
72990 Hwy. 111
Palm Desert, CA 92260
(619)346-6111
Fax: (619)346-3463

SCORE Office (Palm Springs)
650 E. Tahquitz Canyon Way Ste. D
Palm Springs, CA 92262-6706
(760)320-6682
Fax: (760)323-9426

SCORE Office (Lakeside)
2150 Low Tree
Palmdale, CA 93551
(805)948-4518
Fax: (805)949-1212

SCORE Office (Palo Alto)
325 Forest Ave.
Palo Alto, CA 94301
(415)324-3121
Fax: (415)324-1215

SCORE Office (Pasadena)
117 E. Colorado Blvd., Ste. 100
Pasadena, CA 91105
(818)795-3355
Fax: (818)795-5663

SCORE Office (Paso Robles)
1225 Park St.
Paso Robles, CA 93446-2234

(805)238-0506
Fax: (805)238-0527

SCORE Office (Petaluma)
799 Baywood Dr., Ste. 3
Petaluma, CA 94954
(707)762-2785
Fax: (707)762-4721

SCORE Office (Pico Rivera)
9122 E. Washington Blvd.
Pico Rivera, CA 90660

SCORE Office (Pittsburg)
2700 E. Leland Rd.
Pittsburg, CA 94565
(510)439-2181
Fax: (510)427-1599

SCORE Office (Pleasanton)
777 Peters Ave.
Pleasanton, CA 94566
(510)846-9697

SCORE Office (Monterey Park)
485 N. Garey
Pomona, CA 91769

SCORE Office (Pomona)
485 N. Garey Ave.
Pomona, CA 91766
(909)622-1256

SCORE Office (Antelope Valley)
4511 West Ave. M-4
Quartz Hill, CA 93536
(805)272-0087
E-mail: avscore@ptw.com
Website: http://www.score.av.org/

SCORE Office (Shasta)
737 Auditorium Dr.
Redding, CA 96099
(916)225-2770

SCORE Office (Redwood City)
1675 Broadway
Redwood City, CA 94063
(415)364-1722
Fax: (415)364-1729

SCORE Office (Richmond)
3925 MacDonald Ave.
Richmond, CA 94805

SCORE Office (Ridgecrest)
PO Box 771
Ridgecrest, CA 93555
(619)375-8331
Fax: (619)375-0365

SCORE Office (Riverside)
3685 Main St., Ste. 350
Riverside, CA 92501
(909)683-7100

SCORE Office (Sacramento)
9845 Horn Rd., 260-B
Sacramento, CA 95827
(916)361-2322
Fax: (916)361-2164
E-mail: sacchapter@directcon.net

SCORE Office (Salinas)
PO Box 1170
Salinas, CA 93902
(408)424-7611
Fax: (408)424-8639

SCORE Office (Inland Empire)
777 E. Rialto Ave.
Purchasing
San Bernardino, CA 92415-0760
(909)386-8278

SCORE Office (San Carlos)
San Carlos Chamber of Commerce
PO Box 1086
San Carlos, CA 94070
(415)593-1068
Fax: (415)593-9108

SCORE Office (Encinitas)
550 W. C St., Ste. 550
San Diego, CA 92101-3540
(619)557-7272
Fax: (619)557-5894

SCORE Office (San Diego)
550 West C. St., Ste. 550
San Diego, CA 92101-3540
(619)557-7272
Fax: (619)557-5894
Website: http://www.score-sandiego.org

SCORE Office (Menlo Park)
1100 Merrill St.
San Francisco, CA 94105
(415)325-2818
Fax: (415)325-0920

SCORE Office (San Francisco)
455 Market St., 6th Fl.
San Francisco, CA 94105
(415)744-6827
Fax: (415)744-6750
E-mail: sfscore@sfscore.
Website: http://www.sfscore.com

SCORE Office (San Gabriel)
401 W. Las Tunas Dr.
San Gabriel, CA 91776

(818)576-2525
Fax: (818)289-2901

SCORE Office (San Jose)
Deanza College
208 S. 1st. St., Ste. 137
San Jose, CA 95113
(408)288-8479
Fax: (408)535-5541

SCORE Office (Silicon Valley)
84 W. Santa Clara St., Ste. 100
San Jose, CA 95113
(408)288-8479
Fax: (408)535-5541
E-mail: info@svscore.org
Website: http://www.svscore.org

SCORE Office (San Luis Obispo)
3566 S. Hiquera, No. 104
San Luis Obispo, CA 93401
(805)547-0779

SCORE Office (San Mateo)
1021 S. El Camino, 2nd Fl.
San Mateo, CA 94402
(415)341-5679

SCORE Office (San Pedro)
390 W. 7th St.
San Pedro, CA 90731
(310)832-7272

SCORE Office (Orange County)
200 W. Santa Anna Blvd., Ste. 700
Santa Ana, CA 92701
(714)550-7369
Fax: (714)550-0191
Website: http://www.score114.org

SCORE Office (Santa Barbara)
3227 State St.
Santa Barbara, CA 93130
(805)563-0084

SCORE Office (Central Coast)
509 W. Morrison Ave.
Santa Maria, CA 93454
(805)347-7755

SCORE Office (Santa Maria)
614 S. Broadway
Santa Maria, CA 93454-5111
(805)925-2403
Fax: (805)928-7559

SCORE Office (Santa Monica)
501 Colorado, Ste. 150
Santa Monica, CA 90401
(310)393-9825
Fax: (310)394-1868

SCORE Office (Santa Rosa)
777 Sonoma Ave., Rm. 115E
Santa Rosa, CA 95404
(707)571-8342
Fax: (707)541-0331
Website: http://www.pressdemo.com/
community/score/score.html

SCORE Office (Scotts Valley)
4 Camp Evers Ln.
Scotts Valley, CA 95066
(408)438-1010
Fax: (408)438-6544

SCORE Office (Simi Valley)
40 W. Cochran St., Ste. 100
Simi Valley, CA 93065
(805)526-3900
Fax: (805)526-6234

SCORE Office (Sonoma)
453 1st St. E
Sonoma, CA 95476
(707)996-1033

SCORE Office (Los Banos)
222 S. Shepard St.
Sonora, CA 95370
(209)532-4212

SCORE Office (Tuolumne County)
39 North Washington St.
Sonora, CA 95370
(209)588-0128
E-mail: score@mlode.com

SCORE Office (South San Francisco)
445 Market St., Ste. 6th Fl.
South San Francisco, CA 94105
(415)744-6827
Fax: (415)744-6812

SCORE Office (Stockton)
401 N. San Joaquin St., Rm. 215
Stockton, CA 95202
(209)946-6293

SCORE Office (Taft)
314 4th St.
Taft, CA 93268
(805)765-2165
Fax: (805)765-6639

SCORE Office (Conejo Valley)
625 W. Hillcrest Dr.
Thousand Oaks, CA 91360
(805)499-1993
Fax: (805)498-7264

SCORE Office (Torrance)
3400 Torrance Blvd., Ste. 100
Torrance, CA 90503

(310)540-5858
Fax: (310)540-7662

SCORE Office (Truckee)
PO Box 2757
Truckee, CA 96160
(916)587-2757
Fax: (916)587-2439

SCORE Office (Visalia)
113 S. M St,
Tulare, CA 93274
(209)627-0766
Fax: (209)627-8149

SCORE Office (Upland)
433 N. 2nd Ave.
Upland, CA 91786
(909)931-4108

SCORE Office (Vallejo)
2 Florida St.
Vallejo, CA 94590
(707)644-5551
Fax: (707)644-5590

SCORE Office (Van Nuys)
14540 Victory Blvd.
Van Nuys, CA 91411
(818)989-0300
Fax: (818)989-3836

SCORE Office (Ventura)
5700 Ralston St., Ste. 310
Ventura, CA 93001
(805)658-2688
Fax: (805)658-2252
E-mail: scoreven@jps.net
Website: http://www.jps.net/scoreven

SCORE Office (Vista)
201 E. Washington St.
Vista, CA 92084
(619)726-1122
Fax: (619)226-8654

SCORE Office (Watsonville)
PO Box 1748
Watsonville, CA 95077
(408)724-3849
Fax: (408)728-5300

SCORE Office (West Covina)
811 S. Sunset Ave.
West Covina, CA 91790
(818)338-8496
Fax: (818)960-0511

SCORE Office (Westlake)
30893 Thousand Oaks Blvd.
Westlake Village, CA 91362
(805)496-5630
Fax: (818)991-1754

Colorado

SCORE Office (Colorado Springs)
2 N. Cascade Ave., Ste. 110
Colorado Springs, CO 80903
(719)636-3074
Website: http://www.cscc.org/score02/index.html

SCORE Office (Denver)
US Custom's House, 4th Fl.
721 19th St.
Denver, CO 80201-0660
(303)844-3985
Fax: (303)844-6490
E-mail: score62@csn.net
Website: http://www.sni.net/score62

SCORE Office (Tri-River)
1102 Grand Ave.
Glenwood Springs, CO 81601
(970)945-6589

SCORE Office (Grand Junction)
2591 B & 3/4 Rd.
Grand Junction, CO 81503
(970)243-5242

SCORE Office (Gunnison)
608 N. 11th
Gunnison, CO 81230
(303)641-4422

SCORE Office (Montrose)
1214 Peppertree Dr.
Montrose, CO 81401
(970)249-6080

SCORE Office (Pagosa Springs)
PO Box 4381
Pagosa Springs, CO 81157
(970)731-4890

SCORE Office (Rifle)
0854 W. Battlement Pky., Apt. C106
Parachute, CO 81635
(970)285-9390

SCORE Office (Pueblo)
302 N. Santa Fe
Pueblo, CO 81003
(719)542-1704
Fax: (719)542-1624
E-mail: mackey@iex.net
Website: http://www.pueblo.org/score

SCORE Office (Ridgway)
143 Poplar Pl.
Ridgway, CO 81432

SCORE Office (Silverton)
PO Box 480
Silverton, CO 81433
(303)387-5430

SCORE Office (Minturn)
PO Box 2066
Vail, CO 81658
(970)476-1224

Connecticut

SCORE Office (Greater Bridgeport)
230 Park Ave.
Bridgeport, CT 06601-0999
(203)576-4369
Fax: (203)576-4388

SCORE Office (Bristol)
10 Main St. 1st. Fl.
Bristol, CT 06010
(203)584-4718
Fax: (203)584-4722

SCORE office (Greater Danbury)
246 Federal Rd.
Unit LL2, Ste. 7
Brookfield, CT 06804
(203)775-1151

SCORE Office (Greater Danbury)
246 Federal Rd., Unit LL2, Ste. 7
Brookfield, CT 06804
(203)775-1151

SCORE Office (Eastern Connecticut)
Administration Bldg., Rm. 313
PO 625
61 Main St. (Chapter 579)
Groton, CT 06475
(203)388-9508

SCORE Office (Greater Hartford County)
330 Main St.
Hartford, CT 06106
(860)548-1749
Fax: (860)240-4659
Website: http://www.score56.org

SCORE Office (Manchester)
20 Hartford Rd.
Manchester, CT 06040
(203)646-2223
Fax: (203)646-5871

SCORE Office (New Britain)
185 Main St., Ste. 431
New Britain, CT 06051
(203)827-4492
Fax: (203)827-4480

SCORE Office (New Haven)
25 Science Pk., Bldg. 25, Rm. 366
New Haven, CT 06511
(203)865-7645

SCORE Office (Fairfield County)
24 Beldon Ave., 5th Fl.
Norwalk, CT 06850
(203)847-7348
Fax: (203)849-9308

SCORE Office (Old Saybrook)
146 Main St.
Old Saybrook, CT 06475
(860)388-9508

SCORE Office (Simsbury)
Box 244
Simsbury, CT 06070
(203)651-7307
Fax: (203)651-1933

SCORE Office (Torrington)
23 North Rd.
Torrington, CT 06791
(203)482-6586

Delaware

SCORE Office (Dover)
Treadway Towers
PO Box 576
Dover, DE 19903
(302)678-0892
Fax: (302)678-0189

SCORE Office (Lewes)
PO Box 1
Lewes, DE 19958
(302)645-8073
Fax: (302)645-8412

SCORE Office (Milford)
204 NE Front St.
Milford, DE 19963
(302)422-3301

SCORE Office (Wilmington)
824 Market St., Ste. 610
Wilmington, DE 19801
(302)573-6652
Fax: (302)573-6092
Website: http://www.scoredelaware.com

District of Columbia

SCORE Office (George Mason University)
409 3rd St. SW, 4th Fl.
Washington, DC 20024
800-634-0245

SCORE Office (Washington DC)
1110 Vermont Ave. NW, 9th Fl.
Washington, DC 20043
(202)606-4000

Fax: (202)606-4225
E-mail: dcscore@hotmail.com
Website: http://www.scoredc.org/

Florida

SCORE Office (Desota County Chamber of Commerce)
16 South Velucia Ave.
Arcadia, FL 34266
(941)494-4033

SCORE Office (Suncoast/Pinellas)
Airport Business Ctr.
4707 - 140th Ave. N, No. 311
Clearwater, FL 33755
(813)532-6800
Fax: (813)532-6800

SCORE Office (DeLand)
336 N. Woodland Blvd.
DeLand, FL 32720
(904)734-4331
Fax: (904)734-4333

SCORE Office (South Palm Beach)
1050 S. Federal Hwy., Ste. 132
Delray Beach, FL 33483
(561)278-7752
Fax: (561)278-0288

SCORE Office (Ft. Lauderdale)
Federal Bldg., Ste. 123
299 E. Broward Blvd.
Ft. Lauderdale, FL 33301
(954)356-7263
Fax: (954)356-7145

SCORE Office (Southwest Florida)
The Renaissance
8695 College Pky., Ste. 345 & 346
Ft. Myers, FL 33919
(941)489-2935
Fax: (941)489-1170

SCORE Office (Treasure Coast)
Professional Center, Ste. 2
3220 S. US, No. 1
Ft. Pierce, FL 34982
(561)489-0548

SCORE Office (Gainesville)
101 SE 2nd Pl., Ste. 104
Gainesville, FL 32601
(904)375-8278

SCORE Office (Hialeah Dade Chamber)
59 W. 5th St.
Hialeah, FL 33010
(305)887-1515
Fax: (305)887-2453

SCORE Office (Daytona Beach)
921 Nova Rd., Ste. A
Holly Hills, FL 32117
(904)255-6889
Fax: (904)255-0229
E-mail: score87@dbeach.com

SCORE Office (South Broward)
3475 Sheridian St., Ste. 203
Hollywood, FL 33021
(305)966-8415

SCORE Office (Citrus County)
5 Poplar Ct.
Homosassa, FL 34446
(352)382-1037

SCORE Office (Jacksonville)
7825 Baymeadows Way, Ste. 100-B
Jacksonville, FL 32256
(904)443-1911
Fax: (904)443-1980
E-mail: scorejax@juno.com
Website: http://www.scorejax.org/

SCORE Office (Jacksonville Satellite)
3 Independent Dr.
Jacksonville, FL 32256
(904)366-6600
Fax: (904)632-0617

SCORE Office (Central Florida)
5410 S. Florida Ave., No. 3
Lakeland, FL 33801
(941)687-5783
Fax: (941)687-6225

SCORE Office (Lakeland)
100 Lake Morton Dr.
Lakeland, FL 33801
(941)686-2168

SCORE Office (St. Petersburg)
800 W. Bay Dr., Ste. 505
Largo, FL 33712
(813)585-4571

SCORE Office (Leesburg)
9501 US Hwy. 441
Leesburg, FL 34788-8751
(352)365-3556
Fax: (352)365-3501

SCORE Office (Cocoa)
1600 Farno Rd., Unit 205
Melbourne, FL 32935
(407)254-2288

SCORE Office (Melbourne)
Melbourne Professional Complex
1600 Sarno, Ste. 205
Melbourne, FL 32935

(407)254-2288
Fax: (407)245-2288

SCORE Office (Merritt Island)
1600 Sarno Rd., Ste. 205
Melbourne, FL 32935
(407)254-2288
Fax: (407)254-2288

SCORE Office (Space Coast)
Melbourn Professional Complex
1600 Sarno, Ste. 205
Melbourne, FL 32935
(407)254-2288
Fax: (407)254-2288

SCORE Office (Dade)
49 NW 5th St.
Miami, FL 33128
(305)371-6889
Fax: (305)374-1882
E-mail: score@netrox.net
Website: http://www.netrox.net/~score/

SCORE Office (Naples of Collier)
International College
2654 Tamiami Trl. E
Naples, FL 34112
(941)417-1280
Fax: (941)417-1281
E-mail: score@naples.net
Website: http://www.naples.net/clubs/
score/index.htm

SCORE Office (Pasco County)
6014 US Hwy. 19, Ste. 302
New Port Richey, FL 34652
(813)842-4638

SCORE Office (Southeast Volusia)
115 Canal St.
New Smyrna Beach, FL 32168
(904)428-2449
Fax: (904)423-3512

SCORE Office (Ocala)
110 E. Silver Springs Blvd.
Ocala, FL 34470
(352)629-5959

Clay County SCORE Office
Clay County Chamber of Commerce
1734 Kingsdey Ave.
PO Box 1441
Orange Park, FL 32073
(904)264-2651
Fax: (904)269-0363

SCORE Office (Orlando)
80 N. Hughey Ave.
Rm. 445 Federal Bldg.

Orlando, FL 32801
(407)648-6476
Fax: (407)648-6425

SCORE Office (Emerald Coast)
19 W. Garden St., No. 325
Pensacola, FL 32501
(904)444-2060
Fax: (904)444-2070

SCORE Office (Charlotte County)
201 W. Marion Ave., Ste. 211
Punta Gorda, FL 33950
(941)575-1818
E-mail: score@gls3c.com
Website: http://www.charlotte-
florida.com/business/scorepg01.htm

SCORE Office (St. Augustine)
1 Riberia St.
St. Augustine, FL 32084
(904)829-5681
Fax: (904)829-6477

SCORE Office (Bradenton)
2801 Fruitville, Ste. 280
Sarasota, FL 34237
(813)955-1029

SCORE Office (Manasota)
2801 Fruitville Rd., Ste. 280
Sarasota, FL 34237
(941)955-1029
Fax: (941)955-5581
E-mail: score116@gte.net
Website: http://www.score-suncoast.org/

SCORE Office (Tallahassee)
200 W. Park Ave.
Tallahassee, FL 32302
(850)487-2665

SCORE Office (Hillsborough)
4732 Dale Mabry Hwy. N, Ste. 400
Tampa, FL 33614-6509
(813)870-0125

SCORE Office (Lake Sumter)
122 E. Main St.
Tavares, FL 32778-3810
(352)365-3556

SCORE Office (Titusville)
2000 S. Washington Ave.
Titusville, FL 32780
(407)267-3036
Fax: (407)264-0127

SCORE Office (Venice)
257 N. Tamiami Trl.
Venice, FL 34285
(941)488-2236
Fax: (941)484-5903

SCORE Office (Palm Beach)
500 Australian Ave. S, Ste. 100
West Palm Beach, FL 33401
(561)833-1672
Fax: (561)833-1712

SCORE Office (Wildwood)
103 N. Webster St.
Wildwood, FL 34785

Georgia

SCORE Office (Atlanta)
Harris Tower, Suite 1900
233 Peachtree Rd., NE
Atlanta, GA 30309
(404)347-2442
Fax: (404)347-1227

SCORE Office (Augusta)
3126 Oxford Rd.
Augusta, GA 30909
(706)869-9100

SCORE Office (Columbus)
School Bldg.
PO Box 40
Columbus, GA 31901
(706)327-3654

SCORE Office (Dalton-Whitfield)
305 S. Thorton Ave.
Dalton, GA 30720
(706)279-3383

SCORE Office (Gainesville)
PO Box 374
Gainesville, GA 30503
(770)532-6206
Fax: (770)535-8419

SCORE Office (Macon)
711 Grand Bldg.
Macon, GA 31201
(912)751-6160

SCORE Office (Brunswick)
4 Glen Ave.
St. Simons Island, GA 31520
(912)265-0620
Fax: (912)265-0629

SCORE Office (Savannah)
111 E. Liberty St., Ste. 103
Savannah, GA 31401
(912)652-4335
Fax: (912)652-4184
E-mail: info@scoresav.org
Website: http://www.coastalempire.com/
score/index.htm

Guam

SCORE Office (Guam)
Pacific News Bldg., Rm. 103
238 Archbishop Flores St.
Agana, GU 96910-5100
(671)472-7308

Hawaii

SCORE Office (Hawaii, Inc.)
1111 Bishop St., Ste. 204
PO Box 50207
Honolulu, HI 96813
(808)522-8132
Fax: (808)522-8135
E-mail: hnlscore@juno.com

SCORE Office (Kahului)
250 Alamaha, Unit N16A
Kahului, HI 96732
(808)871-7711

SCORE Office (Maui, Inc.)
590 E. Lipoa Pkwy., Ste. 227
Kihei, HI 96753
(808)875-2380

Idaho

SCORE Office (Treasure Valley)
1020 Main St., No. 290
Boise, ID 83702
(208)334-1696
Fax: (208)334-9353

SCORE Office (Eastern Idaho)
2300 N. Yellowstone, Ste. 119
Idaho Falls, ID 83401
(208)523-1022
Fax: (208)528-7127

Illinois

SCORE Office (Fox Valley)
40 W. Downer Pl.
PO Box 277
Aurora, IL 60506
(630)897-9214
Fax: (630)897-7002

SCORE Office (Greater Belvidere)
419 S. State St.
Belvidere, IL 61008
(815)544-4357
Fax: (815)547-7654

SCORE Office (Bensenville)
1050 Busse Hwy. Suite 100
Bensenville, IL 60106
(708)350-2944
Fax: (708)350-2979

SCORE Office (Central Illinois)
402 N. Hershey Rd.
Bloomington, IL 61704
(309)644-0549
Fax: (309)663-8270
E-mail: webmaster@central-
illinois-score.org
Website: http://www.central-
illinois-score.org/

SCORE Office (Southern Illinois)
150 E. Pleasant Hill Rd.
Box 1
Carbondale, IL 62901
(618)453-6654
Fax: (618)453-5040

SCORE Office (Chicago)
Northwest Atrium Ctr.
500 W. Madison St., No. 1250
Chicago, IL 60661
(312)353-7724
Fax: (312)886-5688
Website: http://www.mcs.net/~bic/

SCORE Office (Chicago–Oliver Harvey College)
Pullman Bldg.
1000 E. 11th St., 7th Fl.
Chicago, IL 60628
Fax: (312)468-8086

SCORE Office (Danville)
28 W. N. Street
Danville, IL 61832
(217)442-7232
Fax: (217)442-6228

SCORE Office (Decatur)
Milliken University
1184 W. Main St.
Decatur, IL 62522
(217)424-6297
Fax: (217)424-3993
E-mail: charding@mail.millikin.edu
Website: http://www.millikin.edu/
academics/Tabor/score.html

SCORE Office (Downers Grove)
925 Curtis
Downers Grove, IL 60515
(708)968-4050
Fax: (708)968-8368

SCORE Office (Elgin)
24 E. Chicago, 3rd Fl.
PO Box 648
Elgin, IL 60120
(847)741-5660
Fax: (847)741-5677

SCORE Office (Freeport Area)
26 S. Galena Ave.
Freeport, IL 61032
(815)233-1350
Fax: (815)235-4038

SCORE Office (Galesburg)
292 E. Simmons St.
PO Box 749
Galesburg, IL 61401
(309)343-1194
Fax: (309)343-1195

SCORE Office (Glen Ellyn)
500 Pennsylvania
Glen Ellyn, IL 60137
(708)469-0907
Fax: (708)469-0426

SCORE Office (Greater Alton)
Alden Hall
5800 Godfrey Rd.
Godfrey, IL 62035-2466
(618)467-2280
Fax: (618)466-8289
Website: http://www.altonweb.com/
score/

SCORE Office (Grayslake)
19351 W. Washington St.
Grayslake, IL 60030
(708)223-3633
Fax: (708)223-9371

SCORE Office (Harrisburg)
303 S. Commercial
Harrisburg, IL 62946-1528
(618)252-8528
Fax: (618)252-0210

SCORE Office (Joliet)
100 N. Chicago
Joliet, IL 60432
(815)727-5371
Fax: (815)727-5374

SCORE Office (Kankakee)
101 S. Schuyler Ave.
Kankakee, IL 60901
(815)933-0376
Fax: (815)933-0380

SCORE Office (Macomb)
216 Seal Hall, Rm. 214
Macomb, IL 61455
(309)298-1128
Fax: (309)298-2520

SCORE Office (Matteson)
210 Lincoln Mall
Matteson, IL 60443

(708)709-3750
Fax: (708)503-9322

SCORE Office (Mattoon)
1701 Wabash Ave.
Mattoon, IL 61938
(217)235-5661
Fax: (217)234-6544

SCORE Office (Quad Cities)
622 19th St.
Moline, IL 61265
(309)797-0082
Fax: (309)757-5435
E-mail: score@qconline.com
Website: http://www.qconline.com/
business/score/

SCORE Office (Naperville)
131 W. Jefferson Ave.
Naperville, IL 60540
(708)355-4141
Fax: (708)355-8355

SCORE Office (Northbrook)
2002 Walters Ave.
Northbrook, IL 60062
(847)498-5555
Fax: (847)498-5510

SCORE Office (Palos Hills)
10900 S. 88th Ave.
Palos Hills, IL 60465
(847)974-5468
Fax: (847)974-0078

SCORE Office (Peoria)
124 SW Adams, Ste. 300
Peoria, IL 61602
(309)676-0755
Fax: (309)676-7534

SCORE Office (Prospect Heights)
1375 Wolf Rd.
Prospect Heights, IL 60070
(847)537-8660
Fax: (847)537-7138

SCORE Office (Quincy Tri-State)
300 Civic Center Plz., Ste. 245
Quincy, IL 62301
(217)222-8093
Fax: (217)222-3033

SCORE Office (River Grove)
2000 5th Ave.
River Grove, IL 60171
(708)456-0300
Fax: (708)583-3121

SCORE Office (Northern Illinois)
515 N. Court St.
Rockford, IL 61103

(815)962-0122
Fax: (815)962-0122

SCORE Office (St. Charles)
103 N. 1st Ave.
St. Charles, IL 60174-1982
(847)584-8384
Fax: (847)584-6065

SCORE Office (Springfield)
511 W. Capitol Ave., Ste. 302
Springfield, IL 62704
(217)492-4416
Fax: (217)492-4867

SCORE Office (Sycamore)
112 Somunak St.
Sycamore, IL 60178
(815)895-3456
Fax: (815)895-0125

SCORE Office (University)
Hwy. 50 & Stuenkel Rd. Ste. C3305
University Park, IL 60466
(708)534-5000
Fax: (708)534-8457

Indiana

SCORE Office (Anderson)
205 W. 11th St.
Anderson, IN 46015
(317)642-0264

SCORE Office (Bloomington)
Star Center
216 W. Allen
Bloomington, IN 47403
(812)335-7334
E-mail: wtfische@indiana.edu
Website: http://
www.brainfreezemedia.com/score527/

SCORE Office (South East Indiana)
500 Franklin St.
Box 29
Columbus, IN 47201
(812)379-4457

SCORE Office (Corydon)
310 N. Elm St.
Corydon, IN 47112
(812)738-2137
Fax: (812)738-6438

SCORE Office (Crown Point)
Old Courthouse Sq. Ste. 206
PO Box 43
Crown Point, IN 46307
(219)663-1800

SCORE Office (Elkhart)
418 S. Main St.
Elkhart, IN 46515
(219)293-1531
Fax: (219)294-1859

SCORE Office (Evansville)
1100 W. Lloyd Expy., Ste. 105
Evansville, IN 47708
(812)426-6144

SCORE Office (Fort Wayne)
1300 S. Harrison St.
Ft. Wayne, IN 46802
(219)422-2601
Fax: (219)422-2601

SCORE Office (Gary)
973 W. 6th Ave., Rm. 326
Gary, IN 46402
(219)882-3918

SCORE Office (Hammond)
7034 Indianapolis Blvd.
Hammond, IN 46324
(219)931-1000
Fax: (219)845-9548

SCORE Office (Indianapolis)
429 N. Pennsylvania St., Ste. 100
Indianapolis, IN 46204-1873
(317)226-7264
Fax: (317)226-7259
E-mail: inscore@indy.net
Website: http://www.score-
indianapolis.org/

SCORE Office (Jasper)
PO Box 307
Jasper, IN 47547-0307
(812)482-6866

SCORE Office (Kokomo/Howard Counties)
106 N. Washington St.
Kokomo, IN 46901
(765)457-5301
Fax: (765)452-4564

SCORE Office (Logansport)
300 E. Broadway, Ste. 103
Logansport, IN 46947
(219)753-6388

SCORE Office (Madison)
301 E. Main St.
Madison, IN 47250
(812)265-3135
Fax: (812)265-2923

SCORE Office (Marengo)
Rt. 1 Box 224D
Marengo, IN 47140
Fax: (812)365-2793

SCORE Office (Marion/Grant Counties)
215 S. Adams
Marion, IN 46952
(765)664-5107

SCORE Office (Merrillville)
255 W. 80th Pl.
Merrillville, IN 46410
(219)769-8180
Fax: (219)736-6223

SCORE Office (Michigan City)
200 E. Michigan Blvd.
Michigan City, IN 46360
(219)874-6221
Fax: (219)873-1204

SCORE Office (South Central Indiana)
4100 Charleston Rd.
New Albany, IN 47150-9538
(812)945-0066

SCORE Office (Rensselaer)
104 W. Washington
Rensselaer, IN 47978

SCORE Office (Salem)
210 N. Main St.
Salem, IN 47167
(812)883-4303
Fax: (812)883-1467

SCORE Office (South Bend)
300 N. Michigan St.
South Bend, IN 46601
(219)282-4350
E-mail: chair@southbend-score.org
Website: http://www.southbend-score.org/

SCORE Office (Valparaiso)
150 Lincolnway
Valparaiso, IN 46383
(219)462-1105
Fax: (219)469-5710

SCORE Office (Vincennes)
27 N. 3rd
PO Box 553
Vincennes, IN 47591
(812)882-6440
Fax: (812)882-6441

SCORE Office (Wabash)
PO Box 371
Wabash, IN 46992
(219)563-1168
Fax: (219)563-6920

Iowa

SCORE Office (Burlington)
Federal Bldg.
300 N. Main St.
Burlington, IA 52601
(319)752-2967

SCORE Office (Cedar Rapids)
2750 1st Ave. NE, Ste 350
Cedar Rapids, IA 52401-1806
(319)362-6405
Fax: (319)362-7861
E:mail: score@scorecr.org
Website: http://www.scorecr.org

SCORE Office (Illowa)
333 4th Ave. S
Clinton, IA 52732
(319)242-5702

SCORE Office (Council Bluffs)
7 N. 6th St.
Council Bluffs, IA 51502
(712)325-1000

SCORE Office (Northeast Iowa)
3404 285th St.
Cresco, IA 52136
(319)547-3377

SCORE Office (Des Moines)
Federal Bldg., Rm. 749
210 Walnut St.
Des Moines, IA 50309-2186
(515)284-4760

SCORE Office (Ft. Dodge)
Federal Bldg., Rm. 436
205 S. 8th St.
Ft. Dodge, IA 50501
(515)955-2622

SCORE Office (Independence)
110 1st. St. east
Independence, IA 50644
(319)334-7178
Fax: (319)334-7179

SCORE Office (Iowa City)
210 Federal Bldg.
PO Box 1853
Iowa City, IA 52240-1853
(319)338-1662

SCORE Office (Keokuk)
401 Main St.
Pierce Bldg., No. 1
Keokuk, IA 52632
(319)524-5055

SCORE Office (Central Iowa)
Fisher Community College
709 S. Center
Marshalltown, IA 50158
(515)753-6645

SCORE Office (River City)
15 West State St.
Mason City, IA 50401
(515)423-5724

SCORE Office (South Central)
SBDC, Indian Hills Community College
525 Grandview Ave.
Ottumwa, IA 52501
(515)683-5127
Fax: (515)683-5263

SCORE Office (Dubuque)
10250 Sundown Rd.
Peosta, IA 52068
(319)556-5110

SCORE Office (Southwest Iowa)
614 W. Sheridan
Shenandoah, IA 51601
(712)246-3260

SCORE Office (Sioux City)
Federal Bldg.
320 6th St.
Sioux City, IA 51101
(712)277-2324
Fax: (712)277-2325

SCORE Office (Iowa Lakes)
122 W. 5th St.
Spencer, IA 51301
(712)262-3059

SCORE Office (Vista)
119 W. 6th St.
Storm Lake, IA 50588
(712)732-3780

SCORE Office (Waterloo)
215 E. 4th
Waterloo, IA 50703
(319)233-8431

Kansas

SCORE Office (Southwest Kansas)
501 W. Spruce
Dodge City, KS 67801
(316)227-3119

SCORE Office (Emporia)
811 Homewood
Emporia, KS 66801
(316)342-1600

SCORE Office (Golden Belt)
1307 Williams
Great Bend, KS 67530
(316)792-2401

SCORE Office (Hays)
PO Box 400
Hays, KS 67601
(913)625-6595

SCORE Office (Hutchinson)
1 E. 9th St.
Hutchinson, KS 67501
(316)665-8468
Fax: (316)665-7619

SCORE Office (Southeast Kansas)
404 Westminster Pl.
PO Box 886
Independence, KS 67301
(316)331-4741

SCORE Office (McPherson)
306 N. Main
PO Box 616
McPherson, KS 67460
(316)241-3303

SCORE Office (Salina)
120 Ash St.
Salina, KS 67401
(785)243-4290
Fax: (785)243-1833

SCORE Office (Topeka)
1700 College
Topeka, KS 66621
(785)231-1010

SCORE Office (Wichita)
100 E. English, Ste. 510
Wichita, KS 67202
(316)269-6273
Fax: (316)269-6499

SCORE Office (Ark Valley)
205 E. 9th St.
Winfield, KS 67156
(316)221-1617

Kentucky

SCORE Office (Ashland)
PO Box 830
Ashland, KY 41105
(606)329-8011
Fax: (606)325-4607

SCORE Office (Bowling Green)
812 State St.
PO Box 51
Bowling Green, KY 42101

(502)781-3200
Fax: (502)843-0458

SCORE Office (Tri-Lakes)
508 Barbee Way
Danville, KY 40422-1548
(606)231-9902

SCORE Office (Glasgow)
301 W. Main St.
Glasgow, KY 42141
(502)651-3161
Fax: (502)651-3122

SCORE Office (Hazard)
B & I Technical Center
100 Airport Gardens Rd.
Hazard, KY 41701
(606)439-5856
Fax: (606)439-1808

SCORE Office (Lexington)
410 W. Vine St., Ste. 290, Civic C
Lexington, KY 40507
(606)231-9902
Fax: (606)253-3190
E-mail: scorelex@uky.campus.mci.net

SCORE Office (Louisville)
188 Federal Office Bldg.
600 Dr. Martin L. King Jr. Pl.
Louisville, KY 40202
(502)582-5976

SCORE Office (Madisonville)
257 N. Main
Madisonville, KY 42431
(502)825-1399
Fax: (502)825-1396

SCORE Office (Paducah)
Federal Office Bldg.
501 Broadway, Rm. B-36
Paducah, KY 42001
(502)442-5685

Louisiana

SCORE Office (Central Louisiana)
802 3rd St.
Alexandria, LA 71309
(318)442-6671

SCORE Office (Baton Rouge)
564 Laurel St.
PO Box 3217
Baton Rouge, LA 70801
(504)381-7130
Fax: (504)336-4306

SCORE Office (North Shore)
2 W. Thomas
Hammond, LA 70401

(504)345-4457
Fax: (504)345-4749

SCORE Office (Lafayette)
804 St. Mary Blvd.
Lafayette, LA 70505-1307
(318)233-2705
Fax: (318)234-8671
E-mail: score302@aol.com

SCORE Office (Lake Charles)
120 W. Pujo St.
Lake Charles, LA 70601
(318)433-3632

SCORE Office (New Orleans)
365 Canal St., Ste. 3100
New Orleans, LA 70130
(504)589-2356
Fax: (504)589-2339

SCORE Office (Shreveport)
400 Edwards St.
Shreveport, LA 71101
(318)677-2536
Fax: (318)677-2541

Maine

SCORE Office (Augusta)
40 Western Ave.
Augusta, ME 04330
(207)622-8509

SCORE Office (Bangor)
Peabody Hall, Rm. 229
One College Cir.
Bangor, ME 04401
(207)941-9707

SCORE Office (Central & Northern Arroostock)
111 High St.
Caribou, ME 04736
(207)492-8010
Fax: (207)492-8010

SCORE Office (Penquis)
South St.
Dover Foxcroft, ME 04426
(207)564-7021

SCORE Office (Maine Coastal)
Mill Mall
Box 1105
Ellsworth, ME 04605-1105
(207)667-5800
E-mail: score@arcadia.net

SCORE Office (Lewiston-Auburn)
BIC of Maine-Bates Mill Complex
35 Canal St.

Lewiston, ME 04240-7764
(207)782-3708
Fax: (207)783-7745

SCORE Office (Portland)
66 Pearl St., Rm. 210
Portland, ME 04101
(207)772-1147
Fax: (207)772-5581
E-mail: Score53@score.maine.org
Website: http://www.score.maine.org/
chapter53/

SCORE Office (Western Mountains)
255 River St.
PO Box 252
Rumford, ME 04257-0252
(207)369-9976

SCORE Office (Oxford Hills)
166 Main St.
South Paris, ME 04281
(207)743-0499

Maryland

SCORE Office (Southern Maryland)
2525 Riva Rd., Ste. 110
Annapolis, MD 21401
(410)266-9553
Fax: (410)573-0981
E-mail: score390@aol.com
Website: http://members.aol.com/
score390/index.htm

SCORE Office (Baltimore)
The City Crescent Bldg., 6th Fl.
10 S. Howard St.
Baltimore, MD 21201
(410)962-2233
Fax: (410)962-1805

SCORE Office (Bel Air)
108 S. Bond St.
Bel Air, MD 21014
(410)838-2020
Fax: (410)893-4715

SCORE Office (Bethesda)
7910 Woodmont Ave., Ste. 1204
Bethesda, MD 20814
(301)652-4900
Fax: (301)657-1973

SCORE Office (Bowie)
6670 Race Track Rd.
Bowie, MD 20715
(301)262-0920
Fax: (301)262-0921

SCORE Office (Dorchester County)
203 Sunburst Hwy.
Cambridge, MD 21613
(410)228-3575

SCORE Office (Upper Shore)
210 Marlboro Ave.
Easton, MD 21601
(410)822-4606
Fax: (410)822-7922

SCORE Office (Frederick County)
43A S. Market St.
Frederick, MD 21701
(301)662-8723
Fax: (301)846-4427

SCORE Office (Gaithersburg)
9 Park Ave.
Gaithersburg, MD 20877
(301)840-1400
Fax: (301)963-3918

SCORE Office (Glen Burnie)
103 Crain Hwy. SE
Glen Burnie, MD 21061
(410)766-8282
Fax: (410)766-9722

SCORE Office (Hagerstown)
111 W. Washington St.
Hagerstown, MD 21740
(301)739-2015
Fax: (301)739-1278

SCORE Office (Laurel)
7901 Sandy Spring Rd. Ste. 501
Laurel, MD 20707
(301)725-4000
Fax: (301)725-0776

SCORE Office (Salisbury)
300 E. Main St.
Salisbury, MD 21801
(410)749-0185
Fax: (410)860-9925

Massachusetts

SCORE Office (NE Massachusetts)
100 Cummings Ctr., Ste. 101 K
Beverly, MA 01923
(978)922-9441
Website: http://www1.shore.net/~score/

SCORE Office (Boston)
10 Causeway St., Rm. 265
Boston, MA 02222-1093
(617)565-5591
Fax: (617)565-5598

E-mail: boston-score-
20@worldnet.att.net
Website: http://www.scoreboston.org/

SCORE office (Bristol/Plymouth County)
53 N. 6th St., Federal Bldg.
Bristol, MA 02740
(508)994-5093

SCORE Office (SE Massachusetts)
60 School St.
Brockton, MA 02401
(508)587-2673
Fax: (508)587-1340
Website: http://www.metrosouthchamber.
com/score.html

SCORE Office (North Adams)
820 N. State Rd.
Cheshire, MA 01225
(413)743-5100

SCORE Office (Clinton Satellite)
1 Green St.
Clinton, MA 01510
Fax: (508)368-7689

SCORE Office (Greenfield)
PO Box 898
Greenfield, MA 01302
(413)773-5463
Fax: (413)773-7008

SCORE Office (Haverhill)
87 Winter St.
Haverhill, MA 01830
(508)373-5663
Fax: (508)373-8060

SCORE Office (Hudson Satellite)
PO Box 578
Hudson, MA 01749
(508)568-0360
Fax: (508)568-0360

SCORE Office (Cape Cod)
Independence Pk., Ste. 5B
270 Communications Way
Hyannis, MA 02601
(508)775-4884
Fax: (508)790-2540

SCORE Office (Lawrence)
264 Essex St.
Lawrence, MA 01840
(508)686-0900
Fax: (508)794-9953

SCORE Office (Leominster Satellite)
110 Erdman Way
Leominster, MA 01453

(508)840-4300
Fax: (508)840-4896

SCORE Office (Bristol/Plymouth Counties)
53 N. 6th St., Federal Bldg.
New Bedford, MA 02740
(508)994-5093

SCORE Office (Newburyport)
29 State St.
Newburyport, MA 01950
(617)462-6680

SCORE Office (Pittsfield)
66 West St.
Pittsfield, MA 01201
(413)499-2485

SCORE Office (Haverhill-Salem)
32 Derby Sq.
Salem, MA 01970
(508)745-0330
Fax: (508)745-3855

SCORE Office (Springfield)
1350 Main St.
Federal Bldg.
Springfield, MA 01103
(413)785-0314

SCORE Office (Carver)
12 Taunton Green, Ste. 201
Taunton, MA 02780
(508)824-4068
Fax: (508)824-4069

SCORE Office (Worcester)
33 Waldo St.
Worcester, MA 01608
(508)753-2929
Fax: (508)754-8560

Michigan

SCORE Office (Allegan)
PO Box 338
Allegan, MI 49010
(616)673-2479

SCORE Office (Ann Arbor)
425 S. Main St., Ste. 103
Ann Arbor, MI 48104
(313)665-4433

SCORE Office (Battle Creek)
34 W. Jackson Ste. 4A
Battle Creek, MI 49017-3505
(616)962-4076
Fax: (616)962-6309

SCORE Office (Cadillac)
222 Lake St.
Cadillac, MI 49601
(616)775-9776
Fax: (616)768-4255

SCORE Office (Detroit)
477 Michigan Ave., Rm. 515
Detroit, MI 48226
(313)226-7947
Fax: (313)226-3448

SCORE Office (Flint)
708 Root Rd., Rm. 308
Flint, MI 48503
(810)233-6846

SCORE Office (Grand Rapids)
111 Pearl St. NW
Grand Rapids, MI 49503-2831
(616)771-0305
Fax: (616)771-0328
E-mail: scoreone@iserv.net
Website: http://www.iserv.net/
~scoreone/

SCORE Office (Holland)
480 State St.
Holland, MI 49423
(616)396-9472

SCORE Office (Jackson)
209 East Washington
PO Box 80
Jackson, MI 49204
(517)782-8221
Fax: (517)782-0061

SCORE Office (Kalamazoo)
345 W. Michigan Ave.
Kalamazoo, MI 49007
(616)381-5382
Fax: (616)384-0096
E-mail: score@nucleus.net

SCORE Office (Lansing)
117 E. Allegan
PO Box 14030
Lansing, MI 48901
(517)487-6340
Fax: (517)484-6910

SCORE Office (Livonia)
15401 Farmington Rd.
Livonia, MI 48154
(313)427-2122
Fax: (313)427-6055

SCORE Office (Madison Heights)
26345 John R
Madison Heights, MI 48071

(810)542-5010
Fax: (810)542-6821

SCORE Office (Monroe)
111 E. 1st
Monroe, MI 48161
(313)242-3366
Fax: (313)242-7253

SCORE Office (Mt. Clemens)
58 S/B Gratiot
Mt. Clemens, MI 48043
(810)463-1528
Fax: (810)463-6541

SCORE Office (Muskegon)
PO Box 1087
230 Terrace Plz.
Muskegon, MI 49443
(616)722-3751
Fax: (616)728-7251

SCORE Office (Petoskey)
401 E. Mitchell St.
Petoskey, MI 49770
(616)347-4150

SCORE Office (Pontiac)
Executive Office Bldg.
1200 N. Telegraph Rd.
Pontiac, MI 48341
(810)975-9555

SCORE Office (Pontiac)
PO Box 430025
Pontiac, MI 48343
(810)335-9600

SCORE Office (Port Huron)
920 Pinegrove Ave.
Port Huron, MI 48060
(810)985-7101

SCORE Office (Rochester)
71 Walnut Ste. 110
Rochester, MI 48307
(810)651-6700
Fax: (810)651-5270

SCORE Office (Saginaw)
901 S. Washington Ave.
Saginaw, MI 48601
(517)752-7161
Fax: (517)752-9055

SCORE Office (Upper Peninsula)
2581 I-75 Business Spur
Sault Ste. Marie, MI 49783
(906)632-3301

SCORE Office (Southfield)
21000 W. 10 Mile Rd.
Southfield, MI 48075

(810)204-3050
Fax: (810)204-3099

SCORE Office (Traverse City)
202 E. Grandview Pkwy.
PO Box 387
Traverse City, MI 49685
(616)947-5075
Fax: (616)946-2565

SCORE Office (Warren)
30500 Van Dyke, Ste. 118
Warren, MI 48093
(810)751-3939

Minnesota

SCORE Office (Aitkin)
Aitkin, MN 56431
(218)741-3906

SCORE Office (Albert Lea)
202 N. Broadway Ave.
Albert Lea, MN 56007
(507)373-7487

SCORE Office (Austin)
PO Box 864
Austin, MN 55912
(507)437-4561
Fax: (507)437-4869

SCORE Office (South Metro)
Ames Business Ctr.
2500 W. County Rd., No. 42
Burnsville, MN 55337
(612)898-5645
Fax: (612)435-6972
E-mail: southmetro@scoreminn.org
Website: http://www.scoreminn.org/
southmetro/

SCORE Office (Duluth)
1717 Minnesota Ave.
Duluth, MN 55802
(218)727-8286
Fax: (218)727-3113
E-mail: duluth@scoreminn.org
Website: http://www.scoreminn.org

SCORE Office (Fairmont)
PO Box 826
Fairmont, MN 56031
(507)235-5547
Fax: (507)235-8411

SCORE Office (Southwest Minnesota)
112 Riverfront St.
Box 999
Mankato, MN 56001
(507)345-4519

Fax: (507)345-4451
Website: http://www.scoreminn.org/

SCORE Office (Minneapolis)
North Plaza Bldg., Ste. 51
5217 Wayzata Blvd.
Minneapolis, MN 55416
(612)591-0539
Fax: (612)544-0436
Website: http://www.scoreminn.org/

SCORE Office (Owatonna)
PO Box 331
Owatonna, MN 55060
(507)451-7970
Fax: (507)451-7972

SCORE Office (Red Wing)
2000 W. Main St., Ste. 324
Red Wing, MN 55066
(612)388-4079

SCORE Office (Southeastern Minnesota)
220 S. Broadway, Ste. 100
Rochester, MN 55901
(507)288-1122
Fax: (507)282-8960
Website: http://www.scoreminn.org/

SCORE Office (Brainerd)
St. Cloud, MN 56301

SCORE Office (Central Area)
1527 Northway Dr.
St. Cloud, MN 56301
(320)240-1332
Fax: (320)255-9050
Website: http://www.scoreminn.org/

SCORE Office (St. Paul)
350 St. Peter St., No. 295
Lowry Professional Bldg.
St. Paul, MN 55102
(651)223-5010
Fax: (651)223-5048
Website: http://www.scoreminn.org/

SCORE Office (Winona)
Box 870
Winona, MN 55987
(507)452-2272
Fax: (507)454-8814

SCORE Office (Worthington)
1121 3rd Ave.
Worthington, MN 56187
(507)372-2919
Fax: (507)372-2827

Mississippi

SCORE Office (Delta)
915 Washington Ave.
PO Box 933
Greenville, MS 38701
(601)378-3141

SCORE Office (Gulfcoast)
1 Government Plaza
2909 13th St., Ste. 203
Gulfport, MS 39501
(228)863-0054

SCORE Office (Jackson)
1st Jackson Center, Ste. 400
101 W. Capitol St.
Jackson, MS 39201
(601)965-5533

SCORE Office (Meridian)
5220 16th Ave.
Meridian, MS 39305
(601)482-4412

Missouri

SCORE Office (Lake of the Ozark)
University Extension
113 Kansas St.
PO Box 1405
Camdenton, MO 65020
(573)346-2644
Fax: (573)346-2694
E-mail: score@cdoc.net
Website: http://sites.cdoc.net/score/

Chamber of Commerce (Cape Girardeau)
PO Box 98
Cape Girardeau, MO 63702-0098
(314)335-3312

SCORE Office (Mid-Missouri)
1705 Halstead Ct.
Columbia, MO 65203
(573)874-1132

SCORE Office (Ozark-Gateway)
1486 Glassy Rd.
Cuba, MO 65453-1640
(573)885-4954

SCORE Office (Kansas City)
323 W. 8th St., Ste. 104
Kansas City, MO 64105
(816)374-6675
Fax: (816)374-6692
E-mail: SCOREBIC@AOL.COM
Website: http://www.crn.org/score/

SCORE Office (Sedalia)
Lucas Place
323 W. 8th St., Ste.104
Kansas City, MO 64105
(816)374-6675

SCORE office (Tri-Lakes)
PO Box 1148
Kimberling, MO 65686
(417)739-3041

SCORE Office (Tri-Lakes)
HCRI Box 85
Lampe, MO 65681
(417)858-6798

SCORE Office (Mexico)
111 N. Washington St.
Mexico, MO 65265
(314)581-2765

SCORE Office (Southeast Missouri)
Rte. 1, Box 280
Neelyville, MO 63954
(573)989-3577

SCORE office (Poplar Bluff Area)
806 Emma St.
Poplar Bluff, MO 63901
(573)686-8892

SCORE Office (St. Joseph)
3003 Frederick Ave.
St. Joseph, MO 64506
(816)232-4461

SCORE Office (St. Louis)
815 Olive St., Rm. 242
St. Louis, MO 63101-1569
(314)539-6970
Fax: (314)539-3785
E-mail: info@stlscore.org
Website: http://www.stlscore.org/

SCORE Office (Lewis & Clark)
425 Spencer Rd.
St. Peters, MO 63376
(314)928-2900
Fax: (314)928-2900
E-mail: score01@mail.win.org

SCORE Office (Springfield)
620 S. Glenstone, Ste. 110
Springfield, MO 65802-3200
(417)864-7670
Fax: (417)864-4108

SCORE office (Southeast Kansas)
1206 W. First St.
Webb City, MO 64870
(417)673-3984

Montana

SCORE Office (Billings)
815 S. 27th St.
Billings, MT 59101
(406)245-4111

SCORE Office (Bozeman)
1205 E. Main St.
Bozeman, MT 59715
(406)586-5421

SCORE Office (Butte)
1000 George St.
Butte, MT 59701
(406)723-3177

SCORE Office (Great Falls)
710 First Ave. N
Great Falls, MT 59401
(406)761-4434
E-mail: scoregtf@in.tch.com

SCORE Office (Havre, Montana)
518 First St.
Havre, MT 59501
(406)265-4383

SCORE Office (Helena)
Federal Bldg.
301 S. Park
Helena, MT 59626-0054
(406)441-1081

SCORE Office (Kalispell)
2 Main St.
Kalispell, MT 59901
(406)756-5271
Fax: (406)752-6665

SCORE Office (Missoula)
723 Ronan
Missoula, MT 59806
(406)327-8806
E-mail: score@safeshop.com
Website: http://missoula.bigsky.net/
score/

Nebraska

SCORE Office (Columbus)
Columbus, NE 68601
(402)564-2769

SCORE Office (Fremont)
92 W. 5th St.
Fremont, NE 68025
(402)721-2641

SCORE Office (Hastings)
Hastings, NE 68901
(402)463-3447

SCORE Office (Lincoln)
8800 O St.
Lincoln, NE 68520
(402)437-2409

SCORE Office (Panhandle)
150549 CR 30
Minatare, NE 69356
(308)632-2133
Website: http://www.tandt.com/SCORE

SCORE Office (Norfolk)
3209 S. 48th Ave.
Norfolk, NE 68106
(402)564-2769

SCORE Office (North Platte)
3301 W. 2nd St.
North Platte, NE 69101
(308)532-4466

SCORE Office (Omaha)
11145 Mill Valley Rd.
Omaha, NE 68154
(402)221-3606
Fax: (402)221-3680
E-mail: infoctr@ne.uswest.net
Website: http://www.tandt.com/score/

Nevada

SCORE Office (Incline Village)
969 Tahoe Blvd.
Incline Village, NV 89451
(702)831-7327
Fax: (702)832-1605

SCORE Office (Carson City)
301 E. Stewart
PO Box 7527
Las Vegas, NV 89125
(702)388-6104

SCORE Office (Las Vegas)
300 Las Vegas Blvd. S, Ste. 1100
Las Vegas, NV 89101
(702)388-6104

SCORE Office (Northern Nevada)
SBDC, College of Business
Administration
Univ. of Nevada
Reno, NV 89557-0100
(702)784-4436
Fax: (702)784-4337

New Hampshire

SCORE Office (North Country)
PO Box 34
Berlin, NH 03570
(603)752-1090

SCORE Office (Concord)
143 N. Main St., Rm. 202A
PO Box 1258
Concord, NH 03301
(603)225-1400
Fax: (603)225-1409

SCORE Office (Dover)
299 Central Ave.
Dover, NH 03820
(603)742-2218
Fax: (603)749-6317

SCORE Office (Monadnock)
34 Mechanic St.
Keene, NH 03431-3421
(603)352-0320

SCORE Office (Lakes Region)
67 Water St., Ste. 105
Laconia, NH 03246
(603)524-9168

SCORE Office (Upper Valley)
Citizens Bank Bldg., Rm. 310
20 W. Park St.
Lebanon, NH 03766
(603)448-3491
Fax: (603)448-1908
E-mail: billt@valley.net
Website: http://www.valley.net/~score/

SCORE Office (Merrimack Valley)
275 Chestnut St., Rm. 618
Manchester, NH 03103
(603)666-7561
Fax: (603)666-7925

SCORE Office (Mt. Washington Valley)
PO Box 1066
North Conway, NH 03818
(603)383-0800

SCORE Office (Seacoast)
195 Commerce Way, Unit-A
Portsmouth, NH 03801-3251
(603)433-0575

New Jersey

SCORE Office (Somerset)
Paritan Valley Community College, Rte. 28
Branchburg, NJ 08807
(908)218-8874
E-mail: nj-score@grizbiz.com.
Website: http://www.nj-score.org/

SCORE Office (Chester)
5 Old Mill Rd.
Chester, NJ 07930
(908)879-7080

SCORE Office (Greater Princeton)
4 A George Washington Dr.
Cranbury, NJ 08512
(609)520-1776

SCORE Office (Freehold)
36 W. Main St.
Freehold, NJ 07728
(908)462-3030
Fax: (908)462-2123

SCORE Office (North West)
Picantinny Innovation Ctr.
3159 Schrader Rd.
Hamburg, NJ 07419
(973)209-8525
Fax: (973)209-7252
E-mail: nj-score@grizbiz.com
Website: http://www.nj-score.org/

SCORE Office (Monmouth)
765 Newman Springs Rd.
Lincroft, NJ 07738
(908)224-2573
E-mail: nj-score@grizbiz.com
Website: http://www.nj-score.org/

SCORE Office (Manalapan)
125 Symmes Dr.
Manalapan, NJ 07726
(908)431-7220

SCORE Office (Jersey City)
2 Gateway Ctr., 4th Fl.
Newark, NJ 07102
(973)645-3982
Fax: (973)645-2375

SCORE Office (Newark)
2 Gateway Center, 15th Fl.
Newark, NJ 07102-5553
(973)645-3982
Fax: (973)645-2375
E-mail: nj-score@grizbiz.com
Website: http://www.nj-score.org

SCORE Office (Bergen County)
327 E. Ridgewood Ave.
Paramus, NJ 07652
(201)599-6090
E-mail: nj-score@grizbiz.com
Website: http://www.nj-score.org/

SCORE Office (Pennsauken)
4900 Rte. 70
Pennsauken, NJ 08109
(609)486-3421

SCORE Office (Southern New Jersey)
4900 Rte. 70
Pennsauken, NJ 08109

(609)486-3421
E-mail: nj-score@grizbiz.com
Website: http://www.nj-score.org/

SCORE Office (Greater Princeton)
216 Rockingham Row
Princeton Forrestal Village
Princeton, NJ 08540
(609)520-1776
Fax: (609)520-9107
E-mail: nj-score@grizbiz.com
Website: http://www.nj-score.org/

SCORE Office (Shrewsbury)
Hwy. 35
Shrewsbury, NJ 07702
(908)842-5995
Fax: (908)219-6140

SCORE Office (Ocean County)
33 Washington St.
Toms River, NJ 08754
(732)505-6033
E-mail: nj-score@grizbiz.com
Website: http://www.nj-score.org/

SCORE Office (Wall)
2700 Allaire Rd.
Wall, NJ 07719
(908)449-8877

SCORE Office (Wayne)
2055 Hamburg Tpke.
Wayne, NJ 07470
(201)831-7788
Fax: (201)831-9112

New Mexico

SCORE Office (Albuquerque)
525 Buena Vista, SE
Albuquerque, NM 87106
(505)272-7999
Fax: (505)272-7963

SCORE Office (Las Cruces)
Loretto Towne Center
505 S. Main St., Ste. 125
Las Cruces, NM 88001
(505)523-5627
Fax: (505)524-2101
E-mail: score.397@zianet.com

SCORE Office (Roswell)
Federal Bldg., Rm. 237
Roswell, NM 88201
(505)625-2112
Fax: (505)623-2545

SCORE Office (Santa Fe)
Montoya Federal Bldg.
120 Federal Place, Rm. 307

Santa Fe, NM 87501
(505)988-6302
Fax: (505)988-6300

New York

SCORE Office (Northeast)
1 Computer Dr. S
Albany, NY 12205
(518)446-1118
Fax: (518)446-1228

SCORE Office (Auburn)
30 South St.
PO Box 675
Auburn, NY 13021
(315)252-7291

SCORE Office (South Tier Binghamton)
Metro Center, 2nd Fl.
49 Court St.
PO Box 995
Binghamton, NY 13902
(607)772-8860

SCORE Office (Queens County City)
12055 Queens Blvd., Rm. 333
Borough Hall, NY 11424
(718)263-8961

SCORE Office (Buffalo)
Federal Bldg., Rm. 1311
111 W. Huron St.
Buffalo, NY 14202
(716)551-4301
Website: http://www2.pcom.net/score/
buf45.html

SCORE Office (Canandaigua)
Chamber of Commerce Bldg.
113 S. Main St.
Canandaigua, NY 14424
(716)394-4400
Fax: (716)394-4546

SCORE Office (Chemung)
333 E. Water St., 4th Fl.
Elmira, NY 14901
(607)734-3358

SCORE Office (Geneva)
Chamber of Commerce Bldg.
PO Box 587
Geneva, NY 14456
(315)789-1776
Fax: (315)789-3993

SCORE Office (Glens Falls)
84 Broad St.
Glens Falls, NY 12801

(518)798-8463
Fax: (518)745-1433

SCORE Office (Orange County)
40 Matthews St.
Goshen, NY 10924
(914)294-8080
Fax: (914)294-6121

SCORE Office (Huntington Area)
151 W. Carver St.
Huntington, NY 11743
(516)423-6100

SCORE Office (Tompkins County)
904 E. Shore Dr.
Ithaca, NY 14850
(607)273-7080

SCORE Office (Long Island City)
120-55 Queens Blvd.
Jamaica, NY 11424
(718)263-8961
Fax: (718)263-9032

SCORE Office (Chatauqua)
101 W. 5th St.
Jamestown, NY 14701
(716)484-1103

SCORE Office (Westchester)
2 Caradon Ln.
Katonah, NY 10536
(914)948-3907
Fax: (914)948-4645
E-mail: score@w-w-w.com
Website: http://w-w-w.com/score/

SCORE Office (Queens County)
Queens Borough Hall
120-55 Queens Blvd. Rm. 333
Kew Gardens, NY 11424
(718)263-8961
Fax: (718)263-9032

SCORE Office (Brookhaven)
3233 Rte. 112
Medford, NY 11763
(516)451-6563
Fax: (516)451-6925

SCORE Office (Melville)
35 Pinelawn Rd., Rm. 207-W
Melville, NY 11747
(516)454-0771

SCORE Office (Nassau County)
400 County Seat Dr., No. 140
Mineola, NY 11501
(516)571-3303
E-mail: Counse1998@aol.com

Website: http://members.aol.com/
Counse1998/Default.htm

SCORE Office (Mt. Vernon)
4 N. 7th Ave.
Mt. Vernon, NY 10550
(914)667-7500

SCORE Office (New York)
26 Federal Plz., Rm. 3100
New York, NY 10278
(212)264-4507
Fax: (212)264-4963
E-mail: score1000@erols.com
Website: http://users.erols.com/score-
nyc/

SCORE Office (Newburgh)
47 Grand St.
Newburgh, NY 12550
(914)562-5100

SCORE Office (Owego)
188 Front St.
Owego, NY 13827
(607)687-2020

SCORE Office (Peekskill)
1 S. Division St.
Peekskill, NY 10566
(914)737-3600
Fax: (914)737-0541

SCORE Office (Penn Yan)
2375 Rte. 14A
Penn Yan, NY 14527
(315)536-3111

SCORE Office (Dutchess)
110 Main St.
Poughkeepsie, NY 12601
(914)454-1700

SCORE Office (Rochester)
601 Keating Federal Bldg., Rm. 410
100 State St.
Rochester, NY 14614
(716)263-6473
Fax: (716)263-3146
Website: http://www.ggw.org/score/

SCORE Office (Saranac Lake)
30 Main St.
Saranac Lake, NY 12983
(315)448-0415

SCORE Office (Suffolk)
286 Main St.
Setauket, NY 11733
(516)751-3886

SCORE Office (Staten Island)
130 Bay St.
Staten Island, NY 10301
(718)727-1221

SCORE Office (Ulster)
Clinton Bldg., Rm. 107
Stone Ridge, NY 12484
(914)687-5035
Fax: (914)687-5015
Website: http://www.scoreulster.org/

SCORE Office (Syracuse)
401 S. Salina, 5th Fl.
Syracuse, NY 13202
(315)471-9393

SCORE Office (Utica)
SUNY Institute of Technology,
Route 12
Utica, NY 13504-3050
(315)792-7553

SCORE Office (Watertown)
518 Davidson St.
Watertown, NY 13601
(315)788-1200
Fax: (315)788-8251

North Carolina

SCORE office (Asheboro)
317 E. Dixie Dr.
Asheboro, NC 27203
(336)626-2626
Fax: (336)626-7077

SCORE Office (Asheville)
Federal Bldg., Rm. 259
151 Patton
Asheville, NC 28801-5770
(828)271-4786
Fax: (828)271-4009

SCORE Office (Chapel Hill)
104 S. Estes Dr.
PO Box 2897
Chapel Hill, NC 27514
(919)967-7075

SCORE Office (Coastal Plains)
PO Box 2897
Chapel Hill, NC 27515
(919)967-7075
Fax: (919)968-6874

SCORE Office (Charlotte)
200 N. College St., Ste. A-2015
Charlotte, NC 28202
(704)344-6576
Fax: (704)344-6769

E-mail: CharlotteSCORE47@AOL.com
Website: http://www.charweb.org/
business/score/

SCORE Office (Durham)
411 W. Chapel Hill St.
Durham, NC 27707
(919)541-2171

SCORE Office (Gastonia)
PO Box 2168
Gastonia, NC 28053
(704)864-2621
Fax: (704)854-8723

SCORE Office (Greensboro)
400 W. Market St., Ste. 103
Greensboro, NC 27401-2241
(910)333-5399

SCORE Office (Henderson)
PO Box 917
Henderson, NC 27536
(919)492-2061
Fax: (919)430-0460

SCORE Office (Hendersonville)
Federal Bldg., Rm. 108
W. 4th Ave. & Church St.
Hendersonville, NC 28792
(828)693-8702
E-mail: score@circle.net
Website: http://www.wncguide.com/
score/Welcome.html

SCORE Office (Unifour)
PO Box 1828
Hickory, NC 28603
(704)328-6111

SCORE Office (High Point)
1101 N. Main St.
High Point, NC 27262
(336)882-8625
Fax: (336)889-9499

SCORE Office (Outer Banks)
Collington Rd. and Mustain
Kill Devil Hills, NC 27948
(252)441-8144

SCORE Office (Down East)
312 S. Front St., Ste. 6
New Bern, NC 28560
(252)633-6688
Fax: (252)633-9608

SCORE Office (Kinston)
PO Box 95
New Bern, NC 28561
(919)633-6688

SCORE Office (Raleigh)
Century Post Office Bldg., Ste. 306
300 Federal St. Mall
Raleigh, NC 27601
(919)856-4739
E-mail: jendres@ibm.net
Website: http://www.intrex.net/score96/
score96.htm

SCORE Office (Sanford)
1801 Nash St.
Sanford, NC 27330
(919)774-6442
Fax: (919)776-8739

SCORE Office (Sandhills Area)
1480 Hwy. 15-501
PO Box 458
Southern Pines, NC 28387
(910)692-3926

SCORE Office (Wilmington)
Corps of Engineers Bldg.
96 Darlington Ave., Ste. 207
Wilmington, NC 28403
(910)815-4576
Fax: (910)815-4658

North Dakota

SCORE Office (Bismarck-Mandan)
700 E. Main Ave., 2nd Fl.
PO Box 5509
Bismarck, ND 58506-5509
(701)250-4303

SCORE Office (Fargo)
657 2nd Ave., Rm. 225
Fargo, ND 58108-3083
(701)239-5677

SCORE Office (Upper Red River)
4275 Technology Dr., Rm. 156
Grand Forks, ND 58202-8372
(701)777-3051

SCORE Office (Minot)
100 1st St. SW
Minot, ND 58701-3846
(701)852-6883
Fax: (701)852-6905

Ohio

SCORE Office (Akron)
1 Cascade Plz., 7th Fl.
Akron, OH 44308
(330)379-3163
Fax: (330)379-3164

SCORE Office (Ashland)
Gill Center
47 W. Main St.
Ashland, OH 44805
(419)281-4584

SCORE Office (Canton)
116 Cleveland Ave. NW, Ste. 601
Canton, OH 44702-1720
(330)453-6047

SCORE Office (Chillicothe)
165 S. Paint St.
Chillicothe, OH 45601
(614)772-4530

SCORE Office (Cincinnati)
Ameritrust Bldg., Rm. 850
525 Vine St.
Cincinnati, OH 45202
(513)684-2812
Fax: (513)684-3251
Website: http://www.score.chapter34.org/

SCORE Office (Cleveland)
Eaton Center, Ste. 620
1100 Superior Ave.
Cleveland, OH 44114-2507
(216)522-4194
Fax: (216)522-4844

SCORE Office (Columbus)
2 Nationwide Plz., Ste. 1400
Columbus, OH 43215-2542
(614)469-2357
Fax: (614)469-2391
E-mail: info@scorecolumbus.org
Website: http://www.scorecolumbus.org/

SCORE Office (Dayton)
Dayton Federal Bldg., Rm. 505
200 W. Second St.
Dayton, OH 45402-1430
(513)225-2887
Fax: (513)225-7667

SCORE Office (Defiance)
615 W. 3rd St.
PO Box 130
Defiance, OH 43512
(419)782-7946

SCORE Office (Findlay)
123 E. Main Cross St.
PO Box 923
Findlay, OH 45840
(419)422-3314

SCORE Office (Lima)
147 N. Main St.
Lima, OH 45801

(419)222-6045
Fax: (419)229-0266

SCORE Office (Mansfield)
55 N. Mulberry St.
Mansfield, OH 44902
(419)522-3211

SCORE Office (Marietta)
Thomas Hall
Marietta, OH 45750
(614)373-0268

SCORE Office (Medina)
County Administrative Bldg.
144 N. Broadway
Medina, OH 44256
(216)764-8650

SCORE Office (Licking County)
50 W. Locust St.
Newark, OH 43055
(614)345-7458

SCORE Office (Salem)
2491 State Rte. 45 S
Salem, OH 44460
(216)332-0361

SCORE Office (Tiffin)
62 S. Washington St.
Tiffin, OH 44883
(419)447-4141
Fax: (419)447-5141

SCORE Office (Toledo)
608 Madison Ave, Ste. 910
Toledo, OH 43624
(419)259-7598
Fax: (419)259-6460

SCORE Office (Heart of Ohio)
377 W. Liberty St.
Wooster, OH 44691
(330)262-5735
Fax: (330)262-5745

SCORE Office (Youngstown)
306 Williamson Hall
Youngstown, OH 44555
(330)746-2687

Oklahoma

SCORE Office (Anadarko)
PO Box 366
Anadarko, OK 73005
(405)247-6651

SCORE Office (Ardmore)
410 W. Main
Ardmore, OK 73401
(580)226-2620

SCORE Office (Northeast Oklahoma)
210 S. Main
Grove, OK 74344
(918)787-2796
Fax: (918)787-2796
E-mail: Score595@greencis.net

SCORE Office (Lawton)
4500 W. Lee Blvd., Bldg. 100, Ste. 107
Lawton, OK 73505
(580)353-8727
Fax: (580)250-5677

SCORE Office (Oklahoma City)
210 Park Ave., No. 1300
Oklahoma City, OK 73102
(405)231-5163
Fax: (405)231-4876
E-mail: score212@usa.net

SCORE Office (Stillwater)
439 S. Main
Stillwater, OK 74074
(405)372-5573
Fax: (405)372-4316

SCORE Office (Tulsa)
616 S. Boston, Ste. 406
Tulsa, OK 74119
(918)581-7462
Fax: (918)581-6908
Website: http://www.ionet.net/
~tulscore/

Oregon

SCORE Office (Bend)
63085 N. Hwy. 97
Bend, OR 97701
(541)923-2849
Fax: (541)330-6900

SCORE Office (Willamette)
1401 Willamette St.
PO Box 1107
Eugene, OR 97401-4003
(541)465-6600
Fax: (541)484-4942

SCORE Office (Florence)
3149 Oak St.
Florence, OR 97439
(503)997-8444
Fax: (503)997-8448

SCORE Office (Southern Oregon)
33 N. Central Ave., Ste. 216
Medford, OR 97501
(541)776-4220
E-mail: pgr134f@prodigy.com

SCORE Office (Portland)
1515 SW 5th Ave., Ste. 1050
Portland, OR 97201
(503)326-3441
Fax: (503)326-2808
E-mail: gr134@prodigy.com

SCORE Office (Salem)
416 State St. (corner of Liberty)
Salem, OR 97301
(503)370-2896

Pennsylvania

SCORE Office (Altoona-Blair)
1212 12th Ave.
Altoona, PA 16601-3493
(814)943-8151

SCORE Office (Lehigh Valley)
Rauch Bldg. 37
Lehigh University
621 Taylor St.
Bethlehem, PA 18015
(610)758-4496
Fax: (610)758-5205

SCORE Office (Butler County)
100 N. Main St.
PO Box 1082
Butler, PA 16003
(412)283-2222
Fax: (412)283-0224

SCORE Office (Harrisburg)
4211 Trindle Rd.
Camp Hill, PA 17011
(717)761-4304
Fax: (717)761-4315

SCORE Office (Cumberland Valley)
75 S. 2nd St.
Chambersburg, PA 17201
(717)264-2935

SCORE Office (Monroe County-Stroudsburg)
556 Main St.
East Stroudsburg, PA 18301
(717)421-4433

SCORE Office (Erie)
120 W. 9th St.
Erie, PA 16501
(814)871-5650
Fax: (814)871-7530

SCORE Office (Bucks County)
409 Hood Blvd.
Fairless Hills, PA 19030
(215)943-8850
Fax: (215)943-7404

SCORE Office (Hanover)
146 Broadway
Hanover, PA 17331
(717)637-6130
Fax: (717)637-9127

SCORE Office (Harrisburg)
100 Chestnut, Ste. 309
Harrisburg, PA 17101
(717)782-3874

SCORE Office (East Montgomery County)
Baederwood Shopping Center
1653 The Fairways, Ste. 204
Jenkintown, PA 19046
(215)885-3027

SCORE Office (Kittanning)
2 Butler Rd.
Kittanning, PA 16201
(412)543-1305
Fax: (412)543-6206

SCORE Office (Lancaster)
118 W. Chestnut St.
Lancaster, PA 17603
(717)397-3092

SCORE Office (Westmoreland County)
300 Fraser Purchase Rd.
Latrobe, PA 15650-2690
(412)539-7505
Fax: (412)539-1850

SCORE Office (Lebanon)
252 N. 8th St.
PO Box 899
Lebanon, PA 17042-0899
(717)273-3727
Fax: (717)273-7940

SCORE Office (Lewistown)
3 W. Monument Sq., Ste. 204
Lewistown, PA 17044
(717)248-6713
Fax: (717)248-6714

SCORE Office (Delaware County)
602 E. Baltimore Pike
Media, PA 19063
(610)565-3677
Fax: (610)565-1606

SCORE Office (Milton Area)
112 S. Front St.
Milton, PA 17847
(717)742-7341
Fax: (717)792-2008

SCORE Office (Mon-Valley)
435 Donner Ave.
Monessen, PA 15062

(412)684-4277
Fax: (412)684-7688

SCORE Office (Monroeville)
William Penn Plaza
2790 Mosside Blvd., Ste. 295
Monroeville, PA 15146
(412)856-0622
Fax: (412)856-1030

SCORE Office (Airport Area)
986 Brodhead Rd.
Moon Township, PA 15108-2398
(412)264-6270
Fax: (412)264-1575

SCORE Office (Northeast)
8601 E. Roosevelt Blvd.
Philadelphia, PA 19152
(215)332-3400
Fax: (215)332-6050

SCORE Office (Philadelphia)
1315 Walnut St., Ste. 500
Philadelphia, PA 19107
(215)790-5050
Fax: (215)790-5057
E-mail: score46@bellatlantic.net
Website: http://www.pgweb.net/score46/

SCORE Office (Pittsburgh)
1000 Liberty Ave., Rm. 1122
Pittsburgh, PA 15222
(412)395-6560
Fax: (412)395-6562

SCORE Office (Tri-County)
801 N. Charlotte St.
Pottstown, PA 19464
(610)327-2673

SCORE Office (Reading)
601 Penn St.
Reading, PA 19601
(610)376-3497

SCORE Office (Scranton)
Oppenheim Bldg.
116 N. Washington Ave., Ste. 650
Scranton, PA 18503
(717)347-4611
Fax: (717)347-4611

SCORE Office (Central Pennsylvania)
200 Innovation Blvd., Ste. 242-B
State College, PA 16803
(814)234-9415
Fax: (814)238-9686
Website: http://countrystore.org/
business/score.htm

SCORE Office (Monroe-Stroudsburg)
556 Main St.
Stroudsburg, PA 18360
(717)421-4433

SCORE Office (Uniontown)
Federal Bldg.
Pittsburg St.
PO Box 2065 DTS
Uniontown, PA 15401
(412)437-4222
E-mail: uniontownscore@lcsys.net

SCORE Office (Warren County)
315 2nd Ave.
Warren, PA 16365
(814)723-9017

SCORE Office (Waynesboro)
323 E. Main St.
Waynesboro, PA 17268
(717)762-7123
Fax: (717)962-7124

SCORE Office (Chester County)
Government Service Center, Ste. 281
601 Westtown Rd.
West Chester, PA 19382-4538
(610)344-6910
Fax: (610)344-6919
E-mail: score@locke.ccil.org

SCORE Office (Wilkes-Barre)
7 N. Wilkes-Barre Blvd.
Wilkes Barre, PA 18702-5241
(717)826-6502
Fax: (717)826-6287

SCORE Office (North Central Pennsylvania)
240 W. 3rd St., Rm. 227
PO Box 725
Williamsport, PA 17703
(717)322-3720
Fax: (717)322-1607
E-mail: score234@mail.csrlink.net
Website: http://www.lycoming.org/score/

SCORE Office (York)
Cyber Center
2101 Pennsylvania Ave.
York, PA 17404
(717)845-8830
Fax: (717)854-9333

Puerto Rico

SCORE Office (Puerto Rico & Virgin Islands)
PO Box 12383-96
San Juan, PR 00914-0383

(787)726-8040
Fax: (787)726-8135

Rhode Island

SCORE Office (Barrington)
281 County Rd.
Barrington, RI 02806
(401)247-1920
Fax: (401)247-3763

SCORE Office (Woonsocket)
640 Washington Hwy.
Lincoln, RI 02865
(401)334-1000
Fax: (401)334-1009

SCORE Office (Wickford)
8045 Post Rd.
North Kingstown, RI 02852
(401)295-5566
Fax: (401)295-8987

SCORE Office (J.G.E. Knight)
380 Westminster St.
Providence, RI 02903
(401)528-4571
Fax: (401)528-4539
Website: http://www.riscore.org

SCORE Office (Warwick)
3288 Post Rd.
Warwick, RI 02886
(401)732-1100
Fax: (401)732-1101

SCORE Office (Westerly)
74 Post Rd.
Westerly, RI 02891
(401)596-7761
800-732-7636
Fax: (401)596-2190

South Carolina

SCORE Office (Aiken)
PO Box 892
Aiken, SC 29802
(803)641-1111
800-542-4536
Fax: (803)641-4174

SCORE Office (Anderson)
Anderson Mall
3130 N. Main St.
Anderson, SC 29621
(864)224-0453

SCORE Office (Coastal)
284 King St.
Charleston, SC 29401

(803)727-4778
Fax: (803)853-2529

SCORE Office (Midlands)
Strom Thurmond Bldg., Rm. 358
1835 Assembly St., Rm 358
Columbia, SC 29201
(803)765-5131
Fax: (803)765-5962
Website: http://www.scoremidlands.org/

SCORE Office (Piedmont)
Federal Bldg., Rm. B-02
300 E. Washington St.
Greenville, SC 29601
(864)271-3638

SCORE Office (Greenwood)
PO Drawer 1467
Greenwood, SC 29648
(864)223-8357

SCORE Office (Hilton Head Island)
52 Savannah Trail
Hilton Head, SC 29926
(803)785-7107
Fax: (803)785-7110

SCORE Office (Grand Strand)
937 Broadway
Myrtle Beach, SC 29577
(803)918-1079
Fax: (803)918-1083
E-mail: score381@aol.com

SCORE Office (Spartanburg)
PO Box 1636
Spartanburg, SC 29304
(864)594-5000
Fax: (864)594-5055

South Dakota

SCORE Office (West River)
Rushmore Plz. Civic Ctr.
444 Mount Rushmore Rd., No. 209
Rapid City, SD 57701
(605)394-5311
E-mail: score@gwtc.net

SCORE Office (Sioux Falls)
First Financial Center
110 S. Phillips Ave., Ste. 200
Sioux Falls, SD 57104-6727
(605)330-4231
Fax: (605)330-4231

Tennessee

SCORE Office (Chattanooga)
Federal Bldg., Rm. 26
900 Georgia Ave.

Chattanooga, TN 37402
(423)752-5190
Fax: (423)752-5335

SCORE Office (Cleveland)
PO Box 2275
Cleveland, TN 37320
(423)472-6587
Fax: (423)472-2019

**SCORE Office (Upper Cumberland
Center)**
1225 S. Willow Ave.
Cookeville, TN 38501
(615)432-4111
Fax: (615)432-6010

SCORE Office (Unicoi County)
PO Box 713
Erwin, TN 37650
(423)743-3000
Fax: (423)743-0942

SCORE Office (Greeneville)
115 Academy St.
Greeneville, TN 37743
(423)638-4111
Fax: (423)638-5345

SCORE Office (Jackson)
194 Auditorium St.
Jackson, TN 38301
(901)423-2200

SCORE Office (Northeast Tennessee)
1st Tennessee Bank Bldg.
2710 S. Roan St., Ste. 584
Johnson City, TN 37601
(423)929-7686
Fax: (423)461-8052

SCORE Office (Kingsport)
151 E. Main St.
Kingsport, TN 37662
(423)392-8805

SCORE Office (Greater Knoxville)
Farragot Bldg., Ste. 224
530 S. Gay St.
Knoxville, TN 37902
(423)545-4203
E-mail: scoreknox@ntown.com
Website: http://www.scoreknox.org/

SCORE Office (Maryville)
201 S. Washington St.
Maryville, TN 37804-5728
(423)983-2241
800-525-6834
Fax: (423)984-1386

SCORE Office (Memphis)
Federal Bldg., Ste. 390
167 N. Main St.
Memphis, TN 38103
(901)544-3588

SCORE Office (Nashville)
50 Vantage Way, Ste. 201
Nashville, TN 37228-1500
(615)736-7621

Texas

SCORE Office (Abilene)
2106 Federal Post Office and Court Bldg.
Abilene, TX 79601
(915)677-1857

SCORE Office (Austin)
2501 S. Congress
Austin, TX 78701
(512)442-7235
Fax: (512)442-7528

SCORE Office (Golden Triangle)
450 Boyd St.
Beaumont, TX 77704
(409)838-6581
Fax: (409)833-6718

SCORE Office (Brownsville)
3505 Boca Chica Blvd., Ste. 305
Brownsville, TX 78521
(210)541-4508

SCORE Office (Brazos Valley)
3000 Briarcrest, Ste. 302
Bryan, TX 77802
(409)776-8876
E-mail: 102633.2612@compuserve.com

SCORE Office (Cleburne)
Watergarden Pl., 9th Fl., Ste. 400
Cleburne, TX 76031
(817)871-6002

SCORE Office (Corpus Christi)
651 Upper North Broadway, Ste. 654
Corpus Christi, TX 78477
(512)888-4322
Fax: (512)888-3418

SCORE Office (Dallas)
6260 E. Mockingbird
Dallas, TX 75214-2619
(214)828-2471
Fax: (214)821-8033

SCORE Office (El Paso)
10 Civic Center Plaza
El Paso, TX 79901
(915)534-0541
Fax: (915)534-0513

SCORE Office (Bedford)
100 E. 15th St., Ste. 400
Ft. Worth, TX 76102
(817)871-6002

SCORE Office (Ft. Worth)
100 E. 15th St., No. 24
Ft. Worth, TX 76102
(817)871-6002
Fax: (817)871-6031
E-mail: fwbac@onramp.net

SCORE Office (Garland)
2734 W. Kingsley Rd.
Garland, TX 75041
(214)271-9224

**SCORE Office (Granbury Chamber
of Commerce)**
416 S. Morgan
Granbury, TX 76048
(817)573-1622
Fax: (817)573-0805

**SCORE Office (Lower Rio Grande
Valley)**
222 E. Van Buren, Ste. 500
Harlingen, TX 78550
(956)427-8533
Fax: (956)427-8537

SCORE Office (Houston)
9301 Southwest Fwy., Ste. 550
Houston, TX 77074
(713)773-6565
Fax: (713)773-6550

SCORE Office (Irving)
3333 N. MacArthur Blvd., Ste. 100
Irving, TX 75062
(214)252-8484
Fax: (214)252-6710

SCORE Office (Lubbock)
1205 Texas Ave., Rm. 411D
Lubbock, TX 79401
(806)472-7462
Fax: (806)472-7487

SCORE Office (Midland)
Post Office Annex
200 E. Wall St., Rm. P121
Midland, TX 79701
(915)687-2649

SCORE Office (Orange)
1012 Green Ave.
Orange, TX 77630-5620
(409)883-3536
800-528-4906
Fax: (409)886-3247

SCORE Office (Plano)
1200 E. 15th St.
PO Drawer 940287
Plano, TX 75094-0287
(214)424-7547
Fax: (214)422-5182

SCORE Office (Port Arthur)
4749 Twin City Hwy., Ste. 300
Port Arthur, TX 77642
(409)963-1107
Fax: (409)963-3322

SCORE Office (Richardson)
411 Belle Grove
Richardson, TX 75080
(214)234-4141
800-777-8001
Fax: (214)680-9103

SCORE Office (San Antonio)
Federal Bldg., Rm. A527
727 E. Durango
San Antonio, TX 78206
(210)472-5931
Fax: (210)472-5935

SCORE Office (Texarkana State College)
819 State Line Ave.
Texarkana, TX 75501
(903)792-7191
Fax: (903)793-4304

SCORE Office (East Texas)
RTDC
1530 SSW Loop 323, Ste. 100
Tyler, TX 75701
(903)510-2975
Fax: (903)510-2978

SCORE Office (Waco)
401 Franklin Ave.
Waco, TX 76701
(817)754-8898
Fax: (817)756-0776
Website: http://www.brc-waco.com/

SCORE Office (Wichita Falls)
Hamilton Bldg.
900 8th St.
Wichita Falls, TX 76307
(940)723-2741
Fax: (940)723-8773

Utah

SCORE Office (Northern Utah)
160 N. Main
Logan, UT 84321
(435)746-2269

SCORE Office (Ogden)
1701 E. Windsor Dr.
Ogden, UT 84604
(801)629-8613
E-mail: score158@netscape.net

SCORE Office (Central Utah)
1071 E. Windsor Dr.
Provo, UT 84604
(801)373-8660

SCORE Office (Southern Utah)
225 South 700 East
St. George, UT 84770
(435)652-7751

SCORE Office (Salt Lake)
310 S Main St.
Salt Lake City, UT 84101
(801)746-2269
Fax: (801)746-2273

Vermont

SCORE Office (Champlain Valley)
Winston Prouty Federal Bldg.
11 Lincoln St., Rm. 106
Essex Junction, VT 05452
(802)951-6762

SCORE Office (Montpelier)
87 State St., Rm. 205
PO Box 605
Montpelier, VT 05601
(802)828-4422
Fax: (802)828-4485

SCORE Office (Marble Valley)
256 N. Main St.
Rutland, VT 05701-2413
(802)773-9147

SCORE Office (Northeast Kingdom)
20 Main St.
PO Box 904
St. Johnsbury, VT 05819
(802)748-5101

Virgin Islands

SCORE Office (St. Croix)
United Plaza Shopping Center
PO Box 4010, Christiansted
St. Croix, VI 00822
(809)778-5380

SCORE Office (St. Thomas-St. John)
Federal Bldg., Rm. 21
Veterans Dr.
St. Thomas, VI 00801
(809)774-8530

Virginia

SCORE Office (Arlington)
2009 N. 14th St., Ste. 111
Arlington, VA 22201
(703)525-2400

SCORE Office (Blacksburg)
141 Jackson St.
Blacksburg, VA 24060
(540)552-4061

SCORE Office (Bristol)
20 Volunteer Pkwy.
Bristol, VA 24203
(540)989-4850

SCORE Office (Central Virginia)
1001 E. Market St., Ste. 101
Charlottesville, VA 22902
(804)295-6712
Fax: (804)295-7066

SCORE Office (Alleghany Satellite)
241 W. Main St.
Covington, VA 24426
(540)962-2178
Fax: (540)962-2179

SCORE Office (Central Fairfax)
3975 University Dr., Ste. 350
Fairfax, VA 22030
(703)591-2450

SCORE Office (Falls Church)
PO Box 491
Falls Church, VA 22040
(703)532-1050
Fax: (703)237-7904

SCORE Office (Glenns)
Glenns Campus
Box 287
Glenns, VA 23149
(804)693-9650

SCORE Office (Peninsula)
6 Manhattan Sq.
PO Box 7269
Hampton, VA 23666
(757)766-2000
Fax: (757)865-0339
E-mail: score100@seva.net

SCORE Office (Tri-Cities)
108 N. Main St.
Hopewell, VA 23860
(804)458-5536

SCORE Office (Lynchburg)
Federal Bldg.
1100 Main St.

Lynchburg, VA 24504-1714
(804)846-3235

SCORE Office (Greater Prince William)
8963 Center St
Manassas, VA 20110
(703)368-4813
Fax: (703)368-4733

SCORE Office (Martinsvile)
115 Broad St.
Martinsville, VA 24112-0709
(540)632-6401
Fax: (540)632-5059

SCORE Office (Hampton Roads)
Federal Bldg., Rm. 737
200 Grandby St.
Norfolk, VA 23510
(757)441-3733
Fax: (757)441-3733
E-mail: scorehr60@juno.com

SCORE Office (Norfolk)
Federal Bldg., Rm. 737
200 Granby St.
Norfolk, VA 23510
(757)441-3733
Fax: (757)441-3733

SCORE Office (Virginia Beach)
Chamber of Commerce
200 Grandby St., Rm 737
Norfolk, VA 23510
(804)441-3733

SCORE Office (Radford)
1126 Norwood St.
Radford, VA 24141
(540)639-2202

SCORE Office (Richmond)
Federal Bldg.
400 N. 8th St., Ste. 1150
PO Box 10126
Richmond, VA 23240-0126
(804)771-2400
Fax: (804)771-8018
E-mail: scorechapter12@yahoo.com
Website: http://www.cvco.org/score/

SCORE Office (Roanoke)
Federal Bldg., Rm. 716
250 Franklin Rd.
Roanoke, VA 24011
(540)857-2834
Fax: (540)857-2043
E-mail: scorerva@juno.com
Website: http://hometown.aol.com/
scorerv/Index.html

SCORE Office (Fairfax)
8391 Old Courthouse Rd., Ste. 300
Vienna, VA 22182
(703)749-0400

SCORE Office (Greater Vienna)
513 Maple Ave. West
Vienna, VA 22180
(703)281-1333
Fax: (703)242-1482

SCORE Office (Shenandoah Valley)
301 W. Main St.
Waynesboro, VA 22980
(540)949-8203
Fax: (540)949-7740
E-mail: score427@intelos.net

SCORE Office (Williamsburg)
201 Penniman Rd.
Williamsburg, VA 23185
(757)229-6511
E-mail: wacc@williamsburgcc.com

SCORE Office (Northern Virginia)
1360 S. Pleasant Valley Rd.
Winchester, VA 22601
(540)662-4118

Washington

SCORE Office (Gray's Harbor)
506 Duffy St.
Aberdeen, WA 98520
(360)532-1924
Fax: (360)533-7945

SCORE Office (Bellingham)
101 E. Holly St.
Bellingham, WA 98225
(360)676-3307

SCORE Office (Everett)
2702 Hoyt Ave.
Everett, WA 98201-3556
(206)259-8000

SCORE Office (Gig Harbor)
3125 Judson St.
Gig Harbor, WA 98335
(206)851-6865

SCORE Office (Kennewick)
PO Box 6986
Kennewick, WA 99336
(509)736-0510

SCORE Office (Puyallup)
322 2nd St. SW
PO Box 1298
Puyallup, WA 98371
(206)845-6755
Fax: (206)848-6164

SCORE Office (Seattle)
1200 6th Ave., Ste. 1700
Seattle, WA 98101
(206)553-7320
Fax: (206)553-7044
E-mail: score55@aol.com
Website: http://www.scn.org/civic/score-online/index55.html

SCORE Office (Spokane)
801 W. Riverside Ave., No. 240
Spokane, WA 99201
(509)353-2820
Fax: (509)353-2600
E-mail: score@dmi.net
Website: http://www.dmi.net/score/

SCORE Office (Clover Park)
PO Box 1933
Tacoma, WA 98401-1933
(206)627-2175

SCORE Office (Tacoma)
1101 Pacific Ave.
Tacoma, WA 98402
(253)274-1288
Fax: (253)274-1289

SCORE Office (Fort Vancouver)
1701 Broadway, S-1
Vancouver, WA 98663
(360)699-1079

SCORE Office (Walla Walla)
500 Tausick Way
Walla Walla, WA 99362
(509)527-4681

SCORE Office (Mid-Columbia)
1113 S. 14th Ave.
Yakima, WA 98907
(509)574-4944
Fax: (509)574-2943
Website: http://www.ellensburg.com/~score/

West Virginia

SCORE Office (Charleston)
1116 Smith St.
Charleston, WV 25301
(304)347-5463
E-mail: score256@juno.com

SCORE Office (Virginia Street)
1116 Smith St., Ste. 302
Charleston, WV 25301
(304)347-5463

SCORE Office (Marion County)
PO Box 208
Fairmont, WV 26555-0208
(304)363-0486

SCORE Office (Upper Monongahela Valley)
1000 Technology Dr., Ste. 1111
Fairmont, WV 26555
(304)363-0486
E-mail: score537@hotmail.com

SCORE Office (Huntington)
1101 6th Ave., Ste. 220
Huntington, WV 25701-2309
(304)523-4092

SCORE Office (Wheeling)
1310 Market St.
Wheeling, WV 26003
(304)233-2575
Fax: (304)233-1320

Wisconsin

SCORE Office (Fox Cities)
227 S. Walnut St.
Appleton, WI 54913
(920)734-7101
Fax: (920)734-7161

SCORE Office (Beloit)
136 W. Grand Ave., Ste. 100
PO Box 717
Beloit, WI 53511
(608)365-8835
Fax: (608)365-9170

SCORE Office (Eau Claire)
Federal Bldg., Rm. B11
510 S. Barstow St.
Eau Claire, WI 54701
(715)834-1573
E-mail: score@ecol.net
Website: http://www.ecol.net/~score/

SCORE Office (Fond du Lac)
207 N. Main St.
Fond du Lac, WI 54935
(414)921-9500
Fax: (414)921-9559

SCORE Office (Green Bay)
835 Potts Ave.
Green Bay, WI 54304
(414)496-8930
Fax: (414)496-6009

SCORE Office (Janesville)
20 S. Main St., Ste. 11
PO Box 8008
Janesville, WI 53547
(608)757-3160
Fax: (608)757-3170

SCORE Office (La Crosse)
712 Main St.
La Crosse, WI 54602-0219
(608)784-4880

SCORE Office (Madison)
505 S. Rosa Rd.
Madison, WI 53719
(608)441-2820

SCORE Office (Manitowoc)
1515 Memorial Dr.
PO Box 903
Manitowoc, WI 54221-0903
(414)684-5575
Fax: (414)684-1915

SCORE Office (Milwaukee)
310 W. Wisconsin Ave., Ste. 425
Milwaukee, WI 53203
(414)297-3942
Fax: (414)297-1377

SCORE Office (Central Wisconsin)
1224 Lindbergh Ave.
Stevens Point, WI 54481
(715)344-7729

SCORE Office (Superior)
Superior Business Center Inc.
1423 N. 8th St.
Superior, WI 54880
(715)394-7388
Fax: (715)393-7414

SCORE Office (Waukesha)
223 Wisconsin Ave.
Waukesha, WI 53186-4926
(414)542-4249

SCORE Office (Wausau)
300 3rd St., Ste. 200
Wausau, WI 54402-6190
(715)845-6231

SCORE Office (Wisconsin Rapids)
2240 Kingston Rd.
Wisconsin Rapids, WI 54494
(715)423-1830

Wyoming

SCORE Office (Casper)
Federal Bldg., No. 2215
100 East B St.
Casper, WY 82602
(307)261-6529
Fax: (307)261-6530

Venture capital & financing companies

This section contains a listing of financing and loan companies in the United States and
Canada. These listing are arranged alphabetically by country, then by state or province, then by city, then by organization name.

Canada

Alberta

Launchworks Inc.
1902J 11th St., S.E.
Calgary, AB, Canada T2G 3G2
(403)269-1119
Fax: (403)269-1141
Website: http://www.launchworks.com

Native Venture Capital Company, Inc.
21 Artist View Point, Box 7
Site 25, RR 12
Calgary, AB, Canada T3E 6W3
(903)208-5380

Miralta Capital Inc.
4445 Calgary Trail South
888 Terrace Plaza Alberta
Edmonton, AB, Canada T6H 5R7
(780)438-3535
Fax: (780)438-3129

Vencap Equities Alberta Ltd.
10180-101st St., Ste. 1980
Edmonton, AB, Canada T5J 3S4
(403)420-1171
Fax: (403)429-2541

British Columbia

Discovery Capital
5th Fl., 1199 West Hastings
Vancouver, BC, Canada V6E 3T5
(604)683-3000
Fax: (604)662-3457
E-mail: info@discoverycapital.com
Website: http://www.discoverycapital.com

Greenstone Venture Partners
1177 West Hastings St.
Ste. 400
Vancouver, BC, Canada V6E 2K3
(604)717-1977
Fax: (604)717-1976
Website: http://www.greenstonevc.com

Growthworks Capital
2600-1055 West Georgia St.
Box 11170 Royal Centre
Vancouver, BC, Canada V6E 3R5
(604)895-7259
Fax: (604)669-7605
Website: http://www.wofund.com

MDS Discovery Venture Management, Inc.
555 W. Eighth Ave., Ste. 305
Vancouver, BC, Canada V5Z 1C6
(604)872-8464
Fax: (604)872-2977
E-mail: info@mds-ventures.com

Ventures West Management Inc.
1285 W. Pender St., Ste. 280
Vancouver, BC, Canada V6E 4B1
(604)688-9495
Fax: (604)687-2145
Website: http://www.ventureswest.com

Nova Scotia

ACF Equity Atlantic Inc.
Purdy's Wharf Tower II
Ste. 2106
Halifax, NS, Canada B3J 3R7
(902)421-1965
Fax: (902)421-1808

Montgomerie, Huck & Co.
146 Bluenose Dr.
PO Box 538
Lunenburg, NS, Canada B0J 2C0
(902)634-7125
Fax: (902)634-7130

Ontario

IPS Industrial Promotion Services Ltd.
60 Columbia Way, Ste. 720
Markham, ON, Canada L3R 0C9
(905)475-9400
Fax: (905)475-5003

Betwin Investments Inc.
Box 23110
Sault Ste. Marie, ON, Canada P6A 6W6
(705)253-0744
Fax: (705)253-0744

Bailey & Company, Inc.
594 Spadina Ave.
Toronto, ON, Canada M5S 2H4
(416)921-6930
Fax: (416)925-4670

BCE Capital
200 Bay St.
South Tower, Ste. 3120
Toronto, ON, Canada M5J 2J2
(416)815-0078
Fax: (416)941-1073
Website: http://www.bcecapital.com

Castlehill Ventures
55 University Ave., Ste. 500
Toronto, ON, Canada M5J 2H7

(416)862-8574
Fax: (416)862-8875

CCFL Mezzanine Partners of Canada
70 University Ave.
Ste. 1450
Toronto, ON, Canada M5J 2M4
(416)977-1450
Fax: (416)977-6764
E-mail: info@ccfl.com
Website: http://www.ccfl.com

Celtic House International
100 Simcoe St., Ste. 100
Toronto, ON, Canada M5H 3G2
(416)542-2436
Fax: (416)542-2435
Website: http://www.celtic-house.com

Clairvest Group Inc.
22 St. Clair Ave. East
Ste. 1700
Toronto, ON, Canada M4T 2S3
(416)925-9270
Fax: (416)925-5753

Crosbie & Co., Inc.
One First Canadian Place
9th Fl.
PO Box 116
Toronto, ON, Canada M5X 1A4
(416)362-7726
Fax: (416)362-3447
E-mail: info@crosbieco.com
Website: http://www.crosbieco.com

Drug Royalty Corp.
Eight King St. East
Ste. 202
Toronto, ON, Canada M5C 1B5
(416)863-1865
Fax: (416)863-5161

Grieve, Horner, Brown & Asculai
8 King St. E, Ste. 1704
Toronto, ON, Canada M5C 1B5
(416)362-7668
Fax: (416)362-7660

Jefferson Partners
77 King St. West
Ste. 4010
PO Box 136
Toronto, ON, Canada M5K 1H1
(416)367-1533
Fax: (416)367-5827
Website: http://www.jefferson.com

J.L. Albright Venture Partners
Canada Trust Tower, 161 Bay St.
Ste. 4440

PO Box 215
Toronto, ON, Canada M5J 2S1
(416)367-2440
Fax: (416)367-4604
Website: http://www.jlaventures.com

McLean Watson Capital Inc.
One First Canadian Place
Ste. 1410
PO Box 129
Toronto, ON, Canada M5X 1A4
(416)363-2000
Fax: (416)363-2010
Website: http://www.
mcleanwatson.com

Middlefield Capital Fund
One First Canadian Place
85th Fl.
PO Box 192
Toronto, ON, Canada M5X 1A6
(416)362-0714
Fax: (416)362-7925
Website: http://www.middlefield.com

Mosaic Venture Partners
24 Duncan St.
Ste. 300
Toronto, ON, Canada M5V 3M6
(416)597-8889
Fax: (416)597-2345

Onex Corp.
161 Bay St.
PO Box 700
Toronto, ON, Canada M5J 2S1
(416)362-7711
Fax: (416)362-5765

Penfund Partners Inc.
145 King St. West
Ste. 1920
Toronto, ON, Canada M5H 1J8
(416)865-0300
Fax: (416)364-6912
Website: http://www.penfund.com

Primaxis Technology Ventures Inc.
1 Richmond St. West, 8th Fl.
Toronto, ON, Canada M5H 3W4
(416)313-5210
Fax: (416)313-5218
Website: http://www.primaxis.com

Priveq Capital Funds
240 Duncan Mill Rd., Ste. 602
Toronto, ON, Canada M3B 3P1
(416)447-3330
Fax: (416)447-3331
E-mail: priveq@sympatico.ca

Roynat Ventures
40 King St. West, 26th Fl.
Toronto, ON, Canada M5H 1H1
(416)933-2667
Fax: (416)933-2783
Website: http://www.roynatcapital.com

Tera Capital Corp.
366 Adelaide St. East, Ste. 337
Toronto, ON, Canada M5A 3X9
(416)368-1024
Fax: (416)368-1427

Working Ventures Canadian Fund Inc.
250 Bloor St. East, Ste. 1600
Toronto, ON, Canada M4W 1E6
(416)934-7718
Fax: (416)929-0901
Website: http://www.workingventures.ca

Quebec

Altamira Capital Corp.
202 University
Niveau de Maisoneuve, Bur. 201
Montreal, QC, Canada H3A 2A5
(514)499-1656
Fax: (514)499-9570

Federal Business Development Bank
Venture Capital Division
Five Place Ville Marie, Ste. 600
Montreal, QC, Canada H3B 5E7
(514)283-1896
Fax: (514)283-5455

Hydro-Quebec Capitech Inc.
75 Boul, Rene Levesque Quest
Montreal, QC, Canada H2Z 1A4
(514)289-4783
Fax: (514)289-5420
Website: http://www.hqcapitech.com

Investissement Desjardins
2 complexe Desjardins
C.P. 760
Montreal, QC, Canada H5B 1B8
(514)281-7131
Fax: (514)281-7808
Website: http://www.desjardins.com/id

Marleau Lemire Inc.
One Place Ville-Marie, Ste. 3601
Montreal, QC, Canada H3B 3P2
(514)877-3800
Fax: (514)875-6415

Speirs Consultants Inc.
365 Stanstead
Montreal, QC, Canada H3R 1X5

(514)342-3858
Fax: (514)342-1977

Tecnocap Inc.
4028 Marlowe
Montreal, QC, Canada H4A 3M2
(514)483-6009
Fax: (514)483-6045
Website: http://www.technocap.com

Telsoft Ventures
1000, Rue de la Gauchetiere
Quest, 25eme Etage
Montreal, QC, Canada H3B 4W5
(514)397-8450
Fax: (514)397-8451

Saskatchewan

Saskatchewan Government Growth Fund
1801 Hamilton St., Ste. 1210
Canada Trust Tower
Regina, SK, Canada S4P 4B4
(306)787-2994
Fax: (306)787-2086

United states

Alabama

FHL Capital Corp.
600 20th Street North
Suite 350
Birmingham, AL 35203
(205)328-3098
Fax: (205)323-0001

Harbert Management Corp.
One Riverchase Pkwy. South
Birmingham, AL 35244
(205)987-5500
Fax: (205)987-5707
Website: http://www.harbert.net

Jefferson Capital Fund
PO Box 13129
Birmingham, AL 35213
(205)324-7709

Private Capital Corp.
100 Brookwood Pl., 4th Fl.
Birmingham, AL 35209
(205)879-2722
Fax: (205)879-5121

21st Century Health Ventures
One Health South Pkwy.
Birmingham, AL 35243
(256)268-6250
Fax: (256)970-8928

FJC Growth Capital Corp.
200 W. Side Sq., Ste. 340
Huntsville, AL 35801
(256)922-2918
Fax: (256)922-2909

Hickory Venture Capital Corp.
301 Washington St. NW
Suite 301
Huntsville, AL 35801
(256)539-1931
Fax: (256)539-5130
E-mail: hvcc@hvcc.com
Website: http://www.hvcc.com

Southeastern Technology Fund
7910 South Memorial Pkwy., Ste. F
Huntsville, AL 35802
(256)883-8711
Fax: (256)883-8558

Cordova Ventures
4121 Carmichael Rd., Ste. 301
Montgomery, AL 36106
(334)271-6011
Fax: (334)260-0120
Website: http://
www.cordovaventures.com

Small Business Clinic of Alabama/AG Bartholomew & Associates
PO Box 231074
Montgomery, AL 36123-1074
(334)284-3640

Arizona

Miller Capital Corp.
4909 E. McDowell Rd.
Phoenix, AZ 85008
(602)225-0504
Fax: (602)225-9024
Website: http://www.themillergroup.com

The Columbine Venture Funds
9449 North 90th St., Ste. 200
Scottsdale, AZ 85258
(602)661-9222
Fax: (602)661-6262

Koch Ventures
17767 N. Perimeter Dr., Ste. 101
Scottsdale, AZ 85255
(480)419-3600
Fax: (480)419-3606
Website: http://www.kochventures.com

McKee & Co.
7702 E. Doubletree Ranch Rd.
Suite 230
Scottsdale, AZ 85258

(480)368-0333
Fax: (480)607-7446

Merita Capital Ltd.
7350 E. Stetson Dr., Ste. 108-A
Scottsdale, AZ 85251
(480)947-8700
Fax: (480)947-8766

Valley Ventures / Arizona Growth Partners L.P.
6720 N. Scottsdale Rd., Ste. 208
Scottsdale, AZ 85253
(480)661-6600
Fax: (480)661-6262

Estreetcapital.com
660 South Mill Ave., Ste. 315
Tempe, AZ 85281
(480)968-8400
Fax: (480)968-8480
Website: http://www.estreetcapital.com

Coronado Venture Fund
PO Box 65420
Tucson, AZ 85728-5420
(520)577-3764
Fax: (520)299-8491

Arkansas

Arkansas Capital Corp.
225 South Pulaski St.
Little Rock, AR 72201
(501)374-9247
Fax: (501)374-9425
Website: http://www.arcapital.com

California

Sundance Venture Partners, L.P.
100 Clocktower Place, Ste. 130
Carmel, CA 93923
(831)625-6500
Fax: (831)625-6590

Westar Capital (Costa Mesa)
949 South Coast Dr., Ste. 650
Costa Mesa, CA 92626
(714)481-5160
Fax: (714)481-5166
E-mail: mailbox@westarcapital.com
Website: http://www.westarcapital.com

Alpine Technology Ventures
20300 Stevens Creek Boulevard, Ste. 495
Cupertino, CA 95014
(408)725-1810
Fax: (408)725-1207
Website: http://www.alpineventures.com

Bay Partners
10600 N. De Anza Blvd.
Cupertino, CA 95014-2031
(408)725-2444
Fax: (408)446-4502
Website: http://www.baypartners.com

Novus Ventures
20111 Stevens Creek Blvd., Ste. 130
Cupertino, CA 95014
(408)252-3900
Fax: (408)252-1713
Website: http://www.novusventures.com

Triune Capital
19925 Stevens Creek Blvd., Ste. 200
Cupertino, CA 95014
(310)284-6800
Fax: (310)284-3290

Acorn Ventures
268 Bush St., Ste. 2829
Daly City, CA 94014
(650)994-7801
Fax: (650)994-3305
Website: http://www.acornventures.com

Digital Media Campus
2221 Park Place
El Segundo, CA 90245
(310)426-8000
Fax: (310)426-8010
E-mail: info@thecampus.com
Website: http://www.digitalmedia
campus.com

BankAmerica Ventures / BA Venture Partners
950 Tower Ln., Ste. 700
Foster City, CA 94404
(650)378-6000
Fax: (650)378-6040
Website: http://www.baventurepartners.com

Starting Point Partners
666 Portofino Lane
Foster City, CA 94404
(650)722-1035
Website: http://
www.startingpointpartners.com

Opportunity Capital Partners
2201 Walnut Ave., Ste. 210
Fremont, CA 94538
(510)795-7000
Fax: (510)494-5439
Website: http://www.ocpcapital.com

Imperial Ventures Inc.
9920 S. La Cienega Boulevar, 14th Fl.
Inglewood, CA 90301

(310)417-5409
Fax: (310)338-6115

Ventana Global (Irvine)
18881 Von Karman Ave., Ste. 1150
Irvine, CA 92612
(949)476-2204
Fax: (949)752-0223
Website: http://www.ventanaglobal.com

Integrated Consortium Inc.
50 Ridgecrest Rd.
Kentfield, CA 94904
(415)925-0386
Fax: (415)461-2726

Enterprise Partners
979 Ivanhoe Ave., Ste. 550
La Jolla, CA 92037
(858)454-8833
Fax: (858)454-2489
Website: http://www.epvc.com

Domain Associates
28202 Cabot Rd., Ste. 200
Laguna Niguel, CA 92677
(949)347-2446
Fax: (949)347-9720
Website: http://www.domainvc.com

Cascade Communications Ventures
60 E. Sir Francis Drake Blvd., Ste. 300
Larkspur, CA 94939
(415)925-6500
Fax: (415)925-6501

Allegis Capital
One First St., Ste. Two
Los Altos, CA 94022
(650)917-5900
Fax: (650)917-5901
Website: http://www.allegiscapital.com

Aspen Ventures
1000 Fremont Ave., Ste. 200
Los Altos, CA 94024
(650)917-5670
Fax: (650)917-5677
Website: http://www.aspenventures.com

AVI Capital L.P.
1 First St., Ste. 2
Los Altos, CA 94022
(650)949-9862
Fax: (650)949-8510
Website: http://www.avicapital.com

Bastion Capital Corp.
1999 Avenue of the Stars, Ste. 2960
Los Angeles, CA 90067
(310)788-5700

Fax: (310)277-7582
E-mail: ga@bastioncapital.com
Website: http://www.bastioncapital.com

Davis Group
PO Box 69953
Los Angeles, CA 90069-0953
(310)659-6327
Fax: (310)659-6337

Developers Equity Corp.
1880 Century Park East, Ste. 211
Los Angeles, CA 90067
(213)277-0300

Far East Capital Corp.
350 S. Grand Ave., Ste. 4100
Los Angeles, CA 90071
(213)687-1361
Fax: (213)617-7939
E-mail: free@fareastnationalbank.com

Kline Hawkes & Co.
11726 San Vicente Blvd., Ste. 300
Los Angeles, CA 90049
(310)442-4700
Fax: (310)442-4707
Website: http://www.klinehawkes.com

Lawrence Financial Group
701 Teakwood
PO Box 491773
Los Angeles, CA 90049
(310)471-4060
Fax: (310)472-3155

Riordan Lewis & Haden
300 S. Grand Ave., 29th Fl.
Los Angeles, CA 90071
(213)229-8500
Fax: (213)229-8597

Union Venture Corp.
445 S. Figueroa St., 9th Fl.
Los Angeles, CA 90071
(213)236-4092
Fax: (213)236-6329

Wedbush Capital Partners
1000 Wilshire Blvd.
Los Angeles, CA 90017
(213)688-4545
Fax: (213)688-6642
Website: http://www.wedbush.com

Advent International Corp.
2180 Sand Hill Rd., Ste. 420
Menlo Park, CA 94025
(650)233-7500

Fax: (650)233-7515
Website: http://www.adventinternational.com

Altos Ventures
2882 Sand Hill Rd., Ste. 100
Menlo Park, CA 94025
(650)234-9771
Fax: (650)233-9821
Website: http://www.altosvc.com

Applied Technology
1010 El Camino Real, Ste. 300
Menlo Park, CA 94025
(415)326-8622
Fax: (415)326-8163

APV Technology Partners
535 Middlefield, Ste. 150
Menlo Park, CA 94025
(650)327-7871
Fax: (650)327-7631
Website: http://www.apvtp.com

August Capital Management
2480 Sand Hill Rd., Ste. 101
Menlo Park, CA 94025
(650)234-9900
Fax: (650)234-9910
Website: http://www.augustcap.com

Baccharis Capital Inc.
2420 Sand Hill Rd., Ste. 100
Menlo Park, CA 94025
(650)324-6844
Fax: (650)854-3025

Benchmark Capital
2480 Sand Hill Rd., Ste. 200
Menlo Park, CA 94025
(650)854-8180
Fax: (650)854-8183
E-mail: info@benchmark.com
Website: http://www.benchmark.com

Bessemer Venture Partners (Menlo Park)
535 Middlefield Rd., Ste. 245
Menlo Park, CA 94025
(650)853-7000
Fax: (650)853-7001
Website: http://www.bvp.com

The Cambria Group
1600 El Camino Real Rd., Ste. 155
Menlo Park, CA 94025
(650)329-8600
Fax: (650)329-8601
Website: http://www.cambriagroup.com

Canaan Partners
2884 Sand Hill Rd., Ste. 115
Menlo Park, CA 94025
(650)854-8092
Fax: (650)854-8127
Website: http://www.canaan.com

Capstone Ventures
3000 Sand Hill Rd., Bldg. One, Ste. 290
Menlo Park, CA 94025
(650)854-2523
Fax: (650)854-9010
Website: http://www.capstonevc.com

Comdisco Venture Group (Silicon Valley)
3000 Sand Hill Rd., Bldg. 1, Ste. 155
Menlo Park, CA 94025
(650)854-9484
Fax: (650)854-4026

Commtech International
535 Middlefield Rd., Ste. 200
Menlo Park, CA 94025
(650)328-0190
Fax: (650)328-6442

Compass Technology Partners
1550 El Camino Real, Ste. 275
Menlo Park, CA 94025-4111
(650)322-7595
Fax: (650)322-0588
Website: http://www.compasstechpartners.com

Convergence Partners
3000 Sand Hill Rd., Ste. 235
Menlo Park, CA 94025
(650)854-3010
Fax: (650)854-3015
Website: http://www.convergencepartners.com

The Dakota Group
PO Box 1025
Menlo Park, CA 94025
(650)853-0600
Fax: (650)851-4899
E-mail: info@dakota.com

Delphi Ventures
3000 Sand Hill Rd.
Bldg. One, Ste. 135
Menlo Park, CA 94025
(650)854-9650
Fax: (650)854-2961
Website: http://www.delphiventures.com

El Dorado Ventures
2884 Sand Hill Rd., Ste. 121
Menlo Park, CA 94025

(650)854-1200
Fax: (650)854-1202
Website: http://www.eldoradoventures.com

Glynn Ventures
3000 Sand Hill Rd., Bldg. 4, Ste. 235
Menlo Park, CA 94025
(650)854-2215

Indosuez Ventures
2180 Sand Hill Rd., Ste. 450
Menlo Park, CA 94025
(650)854-0587
Fax: (650)323-5561
Website: http://www.indosuezventures.com

Institutional Venture Partners
3000 Sand Hill Rd., Bldg. 2, Ste. 290
Menlo Park, CA 94025
(650)854-0132
Fax: (650)854-5762
Website: http://www.ivp.com

Interwest Partners (Menlo Park)
3000 Sand Hill Rd., Bldg. 3, Ste. 255
Menlo Park, CA 94025-7112
(650)854-8585
Fax: (650)854-4706
Website: http://www.interwest.com

Kleiner Perkins Caufield & Byers (Menlo Park)
2750 Sand Hill Rd.
Menlo Park, CA 94025
(650)233-2750
Fax: (650)233-0300
Website: http://www.kpcb.com

Magic Venture Capital LLC
1010 El Camino Real, Ste. 300
Menlo Park, CA 94025
(650)325-4149

Matrix Partners
2500 Sand Hill Rd., Ste. 113
Menlo Park, CA 94025
(650)854-3131
Fax: (650)854-3296
Website: http://www.matrixpartners.com

Mayfield Fund
2800 Sand Hill Rd.
Menlo Park, CA 94025
(650)854-5560
Fax: (650)854-5712
Website: http://www.mayfield.com

McCown De Leeuw and Co. (Menlo Park)
3000 Sand Hill Rd., Bldg. 3, Ste. 290
Menlo Park, CA 94025-7111

(650)854-6000
Fax: (650)854-0853
Website: http://www.mdcpartners.com

Menlo Ventures
3000 Sand Hill Rd., Bldg. 4, Ste. 100
Menlo Park, CA 94025
(650)854-8540
Fax: (650)854-7059
Website: http://www.menloventures.com

Merrill Pickard Anderson & Eyre
2480 Sand Hill Rd., Ste. 200
Menlo Park, CA 94025
(650)854-8600
Fax: (650)854-0345

New Enterprise Associates (Menlo Park)
2490 Sand Hill Rd.
Menlo Park, CA 94025
(650)854-9499
Fax: (650)854-9397
Website: http://www.nea.com

Onset Ventures
2400 Sand Hill Rd., Ste. 150
Menlo Park, CA 94025
(650)529-0700
Fax: (650)529-0777
Website: http://www.onset.com

Paragon Venture Partners
3000 Sand Hill Rd., Bldg. 1, Ste. 275
Menlo Park, CA 94025
(650)854-8000
Fax: (650)854-7260

Pathfinder Venture Capital Funds (Menlo Park)
3000 Sand Hill Rd., Bldg. 3, Ste. 255
Menlo Park, CA 94025
(650)854-0650
Fax: (650)854-4706

Rocket Ventures
3000 Sandhill Rd., Bldg. 1, Ste. 170
Menlo Park, CA 94025
(650)561-9100
Fax: (650)561-9183
Website: http://www.rocketventures.com

Sequoia Capital
3000 Sand Hill Rd., Bldg. 4, Ste. 280
Menlo Park, CA 94025
(650)854-3927
Fax: (650)854-2977
E-mail: sequoia@sequioacap.com
Website: http://www.sequoiacap.com

Sierra Ventures
3000 Sand Hill Rd., Bldg. 4, Ste. 210
Menlo Park, CA 94025
(650)854-1000
Fax: (650)854-5593
Website: http://www.sierraventures.com

Sigma Partners
2884 Sand Hill Rd., Ste. 121
Menlo Park, CA 94025-7022
(650)853-1700
Fax: (650)853-1717
E-mail: info@sigmapartners.com
Website: http://www.sigmapartners.com

Sprout Group (Menlo Park)
3000 Sand Hill Rd.
Bldg. 3, Ste. 170
Menlo Park, CA 94025
(650)234-2700
Fax: (650)234-2779
Website: http://www.sproutgroup.com

TA Associates (Menlo Park)
70 Willow Rd., Ste. 100
Menlo Park, CA 94025
(650)328-1210
Fax: (650)326-4933
Website: http://www.ta.com

Thompson Clive & Partners Ltd.
3000 Sand Hill Rd., Bldg. 1, Ste. 185
Menlo Park, CA 94025-7102
(650)854-0314
Fax: (650)854-0670
E-mail: mail@tcvc.com
Website: http://www.tcvc.com

Trinity Ventures Ltd.
3000 Sand Hill Rd., Bldg. 1, Ste. 240
Menlo Park, CA 94025
(650)854-9500
Fax: (650)854-9501
Website: http://www.trinityventures.com

U.S. Venture Partners
2180 Sand Hill Rd., Ste. 300
Menlo Park, CA 94025
(650)854-9080
Fax: (650)854-3018
Website: http://www.usvp.com

USVP-Schlein Marketing Fund
2180 Sand Hill Rd., Ste. 300
Menlo Park, CA 94025
(415)854-9080
Fax: (415)854-3018
Website: http://www.usvp.com

Venrock Associates
2494 Sand Hill Rd., Ste. 200
Menlo Park, CA 94025

(650)561-9580
Fax: (650)561-9180
Website: http://www.venrock.com

Brad Peery Capital Inc.
145 Chapel Pkwy.
Mill Valley, CA 94941
(415)389-0625
Fax: (415)389-1336

Dot Edu Ventures
650 Castro St., Ste. 270
Mountain View, CA 94041
(650)575-5638
Fax: (650)325-5247
Website: http://www.doteduventures.com

Forrest, Binkley & Brown
840 Newport Ctr. Dr., Ste. 480
Newport Beach, CA 92660
(949)729-3222
Fax: (949)729-3226
Website: http://www.fbbvc.com

Marwit Capital LLC
180 Newport Center Dr., Ste. 200
Newport Beach, CA 92660
(949)640-6234
Fax: (949)720-8077
Website: http://www.marwit.com

Kaiser Permanente / National Venture Development
1800 Harrison St., 22nd Fl.
Oakland, CA 94612
(510)267-4010
Fax: (510)267-4036
Website: http://www.kpventures.com

Nu Capital Access Group, Ltd.
7677 Oakport St., Ste. 105
Oakland, CA 94621
(510)635-7345
Fax: (510)635-7068

Inman and Bowman
4 Orinda Way, Bldg. D, Ste. 150
Orinda, CA 94563
(510)253-1611
Fax: (510)253-9037

Accel Partners (San Francisco)
428 University Ave.
Palo Alto, CA 94301
(650)614-4800
Fax: (650)614-4880
Website: http://www.accel.com

Advanced Technology Ventures
485 Ramona St., Ste. 200
Palo Alto, CA 94301
(650)321-8601

Fax: (650)321-0934
Website: http://www.atvcapital.com

Anila Fund
400 Channing Ave.
Palo Alto, CA 94301
(650)833-5790
Fax: (650)833-0590
Website: http://www.anila.com

Asset Management Company Venture Capital
2275 E. Bayshore, Ste. 150
Palo Alto, CA 94303
(650)494-7400
Fax: (650)856-1826
E-mail: postmaster@assetman.com
Website: http://www.assetman.com

BancBoston Capital / BancBoston Ventures
435 Tasso St., Ste. 250
Palo Alto, CA 94305
(650)470-4100
Fax: (650)853-1425
Website: http://www.bancbostoncapital.com

Charter Ventures
525 University Ave., Ste. 1400
Palo Alto, CA 94301
(650)325-6953
Fax: (650)325-4762
Website: http://www.charterventures.com

Communications Ventures
505 Hamilton Avenue, Ste. 305
Palo Alto, CA 94301
(650)325-9600
Fax: (650)325-9608
Website: http://www.comven.com

HMS Group
2468 Embarcadero Way
Palo Alto, CA 94303-3313
(650)856-9862
Fax: (650)856-9864

Jafco America Ventures, Inc.
505 Hamilton Ste. 310
Palto Alto, CA 94301
(650)463-8800
Fax: (650)463-8801
Website: http://www.jafco.com

New Vista Capital
540 Cowper St., Ste. 200
Palo Alto, CA 94301
(650)329-9333
Fax: (650)328-9434
E-mail: fgreene@nvcap.com
Website: http://www.nvcap.com

Norwest Equity Partners (Palo Alto)
245 Lytton Ave., Ste. 250
Palo Alto, CA 94301-1426
(650)321-8000
Fax: (650)321-8010
Website: http://www.norwestvp.com

Oak Investment Partners
525 University Ave., Ste. 1300
Palo Alto, CA 94301
(650)614-3700
Fax: (650)328-6345
Website: http://www.oakinv.com

Patricof & Co. Ventures, Inc. (Palo Alto)
2100 Geng Rd., Ste. 150
Palo Alto, CA 94303
(650)494-9944
Fax: (650)494-6751
Website: http://www.patricof.com

RWI Group
835 Page Mill Rd.
Palo Alto, CA 94304
(650)251-1800
Fax: (650)213-8660
Website: http://www.rwigroup.com

Summit Partners (Palo Alto)
499 Hamilton Ave., Ste. 200
Palo Alto, CA 94301
(650)321-1166
Fax: (650)321-1188
Website: http://www.summitpartners.com

Sutter Hill Ventures
755 Page Mill Rd., Ste. A-200
Palo Alto, CA 94304
(650)493-5600
Fax: (650)858-1854
E-mail: shv@shv.com

Vanguard Venture Partners
525 University Ave., Ste. 600
Palo Alto, CA 94301
(650)321-2900
Fax: (650)321-2902
Website: http://www.vanguardventures.com

Venture Growth Associates
2479 East Bayshore St., Ste. 710
Palo Alto, CA 94303
(650)855-9100
Fax: (650)855-9104

Worldview Technology Partners
435 Tasso St., Ste. 120
Palo Alto, CA 94301
(650)322-3800

Fax: (650)322-3880
Website: http://www.worldview.com

Draper, Fisher, Jurvetson / Draper Associates
400 Seaport Ct., Ste.250
Redwood City, CA 94063
(415)599-9000
Fax: (415)599-9726
Website: http://www.dfj.com

Gabriel Venture Partners
350 Marine Pkwy., Ste. 200
Redwood Shores, CA 94065
(650)551-5000
Fax: (650)551-5001
Website: http://www.gabrielvp.com

Hallador Venture Partners, L.L.C.
740 University Ave., Ste. 110
Sacramento, CA 95825-6710
(916)920-0191
Fax: (916)920-5188
E-mail: chris@hallador.com

Emerald Venture Group
12396 World Trade Dr., Ste. 116
San Diego, CA 92128
(858)451-1001
Fax: (858)451-1003
Website: http://www.emeraldventure.com

Forward Ventures
9255 Towne Centre Dr.
San Diego, CA 92121
(858)677-6077
Fax: (858)452-8799
E-mail: info@forwardventure.com
Website: http://www.forwardventure.com

Idanta Partners Ltd.
4660 La Jolla Village Dr., Ste. 850
San Diego, CA 92122
(619)452-9690
Fax: (619)452-2013
Website: http://www.idanta.com

Kingsbury Associates
3655 Nobel Dr., Ste. 490
San Diego, CA 92122
(858)677-0600
Fax: (858)677-0800

Kyocera International Inc.
Corporate Development
8611 Balboa Ave.
San Diego, CA 92123
(858)576-2600
Fax: (858)492-1456

Sorrento Associates, Inc.
4370 LaJolla Village Dr., Ste. 1040
San Diego, CA 92122
(619)452-3100
Fax: (619)452-7607
Website: http://www.sorrentoventures.com

Western States Investment Group
9191 Towne Ctr. Dr., Ste. 310
San Diego, CA 92122
(619)678-0800
Fax: (619)678-0900

Aberdare Ventures
One Embarcadero Center, Ste. 4000
San Francisco, CA 94111
(415)392-7442
Fax: (415)392-4264
Website: http://www.aberdare.com

Acacia Venture Partners
101 California St., Ste. 3160
San Francisco, CA 94111
(415)433-4200
Fax: (415)433-4250
Website: http://www.acaciavp.com

Access Venture Partners
319 Laidley St.
San Francisco, CA 94131
(415)586-0132
Fax: (415)392-6310
Website: http://www.accessventurepartners.com

Alta Partners
One Embarcadero Center, Ste. 4050
San Francisco, CA 94111
(415)362-4022
Fax: (415)362-6178
E-mail: alta@altapartners.com
Website: http://www.altapartners.com

Bangert Dawes Reade Davis & Thom
220 Montgomery St., Ste. 424
San Francisco, CA 94104
(415)954-9900
Fax: (415)954-9901
E-mail: bdrdt@pacbell.net

Berkeley International Capital Corp.
650 California St., Ste. 2800
San Francisco, CA 94108-2609
(415)249-0450
Fax: (415)392-3929
Website: http://www.berkeleyvc.com

Blueprint Ventures LLC
456 Montgomery St., 22nd Fl.
San Francisco, CA 94104
(415)901-4000

Fax: (415)901-4035
Website: http://www.blueprintventures.com

Blumberg Capital Ventures
580 Howard St., Ste. 401
San Francisco, CA 94105
(415)905-5007
Fax: (415)357-5027
Website: http://www.blumberg-capital.com

Burr, Egan, Deleage, and Co. (San Francisco)
1 Embarcadero Center, Ste. 4050
San Francisco, CA 94111
(415)362-4022
Fax: (415)362-6178

Burrill & Company
120 Montgomery St., Ste. 1370
San Francisco, CA 94104
(415)743-3160
Fax: (415)743-3161
Website: http://www.burrillandco.com

CMEA Ventures
235 Montgomery St., Ste. 920
San Francisco, CA 94401
(415)352-1520
Fax: (415)352-1524
Website: http://www.cmeaventures.com

Crocker Capital
1 Post St., Ste. 2500
San Francisco, CA 94101
(415)956-5250
Fax: (415)959-5710

Dominion Ventures, Inc.
44 Montgomery St., Ste. 4200
San Francisco, CA 94104
(415)362-4890
Fax: (415)394-9245

Dorset Capital
Pier 1
Bay 2
San Francisco, CA 94111
(415)398-7101
Fax: (415)398-7141
Website: http://www.dorsetcapital.com

Gatx Capital
Four Embarcadero Center, Ste. 2200
San Francisco, CA 94904
(415)955-3200
Fax: (415)955-3449

IMinds
135 Main St., Ste. 1350
San Francisco, CA 94105

(415)547-0000
Fax: (415)227-0300
Website: http://www.iminds.com

LF International Inc.
360 Post St., Ste. 705
San Francisco, CA 94108
(415)399-0110
Fax: (415)399-9222
Website: http://www.lfvc.com

Newbury Ventures
535 Pacific Ave., 2nd Fl.
San Francisco, CA 94133
(415)296-7408
Fax: (415)296-7416
Website: http://www.newburyven.com

Quest Ventures (San Francisco)
333 Bush St., Ste. 1750
San Francisco, CA 94104
(415)782-1414
Fax: (415)782-1415

Robertson-Stephens Co.
555 California St., Ste. 2600
San Francisco, CA 94104
(415)781-9700
Fax: (415)781-2556
Website: http://www.omegaadventures.com

Rosewood Capital, L.P.
One Maritime Plaza, Ste. 1330
San Francisco, CA 94111-3503
(415)362-5526
Fax: (415)362-1192
Website: http://www.rosewoodvc.com

Ticonderoga Capital Inc.
555 California St., No. 4950
San Francisco, CA 94104
(415)296-7900
Fax: (415)296-8956

21st Century Internet Venture Partners
Two South Park
2nd Floor
San Francisco, CA 94107
(415)512-1221
Fax: (415)512-2650
Website: http://www.21vc.com

VK Ventures
600 California St., Ste.1700
San Francisco, CA 94111
(415)391-5600
Fax: (415)397-2744

Walden Group of Venture Capital Funds
750 Battery St., Seventh Floor
San Francisco, CA 94111
(415)391-7225
Fax: (415)391-7262

Acer Technology Ventures
2641 Orchard Pkwy.
San Jose, CA 95134
(408)433-4945
Fax: (408)433-5230

Authosis
226 Airport Pkwy., Ste. 405
San Jose, CA 95110
(650)814-3603
Website: http://www.authosis.com

Western Technology Investment
2010 N. First St., Ste. 310
San Jose, CA 95131
(408)436-8577
Fax: (408)436-8625
E-mail: mktg@westerntech.com

Drysdale Enterprises
177 Bovet Rd., Ste. 600
San Mateo, CA 94402
(650)341-6336
Fax: (650)341-1329
E-mail: drysdale@aol.com

Greylock
2929 Campus Dr., Ste. 400
San Mateo, CA 94401
(650)493-5525
Fax: (650)493-5575
Website: http://www.greylock.com

Technology Funding
2000 Alameda de las Pulgas, Ste. 250
San Mateo, CA 94403
(415)345-2200
Fax: (415)345-1797

2M Invest Inc.
1875 S. Grant St.
Suite 750
San Mateo, CA 94402
(650)655-3765
Fax: (650)372-9107
E-mail: 2minfo@2minvest.com
Website: http://www.2minvest.com

Phoenix Growth Capital Corp.
2401 Kerner Blvd.
San Rafael, CA 94901
(415)485-4569
Fax: (415)485-4663

NextGen Partners LLC
1705 East Valley Rd.
Santa Barbara, CA 93108
(805)969-8540
Fax: (805)969-8542
Website: http://www.nextgenpartners.com

Denali Venture Capital
1925 Woodland Ave.
Santa Clara, CA 95050
(408)690-4838
Fax: (408)247-6979
E-mail: wael@denaliventurecapital.com
Website: http://www.denaliventure capital.com

Dotcom Ventures LP
3945 Freedom Circle, Ste. 740
Santa Clara, CA 95045
(408)919-9855
Fax: (408)919-9857
Website: http://www.dotcomventure satl.com

Silicon Valley Bank
3003 Tasman
Santa Clara, CA 95054
(408)654-7400
Fax: (408)727-8728

Al Shugart International
920 41st Ave.
Santa Cruz, CA 95062
(831)479-7852
Fax: (831)479-7852
Website: http://www.alshugart.com

Leonard Mautner Associates
1434 Sixth St.
Santa Monica, CA 90401
(213)393-9788
Fax: (310)459-9918

Palomar Ventures
100 Wilshire Blvd., Ste. 450
Santa Monica, CA 90401
(310)260-6050
Fax: (310)656-4150
Website: http://www.palomarventures.com

Medicus Venture Partners
12930 Saratoga Ave., Ste. D8
Saratoga, CA 95070
(408)447-8600
Fax: (408)447-8599
Website: http://www.medicusvc.com

Redleaf Venture Management
14395 Saratoga Ave., Ste. 130
Saratoga, CA 95070

(408)868-0800
Fax: (408)868-0810
E-mail: nancy@redleaf.com
Website: http://www.redleaf.com

Artemis Ventures
207 Second St., Ste. E
3rd Fl.
Sausalito, CA 94965
(415)289-2500
Fax: (415)289-1789
Website: http://www.artemisventures.com

Deucalion Venture Partners
19501 Brooklime
Sonoma, CA 95476
(707)938-4974
Fax: (707)938-8921

Windward Ventures
PO Box 7688
Thousand Oaks, CA 91359-7688
(805)497-3332
Fax: (805)497-9331

National Investment Management, Inc.
2601 Airport Dr., Ste.210
Torrance, CA 90505
(310)784-7600
Fax: (310)784-7605

Southern California Ventures
406 Amapola Ave. Ste. 125
Torrance, CA 90501
(310)787-4381
Fax: (310)787-4382

Sandton Financial Group
21550 Oxnard St., Ste. 300
Woodland Hills, CA 91367
(818)702-9283

Woodside Fund
850 Woodside Dr.
Woodside, CA 94062
(650)368-5545
Fax: (650)368-2416
Website: http://www.woodsidefund.com

Colorado

Colorado Venture Management
Ste. 300
Boulder, CO 80301
(303)440-4055
Fax: (303)440-4636

Dean & Associates
4362 Apple Way
Boulder, CO 80301
Fax: (303)473-9900

Roser Ventures LLC
1105 Spruce St.
Boulder, CO 80302
(303)443-6436
Fax: (303)443-1885
Website: http://www.roserventures.com

Sequel Venture Partners
4430 Arapahoe Ave., Ste. 220
Boulder, CO 80303
(303)546-0400
Fax: (303)546-9728
E-mail: tom@sequelvc.com
Website: http://www.sequelvc.com

New Venture Resources
445C E. Cheyenne Mtn. Blvd.
Colorado Springs, CO 80906-4570
(719)598-9272
Fax: (719)598-9272

The Centennial Funds
1428 15th St.
Denver, CO 80202-1318
(303)405-7500
Fax: (303)405-7575
Website: http://www.centennial.com

Rocky Mountain Capital Partners
1125 17th St., Ste. 2260
Denver, CO 80202
(303)291-5200
Fax: (303)291-5327

Sandlot Capital LLC
600 South Cherry St., Ste. 525
Denver, CO 80246
(303)893-3400
Fax: (303)893-3403
Website: http://www.sandlotcapital.com

Wolf Ventures
50 South Steele St., Ste. 777
Denver, CO 80209
(303)321-4800
Fax: (303)321-4848
E-mail: businessplan@wolfventures.com
Website: http://www.wolfventures.com

The Columbine Venture Funds
5460 S. Quebec St., Ste. 270
Englewood, CO 80111
(303)694-3222
Fax: (303)694-9007

Investment Securities of Colorado, Inc.
4605 Denice Dr.
Englewood, CO 80111
(303)796-9192

Kinship Partners
6300 S. Syracuse Way, Ste. 484
Englewood, CO 80111
(303)694-0268
Fax: (303)694-1707
E-mail: block@vailsys.com

Boranco Management, L.L.C.
1528 Hillside Dr.
Fort Collins, CO 80524-1969
(970)221-2297
Fax: (970)221-4787

Aweida Ventures
890 West Cherry St., Ste. 220
Louisville, CO 80027
(303)664-9520
Fax: (303)664-9530
Website: http://www.aweida.com

Access Venture Partners
8787 Turnpike Dr., Ste. 260
Westminster, CO 80030
(303)426-8899
Fax: (303)426-8828

Connecticut

Medmax Ventures LP
1 Northwestern Dr., Ste. 203
Bloomfield, CT 06002
(860)286-2960
Fax: (860)286-9960

James B. Kobak & Co.
Four Mansfield Place
Darien, CT 06820
(203)656-3471
Fax: (203)655-2905

Orien Ventures
1 Post Rd.
Fairfield, CT 06430
(203)259-9933
Fax: (203)259-5288

ABP Acquisition Corporation
115 Maple Ave.
Greenwich, CT 06830
(203)625-8287
Fax: (203)447-6187

Catterton Partners
9 Greenwich Office Park
Greenwich, CT 06830
(203)629-4901
Fax: (203)629-4903
Website: http://www.cpequity.com

Consumer Venture Partners
3 Pickwick Plz.
Greenwich, CT 06830
(203)629-8800
Fax: (203)629-2019

Insurance Venture Partners
31 Brookside Dr., Ste. 211
Greenwich, CT 06830
(203)861-0030
Fax: (203)861-2745

The NTC Group
Three Pickwick Plaza
Ste. 200
Greenwich, CT 06830
(203)862-2800
Fax: (203)622-6538

Regulus International Capital Co., Inc.
140 Greenwich Ave.
Greenwich, CT 06830
(203)625-9700
Fax: (203)625-9706

Axiom Venture Partners
City Place II
185 Asylum St., 17th Fl.
Hartford, CT 06103
(860)548-7799
Fax: (860)548-7797
Website: http://www.axiomventures.com

Conning Capital Partners
City Place II
185 Asylum St.
Hartford, CT 06103-4105
(860)520-1289
Fax: (860)520-1299
E-mail: pe@conning.com
Website: http://www.conning.com

First New England Capital L.P.
100 Pearl St.
Hartford, CT 06103
(860)293-3333
Fax: (860)293-3338
E-mail: info@firstnewenglandcapital.com
Website: http://www.firstnewengland
capital.com

Northeast Ventures
One State St., Ste. 1720
Hartford, CT 06103
(860)547-1414
Fax: (860)246-8755

Windward Holdings
38 Sylvan Rd.
Madison, CT 06443
(203)245-6870
Fax: (203)245-6865

Advanced Materials Partners, Inc.
45 Pine St.
PO Box 1022
New Canaan, CT 06840

(203)966-6415
Fax: (203)966-8448
E-mail: wkb@amplink.com

RFE Investment Partners
36 Grove St.
New Canaan, CT 06840
(203)966-2800
Fax: (203)966-3109
Website: http://www.rfeip.com

Connecticut Innovations, Inc.
999 West St.
Rocky Hill, CT 06067
(860)563-5851
Fax: (860)563-4877
E-mail: pamela.hartley@
ctinnovations.com
Website: http://www.ctinnovations.com

Canaan Partners
105 Rowayton Ave.
Rowayton, CT 06853
(203)855-0400
Fax: (203)854-9117
Website: http://www.canaan.com

Landmark Partners, Inc.
10 Mill Pond Ln.
Simsbury, CT 06070
(860)651-9760
Fax: (860)651-8890
Website: http://
www.landmarkpartners.com

Sweeney & Company
PO Box 567
Southport, CT 06490
(203)255-0220
Fax: (203)255-0220
E-mail: sweeney@connix.com

Baxter Associates, Inc.
PO Box 1333
Stamford, CT 06904
(203)323-3143
Fax: (203)348-0622

Beacon Partners Inc.
6 Landmark Sq., 4th Fl.
Stamford, CT 06901-2792
(203)359-5776
Fax: (203)359-5876

Collinson, Howe, and Lennox, LLC
1055 Washington Blvd., 5th Fl.
Stamford, CT 06901
(203)324-7700
Fax: (203)324-3636
E-mail: info@chlmedical.com
Website: http://www.chlmedical.com

Prime Capital Management Co.
550 West Ave.
Stamford, CT 06902
(203)964-0642
Fax: (203)964-0862

Saugatuck Capital Co.
1 Canterbury Green
Stamford, CT 06901
(203)348-6669
Fax: (203)324-6995
Website: http://www.saugatuckcapital.
com

Soundview Financial Group Inc.
22 Gatehouse Rd.
Stamford, CT 06902
(203)462-7200
Fax: (203)462-7350
Website: http://www.sndv.com

TSG Ventures, L.L.C.
177 Broad St., 12th Fl.
Stamford, CT 06901
(203)406-1500
Fax: (203)406-1590

Whitney & Company
177 Broad St.
Stamford, CT 06901
(203)973-1400
Fax: (203)973-1422
Website: http://www.jhwhitney.com

Cullinane & Donnelly Venture Partners L.P.
970 Farmington Ave.
West Hartford, CT 06107
(860)521-7811

The Crestview Investment and Financial Group
431 Post Rd. E, Ste. 1
Westport, CT 06880-4403
(203)222-0333
Fax: (203)222-0000

Marketcorp Venture Associates, L.P. (MCV)
274 Riverside Ave.
Westport, CT 06880
(203)222-3030
Fax: (203)222-3033

Oak Investment Partners (Westport)
1 Gorham Island
Westport, CT 06880
(203)226-8346
Fax: (203)227-0372
Website: http://www.oakinv.com

Oxford Bioscience Partners
315 Post Rd. W
Westport, CT 06880-5200
(203)341-3300
Fax: (203)341-3309
Website: http://www.oxbio.com

Prince Ventures (Westport)
25 Ford Rd.
Westport, CT 06880
(203)227-8332
Fax: (203)226-5302

LTI Venture Leasing Corp.
221 Danbury Rd.
Wilton, CT 06897
(203)563-1100
Fax: (203)563-1111
Website: http://www.ltileasing.com

Delaware

Blue Rock Capital
5803 Kennett Pike, Ste. A
Wilmington, DE 19807
(302)426-0981
Fax: (302)426-0982
Website: http://
www.bluerockcapital.com

District of Columbia

Allied Capital Corp.
1919 Pennsylvania Ave. NW
Washington, DC 20006-3434
(202)331-2444
Fax: (202)659-2053
Website: http://www.alliedcapital.com

Atlantic Coastal Ventures, L.P.
3101 South St. NW
Washington, DC 20007
(202)293-1166
Fax: (202)293-1181
Website: http://www.atlanticcv.com

Columbia Capital Group, Inc.
1660 L St. NW, Ste. 308
Washington, DC 20036
(202)775-8815
Fax: (202)223-0544

Core Capital Partners
901 15th St., NW
9th Fl.
Washington, DC 20005
(202)589-0090
Fax: (202)589-0091
Website: http://www.core-capital.com

Next Point Partners
701 Pennsylvania Ave. NW, Ste. 900
Washington, DC 20004
(202)661-8703
Fax: (202)434-7400
E-mail: mf@nextpoint.vc
Website: http://www.nextpointvc.com

Telecommunications Development Fund
2020 K. St. NW
Ste. 375
Washington, DC 20006
(202)293-8840
Fax: (202)293-8850
Website: http://www.tdfund.com

Wachtel & Co., Inc.
1101 4th St. NW
Washington, DC 20005-5680
(202)898-1144

Winslow Partners LLC
1300 Connecticut Ave. NW
Washington, DC 20036-1703
(202)530-5000
Fax: (202)530-5010
E-mail: winslow@winslowpartners.com

Women's Growth Capital Fund
1054 31st St., NW
Ste. 110
Washington, DC 20007
(202)342-1431
Fax: (202)341-1203
Website: http://www.wgcf.com

Florida

Sigma Capital Corp.
22668 Caravelle Circle
Boca Raton, FL 33433
(561)368-9783

North American Business Development Co., L.L.C.
111 East Las Olas Blvd.
Ft. Lauderdale, FL 33301
(305)463-0681
Fax: (305)527-0904
Website: http://
www.northamericanfund.com

Chartwell Capital Management Co. Inc.
1 Independent Dr., Ste. 3120
Jacksonville, FL 32202
(904)355-3519
Fax: (904)353-5833
E-mail: info@chartwellcap.com

CEO Advisors
1061 Maitland Center Commons
Ste. 209

Maitland, FL 32751
(407)660-9327
Fax: (407)660-2109

Henry & Co.
8201 Peters Rd., Ste. 1000
Plantation, FL 33324
(954)797-7400

Avery Business Development Services
2506 St. Michel Ct.
Ponte Vedra, FL 32082
(904)285-6033

New South Ventures
5053 Ocean Blvd.
Sarasota, FL 34242
(941)358-6000
Fax: (941)358-6078
Website: http://www.newsouthventures.com

Venture Capital Management Corp.
PO Box 2626
Satellite Beach, FL 32937
(407)777-1969

Florida Capital Venture Ltd.
325 Florida Bank Plaza
100 W. Kennedy Blvd.
Tampa, FL 33602
(813)229-2294
Fax: (813)229-2028

Quantum Capital Partners
339 South Plant Ave.
Tampa, FL 33606
(813)250-1999
Fax: (813)250-1998
Website: http://www.quantumcapital
partners.com

South Atlantic Venture Fund
614 W. Bay St.
Tampa, FL 33606-2704
(813)253-2500
Fax: (813)253-2360
E-mail: venture@southatlantic.com
Website: http://www.southatlantic.com

LM Capital Corp.
120 S. Olive, Ste. 400
West Palm Beach, FL 33401
(561)833-9700
Fax: (561)655-6587
Website: http://www.lmcapitalsecurities.com

Georgia

Venture First Associates
4811 Thornwood Dr.
Acworth, GA 30102
(770)928-3733
Fax: (770)928-6455

Alliance Technology Ventures
8995 Westside Pkwy., Ste. 200
Alpharetta, GA 30004
(678)336-2000
Fax: (678)336-2001
E-mail: info@atv.com
Website: http://www.atv.com

Cordova Ventures
2500 North Winds Pkwy., Ste. 475
Alpharetta, GA 30004
(678)942-0300
Fax: (678)942-0301
Website: http://www.cordovaventures.com

Advanced Technology Development Fund
1000 Abernathy, Ste. 1420
Atlanta, GA 30328-5614
(404)668-2333
Fax: (404)668-2333

CGW Southeast Partners
12 Piedmont Center, Ste. 210
Atlanta, GA 30305
(404)816-3255
Fax: (404)816-3258
Website: http://www.cgwlp.com

Cyberstarts
1900 Emery St., NW
3rd Fl.
Atlanta, GA 30318
(404)267-5000
Fax: (404)267-5200
Website: http://www.cyberstarts.com

EGL Holdings, Inc.
10 Piedmont Center, Ste. 412
Atlanta, GA 30305
(404)949-8300
Fax: (404)949-8311

Equity South
1790 The Lenox Bldg.
3399 Peachtree Rd. NE
Atlanta, GA 30326
(404)237-6222
Fax: (404)261-1578

Five Paces
3400 Peachtree Rd., Ste. 200
Atlanta, GA 30326

(404)439-8300
Fax: (404)439-8301
Website: http://www.fivepaces.com

Frontline Capital, Inc.
3475 Lenox Rd., Ste. 400
Atlanta, GA 30326
(404)240-7280
Fax: (404)240-7281

Fuqua Ventures LLC
1201 W. Peachtree St. NW, Ste. 5000
Atlanta, GA 30309
(404)815-4500
Fax: (404)815-4528
Website: http://www.fuquaventures.com

Noro-Moseley Partners
4200 Northside Pkwy., Bldg. 9
Atlanta, GA 30327
(404)233-1966
Fax: (404)239-9280
Website: http://www.noro-moseley.com

Renaissance Capital Corp.
34 Peachtree St. NW, Ste. 2230
Atlanta, GA 30303
(404)658-9061
Fax: (404)658-9064

River Capital, Inc.
Two Midtown Plaza
1360 Peachtree St. NE, Ste. 1430
Atlanta, GA 30309
(404)873-2166
Fax: (404)873-2158

State Street Bank & Trust Co.
3414 Peachtree Rd. NE, Ste. 1010
Atlanta, GA 30326
(404)364-9500
Fax: (404)261-4469

UPS Strategic Enterprise Fund
55 Glenlake Pkwy. NE
Atlanta, GA 30328
(404)828-8814
Fax: (404)828-8088
E-mail: jcacyce@ups.com
Website: http://www.ups.com/sef/sef_home

Wachovia
191 Peachtree St. NE, 26th Fl.
Atlanta, GA 30303
(404)332-1000
Fax: (404)332-1392
Website: http://www.wachovia.com/wca

Brainworks Ventures
4243 Dunwoody Club Dr.
Chamblee, GA 30341
(770)239-7447

First Growth Capital Inc.
Best Western Plaza, Ste. 105
PO Box 815
Forsyth, GA 31029
(912)781-7131

Financial Capital Resources, Inc.
21 Eastbrook Bend, Ste. 116
Peachtree City, GA 30269
(404)487-6650

Hawaii

HMS Hawaii Management Partners
Davies Pacific Center
841 Bishop St., Ste. 860
Honolulu, HI 96813
(808)545-3755
Fax: (808)531-2611

Idaho

Sun Valley Ventures
160 Second St.
Ketchum, ID 83340
(208)726-5005
Fax: (208)726-5094

Illinois

Open Prairie Ventures
115 N. Neil St., Ste. 209
Champaign, IL 61820
(217)351-7000
Fax: (217)351-7051
E-mail: inquire@openprairie.com
Website: http://www.openprairie.com

ABN AMRO Private Equity
208 S. La Salle St., 10th Fl.
Chicago, IL 60604
(312)855-7079
Fax: (312)553-6648
Website: http://www.abnequity.com

Alpha Capital Partners, Ltd.
122 S. Michigan Ave., Ste. 1700
Chicago, IL 60603
(312)322-9800
Fax: (312)322-9808
E-mail: acp@alphacapital.com

Ameritech Development Corp.
30 S. Wacker Dr., 37th Fl.
Chicago, IL 60606
(312)750-5083
Fax: (312)609-0244

Apex Investment Partners
225 W. Washington, Ste. 1450
Chicago, IL 60606

(312)857-2800
Fax: (312)857-1800
E-mail: apex@apexvc.com
Website: http://www.apexvc.com

Arch Venture Partners
8725 W. Higgins Rd., Ste. 290
Chicago, IL 60631
(773)380-6600
Fax: (773)380-6606
Website: http://www.archventure.com

The Bank Funds
208 South LaSalle St., Ste. 1680
Chicago, IL 60604
(312)855-6020
Fax: (312)855-8910

Batterson Venture Partners
303 W. Madison St., Ste. 1110
Chicago, IL 60606-3309
(312)269-0300
Fax: (312)269-0021
Website: http://www.battersonvp.com

William Blair Capital Partners, L.L.C.
222 W. Adams St., Ste. 1300
Chicago, IL 60606
(312)364-8250
Fax: (312)236-1042
E-mail: privateequity@wmblair.com
Website: http://www.wmblair.com

Bluestar Ventures
208 South LaSalle St., Ste. 1020
Chicago, IL 60604
(312)384-5000
Fax: (312)384-5005
Website: http://
www.bluestarventures.com

The Capital Strategy Management Co.
233 S. Wacker Dr.
Box 06334
Chicago, IL 60606
(312)444-1170

DN Partners
77 West Wacker Dr., Ste. 4550
Chicago, IL 60601
(312)332-7960
Fax: (312)332-7979

Dresner Capital Inc.
29 South LaSalle St., Ste. 310
Chicago, IL 60603
(312)726-3600
Fax: (312)726-7448

Eblast Ventures LLC
11 South LaSalle St., 5th Fl.
Chicago, IL 60603

(312)372-2600
Fax: (312)372-5621
Website: http://www.eblastventures.com

Essex Woodlands Health Ventures, L.P.
190 S. LaSalle St., Ste. 2800
Chicago, IL 60603
(312)444-6040
Fax: (312)444-6034
Website: http://
www.essexwoodlands.com

First Analysis Venture Capital
233 S. Wacker Dr., Ste. 9500
Chicago, IL 60606
(312)258-1400
Fax: (312)258-0334
Website: http://www.firstanalysis.com

Frontenac Co.
135 S. LaSalle St., Ste.3800
Chicago, IL 60603
(312)368-0044
Fax: (312)368-9520
Website: http://www.frontenac.com

GTCR Golder Rauner, LLC
6100 Sears Tower
Chicago, IL 60606
(312)382-2200
Fax: (312)382-2201
Website: http://www.gtcr.com

High Street Capital LLC
311 South Wacker Dr., Ste. 4550
Chicago, IL 60606
(312)697-4990
Fax: (312)697-4994
Website: http://www.highstr.com

IEG Venture Management, Inc.
70 West Madison
Chicago, IL 60602
(312)644-0890
Fax: (312)454-0369
Website: http://www.iegventure.com

JK&B Capital
180 North Stetson, Ste. 4500
Chicago, IL 60601
(312)946-1200
Fax: (312)946-1103
E-mail: gspencer@jkbcapital.com
Website: http://www.jkbcapital.com

Kettle Partners L.P.
350 W. Hubbard, Ste. 350
Chicago, IL 60610
(312)329-9300
Fax: (312)527-4519
Website: http://www.kettlevc.com

Lake Shore Capital Partners
20 N. Wacker Dr., Ste. 2807
Chicago, IL 60606
(312)803-3536
Fax: (312)803-3534

LaSalle Capital Group Inc.
70 W. Madison St., Ste. 5710
Chicago, IL 60602
(312)236-7041
Fax: (312)236-0720

Linc Capital, Inc.
303 E. Wacker Pkwy., Ste. 1000
Chicago, IL 60601
(312)946-2670
Fax: (312)938-4290
E-mail: bdemars@linccap.com

Madison Dearborn Partners, Inc.
3 First National Plz., Ste. 3800
Chicago, IL 60602
(312)895-1000
Fax: (312)895-1001
E-mail: invest@mdcp.com
Website: http://www.mdcp.com

Mesirow Private Equity Investments Inc.
350 N. Clark St.
Chicago, IL 60610
(312)595-6950
Fax: (312)595-6211
Website: http://www.
meisrowfinancial.com

Mosaix Ventures LLC
1822 North Mohawk
Chicago, IL 60614
(312)274-0988
Fax: (312)274-0989
Website: http://www.mosaixventures.com

Nesbitt Burns
111 West Monroe St.
Chicago, IL 60603
(312)416-3855
Fax: (312)765-8000
Website: http://www.harrisbank.com

Polestar Capital, Inc.
180 N. Michigan Ave., Ste. 1905
Chicago, IL 60601
(312)984-9090
Fax: (312)984-9877
E-mail: wl@polestarvc.com
Website: http://www.polestarvc.com

Prince Ventures (Chicago)
10 S. Wacker Dr., Ste. 2575
Chicago, IL 60606-7407

(312)454-1408
Fax: (312)454-9125

Prism Capital
444 N. Michigan Ave.
Chicago, IL 60611
(312)464-7900
Fax: (312)464-7915
Website: http://www.prismfund.com

Third Coast Capital
900 N. Franklin St., Ste. 700
Chicago, IL 60610
(312)337-3303
Fax: (312)337-2567
E-mail: manic@earthlink.com
Website: http://www.thirdcoastcapital.com

Thoma Cressey Equity Partners
4460 Sears Tower, 92nd Fl.
233 S. Wacker Dr.
Chicago, IL 60606
(312)777-4444
Fax: (312)777-4445
Website: http://www.thomacressey.com

Tribune Ventures
435 N. Michigan Ave., Ste. 600
Chicago, IL 60611
(312)527-8797
Fax: (312)222-5993
Website: http://www.tribuneventures.com

Wind Point Partners (Chicago)
676 N. Michigan Ave., Ste. 330
Chicago, IL 60611
(312)649-4000
Website: http://www.wppartners.com

Marquette Venture Partners
520 Lake Cook Rd., Ste. 450
Deerfield, IL 60015
(847)940-1700
Fax: (847)940-1724
Website: http://www.marquetteventures.com

Duchossois Investments Limited, LLC
845 Larch Ave.
Elmhurst, IL 60126
(630)530-6105
Fax: (630)993-8644
Website: http://www.duchtec.com

Evanston Business Investment Corp.
1840 Oak Ave.
Evanston, IL 60201
(847)866-1840
Fax: (847)866-1808
E-mail: t-parkinson@nwu.com
Website: http://www.ebic.com

Inroads Capital Partners L.P.
1603 Orrington Ave., Ste. 2050
Evanston, IL 60201-3841
(847)864-2000
Fax: (847)864-9692

The Cerulean Fund/WGC Enterprises
1701 E. Lake Ave., Ste. 170
Glenview, IL 60025
(847)657-8002
Fax: (847)657-8168

Ventana Financial Resources, Inc.
249 Market Sq.
Lake Forest, IL 60045
(847)234-3434

Beecken, Petty & Co.
901 Warrenville Rd., Ste. 205
Lisle, IL 60532
(630)435-0300
Fax: (630)435-0370
E-mail: hep@bpcompany.com
Website: http://www.bpcompany.com

Allstate Private Equity
3075 Sanders Rd., Ste. G5D
Northbrook, IL 60062-7127
(847)402-8247
Fax: (847)402-0880

KB Partners
1101 Skokie Blvd., Ste. 260
Northbrook, IL 60062-2856
(847)714-0444
Fax: (847)714-0445
E-mail: keith@kbpartners.com
Website: http://www.kbpartners.com

Transcap Associates Inc.
900 Skokie Blvd., Ste. 210
Northbrook, IL 60062
(847)753-9600
Fax: (847)753-9090

**Graystone Venture Partners, L.L.C. /
Portage Venture Partners**
One Northfield Plaza, Ste. 530
Northfield, IL 60093
(847)446-9460
Fax: (847)446-9470
Website: http://
www.portageventures.com

Motorola Inc.
1303 E. Algonquin Rd.
Schaumburg, IL 60196-1065
(847)576-4929
Fax: (847)538-2250
Website: http://www.mot.com/mne

Indiana

Irwin Ventures LLC
500 Washington St.
Columbus, IN 47202
(812)373-1434
Fax: (812)376-1709
Website: http://www.irwinventures.com

Cambridge Venture Partners
4181 East 96th St., Ste. 200
Indianapolis, IN 46240
(317)814-6192
Fax: (317)944-9815

CID Equity Partners
One American Square, Ste. 2850
Box 82074
Indianapolis, IN 46282
(317)269-2350
Fax: (317)269-2355
Website: http://www.cidequity.com

Gazelle Techventures
6325 Digital Way, Ste. 460
Indianapolis, IN 46278
(317)275-6800
Fax: (317)275-1101
Website: http://www.gazellevc.com

Monument Advisors Inc.
Bank One Center/Circle
111 Monument Circle, Ste. 600
Indianapolis, IN 46204-5172
(317)656-5065
Fax: (317)656-5060
Website: http://www.monumentadv.com

MWV Capital Partners
201 N. Illinois St., Ste. 300
Indianapolis, IN 46204
(317)237-2323
Fax: (317)237-2325
Website: http://www.mwvcapital.com

First Source Capital Corp.
100 North Michigan St.
PO Box 1602
South Bend, IN 46601
(219)235-2180
Fax: (219)235-2227

Iowa

Allsop Venture Partners
118 Third Ave. SE, Ste. 837
Cedar Rapids, IA 52401
(319)368-6675
Fax: (319)363-9515

InvestAmerica Investment Advisors, Inc.
101 2nd St. SE, Ste. 800
Cedar Rapids, IA 52401
(319)363-8249
Fax: (319)363-9683

Pappajohn Capital Resources
2116 Financial Center
Des Moines, IA 50309
(515)244-5746
Fax: (515)244-2346
Website: http://www.pappajohn.com

Berthel Fisher & Company Planning Inc.
701 Tama St.
PO Box 609
Marion, IA 52302
(319)497-5700
Fax: (319)497-4244

Kansas

Enterprise Merchant Bank
7400 West 110th St., Ste. 560
Overland Park, KS 66210
(913)327-8500
Fax: (913)327-8505

Kansas Venture Capital, Inc. (Overland Park)
6700 Antioch Plz., Ste. 460
Overland Park, KS 66204
(913)262-7117
Fax: (913)262-3509
E-mail: jdalton@kvci.com

Child Health Investment Corp.
6803 W. 64th St., Ste. 208
Shawnee Mission, KS 66202
(913)262-1436
Fax: (913)262-1575
Website: http://www.chca.com

Kansas Technology Enterprise Corp.
214 SW 6th, 1st Fl.
Topeka, KS 66603-3719
(785)296-5272
Fax: (785)296-1160
E-mail: ktec@ktec.com
Website: http://www.ktec.com

Kentucky

Kentucky Highlands Investment Corp.
362 Old Whitley Rd.
London, KY 40741
(606)864-5175
Fax: (606)864-5194
Website: http://www.khic.org

Chrysalis Ventures, L.L.C.
1850 National City Tower
Louisville, KY 40202
(502)583-7644
Fax: (502)583-7648
E-mail: bobsany@chrysalisventures.com
Website: http://www.chrysalisventures.com

Humana Venture Capital
500 West Main St.
Louisville, KY 40202
(502)580-3922
Fax: (502)580-2051
E-mail: gemont@humana.com
George Emont, Director

Summit Capital Group, Inc.
6510 Glenridge Park Pl., Ste. 8
Louisville, KY 40222
(502)332-2700

Louisiana

Bank One Equity Investors, Inc.
451 Florida St.
Baton Rouge, LA 70801
(504)332-4421
Fax: (504)332-7377

Advantage Capital Partners
LLE Tower
909 Poydras St., Ste. 2230
New Orleans, LA 70112
(504)522-4850
Fax: (504)522-4950
Website: http://www.advantagecap.com

Maine

CEI Ventures / Coastal Ventures LP
2 Portland Fish Pier, Ste. 201
Portland, ME 04101
(207)772-5356
Fax: (207)772-5503
Website: http://www.ceiventures.com

Commwealth Bioventures, Inc.
4 Milk St.
Portland, ME 04101
(207)780-0904
Fax: (207)780-0913

Maryland

Annapolis Ventures LLC
151 West St., Ste. 302
Annapolis, MD 21401
(443)482-9555
Fax: (443)482-9565
Website: http://www.annapolisventures.com

Delmag Ventures
220 Wardour Dr.
Annapolis, MD 21401
(410)267-8196
Fax: (410)267-8017
Website: http://www.delmagventures.com

Abell Venture Fund
111 S. Calvert St., Ste. 2300
Baltimore, MD 21202
(410)547-1300
Fax: (410)539-6579
Website: http://www.abell.org

ABS Ventures (Baltimore)
1 South St., Ste. 2150
Baltimore, MD 21202
(410)895-3895
Fax: (410)895-3899
Website: http://www.absventures.com

Anthem Capital, L.P.
16 S. Calvert St., Ste. 800
Baltimore, MD 21202-1305
(410)625-1510
Fax: (410)625-1735
Website: http://www.anthemcapital.com

Catalyst Ventures
1119 St. Paul St.
Baltimore, MD 21202
(410)244-0123
Fax: (410)752-7721

Maryland Venture Capital Trust
217 E. Redwood St., Ste. 2200
Baltimore, MD 21202
(410)767-6361
Fax: (410)333-6931

New Enterprise Associates (Baltimore)
1119 St. Paul St.
Baltimore, MD 21202
(410)244-0115
Fax: (410)752-7721
Website: http://www.nea.com

T. Rowe Price Threshold Partnerships
100 E. Pratt St., 8th Fl.
Baltimore, MD 21202
(410)345-2000
Fax: (410)345-2800

Spring Capital Partners
16 W. Madison St.
Baltimore, MD 21201
(410)685-8000
Fax: (410)727-1436
E-mail: mailbox@springcap.com

Arete Corporation
3 Bethesda Metro Ctr., Ste. 770
Bethesda, MD 20814
(301)657-6268
Fax: (301)657-6254
Website: http://www.arete-microgen.com

Embryon Capital
7903 Sleaford Place
Bethesda, MD 20814
(301)656-6837
Fax: (301)656-8056

Potomac Ventures
7920 Norfolk Ave., Ste. 1100
Bethesda, MD 20814
(301)215-9240
Website: http://www.potomacventures.com

Toucan Capital Corp.
3 Bethesda Metro Center, Ste. 700
Bethesda, MD 20814
(301)961-1970
Fax: (301)961-1969
Website: http://www.toucancapital.com

Kinetic Ventures LLC
2 Wisconsin Cir., Ste. 620
Chevy Chase, MD 20815
(301)652-8066
Fax: (301)652-8310
Website: http://www.kineticventures.com

Boulder Ventures Ltd.
4750 Owings Mills Blvd.
Owings Mills, MD 21117
(410)998-3114
Fax: (410)356-5492
Website: http://www.boulderventures.com

Grotech Capital Group
9690 Deereco Rd., Ste. 800
Timonium, MD 21093
(410)560-2000
Fax: (410)560-1910
Website: http://www.grotech.com

Massachusetts

Adams, Harkness & Hill, Inc.
60 State St.
Boston, MA 02109
(617)371-3900

Advent International
75 State St., 29th Fl.
Boston, MA 02109
(617)951-9400
Fax: (617)951-0566
Website: http://www.adventinernational.
com

American Research and Development
30 Federal St.
Boston, MA 02110-2508
(617)423-7500
Fax: (617)423-9655

Ascent Venture Partners
255 State St., 5th Fl.
Boston, MA 02109
(617)270-9400
Fax: (617)270-9401
E-mail: info@ascentvp.com
Website: http://www.ascentvp.com

Atlas Venture
222 Berkeley St.
Boston, MA 02116
(617)488-2200
Fax: (617)859-9292
Website: http://www.atlasventure.com

Axxon Capital
28 State St., 37th Fl.
Boston, MA 02109
(617)722-0980
Fax: (617)557-6014
Website: http://www.axxoncapital.com

BancBoston Capital/BancBoston Ventures
175 Federal St., 10th Fl.
Boston, MA 02110
(617)434-2509
Fax: (617)434-6175
Website: http://www.
bancbostoncapital.com

Boston Capital Ventures
Old City Hall
45 School St.
Boston, MA 02108
(617)227-6550
Fax: (617)227-3847
E-mail: info@bcv.com
Website: http://www.bcv.com

Boston Financial & Equity Corp.
20 Overland St.
PO Box 15071
Boston, MA 02215
(617)267-2900
Fax: (617)437-7601
E-mail: debbie@bfec.com

Boston Millennia Partners
30 Rowes Wharf
Boston, MA 02110
(617)428-5150
Fax: (617)428-5160
Website: http://www.millenniapartners.com

Bristol Investment Trust
842A Beacon St.
Boston, MA 02215-3199
(617)566-5212
Fax: (617)267-0932

Brook Venture Management LLC
50 Federal St., 5th Fl.
Boston, MA 02110
(617)451-8989
Fax: (617)451-2369
Website: http://www.brookventure.com

Burr, Egan, Deleage, and Co. (Boston)
200 Clarendon St., Ste. 3800
Boston, MA 02116
(617)262-7770
Fax: (617)262-9779

Cambridge/Samsung Partners
One Exeter Plaza
Ninth Fl.
Boston, MA 02116
(617)262-4440
Fax: (617)262-5562

Chestnut Street Partners, Inc.
75 State St., Ste. 2500
Boston, MA 02109
(617)345-7220
Fax: (617)345-7201
E-mail: chestnut@chestnutp.com

Claflin Capital Management, Inc.
10 Liberty Sq., Ste. 300
Boston, MA 02109
(617)426-6505
Fax: (617)482-0016
Website: http://www.claflincapital.com

Copley Venture Partners
99 Summer St., Ste. 1720
Boston, MA 02110
(617)737-1253
Fax: (617)439-0699

Corning Capital / Corning Technology Ventures
121 High Street, Ste. 400
Boston, MA 02110
(617)338-2656
Fax: (617)261-3864
Website: http://www.corningventures.com

Downer & Co.
211 Congress St.
Boston, MA 02110
(617)482-6200
Fax: (617)482-6201
E-mail: cdowner@downer.com
Website: http://www.downer.com

Fidelity Ventures
82 Devonshire St.
Boston, MA 02109
(617)563-6370
Fax: (617)476-9023
Website: http://www.fidelityventures.com

Greylock Management Corp. (Boston)
1 Federal St.
Boston, MA 02110-2065
(617)423-5525
Fax: (617)482-0059

Gryphon Ventures
222 Berkeley St., Ste.1600
Boston, MA 02116
(617)267-9191
Fax: (617)267-4293
E-mail: all@gryphoninc.com

Halpern, Denny & Co.
500 Boylston St.
Boston, MA 02116
(617)536-6602
Fax: (617)536-8535

Harbourvest Partners, LLC
1 Financial Center, 44th Fl.
Boston, MA 02111
(617)348-3707
Fax: (617)350-0305
Website: http://www.hvpllc.com

Highland Capital Partners
2 International Pl.
Boston, MA 02110
(617)981-1500
Fax: (617)531-1550
E-mail: info@hcp.com
Website: http://www.hcp.com

Lee Munder Venture Partners
John Hancock Tower T-53
200 Clarendon St.
Boston, MA 02103
(617)380-5600
Fax: (617)380-5601
Website: http://www.leemunder.com

M/C Venture Partners
75 State St., Ste. 2500
Boston, MA 02109
(617)345-7200
Fax: (617)345-7201
Website: http://www.mcventurepartners.com

Massachusetts Capital Resources Co.
420 Boylston St.
Boston, MA 02116
(617)536-3900
Fax: (617)536-7930

Massachusetts Technology Development Corp. (MTDC)
148 State St.
Boston, MA 02109
(617)723-4920
Fax: (617)723-5983
E-mail: jhodgman@mtdc.com
Website: http://www.mtdc.com

New England Partners
One Boston Place, Ste. 2100
Boston, MA 02108
(617)624-8400
Fax: (617)624-8999
Website: http://www.nepartners.com

North Hill Ventures
Ten Post Office Square
11th Fl.
Boston, MA 02109
(617)788-2112
Fax: (617)788-2152
Website: http://www.northhillventures.com

OneLiberty Ventures
150 Cambridge Park Dr.
Boston, MA 02140
(617)492-7280
Fax: (617)492-7290
Website: http://www.oneliberty.com

Schroder Ventures
Life Sciences
60 State St., Ste. 3650
Boston, MA 02109
(617)367-8100
Fax: (617)367-1590
Website: http://www.shroderventures.com

Shawmut Capital Partners
75 Federal St., 18th Fl.
Boston, MA 02110
(617)368-4900
Fax: (617)368-4910
Website: http://www.shawmutcapital.com

Solstice Capital LLC
15 Broad St., 3rd Fl.
Boston, MA 02109
(617)523-7733
Fax: (617)523-5827
E-mail: solticecapital@solcap.com

Spectrum Equity Investors
One International Pl., 29th Fl.
Boston, MA 02110
(617)464-4600
Fax: (617)464-4601
Website: http://www.spectrumequity.com

Spray Venture Partners
One Walnut St.
Boston, MA 02108
(617)305-4140
Fax: (617)305-4144
Website: http://www.sprayventure.com

The Still River Fund
100 Federal St., 29th Fl.
Boston, MA 02110
(617)348-2327
Fax: (617)348-2371
Website: http://www.stillriverfund.com

Summit Partners
600 Atlantic Ave., Ste. 2800
Boston, MA 02210-2227
(617)824-1000
Fax: (617)824-1159
Website: http://www.summitpartners.com

TA Associates, Inc. (Boston)
High Street Tower
125 High St., Ste. 2500
Boston, MA 02110
(617)574-6700
Fax: (617)574-6728
Website: http://www.ta.com

TVM Techno Venture Management
101 Arch St., Ste. 1950
Boston, MA 02110
(617)345-9320
Fax: (617)345-9377
E-mail: info@tvmvc.com
Website: http://www.tvmvc.com

UNC Ventures
64 Burough St.
Boston, MA 02130-4017
(617)482-7070
Fax: (617)522-2176

Venture Investment Management Company (VIMAC)
177 Milk St.
Boston, MA 02190-3410
(617)292-3300
Fax: (617)292-7979
E-mail: bzeisig@vimac.com
Website: http://www.vimac.com

MDT Advisers, Inc.
125 Cambridge Park Dr.
Cambridge, MA 02140-2314
(617)234-2200
Fax: (617)234-2210
Website: http://www.mdtai.com

TTC Ventures
One Main St., 6th Fl.
Cambridge, MA 02142
(617)528-3137
Fax: (617)577-1715
E-mail: info@ttcventures.com

Zero Stage Capital Co. Inc.
101 Main St., 17th Fl.
Cambridge, MA 02142
(617)876-5355
Fax: (617)876-1248
Website: http://www.zerostage.com

Atlantic Capital
164 Cushing Hwy.
Cohasset, MA 02025
(617)383-9449
Fax: (617)383-6040
E-mail: info@atlanticcap.com
Website: http://www.atlanticcap.com

Seacoast Capital Partners
55 Ferncroft Rd.
Danvers, MA 01923
(978)750-1300
Fax: (978)750-1301
E-mail: gdeli@seacoastcapital.com
Website: http://www.seacoastcapital.com

Sage Management Group
44 South Street
PO Box 2026
East Dennis, MA 02641
(508)385-7172
Fax: (508)385-7272
E-mail: sagemgt@capecod.net

Applied Technology
1 Cranberry Hill
Lexington, MA 02421-7397
(617)862-8622
Fax: (617)862-8367

Royalty Capital Management
5 Downing Rd.
Lexington, MA 02421-6918
(781)861-8490

Argo Global Capital
210 Broadway, Ste. 101
Lynnfield, MA 01940
(781)592-5250
Fax: (781)592-5230
Website: http://www.gsmcapital.com

Industry Ventures
6 Bayne Lane
Newburyport, MA 01950
(978)499-7606
Fax: (978)499-0686
Website: http://www.industryventures.com

Softbank Capital Partners
10 Langley Rd., Ste. 202
Newton Center, MA 02459
(617)928-9300
Fax: (617)928-9305
E-mail: clax@bvc.com

Advanced Technology Ventures (Boston)
281 Winter St., Ste. 350
Waltham, MA 02451
(781)290-0707
Fax: (781)684-0045
E-mail: info@atvcapital.com
Website: http://www.atvcapital.com

Castile Ventures
890 Winter St., Ste. 140
Waltham, MA 02451
(781)890-0060
Fax: (781)890-0065
Website: http://www.castileventures.com

Charles River Ventures
1000 Winter St., Ste. 3300
Waltham, MA 02451
(781)487-7060
Fax: (781)487-7065
Website: http://www.crv.com

Comdisco Venture Group (Waltham)
Totton Pond Office Center
400-1 Totten Pond Rd.
Waltham, MA 02451
(617)672-0250
Fax: (617)398-8099

Marconi Ventures
890 Winter St., Ste. 310
Waltham, MA 02451
(781)839-7177
Fax: (781)522-7477
Website: http://www.marconi.com

Matrix Partners
Bay Colony Corporate Center
1000 Winter St., Ste.4500
Waltham, MA 02451
(781)890-2244
Fax: (781)890-2288
Website: http://www.matrixpartners.com

North Bridge Venture Partners
950 Winter St. Ste. 4600
Waltham, MA 02451
(781)290-0004
Fax: (781)290-0999
E-mail: eta@nbvp.com

Polaris Venture Partners
Bay Colony Corporate Ctr.
1000 Winter St., Ste. 3500

Waltham, MA 02451
(781)290-0770
Fax: (781)290-0880
E-mail: partners@polarisventures.com
Website: http://www.polarisventures.com

Seaflower Ventures
Bay Colony Corporate Ctr.
1000 Winter St. Ste. 1000
Waltham, MA 02451
(781)466-9552
Fax: (781)466-9553
E-mail: moot@seaflower.com
Website: http://www.seaflower.com

Ampersand Ventures
55 William St., Ste. 240
Wellesley, MA 02481
(617)239-0700
Fax: (617)239-0824
E-mail: info@ampersandventures.com
Website: http://
www.ampersandventures.com

Battery Ventures (Boston)
20 William St., Ste. 200
Wellesley, MA 02481
(781)577-1000
Fax: (781)577-1001
Website: http://www.battery.com

Commonwealth Capital Ventures, L.P.
20 William St., Ste.225
Wellesley, MA 02481
(781)237-7373
Fax: (781)235-8627
Website: http://www.ccvlp.com

Fowler, Anthony & Company
20 Walnut St.
Wellesley, MA 02481
(781)237-4201
Fax: (781)237-7718

Gemini Investors
20 William St.
Wellesley, MA 02481
(781)237-7001
Fax: (781)237-7233

Grove Street Advisors Inc.
20 William St., Ste. 230
Wellesley, MA 02481
(781)263-6100
Fax: (781)263-6101
Website: http://www.grovestreet
advisors.com

Mees Pierson Investeringsmaat B.V.
20 William St., Ste. 210
Wellesley, MA 02482

(781)239-7600
Fax: (781)239-0377

Norwest Equity Partners
40 William St., Ste. 305
Wellesley, MA 02481-3902
(781)237-5870
Fax: (781)237-6270
Website: http://www.norwestvp.com

Bessemer Venture Partners (Wellesley Hills)
83 Walnut St.
Wellesley Hills, MA 02481
(781)237-6050
Fax: (781)235-7576
E-mail: travis@bvpny.com
Website: http://www.bvp.com

Venture Capital Fund of New England
20 Walnut St., Ste. 120
Wellesley Hills, MA 02481-2175
(781)239-8262
Fax: (781)239-8263

Prism Venture Partners
100 Lowder Brook Dr., Ste. 2500
Westwood, MA 02090
(781)302-4000
Fax: (781)302-4040
E-mail: dwbaum@prismventure.com

Palmer Partners LP
200 Unicorn Park Dr.
Woburn, MA 01801
(781)933-5445
Fax: (781)933-0698

Michigan

Arbor Partners, L.L.C.
130 South First St.
Ann Arbor, MI 48104
(734)668-9000
Fax: (734)669-4195
Website: http://www.arborpartners.com

EDF Ventures
425 N. Main St.
Ann Arbor, MI 48104
(734)663-3213
Fax: (734)663-7358
E-mail: edf@edfvc.com
Website: http://www.edfvc.com

White Pines Management, L.L.C.
2401 Plymouth Rd., Ste. B
Ann Arbor, MI 48105
(734)747-9401
Fax: (734)747-9704

E-mail: ibund@whitepines.com
Website: http://www.whitepines.com

Wellmax, Inc.
3541 Bendway Blvd., Ste. 100
Bloomfield Hills, MI 48301
(248)646-3554
Fax: (248)646-6220

Venture Funding, Ltd.
Fisher Bldg.
3011 West Grand Blvd., Ste. 321
Detroit, MI 48202
(313)871-3606
Fax: (313)873-4935

Investcare Partners L.P. / GMA Capital LLC
32330 W. Twelve Mile Rd.
Farmington Hills, MI 48334
(248)489-9000
Fax: (248)489-8819
E-mail: gma@gmacapital.com
Website: http://www.gmacapital.com

Liberty Bidco Investment Corp.
30833 Northwestern Highway, Ste. 211
Farmington Hills, MI 48334
(248)626-6070
Fax: (248)626-6072

Seaflower Ventures
5170 Nicholson Rd.
PO Box 474
Fowlerville, MI 48836
(517)223-3335
Fax: (517)223-3337
E-mail: gibbons@seaflower.com
Website: http://www.seaflower.com

Ralph Wilson Equity Fund LLC
15400 E. Jefferson Ave.
Gross Pointe Park, MI 48230
(313)821-9122
Fax: (313)821-9101
Website: http://www.
RalphWilsonEquityFund.com
J. Skip Simms, President

Minnesota

Development Corp. of Austin
1900 Eighth Ave., NW
Austin, MN 55912
(507)433-0346
Fax: (507)433-0361
E-mail: dca@smig.net
Website: http://www.spamtownusa.com

Northeast Ventures Corp.
802 Alworth Bldg.
Duluth, MN 55802

(218)722-9915
Fax: (218)722-9871

Medical Innovation Partners, Inc.
6450 City West Pkwy.
Eden Prairie, MN 55344-3245
(612)828-9616
Fax: (612)828-9596

St. Paul Venture Capital, Inc.
10400 Vicking Dr., Ste. 550
Eden Prairie, MN 55344
(612)995-7474
Fax: (612)995-7475
Website: http://www.stpaulvc.com

Cherry Tree Investments, Inc.
7601 France Ave. S, Ste. 150
Edina, MN 55435
(612)893-9012
Fax: (612)893-9036
Website: http://www.cherrytree.com

Shared Ventures, Inc.
6550 York Ave. S
Edina, MN 55435
(612)925-3411

Sherpa Partners LLC
5050 Lincoln Dr., Ste. 490
Edina, MN 55436
(952)942-1070
Fax: (952)942-1071
Website: http://www.sherpapartners.com

Affinity Capital Management
901 Marquette Ave., Ste. 1810
Minneapolis, MN 55402
(612)252-9900
Fax: (612)252-9911
Website: http://www.affinitycapital.com

Artesian Capital
1700 Foshay Tower
821 Marquette Ave.
Minneapolis, MN 55402
(612)334-5600
Fax: (612)334-5601
E-mail: artesian@artesian.com

Coral Ventures
60 S. 6th St., Ste. 3510
Minneapolis, MN 55402
(612)335-8666
Fax: (612)335-8668
Website: http://www.coralventures.com

Crescendo Venture Management, L.L.C.
800 LaSalle Ave., Ste. 2250
Minneapolis, MN 55402
(612)607-2800

Fax: (612)607-2801
Website: http://www.crescendoventures.
com

Gideon Hixon Venture
1900 Foshay Tower
821 Marquette Ave.
Minneapolis, MN 55402
(612)904-2314
Fax: (612)204-0913

Norwest Equity Partners
3600 IDS Center
80 S. 8th St.
Minneapolis, MN 55402
(612)215-1600
Fax: (612)215-1601
Website: http://www.norwestvp.com

Oak Investment Partners (Minneapolis)
4550 Norwest Center
90 S. 7th St.
Minneapolis, MN 55402
(612)339-9322
Fax: (612)337-8017
Website: http://www.oakinv.com

Pathfinder Venture Capital Funds (Minneapolis)
7300 Metro Blvd., Ste. 585
Minneapolis, MN 55439
(612)835-1121
Fax: (612)835-8389
E-mail: jahrens620@aol.com

U.S. Bancorp Piper Jaffray Ventures, Inc.
800 Nicollet Mall, Ste. 800
Minneapolis, MN 55402
(612)303-5686
Fax: (612)303-1350
Website: http://www.paperjaffrey
ventures.com

The Food Fund, Ltd. Partnership
5720 Smatana Dr., Ste. 300
Minnetonka, MN 55343
(612)939-3950
Fax: (612)939-8106

Mayo Medical Ventures
200 First St. SW
Rochester, MN 55905
(507)266-4586
Fax: (507)284-5410
Website: http://www.mayo.edu

Missouri

Bankers Capital Corp.
3100 Gillham Rd.
Kansas City, MO 64109

(816)531-1600
Fax: (816)531-1334

Capital for Business, Inc. (Kansas City)
1000 Walnut St., 18th Fl.
Kansas City, MO 64106
(816)234-2357
Fax: (816)234-2952
Website: http://www.capitalforbusiness.com

De Vries & Co. Inc.
800 West 47th St.
Kansas City, MO 64112
(816)756-0055
Fax: (816)756-0061

InvestAmerica Venture Group Inc. (Kansas City)
Commerce Tower
911 Main St., Ste. 2424
Kansas City, MO 64105
(816)842-0114
Fax: (816)471-7339

Kansas City Equity Partners
233 W. 47th St.
Kansas City, MO 64112
(816)960-1771
Fax: (816)960-1777
Website: http://www.kcep.com

Bome Investors, Inc.
8000 Maryland Ave., Ste. 1190
St. Louis, MO 63105
(314)721-5707
Fax: (314)721-5135
Website: http://www.gatewayventures.com

Capital for Business, Inc. (St. Louis)
11 S. Meramac St., Ste. 1430
St. Louis, MO 63105
(314)746-7427
Fax: (314)746-8739
Website: http://www.capitalforbusiness.com

Crown Capital Corp.
540 Maryville Centre Dr., Ste. 120
Saint Louis, MO 63141
(314)576-1201
Fax: (314)576-1525
Website: http://www.crown-cap.com

Gateway Associates L.P.
8000 Maryland Ave., Ste. 1190
St. Louis, MO 63105
(314)721-5707
Fax: (314)721-5135

Harbison Corp.
8112 Maryland Ave., Ste. 250
Saint Louis, MO 63105
(314)727-8200
Fax: (314)727-0249

Nebraska

Heartland Capital Fund, Ltd.
PO Box 642117
Omaha, NE 68154
(402)778-5124
Fax: (402)445-2370
Website: http://www.heartland
capitalfund.com

Odin Capital Group
1625 Farnam St., Ste. 700
Omaha, NE 68102
(402)346-6200
Fax: (402)342-9311
Website: http://www.odincapital.com

Nevada

Edge Capital Investment Co. LLC
1350 E. Flamingo Rd., Ste. 3000
Las Vegas, NV 89119
(702)438-3343
E-mail: info@edgecapital.net
Website: http://www.edgecapital.net

The Benefit Capital Companies Inc.
PO Box 542
Logandale, NV 89021
(702)398-3222
Fax: (702)398-3700

Millennium Three Venture Group LLC
6880 South McCarran Blvd., Ste. A-11
Reno, NV 89509
(775)954-2020
Fax: (775)954-2023
Website: http://www.m3vg.com

New Jersey

Alan I. Goldman & Associates
497 Ridgewood Ave.
Glen Ridge, NJ 07028
(973)857-5680
Fax: (973)509-8856

CS Capital Partners LLC
328 Second St., Ste. 200
Lakewood, NJ 08701
(732)901-1111
Fax: (212)202-5071
Website: http://www.cs-capital.com

Edison Venture Fund
1009 Lenox Dr., Ste. 4
Lawrenceville, NJ 08648

(609)896-1900
Fax: (609)896-0066
E-mail: info@edisonventure.com
Website: http://www.edisonventure.com

Tappan Zee Capital Corp. (New Jersey)
201 Lower Notch Rd.
PO Box 416
Little Falls, NJ 07424
(973)256-8280
Fax: (973)256-2841

The CIT Group/Venture Capital, Inc.
650 CIT Dr.
Livingston, NJ 07039
(973)740-5429
Fax: (973)740-5555
Website: http://www.cit.com

Capital Express, L.L.C.
1100 Valleybrook Ave.
Lyndhurst, NJ 07071
(201)438-8228
Fax: (201)438-5131
E-mail: niles@capitalexpress.com
Website: http://www.capitalexpress.com

Westford Technology Ventures, L.P.
17 Academy St.
Newark, NJ 07102
(973)624-2131
Fax: (973)624-2008

Accel Partners
1 Palmer Sq.
Princeton, NJ 08542
(609)683-4500
Fax: (609)683-4880
Website: http://www.accel.com

Cardinal Partners
221 Nassau St.
Princeton, NJ 08542
(609)924-6452
Fax: (609)683-0174
Website: http://www.cardinalhealth
partners.com

Domain Associates L.L.C.
One Palmer Sq., Ste. 515
Princeton, NJ 08542
(609)683-5656
Fax: (609)683-9789
Website: http://www.domainvc.com

Johnston Associates, Inc.
181 Cherry Valley Rd.
Princeton, NJ 08540
(609)924-3131
Fax: (609)683-7524
E-mail: jaincorp@aol.com

Kemper Ventures
Princeton Forrestal Village
155 Village Blvd.
Princeton, NJ 08540
(609)936-3035
Fax: (609)936-3051

Penny Lane Parnters
One Palmer Sq., Ste. 309
Princeton, NJ 08542
(609)497-4646
Fax: (609)497-0611

Early Stage Enterprises L.P.
995 Route 518
Skillman, NJ 08558
(609)921-8896
Fax: (609)921-8703
Website: http://www.esevc.com

MBW Management Inc.
1 Springfield Ave.
Summit, NJ 07901
(908)273-4060
Fax: (908)273-4430

BCI Advisors, Inc.
Glenpointe Center W.
Teaneck, NJ 07666
(201)836-3900
Fax: (201)836-6368
E-mail: info@bciadvisors.com
Website: http://www.bcipartners.com

Demuth, Folger & Wetherill / DFW Capital Partners
Glenpointe Center E., 5th Fl.
300 Frank W. Burr Blvd.
Teaneck, NJ 07666
(201)836-2233
Fax: (201)836-5666
Website: http://www.dfwcapital.com

First Princeton Capital Corp.
189 Berdan Ave., No. 131
Wayne, NJ 07470-3233
(973)278-3233
Fax: (973)278-4290
Website: http://www.lytellcatt.net

Edelson Technology Partners
300 Tice Blvd.
Woodcliff Lake, NJ 07675
(201)930-9898
Fax: (201)930-8899
Website: http://www.edelsontech.com

New Mexico

Bruce F. Glaspell & Associates
10400 Academy Rd. NE, Ste. 313
Albuquerque, NM 87111

(505)292-4505
Fax: (505)292-4258

High Desert Ventures, Inc.
6101 Imparata St. NE, Ste. 1721
Albuquerque, NM 87111
(505)797-3330
Fax: (505)338-5147

New Business Capital Fund, Ltd.
5805 Torreon NE
Albuquerque, NM 87109
(505)822-8445

SBC Ventures
10400 Academy Rd. NE, Ste. 313
Albuquerque, NM 87111
(505)292-4505
Fax: (505)292-4528

Technology Ventures Corp.
1155 University Blvd. SE
Albuquerque, NM 87106
(505)246-2882
Fax: (505)246-2891

New York

New York State Science & Technology Foundation
Small Business Technology Investment Fund
99 Washington Ave., Ste. 1731
Albany, NY 12210
(518)473-9741
Fax: (518)473-6876

Rand Capital Corp.
2200 Rand Bldg.
Buffalo, NY 14203
(716)853-0802
Fax: (716)854-8480
Website: http://www.randcapital.com

Seed Capital Partners
620 Main St.
Buffalo, NY 14202
(716)845-7520
Fax: (716)845-7539
Website: http://www.seedcp.com

Coleman Venture Group
5909 Northern Blvd.
PO Box 224
East Norwich, NY 11732
(516)626-3642
Fax: (516)626-9722

Vega Capital Corp.
45 Knollwood Rd.
Elmsford, NY 10523

(914)345-9500
Fax: (914)345-9505

Herbert Young Securities, Inc.
98 Cuttermill Rd.
Great Neck, NY 11021
(516)487-8300
Fax: (516)487-8319

Sterling/Carl Marks Capital, Inc.
175 Great Neck Rd., Ste. 408
Great Neck, NY 11021
(516)482-7374
Fax: (516)487-0781
E-mail: stercrlmar@aol.com
Website: http://www.serlingcarlmarks.com

Impex Venture Management Co.
PO Box 1570
Green Island, NY 12183
(518)271-8008
Fax: (518)271-9101

Corporate Venture Partners L.P.
200 Sunset Park
Ithaca, NY 14850
(607)257-6323
Fax: (607)257-6128

Arthur P. Gould & Co.
One Wilshire Dr.
Lake Success, NY 11020
(516)773-3000
Fax: (516)773-3289

Dauphin Capital Partners
108 Forest Ave.
Locust Valley, NY 11560
(516)759-3339
Fax: (516)759-3322
Website: http://www.dauphincapital.com

550 Digital Media Ventures
555 Madison Ave., 10th Fl.
New York, NY 10022
Website: http://www.550dmv.com

Aberlyn Capital Management Co., Inc.
500 Fifth Ave.
New York, NY 10110
(212)391-7750
Fax: (212)391-7762

Adler & Company
342 Madison Ave., Ste. 807
New York, NY 10173
(212)599-2535
Fax: (212)599-2526

Alimansky Capital Group, Inc.
605 Madison Ave., Ste. 300
New York, NY 10022-1901

(212)832-7300
Fax: (212)832-7338

Allegra Partners
515 Madison Ave., 29th Fl.
New York, NY 10022
(212)826-9080
Fax: (212)759-2561

The Argentum Group
The Chyrsler Bldg.
405 Lexington Ave.
New York, NY 10174
(212)949-6262
Fax: (212)949-8294
Website: http://www.argentumgroup.com

Axavision Inc.
14 Wall St., 26th Fl.
New York, NY 10005
(212)619-4000
Fax: (212)619-7202

Bedford Capital Corp.
18 East 48th St., Ste. 1800
New York, NY 10017
(212)688-5700
Fax: (212)754-4699
E-mail: info@bedfordnyc.com
Website: http://www.bedfordnyc.com

Bloom & Co.
950 Third Ave.
New York, NY 10022
(212)838-1858
Fax: (212)838-1843

Bristol Capital Management
300 Park Ave., 17th Fl.
New York, NY 10022
(212)572-6306
Fax: (212)705-4292

Citicorp Venture Capital Ltd. (New York City)
399 Park Ave., 14th Fl.
Zone 4
New York, NY 10043
(212)559-1127
Fax: (212)888-2940

CM Equity Partners
135 E. 57th St.
New York, NY 10022
(212)909-8428
Fax: (212)980-2630

Cohen & Co., L.L.C.
800 Third Ave.
New York, NY 10022
(212)317-2250

Fax: (212)317-2255
E-mail: nlcohen@aol.com

Cornerstone Equity Investors, L.L.C.
717 5th Ave., Ste. 1100
New York, NY 10022
(212)753-0901
Fax: (212)826-6798
Website: http://www.cornerstone-equity.com

CW Group, Inc.
1041 3rd Ave., 2nd fl.
New York, NY 10021
(212)308-5266
Fax: (212)644-0354
Website: http://www.cwventures.com

DH Blair Investment Banking Corp.
44 Wall St., 2nd Fl.
New York, NY 10005
(212)495-5000
Fax: (212)269-1438

Dresdner Kleinwort Capital
75 Wall St.
New York, NY 10005
(212)429-3131
Fax: (212)429-3139
Website: http://www.dresdnerkb.com

East River Ventures, L.P.
645 Madison Ave., 22nd Fl.
New York, NY 10022
(212)644-2322
Fax: (212)644-5498

Easton Hunt Capital Partners
641 Lexington Ave., 21st Fl.
New York, NY 10017
(212)702-0950
Fax: (212)702-0952
Website: http://www.eastoncapital.com

Elk Associates Funding Corp.
747 3rd Ave., Ste. 4C
New York, NY 10017
(212)355-2449
Fax: (212)759-3338

EOS Partners, L.P.
320 Park Ave., 22nd Fl.
New York, NY 10022
(212)832-5800
Fax: (212)832-5815
E-mail: mfirst@eospartners.com
Website: http://www.eospartners.com

Euclid Partners
45 Rockefeller Plaza, Ste. 3240
New York, NY 10111

(212)218-6880
Fax: (212)218-6877
E-mail: graham@euclidpartners.com
Website: http://www.euclidpartners.com

Evergreen Capital Partners, Inc.
150 East 58th St.
New York, NY 10155
(212)813-0758
Fax: (212)813-0754

Exeter Capital L.P.
10 E. 53rd St.
New York, NY 10022
(212)872-1172
Fax: (212)872-1198
E-mail: exeter@usa.net

Financial Technology Research Corp.
518 Broadway
Penthouse
New York, NY 10012
(212)625-9100
Fax: (212)431-0300
E-mail: fintek@financier.com

4C Ventures
237 Park Ave., Ste. 801
New York, NY 10017
(212)692-3680
Fax: (212)692-3685
Website: http://www.4cventures.com

Fusient Ventures
99 Park Ave., 20th Fl.
New York, NY 10016
(212)972-8999
Fax: (212)972-9876
E-mail: info@fusient.com
Website: http://www.fusient.com

Generation Capital Partners
551 Fifth Ave., Ste. 3100
New York, NY 10176
(212)450-8507
Fax: (212)450-8550
Website: http://www.genpartners.com

Golub Associates, Inc.
555 Madison Ave.
New York, NY 10022
(212)750-6060
Fax: (212)750-5505

Hambro America Biosciences Inc.
650 Madison Ave., 21st Floor
New York, NY 10022
(212)223-7400
Fax: (212)223-0305

Hanover Capital Corp.
505 Park Ave., 15th Fl.
New York, NY 10022
(212)755-1222
Fax: (212)935-1787

Harvest Partners, Inc.
280 Park Ave, 33rd Fl.
New York, NY 10017
(212)559-6300
Fax: (212)812-0100
Website: http://www.harvpart.com

Holding Capital Group, Inc.
10 E. 53rd St., 30th Fl.
New York, NY 10022
(212)486-6670
Fax: (212)486-0843

Hudson Venture Partners
660 Madison Ave., 14th Fl.
New York, NY 10021-8405
(212)644-9797
Fax: (212)644-7430
Website: http://www.hudsonptr.com

IBJS Capital Corp.
1 State St., 9th Fl.
New York, NY 10004
(212)858-2018
Fax: (212)858-2768

InterEquity Capital Partners, L.P.
220 5th Ave.
New York, NY 10001
(212)779-2022
Fax: (212)779-2103
Website: http://www.interequity-capital.com

The Jordan Edmiston Group Inc.
150 East 52nd St., 18th Fl.
New York, NY 10022
(212)754-0710
Fax: (212)754-0337

Josephberg, Grosz and Co., Inc.
633 3rd Ave., 13th Fl.
New York, NY 10017
(212)974-9926
Fax: (212)397-5832

J.P. Morgan Capital Corp.
60 Wall St.
New York, NY 10260-0060
(212)648-9000
Fax: (212)648-5002
Website: http://www.jpmorgan.com

The Lambda Funds
380 Lexington Ave., 54th Fl.
New York, NY 10168

(212)682-3454
Fax: (212)682-9231

Lepercq Capital Management Inc.
1675 Broadway
New York, NY 10019
(212)698-0795
Fax: (212)262-0155

Loeb Partners Corp.
61 Broadway, Ste. 2400
New York, NY 10006
(212)483-7000
Fax: (212)574-2001

Madison Investment Partners
660 Madison Ave.
New York, NY 10021
(212)223-2600
Fax: (212)223-8208

MC Capital Inc.
520 Madison Ave., 16th Fl.
New York, NY 10022
(212)644-0841
Fax: (212)644-2926

McCown, De Leeuw and Co. (New York)
65 E. 55th St., 36th Fl.
New York, NY 10022
(212)355-5500
Fax: (212)355-6283
Website: http://www.mdcpartners.com

Morgan Stanley Venture Partners
1221 Avenue of the Americas, 33rd Fl.
New York, NY 10020
(212)762-7900
Fax: (212)762-8424
E-mail: msventures@ms.com
Website: http://www.msvp.com

Nazem and Co.
645 Madison Ave., 12th Fl.
New York, NY 10022
(212)371-7900
Fax: (212)371-2150

Needham Capital Management, L.L.C.
445 Park Ave.
New York, NY 10022
(212)371-8300
Fax: (212)705-0299
Website: http://www.needhamco.com

Norwood Venture Corp.
1430 Broadway, Ste. 1607
New York, NY 10018
(212)869-5075
Fax: (212)869-5331

E-mail: nvc@mail.idt.net
Website: http://www.norven.com

Noveltek Venture Corp.
521 Fifth Ave., Ste. 1700
New York, NY 10175
(212)286-1963

Paribas Principal, Inc.
787 7th Ave.
New York, NY 10019
(212)841-2005
Fax: (212)841-3558

**Patricof & Co. Ventures, Inc.
(New York)**
445 Park Ave.
New York, NY 10022
(212)753-6300
Fax: (212)319-6155
Website: http://www.patricof.com

The Platinum Group, Inc.
350 Fifth Ave, Ste. 7113
New York, NY 10118
(212)736-4300
Fax: (212)736-6086
Website: http://www.platinumgroup.com

Pomona Capital
780 Third Ave., 28th Fl.
New York, NY 10017
(212)593-3639
Fax: (212)593-3987
Website: http://www.pomonacapital.com

Prospect Street Ventures
10 East 40th St., 44th Fl.
New York, NY 10016
(212)448-0702
Fax: (212)448-9652
E-mail: wkohler@prospectstreet.com
Website: http://www.prospectstreet.com

Regent Capital Management
505 Park Ave., Ste. 1700
New York, NY 10022
(212)735-9900
Fax: (212)735-9908

Rothschild Ventures, Inc.
1251 Avenue of the Americas, 51st Fl.
New York, NY 10020
(212)403-3500
Fax: (212)403-3652
Website: http://www.nmrothschild.com

Sandler Capital Management
767 Fifth Ave., 45th Fl.
New York, NY 10153

(212)754-8100
Fax: (212)826-0280

Siguler Guff & Company
630 Fifth Ave., 16th Fl.
New York, NY 10111
(212)332-5100
Fax: (212)332-5120

Spencer Trask Ventures Inc.
535 Madison Ave.
New York, NY 10022
(212)355-5565
Fax: (212)751-3362
Website: http://www.spencertrask.com

Sprout Group (New York City)
277 Park Ave.
New York, NY 10172
(212)892-3600
Fax: (212)892-3444
E-mail: info@sproutgroup.com
Website: http://www.sproutgroup.com

US Trust Private Equity
114 W.47th St.
New York, NY 10036
(212)852-3949
Fax: (212)852-3759
Website: http://www.ustrust.com/
privateequity

Vencon Management Inc.
301 West 53rd St., Ste. 10F
New York, NY 10019
(212)581-8787
Fax: (212)397-4126
Website: http://www.venconinc.com

Venrock Associates
30 Rockefeller Plaza, Ste. 5508
New York, NY 10112
(212)649-5600
Fax: (212)649-5788
Website: http://www.venrock.com

**Venture Capital Fund of America,
Inc.**
509 Madison Ave., Ste. 812
New York, NY 10022
(212)838-5577
Fax: (212)838-7614
E-mail: mail@vcfa.com
Website: http://www.vcfa.com

Venture Opportunities Corp.
150 E. 58th St.
New York, NY 10155
(212)832-3737
Fax: (212)980-6603

Warburg Pincus Ventures, Inc.
466 Lexington Ave., 11th Fl.
New York, NY 10017
(212)878-9309
Fax: (212)878-9200
Website: http://www.warburgpincus.com

Wasserstein, Perella & Co. Inc.
31 W. 52nd St., 27th Fl.
New York, NY 10019
(212)702-5691
Fax: (212)969-7879

Welsh, Carson, Anderson, & Stowe
320 Park Ave., Ste. 2500
New York, NY 10022-6815
(212)893-9500
Fax: (212)893-9575

Whitney and Co. (New York)
630 Fifth Ave. Ste. 3225
New York, NY 10111
(212)332-2400
Fax: (212)332-2422
Website: http://www.jhwitney.com

Winthrop Ventures
74 Trinity Place, Ste. 600
New York, NY 10006
(212)422-0100

The Pittsford Group
8 Lodge Pole Rd.
Pittsford, NY 14534
(716)223-3523

Genesee Funding
70 Linden Oaks, 3rd Fl.
Rochester, NY 14625
(716)383-5550
Fax: (716)383-5305

Gabelli Multimedia Partners
One Corporate Center
Rye, NY 10580
(914)921-5395
Fax: (914)921-5031

Stamford Financial
108 Main St.
Stamford, NY 12167
(607)652-3311
Fax: (607)652-6301
Website: http://www.stamfordfinancial.
com

Northwood Ventures LLC
485 Underhill Blvd., Ste. 205
Syosset, NY 11791
(516)364-5544
Fax: (516)364-0879

E-mail: northwood@northwood.com
Website: http://www.northwood
ventures.com

**Exponential Business
Development Co.**
216 Walton St.
Syracuse, NY 13202-1227
(315)474-4500
Fax: (315)474-4682
E-mail: dirksonn@aol.com
Website: http://www.exponential-ny.com

Onondaga Venture Capital Fund Inc.
714 State Tower Bldg.
Syracuse, NY 13202
(315)478-0157
Fax: (315)478-0158

Bessemer Venture Partners (Westbury)
1400 Old Country Rd., Ste. 109
Westbury, NY 11590
(516)997-2300
Fax: (516)997-2371
E-mail: bob@bvpny.com
Website: http://www.bvp.com

Ovation Capital Partners
120 Bloomingdale Rd., 4th Fl.
White Plains, NY 10605
(914)258-0011
Fax: (914)684-0848
Website: http://www.ovationcapital.com

North Carolina

Carolinas Capital Investment Corp.
1408 Biltmore Dr.
Charlotte, NC 28207
(704)375-3888
Fax: (704)375-6226

First Union Capital Partners
1st Union Center, 12th Fl.
301 S. College St.
Charlotte, NC 28288-0732
(704)383-0000
Fax: (704)374-6711
Website: http://www.fucp.com

Frontier Capital LLC
525 North Tryon St., Ste. 1700
Charlotte, NC 28202
(704)414-2880
Fax: (704)414-2881
Website: http://www.frontierfunds.com

Kitty Hawk Capital
2700 Coltsgate Rd., Ste. 202
Charlotte, NC 28211
(704)362-3909

Fax: (704)362-2774
Website: http://www.kittyhawkcapital.com

Piedmont Venture Partners
One Morrocroft Centre
6805 Morisson Blvd., Ste. 380
Charlotte, NC 28211
(704)731-5200
Fax: (704)365-9733
Website: http://www.piedmontvp.com

Ruddick Investment Co.
1800 Two First Union Center
Charlotte, NC 28282
(704)372-5404
Fax: (704)372-6409

The Shelton Companies Inc.
3600 One First Union Center
301 S. College St.
Charlotte, NC 28202
(704)348-2200
Fax: (704)348-2260

Wakefield Group
1110 E. Morehead St.
PO Box 36329
Charlotte, NC 28236
(704)372-0355
Fax: (704)372-8216
Website: http://www.wakefieldgroup.com

Aurora Funds, Inc.
2525 Meridian Pkwy., Ste. 220
Durham, NC 27713
(919)484-0400
Fax: (919)484-0444
Website: http://www.aurorafunds.com

Intersouth Partners
3211 Shannon Rd., Ste. 610
Durham, NC 27707
(919)493-6640
Fax: (919)493-6649
E-mail: info@intersouth.com
Website: http://www.intersouth.com

Geneva Merchant Banking Partners
PO Box 21962
Greensboro, NC 27420
(336)275-7002
Fax: (336)275-9155
Website: http://www.
genevamerchantbank.com

The North Carolina Enterprise Fund, L.P.
3600 Glenwood Ave., Ste. 107
Raleigh, NC 27612
(919)781-2691
Fax: (919)783-9195
Website: http://www.ncef.com

Ohio

Senmend Medical Ventures
4445 Lake Forest Dr., Ste. 600
Cincinnati, OH 45242
(513)563-3264
Fax: (513)563-3261

The Walnut Group
312 Walnut St., Ste. 1151
Cincinnati, OH 45202
(513)651-3300
Fax: (513)929-4441
Website: http://
www.thewalnutgroup.com

Brantley Venture Partners
20600 Chagrin Blvd., Ste. 1150
Cleveland, OH 44122
(216)283-4800
Fax: (216)283-5324

Clarion Capital Corp.
1801 E. 9th St., Ste. 1120
Cleveland, OH 44114
(216)687-1096
Fax: (216)694-3545

Crystal Internet Venture Fund, L.P.
1120 Chester Ave., Ste. 418
Cleveland, OH 44114
(216)263-5515
Fax: (216)263-5518
E-mail: jf@crystalventure.com
Website: http://www.crystalventure.com

Key Equity Capital Corp.
127 Public Sq., 28th Fl.
Cleveland, OH 44114
(216)689-3000
Fax: (216)689-3204
Website: http://www.keybank.com

Morgenthaler Ventures
Terminal Tower
50 Public Square, Ste. 2700
Cleveland, OH 44113
(216)416-7500
Fax: (216)416-7501
Website: http://www.morgenthaler.com

National City Equity Partners Inc.
1965 E. 6th St.
Cleveland, OH 44114
(216)575-2491
Fax: (216)575-9965
E-mail: nccap@aol.com
Website: http://www.nccapital.com

Primus Venture Partners, Inc.
5900 LanderBrook Dr., Ste. 2000

Cleveland, OH 44124-4020
(440)684-7300
Fax: (440)684-7342
E-mail: info@primusventure.com
Website: http://www.primusventure.com

Banc One Capital Partners (Columbus)
150 East Gay St., 24th Fl.
Columbus, OH 43215
(614)217-1100
Fax: (614)217-1217

Battelle Venture Partners
505 King Ave.
Columbus, OH 43201
(614)424-7005
Fax: (614)424-4874

Ohio Partners
62 E. Board St., 3rd Fl.
Columbus, OH 43215
(614)621-1210
Fax: (614)621-1240

Capital Technology Group, L.L.C.
400 Metro Place North, Ste. 300
Dublin, OH 43017
(614)792-6066
Fax: (614)792-6036
E-mail: info@capitaltech.com
Website: http://www.capitaltech.com

Northwest Ohio Venture Fund
4159 Holland-Sylvania R., Ste. 202
Toledo, OH 43623
(419)824-8144
Fax: (419)882-2035
E-mail: bwalsh@novf.com

Oklahoma

Moore & Associates
1000 W. Wilshire Blvd., Ste. 370
Oklahoma City, OK 73116
(405)842-3660
Fax: (405)842-3763

Chisholm Private Capital Partners
100 West 5th St., Ste. 805
Tulsa, OK 74103
(918)584-0440
Fax: (918)584-0441
Website: http://www.chisholmvc.com

Davis, Tuttle Venture Partners (Tulsa)
320 S. Boston, Ste. 1000
Tulsa, OK 74103-3703
(918)584-7272
Fax: (918)582-3404
Website: http://www.davistuttle.com

RBC Ventures
2627 E. 21st St.
Tulsa, OK 74114
(918)744-5607
Fax: (918)743-8630

Oregon

Utah Ventures II LP
10700 SW Beaverton-Hillsdale Hwy., Ste. 548
Beaverton, OR 97005
(503)574-4125
E-mail: adishlip@uven.com
Website: http://www.uven.com

Orien Ventures
14523 SW Westlake Dr.
Lake Oswego, OR 97035
(503)699-1680
Fax: (503)699-1681

**OVP Venture Partners
(Lake Oswego)**
340 Oswego Pointe Dr., Ste. 200
Lake Oswego, OR 97034
(503)697-8766
Fax: (503)697-8863
E-mail: info@ovp.com
Website: http://www.ovp.com

**Oregon Resource and Technology
Development Fund**
4370 NE Halsey St., Ste. 233
Portland, OR 97213-1566
(503)282-4462
Fax: (503)282-2976

Shaw Venture Partners
400 SW 6th Ave., Ste. 1100
Portland, OR 97204-1636
(503)228-4884
Fax: (503)227-2471
Website: http://www.shawventures.com

Pennsylvania

Mid-Atlantic Venture Funds
125 Goodman Dr.
Bethlehem, PA 18015
(610)865-6550
Fax: (610)865-6427
Website: http://www.mavf.com

Newspring Ventures
100 W. Elm St., Ste. 101
Conshohocken, PA 19428
(610)567-2380
Fax: (610)567-2388
Website: http://www.newsprintventures.com

Patricof & Co. Ventures, Inc.
455 S. Gulph Rd., Ste. 410
King of Prussia, PA 19406
(610)265-0286
Fax: (610)265-4959
Website: http://www.patricof.com

Loyalhanna Venture Fund
527 Cedar Way, Ste. 104
Oakmont, PA 15139
(412)820-7035
Fax: (412)820-7036

Innovest Group Inc.
2000 Market St., Ste. 1400
Philadelphia, PA 19103
(215)564-3960
Fax: (215)569-3272

**Keystone Venture Capital
Management Co.**
1601 Market St., Ste. 2500
Philadelphia, PA 19103
(215)241-1200
Fax: (215)241-1211
Website: http://www.keystonevc.com

Liberty Venture Partners
2005 Market St., Ste. 200
Philadelphia, PA 19103
(215)282-4484
Fax: (215)282-4485
E-mail: info@libertyvp.com
Website: http://www.libertyvp.com

Penn Janney Fund, Inc.
1801 Market St., 11th Fl.
Philadelphia, PA 19103
(215)665-4447
Fax: (215)557-0820

Philadelphia Ventures, Inc.
The Bellevue
200 S. Broad St.
Philadelphia, PA 19102
(215)732-4445
Fax: (215)732-4644

Birchmere Ventures Inc.
2000 Technology Dr.
Pittsburgh, PA 15219-3109
(412)803-8000
Fax: (412)687-8139
Website: http://www.birchmerevc.com

CEO Venture Fund
2000 Technology Dr., Ste. 160
Pittsburgh, PA 15219-3109
(412)687-3451
Fax: (412)687-8139

E-mail: ceofund@aol.com
Website: http://www.ceoventurefund.com

Innovation Works Inc.
2000 Technology Dr., Ste. 250
Pittsburgh, PA 15219
(412)681-1520
Fax: (412)681-2625
Website: http://www.innovationworks.org

**Keystone Minority Capital
Fund L.P.**
1801 Centre Ave., Ste. 201
Williams Sq.
Pittsburgh, PA 15219
(412)338-2230
Fax: (412)338-2224

Mellon Ventures, Inc.
One Mellon Bank Ctr., Rm. 3500
Pittsburgh, PA 15258
(412)236-3594
Fax: (412)236-3593
Website: http://
www.mellonventures.com

Pennsylvania Growth Fund
5850 Ellsworth Ave., Ste. 303
Pittsburgh, PA 15232
(412)661-1000
Fax: (412)361-0676

Point Venture Partners
The Century Bldg.
130 Seventh St., 7th Fl.
Pittsburgh, PA 15222
(412)261-1966
Fax: (412)261-1718

Cross Atlantic Capital Partners
5 Radnor Corporate Center, Ste. 555
Radnor, PA 19087
(610)995-2650
Fax: (610)971-2062
Website: http://www.xacp.com

**Meridian Venture Partners
(Radnor)**
The Radnor Court Bldg., Ste. 140
259 Radnor-Chester Rd.
Radnor, PA 19087
(610)254-2999
Fax: (610)254-2996
E-mail: mvpart@ix.netcom.com

TDH
919 Conestoga Rd., Bldg. 1, Ste. 301
Rosemont, PA 19010
(610)526-9970
Fax: (610)526-9971

Adams Capital Management
500 Blackburn Ave.
Sewickley, PA 15143
(412)749-9454
Fax: (412)749-9459
Website: http://www.acm.com

S.R. One, Ltd.
Four Tower Bridge
200 Barr Harbor Dr., Ste. 250
W. Conshohocken, PA 19428
(610)567-1000
Fax: (610)567-1039

**Greater Philadelphia Venture
Capital Corp.**
351 East Conestoga Rd.
Wayne, PA 19087
(610)688-6829
Fax: (610)254-8958

PA Early Stage
435 Devon Park Dr., Bldg. 500, Ste. 510
Wayne, PA 19087
(610)293-4075
Fax: (610)254-4240
Website: http://www.paearlystage.com

The Sandhurst Venture Fund, L.P.
351 E. Constoga Rd.
Wayne, PA 19087
(610)254-8900
Fax: (610)254-8958

TL Ventures
700 Bldg.
435 Devon Park Dr.
Wayne, PA 19087-1990
(610)975-3765
Fax: (610)254-4210
Website: http://www.tlventures.com

Rockhill Ventures, Inc.
100 Front St., Ste. 1350
West Conshohocken, PA 19428
(610)940-0300
Fax: (610)940-0301

Puerto Rico

Advent-Morro Equity Partners
Banco Popular Bldg.
206 Tetuan St., Ste. 903
San Juan, PR 00902
(787)725-5285
Fax: (787)721-1735

North America Investment Corp.
Mercantil Plaza, Ste. 813
PO Box 191831
San Juan, PR 00919

(787)754-6178
Fax: (787)754-6181

Rhode Island

Manchester Humphreys, Inc.
40 Westminster St., Ste. 900
Providence, RI 02903
(401)454-0400
Fax: (401)454-0403

Navis Partners
50 Kennedy Plaza, 12th Fl.
Providence, RI 02903
(401)278-6770
Fax: (401)278-6387
Website: http://www.navispartners.com

South Carolina

Capital Insights, L.L.C.
PO Box 27162
Greenville, SC 29616-2162
(864)242-6832
Fax: (864)242-6755
E-mail: jwarner@capitalinsights.com
Website: http://www.capitalinsights.com

Transamerica Mezzanine Financing
7 N. Laurens St., Ste. 603
Greenville, SC 29601
(864)232-6198
Fax: (864)241-4444

Tennessee

Valley Capital Corp.
Krystal Bldg.
100 W. Martin Luther King Blvd., Ste. 212
Chattanooga, TN 37402
(423)265-1557
Fax: (423)265-1588

Coleman Swenson Booth Inc.
237 2nd Ave. S
Franklin, TN 37064-2649
(615)791-9462
Fax: (615)791-9636
Website: http://www.colemanswenson.com

Capital Services & Resources, Inc.
5159 Wheelis Dr., Ste. 106
Memphis, TN 38117
(901)761-2156
Fax: (907)767-0060

Paradigm Capital Partners LLC
6410 Poplar Ave., Ste. 395
Memphis, TN 38119
(901)682-6060
Fax: (901)328-3061

SSM Ventures
845 Crossover Ln., Ste. 140
Memphis, TN 38117
(901)767-1131
Fax: (901)767-1135
Website: http://www.ssmventures.com

Capital Across America L.P.
501 Union St., Ste. 201
Nashville, TN 37219
(615)254-1414
Fax: (615)254-1856
Website: http://www.capitalacross
america.com

Equitas L.P.
2000 Glen Echo Rd., Ste. 101
PO Box 158838
Nashville, TN 37215-8838
(615)383-8673
Fax: (615)383-8693

Massey Burch Capital Corp.
One Burton Hills Blvd., Ste. 350
Nashville, TN 37215
(615)665-3221
Fax: (615)665-3240
E-mail: tcalton@masseyburch.com
Website: http://www.masseyburch.com

Nelson Capital Corp.
3401 West End Ave., Ste. 300
Nashville, TN 37203
(615)292-8787
Fax: (615)385-3150

Texas

Phillips-Smith Specialty Retail Group
5080 Spectrum Dr., Ste. 805 W
Addison, TX 75001
(972)387-0725
Fax: (972)458-2560
E-mail: pssrg@aol.com
Website: http://www.phillips-smith.com

Austin Ventures, L.P.
701 Brazos St., Ste. 1400
Austin, TX 78701
(512)485-1900
Fax: (512)476-3952
E-mail: info@ausven.com
Website: http://www.austinventures.com

The Capital Network
3925 West Braker Lane, Ste. 406
Austin, TX 78759-5321
(512)305-0826
Fax: (512)305-0836

Techxas Ventures LLC
5000 Plaza on the Lake
Austin, TX 78746
(512)343-0118
Fax: (512)343-1879
E-mail: bruce@techxas.com
Website: http://www.techxas.com

Alliance Financial of Houston
218 Heather Ln.
Conroe, TX 77385-9013
(936)447-3300
Fax: (936)447-4222

Amerimark Capital Corp.
1111 W. Mockingbird, Ste. 1111
Dallas, TX 75247
(214)638-7878
Fax: (214)638-7612
E-mail: amerimark@amcapital.com
Website: http://www.amcapital.com

AMT Venture Partners / AMT Capital Ltd.
5220 Spring Valley Rd., Ste. 600
Dallas, TX 75240
(214)905-9757
Fax: (214)905-9761
Website: http://www.amtcapital.com

Arkoma Venture Partners
5950 Berkshire Lane, Ste. 1400
Dallas, TX 75225
(214)739-3515
Fax: (214)739-3572
E-mail: joelf@arkomavp.com

Capital Southwest Corp.
12900 Preston Rd., Ste. 700
Dallas, TX 75230
(972)233-8242
Fax: (972)233-7362
Website: http://
www.capitalsouthwest.com

Dali, Hook Partners
One Lincoln Center, Ste. 1550
5400 LBJ Freeway
Dallas, TX 75240
(972)991-5457
Fax: (972)991-5458
E-mail: dhook@hookpartners.com
Website: http://www.hookpartners.com

HO2 Partners
Two Galleria Tower
13455 Noel Rd., Ste. 1670
Dallas, TX 75240
(972)702-1144
Fax: (972)702-8234
Website: http://www.ho2.com

Interwest Partners (Dallas)
2 Galleria Tower
13455 Noel Rd., Ste. 1670
Dallas, TX 75240
(972)392-7279
Fax: (972)490-6348
Website: http://www.interwest.com

Kahala Investments, Inc.
8214 Westchester Dr., Ste. 715
Dallas, TX 75225
(214)987-0077
Fax: (214)987-2332

MESBIC Ventures Holding Co.
2435 North Central Expressway,
Ste. 200
Dallas, TX 75080
(972)991-1597
Fax: (972)991-4770
Website: http://www.mvhc.com

North Texas MESBIC, Inc.
9500 Forest Lane, Ste. 430
Dallas, TX 75243
(214)221-3565
Fax: (214)221-3566

Richard Jaffe & Company, Inc,
7318 Royal Cir.
Dallas, TX 75230
(214)265-9397
Fax: (214)739-1845

Sevin Rosen Management Co.
13455 Noel Rd., Ste. 1670
Dallas, TX 75240
(972)702-1100
Fax: (972)702-1103
E-mail: info@srfunds.com
Website: http://www.srfunds.com

Stratford Capital Partners, L.P.
300 Crescent Ct., Ste. 500
Dallas, TX 75201
(214)740-7377
Fax: (214)720-7393
E-mail: stratcap@hmtf.com

Sunwestern Investment Group
12221 Merit Dr., Ste. 935
Dallas, TX 75251
(972)239-5650
Fax: (972)701-0024

Wingate Partners
750 N. St. Paul St., Ste. 1200
Dallas, TX 75201
(214)720-1313
Fax: (214)871-8799

Buena Venture Associates
201 Main St., 32nd Fl.
Fort Worth, TX 76102
(817)339-7400
Fax: (817)390-8408
Website: http://www.buenaventure.com

The Catalyst Group
3 Riverway, Ste. 770
Houston, TX 77056
(713)623-8133
Fax: (713)623-0473
E-mail: herman@thecatalystgroup.net
Website: http://www.thecatalystgroup.net

Cureton & Co., Inc.
1100 Louisiana, Ste. 3250
Houston, TX 77002
(713)658-9806
Fax: (713)658-0476

Davis, Tuttle Venture Partners (Dallas)
8 Greenway Plaza, Ste. 1020
Houston, TX 77046
(713)993-0440
Fax: (713)621-2297
Website: http://www.davistuttle.com

Houston Partners
401 Louisiana, 8th Fl.
Houston, TX 77002
(713)222-8600
Fax: (713)222-8932

Southwest Venture Group
10878 Westheimer, Ste. 178
Houston, TX 77042
(713)827-8947
(713)461-1470

AM Fund
4600 Post Oak Place, Ste. 100
Houston, TX 77027
(713)627-9111
Fax: (713)627-9119

Ventex Management, Inc.
3417 Milam St.
Houston, TX 77002-9531
(713)659-7870
Fax: (713)659-7855

MBA Venture Group
1004 Olde Town Rd., Ste. 102
Irving, TX 75061
(972)986-6703

First Capital Group Management Co.
750 East Mulberry St., Ste. 305
PO Box 15616
San Antonio, TX 78212

(210)736-4233
Fax: (210)736-5449

The Southwest Venture Partnerships
16414 San Pedro, Ste. 345
San Antonio, TX 78232
(210)402-1200
Fax: (210)402-1221
E-mail: swvp@aol.com

Medtech International Inc.
1742 Carriageway
Sugarland, TX 77478
(713)980-8474
Fax: (713)980-6343

Utah

First Security Business Investment Corp.
15 East 100 South, Ste. 100
Salt Lake City, UT 84111
(801)246-5737
Fax: (801)246-5740

Utah Ventures II, L.P.
423 Wakara Way, Ste. 206
Salt Lake City, UT 84108
(801)583-5922
Fax: (801)583-4105
Website: http://www.uven.com

Wasatch Venture Corp.
1 S. Main St., Ste. 1400
Salt Lake City, UT 84133
(801)524-8939
Fax: (801)524-8941
E-mail: mail@wasatchvc.com

Vermont

North Atlantic Capital Corp.
76 Saint Paul St., Ste. 600
Burlington, VT 05401
(802)658-7820
Fax: (802)658-5757
Website: http://www.
northatlanticcapital.com

Green Mountain Advisors Inc.
PO Box 1230
Quechee, VT 05059
(802)296-7800
Fax: (802)296-6012
Website: http://www.gmtcap.com

Virginia

Oxford Financial Services Corp.
Alexandria, VA 22314
(703)519-4900
Fax: (703)519-4910
E-mail: oxford133@aol.com

Continental SBIC
4141 N. Henderson Rd.
Arlington, VA 22203
(703)527-5200
Fax: (703)527-3700

Novak Biddle Venture Partners
1750 Tysons Blvd., Ste. 1190
McLean, VA 22102
(703)847-3770
Fax: (703)847-3771
E-mail: roger@novakbiddle.com
Website: http://www.novakbiddle.com

Spacevest
11911 Freedom Dr., Ste. 500
Reston, VA 20190
(703)904-9800
Fax: (703)904-0571
E-mail: spacevest@spacevest.com
Website: http://www.spacevest.com

Virginia Capital
1801 Libbie Ave., Ste. 201
Richmond, VA 23226
(804)648-4802
Fax: (804)648-4809
E-mail: webmaster@vacapital.com
Website: http://www.vacapital.com

Calvert Social Venture Partners
402 Maple Ave. W
Vienna, VA 22180
(703)255-4930
Fax: (703)255-4931
E-mail: calven2000@aol.com

Fairfax Partners
8000 Towers Crescent Dr., Ste. 940
Vienna, VA 22182
(703)847-9486
Fax: (703)847-0911

Global Internet Ventures
8150 Leesburg Pike, Ste. 1210
Vienna, VA 22182
(703)442-3300
Fax: (703)442-3388
Website: http://www.givinc.com

Walnut Capital Corp. (Vienna)
8000 Towers Crescent Dr., Ste. 1070
Vienna, VA 22182
(703)448-3771
Fax: (703)448-7751

Washington

Encompass Ventures
777 108th Ave. NE, Ste. 2300
Bellevue, WA 98004

Organizations, Agencies, & Consultants

(425)486-3900
Fax: (425)486-3901
E-mail: info@evpartners.com
Website: http://www.encompassventures.
com

Fluke Venture Partners
11400 SE Sixth St., Ste. 230
Bellevue, WA 98004
(425)453-4590
Fax: (425)453-4675
E-mail: gabelein@flukeventures.com
Website: http://www.flukeventures.com

Pacific Northwest Partners SBIC, L.P.
15352 SE 53rd St.
Bellevue, WA 98006
(425)455-9967
Fax: (425)455-9404

Materia Venture Associates, L.P.
3435 Carillon Pointe
Kirkland, WA 98033-7354
(425)822-4100
Fax: (425)827-4086

OVP Venture Partners (Kirkland)
2420 Carillon Pt.
Kirkland, WA 98033
(425)889-9192
Fax: (425)889-0152
E-mail: info@ovp.com
Website: http://www.ovp.com

Digital Partners
999 3rd Ave., Ste. 1610
Seattle, WA 98104
(206)405-3607

Fax: (206)405-3617
Website: http://www.digitalpartners.com

Frazier & Company
601 Union St., Ste. 3300
Seattle, WA 98101
(206)621-7200
Fax: (206)621-1848
E-mail: jon@frazierco.com

Kirlan Venture Capital, Inc.
221 First Ave. W, Ste. 108
Seattle, WA 98119-4223
(206)281-8610
Fax: (206)285-3451
Website: http://www.kirlanventure.com

Phoenix Partners
1000 2nd Ave., Ste. 3600
Seattle, WA 98104
(206)624-8968
Fax: (206)624-1907

Voyager Capital
800 5th St., Ste. 4100
Seattle, WA 98103
(206)470-1180
Fax: (206)470-1185
E-mail: info@voyagercap.com
Website: http://www.voyagercap.com

Northwest Venture Associates
221 N. Wall St., Ste. 628
Spokane, WA 99201
(509)747-0728
Fax: (509)747-0758
Website: http://www.nwva.com

Wisconsin

Venture Investors Management, L.L.C.
University Research Park
505 S. Rosa Rd.
Madison, WI 53719
(608)441-2700
Fax: (608)441-2727
E-mail: roger@ventureinvestors.com
Website: http://www.ventureinvesters.com

Capital Investments, Inc.
1009 West Glen Oaks Lane, Ste. 103
Mequon, WI 53092
(414)241-0303
Fax: (414)241-8451
Website: http://www.capitalinvest
mentsinc.com

Future Value Venture, Inc.
2745 N. Martin Luther King Dr., Ste. 204
Milwaukee, WI 53212-2300
(414)264-2252
Fax: (414)264-2253
E-mail: fvvventures@aol.com
William Beckett, President

Lubar and Co., Inc.
700 N. Water St., Ste. 1200
Milwaukee, WI 53202
(414)291-9000
Fax: (414)291-9061

GCI
20875 Crossroads Cir., Ste. 100
Waukesha, WI 53186
(262)798-5080
Fax: (262)798-5087

Glossary of Small Business Terms

Absolute liability
Liability that is incurred due to product defects or negligent actions. Manufacturers or retail establishments are held responsible, even though the defect or action may not have been intentional or negligent.

ACE
See Active Corps of Executives

Accident and health benefits
Benefits offered to employees and their families in order to offset the costs associated with accidental death, accidental injury, or sickness.

Account statement
A record of transactions, including payments, new debt, and deposits, incurred during a defined period of time.

Accounting system
System capturing the costs of all employees and/or machinery included in business expenses.

Accounts payable
See Trade credit

Accounts receivable
Unpaid accounts which arise from unsettled claims and transactions from the sale of a company's products or services to its customers.

Active Corps of Executives (ACE)
A group of volunteers for a management assistance program of the U.S. Small Business Administration; volunteers provide one-on-one counseling and teach workshops and seminars for small firms.

ADA
See Americans with Disabilities Act

Adaptation
The process whereby an invention is modified to meet the needs of users.

Adaptive engineering
The process whereby an invention is modified to meet the manufacturing and commercial requirements of a targeted market.

Adverse selection
The tendency for higher-risk individuals to purchase health care and more comprehensive plans, resulting in increased costs.

Advertising
A marketing tool used to capture public attention and influence purchasing decisions for a product or service. Utilizes various forms of media to generate consumer response, such as flyers, magazines, newspapers, radio, and television.

Age discrimination
The denial of the rights and privileges of employment based solely on the age of an individual.

Agency costs
Costs incurred to insure that the lender or investor maintains control over assets while allowing the borrower or entrepreneur to use them. Monitoring and information costs are the two major types of agency costs.

Agribusiness
The production and sale of commodities and products from the commercial farming industry.

America Online
An online service which is accessible by computer modem. The service features Internet access, bulletin boards, online periodicals, electronic mail, and other services for subscribers.

Americans with Disabilities Act (ADA)
Law designed to ensure equal access and opportunity to handicapped persons.

Annual report
Yearly financial report prepared by a business that adheres to the requirements set forth by the Securities and Exchange Commission (SEC).

Antitrust immunity
Exemption from prosecution under antitrust laws. In the transportation industry, firms with antitrust immunity are permitted under certain conditions to set schedules and sometimes prices for the public benefit.

Applied research
Scientific study targeted for use in a product or process.

Asians
A minority category used by the U.S. Bureau of the Census to represent a diverse group that includes Aleuts, Eskimos, American Indians, Asian Indians, Chinese, Japanese, Koreans, Vietnamese, Filipinos, Hawaiians, and other Pacific Islanders.

Assets
Anything of value owned by a company.

Audit
The verification of accounting records and business procedures conducted by an outside accounting service.

Average cost
Total production costs divided by the quantity produced.

Balance Sheet
A financial statement listing the total assets and liabilities of a company at a given time.

Bankruptcy
The condition in which a business cannot meet its debt obligations and petitions a federal district court either for reorganization of its debts (Chapter 11) or for liquidation of its assets (Chapter 7).

Basic research
Theoretical scientific exploration not targeted to application.

Basket clause
A provision specifying the amount of public pension funds that may be placed in investments not included on a state's legal list (see separate citation).

BBS
See Bulletin Board Service

BDC
See Business development corporation

Benefit
Various services, such as health care, flextime, day care, insurance, and vacation, offered to employees as part of a hiring package. Typically subsidized in whole or in part by the business.

BIDCO
See Business and industrial development company

Billing cycle
A system designed to evenly distribute customer billing throughout the month, preventing clerical backlogs.

Birth
See Business birth

Blue chip security
A low-risk, low-yield security representing an interest in a very stable company.

Blue sky laws
A general term that denotes various states' laws regulating securities.

Bond
A written instrument executed by a bidder or contractor (the principal) and a second party (the surety or sureties) to assure fulfillment of the principal's obligations to a third party (the obligee or government) identified in the bond. If the principal's obligations are not met, the bond assures payment to the extent stipulated of any loss sustained by the obligee.

Bonding requirements
Terms contained in a bond (see separate citation).

Bonus
An amount of money paid to an employee as a reward for achieving certain business goals or objectives.

Brainstorming
A group session where employees contribute their ideas for solving a problem or meeting a company objective without fear of retribution or ridicule.

Brand name
The part of a brand, trademark, or service mark that can be spoken. It can be a word, letter, or group of words or letters.

Bridge financing
A short-term loan made in expectation of intermediateterm or long-term financing. Can be used when a company plans to go public in the near future.

Broker
One who matches resources available for innovation with those who need them.

Budget
An estimate of the spending necessary to complete a project or offer a service in comparison to cash-on-hand and expected earnings for the coming year, with an emphasis on cost control.

Bulletin Board Service (BBS)
An online service enabling users to communicate with each other about specific topics.

Business and industrial development company (BIDCO)
A private, for-profit financing corporation chartered by the state to provide both equity and long-term debt capital to small business owners (see separate citations for equity and debt capital).

Business birth
The formation of a new establishment or enterprise. The appearance of a new establishment or enterprise in the Small Business Data Base (see separate citation).

Business conditions
Outside factors that can affect the financial performance of a business.

Business contractions
The number of establishments that have decreased in employment during a specified time.

Business cycle
A period of economic recession and recovery. These cycles vary in duration.

Business death
The voluntary or involuntary closure of a firm or establishment. The disappearance of an establishment or enterprise from the Small Business Data Base (see separate citation).

Business development corporation (BDC)
A business financing agency, usually composed of the financial institutions in an area or state, organized to assist in financing businesses unable to obtain assistance through normal channels; the risk is spread among various members of the business development corporation, and interest rates may vary somewhat from those charged by member institutions. A venture capital firm in which shares of ownership are publicly held and to which the Investment Act of 1940 applies.

Business dissolution
For enumeration purposes, the absence of a business that was present in the prior time period from any current record.

Business entry
See Business birth

Business ethics
Moral values and principles espoused by members of the business community as a guide to fair and honest business practices.

Business exit
See Business death

Business expansions
The number of establishments that added employees during a specified time.

Business failure
Closure of a business causing a loss to at least one creditor.

Business format franchising
The purchase of the name, trademark, and an ongoing business plan of the parent corporation or franchisor by the franchisee.

Business license
A legal authorization issued by municipal and state governments and required for business operations.

Business name
Enterprises must register their business names with local governments usually on a "doing business as" (DBA) form. (This name is sometimes referred to as a

"fictional name.") The procedure is part of the business licensing process and prevents any other business from using that same name for a similar business in the same locality.

Business norms
See Financial ratios

Business permit
See Business license

Business plan
A document that spells out a company's expected course of action for a specified period, usually including a detailed listing and analysis of risks and uncertainties. For the small business, it should examine the proposed products, the market, the industry, the management policies, the marketing policies, production needs, and financial needs. Frequently, it is used as a prospectus for potential investors and lenders.

Business proposal
See Business plan

Business service firm
An establishment primarily engaged in rendering services to other business organizations on a fee or contract basis.

Business start
For enumeration purposes, a business with a name or similar designation that did not exist in a prior time period.

Cafeteria plan
See Flexible benefit plan

Capacity
Level of a firm's, industry's, or nation's output corresponding to full practical utilization of available resources.

Capital
Assets less liabilities, representing the ownership interest in a business. A stock of accumulated goods, especially at a specified time and in contrast to income received during a specified time period. Accumulated goods devoted to production. Accumulated possessions calculated to bring income.

Capital expenditure
Expenses incurred by a business for improvements that will depreciate over time.

Capital gain
The monetary difference between the purchase price and the selling price of capital. Capital gains are taxed at a rate of 28% by the federal government.

Capital intensity
The relative importance of capital in the production process, usually expressed as the ratio of capital to labor but also sometimes as the ratio of capital to output.

Capital resource
The equipment, facilities and labor used to create products and services.

Caribbean Basin Initiative
An interdisciplinary program to support commerce among the businesses in the nations of the Caribbean Basin and the United States. Agencies involved include: the Agency for International Development, the U.S. Small Business Administration, the International Trade Administration of the U.S. Department of Commerce, and various private sector groups.

Catastrophic care
Medical and other services for acute and long-term illnesses that cost more than insurance coverage limits or that cost the amount most families may be expected to pay with their own resources.

CDC
See Certified development corporation

CD-ROM
Compact disc with read-only memory used to store large amounts of digitized data.

Certified development corporation (CDC)
A local area or statewide corporation or authority (for profit or nonprofit) that packages U.S. Small Business Administration (SBA), bank, state, and/or private money into financial assistance for existing business capital improvements. The SBA holds the second lien on its maximum share of 40 percent involvement. Each state has at least one certified

development corporation. This program is called the SBA 504 Program.

Certified lenders

Banks that participate in the SBA guaranteed loan program (see separate citation). Such banks must have a good track record with the U.S. Small Business Administration (SBA) and must agree to certain conditions set forth by the agency. In return, the SBA agrees to process any guaranteed loan application within three business days.

Champion

An advocate for the development of an innovation.

Channel of distribution

The means used to transport merchandise from the manufacturer to the consumer.

Chapter 7 of the 1978 Bankruptcy Act

Provides for a court-appointed trustee who is responsible for liquidating a company's assets in order to settle outstanding debts.

Chapter 11 of the 1978 Bankruptcy Act

Allows the business owners to retain control of the company while working with their creditors to reorganize their finances and establish better business practices to prevent liquidation of assets.

Closely held corporation

A corporation in which the shares are held by a few persons, usually officers, employees, or others close to the management; these shares are rarely offered to the public.

Code of Federal Regulations

Codification of general and permanent rules of the federal government published in the Federal Register.

Code sharing

See Computer code sharing

Coinsurance

Upon meeting the deductible payment, health insurance participants may be required to make additional health care cost-sharing payments. Coinsurance is a payment of a fixed percentage of the cost of each service; copayment is usually a fixed amount to be paid with each service.

Collateral

Securities, evidence of deposit, or other property pledged by a borrower to secure repayment of a loan.

Collective ratemaking

The establishment of uniform charges for services by a group of businesses in the same industry.

Commercial insurance plan

See Underwriting

Commercial loans

Short-term renewable loans used to finance specific capital needs of a business.

Commercialization

The final stage of the innovation process, including production and distribution.

Common stock

The most frequently used instrument for purchasing ownership in private or public companies. Common stock generally carries the right to vote on certain corporate actions and may pay dividends, although it rarely does in venture investments. In liquidation, common stockholders are the last to share in the proceeds from the sale of a corporation's assets; bondholders and preferred shareholders have priority. Common stock is often used in firstround start-up financing.

Community development corporation

A corporation established to develop economic programs for a community and, in most cases, to provide financial support for such development.

Competitor

A business whose product or service is marketed for the same purpose/use and to the same consumer group as the product or service of another.

Computer code sharing

An arrangement whereby flights of a regional airline are identified by the two-letter code of a major carrier in the computer reservation system to help direct passengers to new regional carriers.

Consignment

A merchandising agreement, usually referring to secondhand shops, where the dealer pays the owner of an item a percentage of the profit when the item is sold.

Consortium
A coalition of organizations such as banks and corporations for ventures requiring large capital resources.

Consultant
An individual that is paid by a business to provide advice and expertise in a particular area.

Consumer price index
A measure of the fluctuation in prices between two points in time.

Consumer research
Research conducted by a business to obtain information about existing or potential consumer markets.

Continuation coverage
Health coverage offered for a specified period of time to employees who leave their jobs and to their widows, divorced spouses, or dependents.

Contractions
See Business contractions

Convertible preferred stock
A class of stock that pays a reasonable dividend and is convertible into common stock (see separate citation). Generally the convertible feature may only be exercised after being held for a stated period of time. This arrangement is usually considered second-round financing when a company needs equity to maintain its cash flow.

Convertible securities
A feature of certain bonds, debentures, or preferred stocks that allows them to be exchanged by the owner for another class of securities at a future date and in accordance with any other terms of the issue.

Copayment
See Coinsurance

Copyright
A legal form of protection available to creators and authors to safeguard their works from unlawful use or claim of ownership by others. Copyrights may be acquired for works of art, sculpture, music, and published or unpublished manuscripts. All copyrights should be registered at the Copyright Office of the Library of Congress.

Corporate financial ratios
The relationship between key figures found in a company's financial statement expressed as a numeric value. Used to evaluate risk and company performance. Also known as Financial averages, Operating ratios, and Business ratios.

Corporation
A legal entity, chartered by a state or the federal government, recognized as a separate entity having its own rights, privileges, and liabilities distinct from those of its members.

Cost containment
Actions taken by employers and insurers to curtail rising health care costs; for example, increasing employee cost sharing (see separate citation), requiring second opinions, or preadmission screening.

Cost sharing
The requirement that health care consumers contribute to their own medical care costs through deductibles and coinsurance (see separate citations). Cost sharing does not include the amounts paid in premiums. It is used to control utilization of services; for example, requiring a fixed amount to be paid with each health care service.

Cottage industry
Businesses based in the home in which the family members are the labor force and family-owned equipment is used to process the goods.

Credit Rating
A letter or number calculated by an organization (such as Dun & Bradstreet) to represent the ability and disposition of a business to meet its financial obligations.

Customer service
Various techniques used to ensure the satisfaction of a customer.

Cyclical peak
The upper turning point in a business cycle.

Cyclical trough
The lower turning point in a business cycle.

DBA
See Business name

Death
See Business death

Debenture
A certificate given as acknowledgment of a debt (see separate citation) secured by the general credit of the issuing corporation. A bond, usually without security, issued by a corporation and sometimes convertible to common stock.

Debt
Something owed by one person to another. Financing in which a company receives capital that must be repaid; no ownership is transferred.

Debt capital
Business financing that normally requires periodic interest payments and repayment of the principal within a specified time.

Debt financing
See Debt capital

Debt securities
Loans such as bonds and notes that provide a specified rate of return for a specified period of time.

Deductible
A set amount that an individual must pay before any benefits are received.

Demand shock absorbers
A term used to describe the role that some small firms play by expanding their output levels to accommodate a transient surge in demand.

Demographics
Statistics on various markets, including age, income, and education, used to target specific products or services to appropriate consumer groups.

Demonstration
Showing that a product or process has been modified sufficiently to meet the needs of users.

Deregulation
The lifting of government restrictions; for example, the lifting of government restrictions on the entry of new businesses, the expansion of services, and the setting of prices in particular industries.

Desktop Publishing
Using personal computers and specialized software to produce camera-ready copy for publications.

Disaster loans
Various types of physical and economic assistance available to individuals and businesses through the U.S. Small Business Administration (SBA). This is the only SBA loan program available for residential purposes.

Discrimination
The denial of the rights and privileges of employment based on factors such as age, race, religion, or gender.

Diseconomies of scale
The condition in which the costs of production increase faster than the volume of production.

Dissolution
See Business dissolution

Distribution
Delivering a product or process to the user.

Distributor
One who delivers merchandise to the user.

Diversified company
A company whose products and services are used by several different markets.

Doing business as (DBA)
See Business name

Dow Jones
An information services company that publishes the Wall Street Journal and other sources of financial information.

Dow Jones Industrial Average
An indicator of stock market performance.

Earned income
A tax term that refers to wages and salaries earned by the recipient, as opposed to monies earned through interest and dividends.

Economic efficiency
The use of productive resources to the fullest practical extent in the provision of the set of goods and services that is most preferred by purchasers in the economy.

Economic indicators
Statistics used to express the state of the economy. These include the length of the average work week, the rate of unemployment, and stock prices.

Economically disadvantaged
See Socially and economically disadvantaged

Economies of scale
See Scale economies

EEOC
See Equal Employment Opportunity Commission

8(a) Program
A program authorized by the Small Business Act that directs federal contracts to small businesses owned and operated by socially and economically disadvantaged individuals.

Electronic mail (e-mail)
The electronic transmission of mail via phone lines.

E-mail
See Electronic mail

Employee leasing
A contract by which employers arrange to have their workers hired by a leasing company and then leased back to them for a management fee. The leasing company typically assumes the administrative burden of payroll and provides a benefit package to the workers.

Employee tenure
The length of time an employee works for a particular employer.

Employer identification number
The business equivalent of a social security number. Assigned by the U.S. Internal Revenue Service.

Enterprise
An aggregation of all establishments owned by a parent company. An enterprise may consist of a single, independent establishment or include subsidiaries and other branches under the same ownership and control.

Enterprise zone
A designated area, usually found in inner cities and other areas with significant unemployment, where

businesses receive tax credits and other incentives to entice them to establish operations there.

Entrepreneur
A person who takes the risk of organizing and operating a new business venture.

Entry
See Business entry

Equal Employment Opportunity Commission (EEOC)
A federal agency that ensures nondiscrimination in the hiring and firing practices of a business.

Equal opportunity employer
An employer who adheres to the standards set by the Equal Employment Opportunity Commission (see separate citation).

Equity
The ownership interest. Financing in which partial or total ownership of a company is surrendered in exchange for capital. An investor's financial return comes from dividend payments and from growth in the net worth of the business.

Equity capital
See Equity; Equity midrisk venture capital

Equity financing
See Equity; Equity midrisk venture capital

Equity midrisk venture capital
An unsecured investment in a company. Usually a purchase of ownership interest in a company that occurs in the later stages of a company's development.

Equity partnership
A limited partnership arrangement for providing start-up and seed capital to businesses.

Equity securities
See Equity

Equity-type
Debt financing subordinated to conventional debt.

Establishment
A single-location business unit that may be independent (a single-establishment enterprise) or owned by a parent enterprise.

Establishment and Enterprise Microdata File
See U.S. Establishment and Enterprise Microdata File

Establishment birth
See Business birth

Establishment Longitudinal Microdata File
See U.S. Establishment Longitudinal Microdata File

Ethics
See Business ethics

Evaluation
Determining the potential success of translating an invention into a product or process.

Exit
See Business exit

Experience rating
See Underwriting

Export
A product sold outside of the country.

Export license
A general or specific license granted by the U.S. Department of Commerce required of anyone wishing to export goods. Some restricted articles need approval from the U.S. Departments of State, Defense, or Energy.

Failure
See Business failure

Fair share agreement
An agreement reached between a franchisor and a minority business organization to extend business ownership to minorities by either reducing the amount of capital required or by setting aside certain marketing areas for minority business owners.

Feasibility study
A study to determine the likelihood that a proposed product or development will fulfill the objectives of a particular investor.

Federal Trade Commission (FTC)
Federal agency that promotes free enterprise and competition within the U.S.

Federal Trade Mark Act of 1946
See Lanham Act

Fictional name
See Business name

Fiduciary
An individual or group that hold assets in trust for a beneficiary.

Financial analysis
The techniques used to determine money needs in a business. Techniques include ratio analysis, calculation of return on investment, guides for measuring profitability, and break-even analysis to determine ultimate success.

Financial intermediary
A financial institution that acts as the intermediary between borrowers and lenders. Banks, savings and loan associations, finance companies, and venture capital companies are major financial intermediaries in the United States.

Financial ratios
See Corporate financial ratios; Industry financial ratios

Financial statement
A written record of business finances, including balance sheets and profit and loss statements.

Financing
See First-stage financing; Second-stage financing; Thirdstage financing

First-stage financing
Financing provided to companies that have expended their initial capital, and require funds to start full-scale manufacturing and sales. Also known as First-round financing.

Fiscal year
Any twelve-month period used by businesses for accounting purposes.

504 Program
See Certified development corporation

Flexible benefit plan
A plan that offers a choice among cash and/or qualified benefits such as group term life insurance, accident and health insurance, group legal services, dependent care assistance, and vacations.

FOB
See Free on board

Format franchising
See Business format franchising; Franchising

401(k) plan
A financial plan where employees contribute a percentage of their earnings to a fund that is invested in stocks, bonds, or money markets for the purpose of saving money for retirement.

Four Ps
Marketing terms referring to Product, Price, Place, and Promotion.

Franchising
A form of licensing by which the owner-the franchisor- distributes or markets a product, method, or service through affiliated dealers called franchisees. The product, method, or service being marketed is identified by a brand name, and the franchisor maintains control over the marketing methods employed. The franchisee is often given exclusive access to a defined geographic area.

Free on board (FOB)
A pricing term indicating that the quoted price includes the cost of loading goods into transport vessels at a specified place.

Frictional unemployment
See Unemployment

FTC
See Federal Trade Commission

Fulfillment
The systems necessary for accurate delivery of an ordered item, including subscriptions and direct marketing.

Full-time workers
Generally, those who work a regular schedule of more than 35 hours per week.

Garment registration number
A number that must appear on every garment sold in the U.S. to indicate the manufacturer of the garment, which may or may not be the same as the label under which the garment is sold. The U.S. Federal Trade Commission assigns and regulates garment registration numbers.

Gatekeeper
A key contact point for entry into a network.

GDP
See Gross domestic product

General obligation bond
A municipal bond secured by the taxing power of the municipality. The Tax Reform Act of 1986 limits the purposes for which such bonds may be issued and establishes volume limits on the extent of their issuance.

GNP
See Gross national product

Good Housekeeping Seal
Seal appearing on products that signifies the fulfillment of the standards set by the Good Housekeeping Institute to protect consumer interests.

Goods sector
All businesses producing tangible goods, including agriculture, mining, construction, and manufacturing businesses.

GPO
See Gross product originating

Gross domestic product (GDP)
The part of the nation's gross national product (see separate citation) generated by private business using resources from within the country.

Gross national product (GNP)
The most comprehensive single measure of aggregate economic output. Represents the market value of the total output of goods and services produced by a nation's economy.

Gross product originating (GPO)
A measure of business output estimated from the income or production side using employee compensation, profit income, net interest, capital consumption, and indirect business taxes.

HAL
See Handicapped assistance loan program

Handicapped assistance loan program (HAL)
Low-interest direct loan program through the U.S. Small Business Administration (SBA) for handicapped

persons. The SBA requires that these persons demonstrate that their disability is such that it is impossible for them to secure employment, thus making it necessary to go into their own business to make a living.

Health maintenance organization (HMO)
Organization of physicians and other health care professionals that provides health services to subscribers and their dependents on a prepaid basis.

Health provider
An individual or institution that gives medical care. Under Medicare, an institutional provider is a hospital, skilled nursing facility, home health agency, or provider of certain physical therapy services.

Hispanic
A person of Cuban, Mexican, Puerto Rican, Latin American (Central or South American), European Spanish, or other Spanish-speaking origin or ancestry.

HMO
See Health maintenance organization

Home-based business
A business with an operating address that is also a residential address (usually the residential address of the proprietor).

Hub-and-spoke system
A system in which flights of an airline from many different cities (the spokes) converge at a single airport (the hub). After allowing passengers sufficient time to make connections, planes then depart for different cities.

Human Resources Management
A business program designed to oversee recruiting, pay, benefits, and other issues related to the company's work force, including planning to determine the optimal use of labor to increase production, thereby increasing profit.

Idea
An original concept for a new product or process.

Import
Products produced outside the country in which they are consumed.

Income
Money or its equivalent, earned or accrued, resulting from the sale of goods and services.

Income statement
A financial statement that lists the profits and losses of a company at a given time.

Incorporation
The filing of a certificate of incorporation with a state's secretary of state, thereby limiting the business owner's liability.

Incubator
A facility designed to encourage entrepreneurship and minimize obstacles to new business formation and growth, particularly for high-technology firms, by housing a number of fledgling enterprises that share an array of services, such as meeting areas, secretarial services, accounting, research library, on-site financial and management counseling, and word processing facilities.

Independent contractor
An individual considered self-employed (see separate citation) and responsible for paying Social Security taxes and income taxes on earnings.

Indirect health coverage
Health insurance obtained through another individual's health care plan; for example, a spouse's employersponsored plan.

Industrial development authority
The financial arm of a state or other political subdivision established for the purpose of financing economic development in an area, usually through loans to nonprofit organizations, which in turn provide facilities for manufacturing and other industrial operations.

Industry financial ratios
Corporate financial ratios averaged for a specified industry. These are used for comparison purposes and reveal industry trends and identify differences between the performance of a specific company and the performance of its industry. Also known as Industrial averages, Industry ratios, Financial averages, and Business or Industrial norms.

Inflation
Increases in volume of currency and credit, generally resulting in a sharp and continuing rise in price levels.

Informal capital
Financing from informal, unorganized sources; includes informal debt capital such as trade credit or loans from friends and relatives and equity capital from informal investors.

Initial public offering (IPO)
A corporation's first offering of stock to the public.

Innovation
The introduction of a new idea into the marketplace in the form of a new product or service or an improvement in organization or process.

Intellectual property
Any idea or work that can be considered proprietary in nature and is thus protected from infringement by others.

Internal capital
Debt or equity financing obtained from the owner or through retained business earnings.

Internet
A government-designed computer network that contains large amounts of information and is accessible through various vendors for a fee.

Intrapreneurship
The state of employing entrepreneurial principles to nonentrepreneurial situations.

Invention
The tangible form of a technological idea, which could include a laboratory prototype, drawings, formulas, etc.

IPO
See Initial public offering

Job description
The duties and responsibilities required in a particular position.

Job tenure
A period of time during which an individual is continuously employed in the same job.

Joint marketing agreements
Agreements between regional and major airlines, often involving the coordination of flight schedules, fares, and baggage transfer. These agreements help regional carriers operate at lower cost.

Joint venture
Venture in which two or more people combine efforts in a particular business enterprise, usually a single transaction or a limited activity, and agree to share the profits and losses jointly or in proportion to their contributions.

Keogh plan
Designed for self-employed persons and unincorporated businesses as a tax-deferred pension account.

Labor force
Civilians considered eligible for employment who are also willing and able to work.

Labor force participation rate
The civilian labor force as a percentage of the civilian population.

Labor intensity
The relative importance of labor in the production process, usually measured as the capital-labor ratio; i.e., the ratio of units of capital (typically, dollars of tangible assets) to the number of employees. The higher the capital-labor ratio exhibited by a firm or industry, the lower the capital intensity of that firm or industry is said to be.

Labor surplus area
An area in which there exists a high unemployment rate. In procurement (see separate citation), extra points are given to firms in counties that are designated a labor surplus area; this information is requested on procurement bid sheets.

Labor union
An organization of similarly-skilled workers who collectively bargain with management over the conditions of employment.

Laboratory prototype
See Prototype

LAN
See Local Area Network

Lanham Act
Refers to the Federal Trade Mark Act of 1946. Protects registered trademarks, trade names, and other service marks used in commerce.

Large business-dominated industry
Industry in which a minimum of 60 percent of employment or sales is in firms with more than 500 workers.

LBO
See Leveraged buy-out

Leader pricing
A reduction in the price of a good or service in order to generate more sales of that good or service.

Legal list
A list of securities selected by a state in which certain institutions and fiduciaries (such as pension funds, insurance companies, and banks) may invest. Securities not on the list are not eligible for investment. Legal lists typically restrict investments to high quality securities meeting certain specifications. Generally, investment is limited to U.S. securities and investment-grade blue chip securities (see separate citation).

Leveraged buy-out (LBO)
The purchase of a business or a division of a corporation through a highly leveraged financing package.

Liability
An obligation or duty to perform a service or an act. Also defined as money owed.

License
A legal agreement granting to another the right to use a technological innovation.

Limited partnerships
See Venture capital limited partnerships

Liquidity
The ability to convert a security into cash promptly.

Loans
See Commercial loans; Disaster loans; SBA direct loans; SBA guaranteed loans; SBA special lending institution categories Local Area Network (LAN) Computer

networks contained within a single building or small area; used to facilitate the sharing of information.

Local development corporation
An organization, usually made up of local citizens of a community, designed to improve the economy of the area by inducing business and industry to locate and expand there. A local development corporation establishes a capability to finance local growth.

Long-haul rates
Rates charged by a transporter in which the distance traveled is more than 800 miles.

Long-term debt
An obligation that matures in a period that exceeds five years.

Low-grade bond
A corporate bond that is rated below investment grade by the major rating agencies (Standard and Poor's, Moody's).

Macro-efficiency
Efficiency as it pertains to the operation of markets and market systems.

Managed care
A cost-effective health care program initiated by employers whereby low-cost health care is made available to the employees in return for exclusive patronage to program doctors.

Management Assistance Programs
See SBA Management Assistance Programs

Management and technical assistance
A term used by many programs to mean business (as opposed to technological) assistance.

Mandated benefits
Specific treatments, providers, or individuals required by law to be included in commercial health plans.

Market evaluation
The use of market information to determine the sales potential of a specific product or process.

Market failure
The situation in which the workings of a competitive market do not produce the best results from the point of view of the entire society.

Market information
Data of any type that can be used for market evaluation, which could include demographic data, technology forecasting, regulatory changes, etc.

Market research
A systematic collection, analysis, and reporting of data about the market and its preferences, opinions, trends, and plans; used for corporate decision-making.

Market share
In a particular market, the percentage of sales of a specific product.

Marketing
Promotion of goods or services through various media.

Master Establishment List (MEL)
A list of firms in the United States developed by the U.S. Small Business Administration; firms can be selected by industry, region, state, standard metropolitan statistical area (see separate citation), county, and zip code.

Maturity
The date upon which the principal or stated value of a bond or other indebtedness becomes due and payable.

Medicaid (Title XIX)
A federally aided, state-operated and administered program that provides medical benefits for certain low income persons in need of health and medical care who are eligible for one of the government's welfare cash payment programs, including the aged, the blind, the disabled, and members of families with dependent children where one parent is absent, incapacitated, or unemployed.

Medicare (Title XVIII)
A nationwide health insurance program for disabled and aged persons. Health insurance is available to insured persons without regard to income. Monies from payroll taxes cover hospital insurance and monies from general revenues and beneficiary premiums pay for supplementary medical insurance.

MEL
See Master Establishment List

MESBIC
See Minority enterprise small business investment corporation

MET
See Multiple employer trust

Metropolitan statistical area (MSA)
A means used by the government to define large population centers that may transverse different governmental jurisdictions. For example, the Washington, D.C. MSA includes the District of Columbia and contiguous parts of Maryland and Virginia because all of these geopolitical areas comprise one population and economic operating unit.

Mezzanine financing
See Third-stage financing

Micro-efficiency
Efficiency as it pertains to the operation of individual firms.

Microdata
Information on the characteristics of an individual business firm.

Mid-term debt
An obligation that matures within one to five years.

Midrisk venture capital
See Equity midrisk venture capital

Minimum premium plan
A combination approach to funding an insurance plan aimed primarily at premium tax savings. The employer self-funds a fixed percentage of estimated monthly claims and the insurance company insures the excess.

Minimum wage
The lowest hourly wage allowed by the federal government.

Minority Business Development Agency
Contracts with private firms throughout the nation to sponsor Minority Business Development Centers which provide minority firms with advice and technical assistance on a fee basis.

Minority Enterprise Small Business Investment Corporation (MESBIC)
A federally funded private venture capital firm licensed by the U.S. Small Business Administration to provide capital to minority-owned businesses (see separate citation).

Minority-owned business
Businesses owned by those who are socially or economically disadvantaged (see separate citation).

Mom and Pop business
A small store or enterprise having limited capital, principally employing family members.

Moonlighter
A wage-and-salary worker with a side business.

MSA
See Metropolitan statistical area

Multi-employer plan
A health plan to which more than one employer is required to contribute and that may be maintained through a collective bargaining agreement and required to meet standards prescribed by the U.S. Department of Labor.

Multi-level marketing
A system of selling in which you sign up other people to assist you and they, in turn, recruit others to help them. Some entrepreneurs have built successful companies on this concept because the main focus of their activities is their product and product sales.

Multimedia
The use of several types of media to promote a product or service. Also, refers to the use of several different types of media (sight, sound, pictures, text) in a CD-ROM (see separate citation) product.

Multiple employer trust (MET)
A self-funded benefit plan generally geared toward small employers sharing a common interest.

NAFTA
See North American Free Trade Agreement

NASDAQ
See National Association of Securities Dealers Automated Quotations

National Association of Securities Dealers Automated Quotations
Provides price quotes on over-the-counter securities as well as securities listed on the New York Stock Exchange.

National income
Aggregate earnings of labor and property arising from the production of goods and services in a nation's economy.

Net assets
See Net worth

Net income
The amount remaining from earnings and profits after all expenses and costs have been met or deducted. Also known as Net earnings.

Net profit
Money earned after production and overhead expenses (see separate citations) have been deducted.

Net worth
The difference between a company's total assets and its total liabilities.

Network
A chain of interconnected individuals or organizations sharing information and/or services.

New York Stock Exchange (NYSE)
The oldest stock exchange in the U.S. Allows for trading in stocks, bonds, warrants, options, and rights that meet listing requirements.

Niche
A career or business for which a person is well-suited. Also, a product which fulfills one need of a particular market segment, often with little or no competition.

Nodes
One workstation in a network, either local area or wide area (see separate citations).

Nonbank bank
A bank that either accepts deposits or makes loans, but not both. Used to create many new branch banks.

Noncompetitive awards
A method of contracting whereby the federal government negotiates with only one contractor to supply a product or service.

Nonmember bank
A state-regulated bank that does not belong to the federal bank system.

Nonprofit
An organization that has no shareholders, does not distribute profits, and is without federal and state tax liabilities.

Norms
See Financial ratios

North American Free Trade Agreement (NAFTA)
Passed in 1993, NAFTA eliminates trade barriers among businesses in the U.S., Canada, and Mexico.

NYSE
See New York Stock Exchange

Occupational Safety & Health Administration (OSHA)
Federal agency that regulates health and safety standards within the workplace.

Optimal firm size
The business size at which the production cost per unit of output (average cost) is, in the long run, at its minimum.

Organizational chart
A hierarchical chart tracking the chain of command within an organization.

OSHA
See Occupational Safety & Health Administration

Overhead
Expenses, such as employee benefits and building utilities, incurred by a business that are unrelated to the actual product or service sold.

Owner's capital
Debt or equity funds provided by the owner(s) of a business; sources of owner's capital are personal savings, sales of assets, or loans from financial institutions.

P & L
See Profit and loss statement

Part-time workers
Normally, those who work less than 35 hours per week. The Tax Reform Act indicated that part-time workers who work less than 17.5 hours per week may be excluded from health plans for purposes of complying with federal nondiscrimination rules.

Part-year workers
Those who work less than 50 weeks per year.

Partnership
Two or more parties who enter into a legal relationship to conduct business for profit. Defined by the U.S. Internal Revenue Code as joint ventures, syndicates, groups, pools, and other associations of two or more persons organized for profit that are not specifically classified in the IRS code as corporations or proprietorships.

Patent
A grant made by the government assuring an inventor the sole right to make, use, and sell an invention for a period of 17 years.

PC
See Professional corporation

Peak
See Cyclical peak

Pension
A series of payments made monthly, semiannually, annually, or at other specified intervals during the lifetime of the pensioner for distribution upon retirement. The term is sometimes used to denote the portion of the retirement allowance financed by the employer's contributions.

Pension fund
A fund established to provide for the payment of pension benefits; the collective contributions made by all of the parties to the pension plan.

Performance appraisal
An established set of objective criteria, based on job description and requirements, that is used to evaluate the performance of an employee in a specific job.

Permit
See Business license

Plan
See Business plan

Pooling
An arrangement for employers to achieve efficiencies and lower health costs by joining together to purchase group health insurance or self-insurance.

PPO
See Preferred provider organization

Preferred lenders program
See SBA special lending institution categories

Preferred provider organization (PPO)
A contractual arrangement with a health care services organization that agrees to discount its health care rates in return for faster payment and/or a patient base.

Premiums
The amount of money paid to an insurer for health insurance under a policy. The premium is generally paid periodically (e.g., monthly), and often is split between the employer and the employee. Unlike deductibles and coinsurance or copayments, premiums are paid for coverage whether or not benefits are actually used.

Prime-age workers
Employees 25 to 54 years of age.

Prime contract
A contract awarded directly by the U.S. Federal Government.

Private company
See Closely held corporation

Private placement
A method of raising capital by offering for sale an investment or business to a small group of investors (generally avoiding registration with the Securities and Exchange Commission or state securities registration agencies). Also known as Private financing or Private offering.

Pro forma
The use of hypothetical figures in financial statements to represent future expenditures, debts, and other potential financial expenses.

Proactive
Taking the initiative to solve problems and anticipate future events before they happen, instead of reacting to an already existing problem or waiting for a difficult situation to occur.

Procurement
A contract from an agency of the federal government for goods or services from a small business.

Prodigy
An online service which is accessible by computer modem. The service features Internet access, bulletin boards, online periodicals, electronic mail, and other services for subscribers.

Product development
The stage of the innovation process where research is translated into a product or process through evaluation, adaptation, and demonstration.

Product franchising
An arrangement for a franchisee to use the name and to produce the product line of the franchisor or parent corporation.

Production
The manufacture of a product.

Production prototype
See Prototype

Productivity
A measurement of the number of goods produced during a specific amount of time.

Professional corporation (PC)
Organized by members of a profession such as medicine, dentistry, or law for the purpose of conducting their professional activities as a corporation. Liability of a member or shareholder is limited in the same manner as in a business corporation.

Profit and loss statement (P & L)
The summary of the incomes (total revenues) and costs of a company's operation during a specific period of time. Also known as Income and expense statement.

Proposal
See Business plan

Proprietorship
The most common legal form of business ownership; about 85 percent of all small businesses are proprietorships. The liability of the owner is unlimited in this form of ownership.

Prospective payment system
A cost-containment measure included in the Social Security Amendments of 1983 whereby Medicare

payments to hospitals are based on established prices, rather than on cost reimbursement.

Prototype
A model that demonstrates the validity of the concept of an invention (laboratory prototype); a model that meets the needs of the manufacturing process and the user (production prototype).

Prudent investor rule or standard
A legal doctrine that requires fiduciaries to make investments using the prudence, diligence, and intelligence that would be used by a prudent person in making similar investments. Because fiduciaries make investments on behalf of third-party beneficiaries, the standard results in very conservative investments. Until recently, most state regulations required the fiduciary to apply this standard to each investment. Newer, more progressive regulations permit fiduciaries to apply this standard to the portfolio taken as a whole, thereby allowing a fiduciary to balance a portfolio with higher-yield, higher-risk investments. In states with more progressive regulations, practically every type of security is eligible for inclusion in the portfolio of investments made by a fiduciary, provided that the portfolio investments, in their totality, are those of a prudent person.

Public equity markets
Organized markets for trading in equity shares such as common stocks, preferred stocks, and warrants. Includes markets for both regularly traded and nonregularly traded securities.

Public offering
General solicitation for participation in an investment opportunity. Interstate public offerings are supervised by the U.S. Securities and Exchange Commission (see separate citation).

Quality control
The process by which a product is checked and tested to ensure consistent standards of high quality.

Rate of return
The yield obtained on a security or other investment based on its purchase price or its current market price.

The total rate of return is current income plus or minus capital appreciation or depreciation.

Real property
Includes the land and all that is contained on it.

Realignment
See Resource realignment

Recession
Contraction of economic activity occurring between the peak and trough (see separate citations) of a business cycle.

Regulated market
A market in which the government controls the forces of supply and demand, such as who may enter and what price may be charged.

Regulation D
A vehicle by which small businesses make small offerings and private placements of securities with limited disclosure requirements. It was designed to ease the burdens imposed on small businesses utilizing this method of capital formation.

Regulatory Flexibility Act
An act requiring federal agencies to evaluate the impact of their regulations on small businesses before the regulations are issued and to consider less burdensome alternatives.

Research
The initial stage of the innovation process, which includes idea generation and invention.

Research and development financing
A tax-advantaged partnership set up to finance product development for start-ups as well as more mature companies.

Resource mobility
The ease with which labor and capital move from firm to firm or from industry to industry.

Resource realignment
The adjustment of productive resources to interindustry changes in demand.

Resources
The sources of support or help in the innovation process, including sources of financing, technical

evaluation, market evaluation, management and business assistance, etc.

Retained business earnings
Business profits that are retained by the business rather than being distributed to the shareholders as dividends.

Revolving credit
An agreement with a lending institution for an amount of money, which cannot exceed a set maximum, over a specified period of time. Each time the borrower repays a portion of the loan, the amount of the repayment may be borrowed yet again.

Risk capital
See Venture capital

Risk management
The act of identifying potential sources of financial loss and taking action to minimize their negative impact.

Routing
The sequence of steps necessary to complete a product during production.

S corporations
See Sub chapter S corporations

SBA
See Small Business Administration

SBA direct loans
Loans made directly by the U.S. Small Business Administration (SBA); monies come from funds appropriated specifically for this purpose. In general, SBA direct loans carry interest rates slightly lower than those in the private financial markets and are available only to applicants unable to secure private financing or an SBA guaranteed loan.

SBA 504 Program
See Certified development corporation

SBA guaranteed loans
Loans made by lending institutions in which the U.S. Small Business Administration (SBA) will pay a prior agreed-upon percentage of the outstanding principal in the event the borrower of the loan defaults. The

terms of the loan and the interest rate are negotiated between theborrower and the lending institution, within set parameters.

SBA loans
See Disaster loans; SBA direct loans; SBA guaranteed loans; SBA special lending institution categories

SBA Management Assistance Programs
Classes, workshops, counseling, and publications offered by the U.S. Small Business Administration.

SBA special lending institution categories
U.S. Small Business Administration (SBA) loan program in which the SBA promises certified banks a 72-hour turnaround period in giving its approval for a loan, and in which preferred lenders in a pilot program are allowed to write SBA loans without seeking prior SBA approval.

SBDB
See Small Business Data Base

SBDC
See Small business development centers

SBI
See Small business institutes program

SBIC
See Small business investment corporation

SBIR Program
See Small Business Innovation Development Act of 1982

Scale economies
The decline of the production cost per unit of output (average cost) as the volume of output increases.

Scale efficiency
The reduction in unit cost available to a firm when producing at a higher output volume.

SCORE
See Service Corps of Retired Executives

SEC
See Securities and Exchange Commission

SECA
See Self-Employment Contributions Act

Second-stage financing
Working capital for the initial expansion of a company that is producing, shipping, and has growing accounts receivable and inventories. Also known as Second-round financing.

Secondary market
A market established for the purchase and sale of outstanding securities following their initial distribution.

Secondary worker
Any worker in a family other than the person who is the primary source of income for the family.

Secondhand capital
Previously used and subsequently resold capital equipment (e.g., buildings and machinery).

Securities and Exchange Commission (SEC)
Federal agency charged with regulating the trade of securities to prevent unethical practices in the investor market.

Securitized debt
A marketing technique that converts long-term loans to marketable securities.

Seed capital
Venture financing provided in the early stages of the innovation process, usually during product development.

Self-employed person
One who works for a profit or fees in his or her own business, profession, or trade, or who operates a farm.

Self-Employment Contributions Act (SECA)
Federal law that governs the self-employment tax (see separate citation).

Self-employment income
Income covered by Social Security if a business earns a net income of at least $400.00 during the year. Taxes are paid on earnings that exceed $400.00.

Self-employment retirement plan
See Keogh plan

Self-employment tax
Required tax imposed on self-employed individuals for the provision of Social Security and Medicare. The tax must be paid quarterly with estimated income tax statements.

Self-funding
A health benefit plan in which a firm uses its own funds to pay claims, rather than transferring the financial risks of paying claims to an outside insurer in exchange for premium payments.

Service Corps of Retired Executives (SCORE)
Volunteers for the SBA Management Assistance Program who provide one-on-one counseling and teach workshops and seminars for small firms.

Service firm
See Business service firm

Service sector
Broadly defined, all U.S. industries that produce intangibles, including the five major industry divisions of transportation, communications, and utilities; wholesale trade; retail trade; finance, insurance, and real estate; and services.

Set asides
See Small business set asides

Short-haul service
A type of transportation service in which the transporter supplies service between cities where the maximum distance is no more than 200 miles.

Short-term debt
An obligation that matures in one year.

SIC codes
See Standard Industrial Classification codes

Single-establishment enterprise
See Establishment

Small business
An enterprise that is independently owned and operated, is not dominant in its field, and employs fewer than 500 people. For SBA purposes, the U.S. Small Business Administration (SBA) considers various other factors (such as gross annual sales) in determining size of a business.

Small Business Administration (SBA)
An independent federal agency that provides assistance with loans, management, and advocating interests before other federal agencies.

Small Business Data Base
A collection of microdata (see separate citation) files on individual firms developed and maintained by the U.S. Small Business Administration.

Small business development centers (SBDC)
Centers that provide support services to small businesses, such as individual counseling, SBA advice, seminars and conferences, and other learning center activities. Most services are free of charge, or available at minimal cost.

Small business development corporation
See Certified development corporation

Small business-dominated industry
Industry in which a minimum of 60 percent of employment or sales is in firms with fewer than 500 employees.

Small Business Innovation Development Act of 1982
Federal statute requiring federal agencies with large extramural research and development budgets to allocate a certain percentage of these funds to small research and development firms. The program, called the Small Business Innovation Research (SBIR) Program, is designed to stimulate technological innovation and make greater use of small businesses in meeting national innovation needs.

Small business institutes (SBI) program
Cooperative arrangements made by U.S. Small Business Administration district offices and local colleges and universities to provide small business firms with graduate students to counsel them without charge.

Small business investment corporation (SBIC)
A privately owned company licensed and funded through the U.S. Small Business Administration and private sector sources to provide equity or debt capital to small businesses.

Small business set asides
Procurement (see separate citation) opportunities required by law to be on all contracts under $10,000 or a certain percentage of an agency's total procurement expenditure.

Smaller firms
For U.S. Department of Commerce purposes, those firms not included in the Fortune 1000.

SMSA
See Metropolitan statistical area

Socially and economically disadvantaged
Individuals who have been subjected to racial or ethnic prejudice or cultural bias without regard to their qualities as individuals, and whose abilities to compete are impaired because of diminished opportunities to obtain capital and credit.

Sole proprietorship
An unincorporated, one-owner business, farm, or professional practice.

Special lending institution categories
See SBA special lending institution categories

Standard Industrial Classification (SIC) codes
Four-digit codes established by the U.S. Federal Government to categorize businesses by type of economic activity; the first two digits correspond to major groups such as construction and manufacturing, while the last two digits correspond to subgroups such as home construction or highway construction.

Standard metropolitan statistical area (SMSA)
See Metropolitan statistical area

Start-up
A new business, at the earliest stages of development and financing.

Start-up costs
Costs incurred before a business can commence operations.

Start-up financing
Financing provided to companies that have either completed product development and initial marketing or have been in business for less than one year but have not yet sold their product commercially.

Stock
A certificate of equity ownership in a business.

Stop-loss coverage
Insurance for a self-insured plan that reimburses the company for any losses it might incur in its health claims beyond a specified amount.

Glossary

Strategic planning
Projected growth and development of a business to establish a guiding direction for the future. Also used to determine which market segments to explore for optimal sales of products or services.

Structural unemployment
See Unemployment

Sub chapter S corporations
Corporations that are considered noncorporate for tax purposes but legally remain corporations.

Subcontract
A contract between a prime contractor and a subcontractor, or between subcontractors, to furnish supplies or services for performance of a prime contract (see separate citation) or a subcontract.

Surety bonds
Bonds providing reimbursement to an individual, company, or the government if a firm fails to complete a contract. The U.S. Small Business Administration guarantees surety bonds in a program much like the SBA guaranteed loan program (see separate citation).

Swing loan
See Bridge financing

Target market
The clients or customers sought for a business' product or service.

Targeted Jobs Tax Credit
Federal legislation enacted in 1978 that provides a tax credit to an employer who hires structurally unemployed individuals.

Tax number
A number assigned to a business by a state revenue department that enables the business to buy goods without paying sales tax.

Taxable bonds
An interest-bearing certificate of public or private indebtedness. Bonds are issued by public agencies to finance economic development.

Technical assistance
See Management and technical assistance

Technical evaluation
Assessment of technological feasibility.

Technology
The method in which a firm combines and utilizes labor and capital resources to produce goods or services; the application of science for commercial or industrial purposes.

Technology transfer
The movement of information about a technology or intellectual property from one party to another for use.

Tenure
See Employee tenure

Term
The length of time for which a loan is made.

Terms of a note
The conditions or limits of a note; includes the interest rate per annum, the due date, and transferability and convertibility features, if any.

Third-party administrator
An outside company responsible for handling claims and performing administrative tasks associated with health insurance plan maintenance.

Third-stage financing
Financing provided for the major expansion of a company whose sales volume is increasing and that is breaking even or profitable. These funds are used for further plant expansion, marketing, working capital, or development of an improved product. Also known as Third-round or Mezzanine financing.

Time deposit
A bank deposit that cannot be withdrawn before a specified future time.

Time management
Skills and scheduling techniques used to maximize productivity.

Trade credit
Credit extended by suppliers of raw materials or finished products. In an accounting statement, trade credit is referred to as "accounts payable."

Trade name

The name under which a company conducts business, or by which its business, goods, or services are identified. It may or may not be registered as a trademark.

Trade periodical

A publication with a specific focus on one or more aspects of business and industry.

Trade secret

Competitive advantage gained by a business through the use of a unique manufacturing process or formula.

Trade show

An exhibition of goods or services used in a particular industry. Typically held in exhibition centers where exhibitors rent space to display their merchandise.

Trademark

A graphic symbol, device, or slogan that identifies a business. A business has property rights to its trademark from the inception of its use, but it is still prudent to register all trademarks with the Trademark Office of the U.S. Department of Commerce.

Translation

See Product development

Treasury bills

Investment tender issued by the Federal Reserve Bank in amounts of $10,000 that mature in 91 to 182 days.

Treasury bonds

Long-term notes with maturity dates of not less than seven and not more than twenty-five years.

Treasury notes

Short-term notes maturing in less than seven years.

Trend

A statistical measurement used to track changes that occur over time.

Trough

See Cyclical trough

UCC

See Uniform Commercial Code

UL

See Underwriters Laboratories

Underwriters Laboratories (UL)

One of several private firms that tests products and processes to determine their safety. Although various firms can provide this kind of testing service, many local and insurance codes specify UL certification.

Underwriting

A process by which an insurer determines whether or not and on what basis it will accept an application for insurance. In an experience-rated plan, premiums are based on a firm's or group's past claims; factors other than prior claims are used for community-rated or manually rated plans.

Unfair competition

Refers to business practices, usually unethical, such as using unlicensed products, pirating merchandise, or misleading the public through false advertising, which give the offending business an unequitable advantage over others.

Unfunded accrued liability

The excess of total liabilities, both present and prospective, over present and prospective assets.

Unemployment

The joblessness of individuals who are willing to work, who are legally and physically able to work, and who are seeking work. Unemployment may represent the temporary joblessness of a worker between jobs (frictional unemployment) or the joblessness of a worker whose skills are not suitable for jobs available in the labor market (structural unemployment).

Uniform Commercial Code (UCC)

A code of laws governing commercial transactions across the U.S., except Louisiana. Their purpose is to bring uniformity to financial transactions.

Uniform product code (UPC symbol)

A computer-readable label comprised of ten digits and stripes that encodes what a product is and how much it costs. The first five digits are assigned by the Uniform Product Code Council, and the last five digits by the individual manufacturer.

Unit cost

See Average cost

UPC symbol
See Uniform product code

U.S. Establishment and Enterprise Microdata (USEEM) File
A cross-sectional database containing information on employment, sales, and location for individual enterprises and establishments with employees that have a Dun & Bradstreet credit rating.

U.S. Establishment Longitudinal Microdata (USELM) File
A database containing longitudinally linked sample microdata on establishments drawn from the U.S. Establishment and Enterprise Microdata file (see separate citation).

U.S. Small Business Administration 504 Program
See Certified development corporation

USEEM
See U.S. Establishment and Enterprise Microdata File

USELM
See U.S. Establishment Longitudinal Microdata File

VCN
See Venture capital network

Venture capital
Money used to support new or unusual business ventures that exhibit above-average growth rates, significant potential for market expansion, and are in need of additional financing to sustain growth or further research and development; equity or equity-type financing traditionally provided at the commercialization stage, increasingly available prior to commercialization.

Venture capital company
A company organized to provide seed capital to a business in its formation stage, or in its first or second stage of expansion. Funding is obtained through public or private pension funds, commercial banks and bank holding companies, small business investment corporations licensed by the U.S. Small Business Administration, private venture capital firms, insurance companies, investment management companies, bank trust departments, industrial companies seeking to diversify their investment, and investment bankers acting as intermediaries for other investors or directly investing on their own behalf.

Venture capital limited partnerships
Designed for business development, these partnerships are an institutional mechanism for providing capital for young, technology-oriented businesses. The investors' money is pooled and invested in money market assets until venture investments have been selected. The general partners are experienced investment managers who select and invest the equity and debt securities of firms with high growth potential and the ability to go public in the near future.

Venture capital network (VCN)
A computer database that matches investors with entrepreneurs.

WAN
See Wide Area Network

Wide Area Network (WAN)
Computer networks linking systems throughout a state or around the world in order to facilitate the sharing of information.

Withholding
Federal, state, social security, and unemployment taxes withheld by the employer from employees' wages; employers are liable for these taxes and the corporate umbrella and bankruptcy will not exonerate an employer from paying back payroll withholding. Employers should escrow these funds in a separate account and disperse them quarterly to withholding authorities.

Workers' compensation
A state-mandated form of insurance covering workers injured in job-related accidents. In some states, the state is the insurer; in other states, insurance must be acquired from commercial insurance firms. Insurance rates are based on a number of factors, including salaries, firm history, and risk of occupation.

Working capital
Refers to a firm's short-term investment of current assets, including cash, short-term securities, accounts receivable, and inventories.

Yield

The rate of income returned on an investment, expressed as a percentage. Income yield is obtained by dividing the current dollar income by the current market price of the security. Net yield or yield to maturity is the current income yield minus any premium above par or plus any discount from par in purchase price, with the adjustment spread over the period from the date of purchase to the date of maturity.

Index

Index